Practical Solutions to Practically Every Problem

Practical Solutions to Practically Every Problem

The Survival Guide for Early Childhood Professionals

Third Edition

Steffen Saifer

Redleaf Press®
www.redleafpress.org
800-423-8309

Published by Redleaf Press
10 Yorkton Court
St. Paul, MN 55117
www.redleafpress.org

Third edition 2017
Cover design by Jim Handrigan
Cover photograph by TatyanaGI / iStock
Interior design by Wendy Holdman
Typeset in Arno Pro and Open Sans
Printed in the United States of America
23 22 21 20 19 18 17 16   1 2 3 4 5 6 7 8

Library of Congress Cataloging-in-Publication Data
Names: Saifer, Steffen, 1951– author.
Title: Practical solutions to practically every problem : the survival guide for early childhood
    professionals / Steffen Saifer.
Description: Third edition. | St. Paul, MN : Redleaf Press, [2017] |
    Includes bibliographical references.
Identifiers: LCCN 2016017676 (print) | LCCN 2016029544 (ebook) | ISBN 9781605545127
    (pbk. : acid-free paper) | ISBN 9781605545134
Subjects: LCSH: Education, Preschool—United States—Handbooks, manuals, etc. | Preschool
    teaching—United States—Handbooks, manuals, etc. | Preschool teachers—United States—
    Handbooks, manuals, etc.
Classification: LCC LB1140.2 .S235 2017 (print) | LCC LB1140.2 (ebook) | DDC 372.21—dc23
LC record available at https://lccn.loc.gov/2016017676

This third edition is dedicated to the world's children.
May their caretakers be loving and wise,
may their communities be peaceful and safe,
and may their early years be joyful and free.

Table of Contents

Acknowledgments   xvii

Introduction   1

How to Be the "Pro" in Problem-Solver   2

Choose the Problems You Like to Solve   2

Have an Effective Approach to Solving Problems in General   2

Take Time If You Can   3

All You Can Do Is Good Enough . . . If You Have the Tools   3

How Is Criticism Like a Mosquito Bite?   4

There May Be a Good Reason for Being Unreasonable   4

Rules Rule   4

Is There a Solution to Every Problem?   5

What's New to This Edition?   5

New Knowledge   5

Essential Life Skills   5

Higher-Order Thinking Skills   6

Brain Development   6

Praise Effort, Not Ability   6

Consequences Are Not Effective   6

The Value of Social Imaginary Play   7

Cultural Responsiveness   7

Intentional Teaching   7

Globalization: New (and Continuing) Inspirations from Europe and Oceania   8

New Issues, Trends, and Challenges   8

Preschool Expulsions and Suspensions   8

Sustainability and Environmental Issues   9

Technology Everywhere!   9

The Quantification of Early Childhood Programs   9

Common Core State Standards (CCSS)   9

Early Learning and Development Standards (ELDS)   10

The Score: Superficial Skills = 1; Exploration, Understanding, Play = 0   10

Terminology   11

New Terms   11

Clarification of Terms   12

PART 1

Daily Dilemmas   13

1. Right from the Start   14

Anticipating and Preventing Problems Related to Starting the Day   14

Solving Problems Related to Starting the Day   15

Children who have a hard time separating from their parents   15

Children who are fussy at the start of the day   16

Chaos: Too much going on at once   17

2. Circle Time and Group Time: All for One and One for All   18

Anticipating and Preventing Problems Related to Circle and Group Times   19

Solving Problems Related to Circle and Group Times   20

Hitting, arguing, or talking with others   20

Can't sit still   21

Interruptions directed to the teacher   22

When "show-and-tell" does not go well   22

3. Work-Play Time: Meaningful Play, Playful Work   23

Anticipating and Preventing Problems Related to Work-Play Time   23

Solving Problems Related to Work-Play Time   24

The child who spends most of his time in one area   24

The child who spends very little time in any one area   24

Too loud, too boisterous   25

Too messy   26

Unimaginative imaginary play   27

War, gun, superhero, and violent play   27

4. Small-Group Time: Small Is Beautiful (and Productive)   28

Anticipating and Preventing Problems Related to Small-Group Time   29

Solving Problems Related to Small-Group Time   30

Not enough staff   30

Bored or resistant children   30

5. Mellow Mealtimes: The Cure for Whole-Class Heartburn   **31**

Anticipating and Preventing Problems Related to Mealtimes   31

Solving Problems Related to Mealtimes   33

    The overzealous eater   33

    The messy eater   34

    The picky eater   34

    Unappealing food   35

    Wasted food   35

    Too much noise   36

    Losing silverware in the trash   36

6. Creative Art: Mess without Stress   **36**

Anticipating and Preventing Problems Related to Art Activities   36

Solving Problems Related to Art Activities   38

    Drippy paint   38

    Paint spills and waste   38

    Gluing   38

7. Moving Muscles: Safe Fun Outside or in the Gym   **39**

Anticipating and Preventing Problems Related to Outside or Gym Play   39

Solving Problems Related to Outside or Gym Play   40

    Limited or unsafe play equipment   40

    Play areas with hard surfaces   41

    No indoor gym space for when the weather is bad   41

8. No More Gnarly Naptimes   **41**

Anticipating and Preventing Problems Related to Naptimes   42

Solving Problems Related to Naptimes   42

    Squirmers   42

    Non-nappers   42

    Noisemakers   43

    Socializers   43

    No rewards necessary   43

9. Technology Center: Keeping the Connection to Creative Play   **43**

Anticipating and Preventing Problems Related to Using Technology   44

Solving Problems Related to Using Technology   45

    Children who do not use the computer correctly or carefully   45

    Too many users   45

    Children who do not want to use the computer   46

    Pressure to eliminate computers, to have more computers, or to use age-inappropriate software   46

10. Trouble-Free Transitions: Getting from Here to There without Getting Lost   **47**

Anticipating and Preventing Problems Related to Transitions   47

Solving Problems Related to Transitions   48

    Transition from eating   48

    Transition to outdoor time   48

    Transition from outdoors or from work-play   49

    Clean-up   49

    Transition from nap   49

    Transition to going home   50

11. Successful Scheduling: A Day in the Life   **50**

Half-Day Toddler Program (2.5 to 3.5 years)   51

Full-Day Toddler Program (2.5 to 3.5 years)   51

Half-Day Preschool (3.5 to 5.5 years)   52

Full-Day Preschool (3.5 to 5.5 years)   52

Half-Day Kindergarten (5.5 to 6.5 years)   53

Full-Day Kindergarten (5.5 to 6.5 years)   53

School-Day Kindergarten (5.5 to 6.5 years)   54

PART 2

Classroom Concerns: In Control but Not Controlling   **55**

1. The Environment: Efficient, Effective, and Aesthetic   **56**

Anticipating and Preventing Problems Related to the Physical Environment   56

Solving Problems Related to the Physical Environment   57

    Small spaces   57

Not enough storage space   57

High ceilings and large open spaces   58

Little money for supplies or equipment   58

Sharing your classroom, sharing control   59

2. Curriculum Conundrums   59

Anticipating and Preventing Problems
Related to Curriculum   62

Solving Problems Related to Curriculum   62

The curriculum is changing   62

A prescription for programmed,
predetermined curricula   63

Thinking up thoughtful themes   64

3. "Of Course I Teach Children to Read": Pressure to Teach Reading and to Teach It Inappropriately   68

Anticipating and Preventing Problems
Related to the Pressure to Teach Reading
Inappropriately   68

Solving Problems Related to the Pressure
to Teach Reading Inappropriately   69

4. Testing without Tears . . . Except for the Teacher's   71

Anticipating and Preventing Problems
Related to Testing   72

Solving Problems Related to Testing   74

It's not the right test or it's not a good test   74

The child is not responding to the questions
or is becoming stressed or discouraged   75

The child misinterprets questions or
the directions   75

Sharing test results with parents and
others—the good news and the
not-such-good news   76

Pressure to teach to the test   76

5. Individualizing: Differentiated Instruction Goes to Preschool   77

Anticipating and Preventing Problems
Related to Individualizing   78

Solving Problems Related to Individualizing   79

Is it really possible to plan for the
whole group, subgroups, and every
individual child too?   79

In spite of careful planning, the activity still
does not meet the needs of some children   80

If children are "out of sorts" much of
the day, it may be the schedule   81

6. Multiage Groups: Multiple Benefits, Many Challenges, Much Satisfaction   82

Anticipating and Preventing Problems
Related to Multiage Groups   82

Solving Problems Related to Multiage Groups   83

Issues with the older children   83

Issues with the younger children   83

Meeting needs and individualizing
across the wide age/developmental range   84

7. Are We Having Fun Yet?: Facilitating Fiasco-free Field Trips   84

Anticipating and Preventing Problems
Related to Field Trips   85

Solving Problems Related to Field Trips   86

The group is overly excited, not following
rules, or not listening to directions   86

No transportation or funds for field trips   87

8. Toys from Home: Confiscate, Tolerate, or Regulate?   88

Anticipating and Preventing Problems
Related to Toys from Home   88

Solving Problems Related to Toys from Home   89

9. Disappearing Dinosaurs, Lost Lego Blocks, Missing Mittens, and Other Mysteries   90

Anticipating and Preventing Problems
Related to Missing Items   90

Missing clothes   90

Missing toys or toy parts   90

Solving Problems Related to Missing Items   91

When clothing is missing   91

When a toy or toy part is missing   91

10. Accidents and Injuries: Reduce Risks and Offer First-Aid Fast   92

Anticipating and Preventing Accidents
and Injuries   92

Solving Problems Related to Accidents
and Injuries   94

When a child wants to do or does
something dangerous or risky   94

If a child is injured   95

If a child eats or drinks something
poisonous   95

11. Emergency and Disaster Preparedness: Prepare for What You Can't Prevent   **96**

Anticipating and Preventing Problems Related to Emergencies and Disasters   96

Solving Problems Related to Emergencies and Disasters   97

    Noisy, disorganized, or slow evacuation drills   97

12. Children Who Are Ill and Other Health Concerns: Stifle the Sneeze, Cover the Cough, Snuff the Sniffle   **98**

Anticipating and Preventing Illnesses   98

Solving Problems Related to Illnesses   100

    Children who come to school sick or become sick during the day   100

    Children who are extremely allergic   101

    Head lice: A "lousy" problem, but not a health threat   102

    Children with asthma   102

    Children who need to take medication during school hours   103

    Children who are excessively dirty   104

    Children who are overweight or obese   105

13. Babies, Breasts, Bottoms, and Boundaries: Talking with Children about Bodies, Relationships, and Personal Safety   **106**

Anticipating and Preventing Problems Related to Talking about Bodies, Relationships, and Personal Safety   107

Solving Problems Related to Talking about Bodies, Relationships, and Personal Safety   108

    Inappropriate words   108

    Questions about sex   108

    Mutual exploration   109

PART 3

Children with Challenges: Abilities, Disabilities, and Vulnerabilities   **111**

1. Is the Child Just Immature or Is There Really Something Wrong?   **112**

Anticipating and Preventing Problems Related to Identifying Children with Special Needs   112

Solving Problems Related to Identifying Children with Special Needs   113

    Observing every child and still finding time to be a teacher   113

    The screening test results are not good   114

    Parents who deny there is a problem   114

    Health professionals who believe there is no problem   115

    Difficulty in finding or affording professional services   116

2. In the Mix: Including Children with Disabilities and Special Needs   **116**

Anticipating and Preventing Problems Related to Inclusion   117

Solving Problems Related to Inclusion   119

    Questions from children that may be hurtful or difficult to answer   119

    Conflicts with special educators, therapists, or other specialists   119

    The overly involved parent   120

    The child with a disability who does not play with others   121

    The child who takes too much time and effort   121

3. Diversity, Difference, and Democracy: Cultural Responsiveness   **122**

Anticipating and Preventing Problems Related to Biases and Diversity   123

Solving Problems Related to Biases and Diversity   125

    Questions from children about differences   125

    Responding to biased behaviors   125

    Cultural differences in learning styles and priorities   126

    Multiracial and multicultural children   127

4. A Different Kind of Special Need: Gifted and Talented Children   **128**

Anticipating and Preventing Problems Related to Gifted and Talented Children   128

Solving Problems Related to Gifted and Talented Children   130

    Lack of access to supports and resources   131

    Problematic behaviors of some gifted children   132

5. Is It Introversion, Insecurity, or Something Else?: Shy, Quiet, and Solitary Children 133

Anticipating and Preventing Problems Related to Shy, Quiet, and Solitary Children 134

Solving Problems Related to Shy, Quiet, and Solitary Children 134

Too clingy 135

6. Modern Family: Children in Nontraditional Families 136

Anticipating and Preventing Problems Related to Children in Nontraditional Families 136

Solving Problems Related to Children in Nontraditional Families 137

Same-sex parents 137

Children who have been adopted 137

Children in foster families 138

Families with nontraditional beliefs and practices 138

7. Going with the FLOE: Children Whose Family Language Is Other than English (FLOEs) 139

Anticipating and Preventing Problems Related to FLOEs 140

Solving Problems Related to FLOEs 141

Subgroups of children who speak the same language 141

Problems with a bilingual assistant 141

The child who won't speak at all 142

8. Every Day Is Like Halloween . . . without the Candy: Children with Extreme Fears 142

Anticipating and Preventing Problems Related to Fears 143

Solving Problems Related to Fears 144

9. Too Much Too Soon: The Sexually Precocious Child 145

Anticipating and Preventing Sexually Precocious Behavior 146

Solving Problems Related to the Sexually Precocious Child 147

When a child manipulates other children 147

Grown-up play in the imaginary play area 147

Appropriate affection 147

Determining if the child is being sexually abused 147

10. Equal Play for Equal Worth: Gender Identity, Gender Equity, and Sex-Role Issues 148

Anticipating and Preventing Problems Related to Gender Issues 148

Solving Problems Related to Gender Issues 150

Teasing 150

Exaggerated sex-role behaviors 150

Helping parents 150

11. Reversed Roles: Children Who Are Too Responsible 151

Anticipating and Preventing Problems Related to Children Who Are Too Responsible 151

Solving Problems Related to Children Who Are Too Responsible 152

12. Adults' Problems, Children's Troubles: Children Who Experience Trauma 153

Anticipating and Preventing Problems Related to the Impacts of Trauma 153

Solving Problems Related to the Impacts of Trauma 153

13. No One Likes Me!: Children Who Are Social Outcasts or Easily Victimized 155

Anticipating and Preventing Children from Becoming Social Outcasts or Easily Victimized 155

Solving Problems Related to Children Who Are Social Outcasts or Easily Victimized 155

PART 4

Big Troubles on Small Shoulders: Children Coping with Change 157

1. New Kid on the Block 158

Anticipating and Preventing Problems Related to a Child Whose Family Has Recently Moved 158

Solving Problems Related to a Child Whose Family Has Recently Moved 158

The child who is having a hard time adjusting 158

The child who has recently moved 159

2. Mommy's House, Daddy's House: Children Whose Parents Are Divorcing   160

Anticipating and Preventing Problems Related to the Impact of a Divorce on Children   160

Solving Problems Related to the Impact of a Divorce on Children   161

3. Adorable Baby Sister or Alien Space Invader: A New Baby in the Family   162

Anticipating and Preventing Problems Related to a New Sibling   162

Solving Problems Related to a New Sibling   162

4. Get Well Soon, Big Baboon! We Miss Your Smile, Crocodile!: Hospitalization   163

Anticipating and Preventing Problems Related to Hospitalization   163

Solving Problems Related to Hospitalization   164

5. Healing a Hurting Heart: Death of a Loved One   165

Anticipating and Preventing Problems Related to Coping with Death   165

Solving Problems Related to Coping with Death   166

Questions about death   167

Death of a classroom pet   167

6. Growing Up and Moving On: Transitioning to the Next Grade or to the "Big School"   168

Anticipating and Preventing Problems Related to Transitioning to the Next Grade or School   168

Solving Problems Related to Transitioning to the Next Grade or School   170

Children who are worried about moving to the next grade   170

Conflicting styles and expectations among teachers in the next grade   170

Celebrations are child-centered, graduations are not   170

PART 5

Problematic Behaviors: Helping Children Who Hurt   173

Understanding Problematic Behaviors   174

The 10 "Ates" Approach for Effectively Dealing with Problematic Behaviors   175

Anticipate Problems   175

Accommodate Needs   175

Accommodating the needs of a child with problematic behaviors   179

Mediate Solutions   180

Investigate Causes   182

Update Strategies   184

1. Little Volcanoes: Children with Extreme or Dangerous Behaviors   185

Anticipating and Preventing Extreme or Dangerous Behaviors   186

Solving Problems Related to Extreme or Dangerous Behaviors   187

Anger   188

Restraining a child   189

2. You Can't Make Me!: Defiant Behavior and Power Struggles   190

Anticipating and Preventing Defiant Behaviors   190

Solving Problems Related to Defiant Behaviors   190

3. Perpetual(ly in) Motion: Active and Easily Distracted/Attracted   191

Anticipating and Preventing Problems Related to Children Who Are Active and Easily Distracted/ Attracted   192

Solving Problems Related to Children Who Are Active and Easily Distracted/ Attracted   192

4. This Problem Really Bites!   194

Anticipating and Preventing Biting   194

Solving Problems Related to Biting   195

5. **He Said a Bad Word, Teacher: Cursing, Name-Calling, and Foul Language** **196**

Anticipating and Preventing Foul Language 196

Solving Problems Related to Foul Language 197

Complaints from parents about foul language 197

6. **The Art of Nonverbal Communication: Excessive Crying or Whining** **198**

Anticipating and Preventing Excessive Crying or Whining 198

Solving Problems Related to Excessive Crying or Whining 199

7. **The Hits Just Keep on Coming: Physical Aggression** **200**

Anticipating and Preventing Physical Aggression 200

Solving Problems Related to Physical Aggression 201

Grabbing toys 202

Wrecking other children's projects 202

8. **Too Bossy: Getting Controlling under Control** **202**

Anticipating and Preventing Problems Related to Children Who Act Bossy 203

Solving Problems Related to Children Who Act Bossy 203

9. **Mean Girls, The Prequel: Verbal and Social Aggression** **204**

Anticipating and Preventing Verbal and Social Aggression 205

Solving Problems Related to Verbal Aggression 205

10. **I Didn't Do It, Teacher!: The Truth about Lying** **206**

Anticipating and Preventing Lying 206

Solving Problems Related to Lying 207

11. **In Their Comfort Zone: Masturbation and Self-Pleasuring** **208**

Anticipating and Preventing Self-Pleasuring 208

Solving Problems Related to Self-Pleasuring 209

12. **Puppies at Play: Roughhousing** **209**

Anticipating and Preventing Roughhousing 209

Solving Problems Related to Roughhousing 210

13. **These Boots Were Made for Walking: Running Inside** **211**

Anticipating and Preventing Running Inside 211

Solving Problems Related to Running Inside 211

14. **Children Who Are Too Silly: Better to Be Goofy Than Be Nobody** **212**

Anticipating and Preventing Silly Behavior 212

Solving Problems Related to Silly Behavior 212

15. **Spit Happens!** **213**

Anticipating and Preventing Spitting 213

Solving Problems Related to Spitting 214

16. **Stealing: The Need Is Too Much and the Temptation Too Great** **214**

Anticipating and Preventing Stealing 214

Solving Problems Related to Stealing 215

17. **Do Tell!: Tattling** **216**

Anticipating and Preventing Tattling 216

Solving Problems Related to Tattling 216

18. **Temper Tantrums: Save Yours for After Class!** **217**

Anticipating and Preventing Tantrums 217

Solving Problems Related to Tantrums 218

19. **Thumb Sucking: Comfort Always at Hand** **219**

Anticipating and Preventing Problems Related to Thumb Sucking 219

Solving Problems Related to Thumb Sucking 219

20. **Too Loud: Silence Isn't Golden but Neither Is Noise** **220**

Anticipating and Preventing Problems Related to Children Who Are Too Loud 220

Solving Problems Related to Children Who Are Too Loud 220

21. Cat Herding 101: Children Who Don't Listen or Follow Instructions   221

Anticipating and Preventing Problems Related to Children Who Won't Listen   221

Solving Problems Related to Children Who Won't Listen   221

PART 6

Partnering with Families to Raise Happy Children: It's a Team Effort   223

What Teachers Bring to the Partnership   224

What Parents Bring to the Partnership   224

Approach All Interactions as a Partnership   224

1. Nontraditional Families: They're Quickly Becoming Traditional   226

Anticipating and Preventing Problems Related to Partnering with Nontraditional Families   226

Solving Problems Related to Partnering with Nontraditional Families   226

2. A Special Partnership: Parents with Special Needs   227

Anticipating and Preventing Problems Related to Partnering with Parents with Special Needs   227

Solving Problems Related to Partnering with Parents with Special Needs   227

3. Beyond Feedback: Parents Who Complain   228

Anticipating and Preventing Complaints from Parents   228

Solving Problems Related to Parents who Complain   229

The chronic complainer   229

Behind your back   230

The angry parent   230

Complaints about your curriculum or style   231

A last resort   231

4. Beyond Busy: Parents Who Are Almost Always in a Hurry   231

Anticipating and Preventing Problems Related to Parents Who Are in a Hurry   232

Solving Problems Related to Parents Who Are in a Hurry   232

5. Beyond Helpful and Friendly: Parents Who Linger   232

Anticipating and Preventing Problems Related to Parents Who Linger   233

Solving Problems Related to Parents Who Linger   233

6. Beyond Late: Parents Who Arrive after the Center Closes   234

Anticipating and Preventing Parents from Arriving after the Center Closes   234

Solving Problems Related to Parents Who Arrive after the Center Closes   234

7. Having "The Talk": Discussing Children's Problematic Behavior with Their Parents   235

Anticipating and Preventing Problems Related to Discussing Children's Problematic Behavior   235

Solving Problems Related to Discussing Children's Problematic Behavior   236

8. Save the Children: Parents Who May Be Abusive or Neglectful   237

Anticipating and Preventing Problems Related to Parents Who May Be Abusive or Neglectful   237

Solving Problems Related to Parents Who May Be Abusive or Neglectful   237

Signs or indicators of abuse and neglect   238

What to do (and not to do) when you suspect abuse or neglect   239

If a parent asks for your help   239

PART 7

Problematic Behaviors Take 2: This Time It's the Adults!   241

1. Bullies, Bumblers, and Other Bad Bosses   242

Anticipating and Preventing Problems Related to Difficult Bosses   242

Solving Problems Related to Difficult Bosses   243

When you have a new boss   243

The authoritarian boss   243

The incompetent boss   244

If all else fails   244

2. Being a Boss without Bullying or Bumbling: Managing Assistants, Volunteers, and Others   245

Anticipating and Preventing Problems Related to Managing Others   245

Solving Problems Related to Managing Others   246

3. Coping with Confounding Coworkers   247

Anticipating and Preventing Problems with Coworkers   247

Solving Problems Related to Confounding Coworkers   248

Problems with coworkers that affect you directly   248

Problems with coworkers that affect children, families, and the program or school   249

PART 8

Take Care of the Caretaker: Attending to Your Own Needs   251

1. Never Enough Time: When Life Feels Like a Game of Beat the Clock   252

Anticipating and Preventing Problems Related to Never Having Enough Time   252

Solving Problems Related to Never Having Enough Time   253

Short on planning time   253

Time seems to slip away   253

Too many committees and meetings   254

Rushed and hassled   254

Procrastinating   254

2. Just Not Feelin' It: Burned Out and Fed Up   255

Anticipating and Preventing Burnout   255

Solving Problems Related to Feeling Burned Out   257

3. Wage Outrage: Underpaid Is an Understatement   259

Anticipating and Preventing Problems Related to Being Underpaid   259

Solving Problems Related to Being Underpaid   259

Finding the better paying jobs in early childhood education   260

Grants   261

4. In Over Your Head and Overwhelmed: How to Tread Water Until You Learn to Swim   261

Anticipating and Preventing Problems Related to Being Overwhelmed   261

Solving Problems Related to Feeling Overwhelmed   262

PART 9

Being a Professional in a Semi-Professional Profession: The A, B, C, D, and E of Working in the Field of Early Childhood   263

1. "A" Is for Advocacy   266

Social Advocacy   266

Child Advocacy   266

2. "B" Is for Brave: Male Teachers of Young Children   267

Female Teachers with Male Coworkers or Assistants   268

Male Teachers   269

3. "C" Is for Comportment: Promoting a Professional Image and Reputation   270

4. "D" Is for Dilemmas: Everyday Ethical Issues   271

A Third Way: Resolving Ethical Dilemmas   271

5. "E" Is for Egregious: How Can We Solve Our Profession's Most Pressing, Long-Standing Problems?   273

Is There Any Good News for Our Field from the Last Twenty-Five Years?   275

What Are Some Lessons Learned?   276

So, What Are Some Practical Solutions?   276

What Will It Take to Reinvent Our Profession? 277

Could This Ever Really Happen? 277

Resources 279

Comprehensive Resources 280

Print Materials 280

Websites—categorized by the type of host organization 280

Videos and Video Collections 281

Resources by Topic 282

Advocacy, Public Policy, and Research 282

Art and Aesthetics 282

Behavior Issues, Positive Guidance, Classroom Management, and Social/ Emotional Development 283

Brain Development 284

Child Development 284

Cultural Responsiveness and Diversity 285

Curriculum and Project-Based Learning 286

Disabilities, Inclusion, and Children with Special Needs 288

Environments: Indoor and Outside 289

Family Language Is Other Than English 289

Family Partnerships 290

Health, Safety, and Nutrition 290

Literacy and Language 291

Math 291

Observation, Assessment, Reflection, and Documentation 292

Play 293

Professionalism: Professional Development and Quality Programs, Classrooms, and Teaching 293

School Readiness 294

Science 294

Sexual Development, Sex Roles, and Gender Identity 295

Standards 296

Technology and Media Literacy 296

Testing 297

Glossary of Common Terms and Jargon 299

References 309

Acknowledgments

This book reflects the collective wisdom and inspiration of many, many dedicated and caring teachers, administrators, and early childhood professionals (of all stripes) that I have had the good fortune to observe, work with, and learn from. I have been very lucky to have been given opportunities to experience and participate in a wide variety of programs across four continents. I am compelled to name as many of the amazing people who have influenced me and whom I so admire as I can recall. All are tireless crusaders for the right of every young child to have a happy childhood. I know I will forget to mention some, so please accept my apology in advance.

My first job was as an assistant teacher in Baltimore in the mid-seventies in one of the first YMCA-sponsored child care programs in the U.S. My supervisor and lead teacher was Sarah Watson, who taught me that having fun was an important element of a quality program.

In the early eighties, at Clark College in Vancouver, WA, the professionalism of Maggie Anderson, Kathy Bobula, and Harriet Levi was inspiring. And later, as a Head Start director in the mid-eighties, I learned a great deal from Joe Verano and Sue Bernt.

My thirteen years at Portland State University were amazing. During this time I wrote the first version of this book and worked with Head Start Programs in Oregon, Washington, Idaho, and Alaska. My boss, Cari Olmstead, who continues to be my dear friend, was a master diplomat who led with grace, humor, and one of the sharpest minds I've ever met. Incredible colleagues included Linda Crum, Mary Perkins, Mary Foltz, Melissa Endicott, Jenna Bauman Adams, Margie Tattersfield, Johnnie Cain, Chuck Smith, Sally Skelding, Olga Talley, Sally Mead, Bonny Headley, Bonnie Kitteridge, Beryl Cheal, and Ginger Fink. Other important colleagues at PSU were Barbara Friesen, Nancy Koroloff, and Amy Driscoll (also my doctoral thesis advisor), among many others. In the Department of Ed, I learned so much from Dell White Ford, Gayle McMurria-Bachik, Maya Close, and Anita McClanahan. The brilliant Head Start RAP network (many of whom I worked with later in the Open Society Foundations' Step by Step program) included Joanne Brady, Roxane Kaufmann, Kris Hansen, Barbara Wolfe, Sue Smith, Luis Hernandez, and Alan Taylor. On the front lines in Head Start programs were amazing teachers and administrators such as Ronnie Herndon, Elaine Harrison, Alan Berlin, Marilyn Harrison, Pam Greenough, Michael Eichman, Jennifer Cahill, Susan Brady, Suzanne VanOrman, Annie Soto, Jo O'Leary, Jan Elyse Witt, Dennis Huft, Caroline Huft, John Bancroft, Doug Fagerness, and Nanette Sieman.

In the 2000s, I had the pleasure of working with and knowing Tim Speth, Lena Ko, Debbie Ellis, Amy Stuczynski, Becky Harmon, Delia Palomeque Morales, Rex Hagan, Nancy Henry, and many more at Education Northwest. An Early Reading First grant gave me the opportunity to collaborate with Deborah Leong, Elena Bodrova, and Ruth Hensen.

Among my professional colleagues, I want to particularly acknowledge Nico Van Oudenhoven, Bengt Ageros, Lory Britain, Kim Browning, Sam Meisels, Roger Neugebauer, Martin Whitehead, David Hawker, Stephanie Feeney, Sue Bredekamp, and Ellen Galinsky.

I greatly appreciate George Soros, Sarah Klaus, Divya Lata, Hugh McLean, Tina Hyder, Kate Lapham, Almaz Ismayilova, and others at the Open Society Foundations for giving me the opportunity to do international work and for their unrelenting commitment to equity and justice for all young children and families. I was lucky enough to have worked with Cassie

Landers on several projects. She has been a role model, mentor, supporter, and friend whose caring, creativity, drive, and intellect are boundless. My terrific Step by Step colleagues included Iryna Lapitskaya, Radu Jusovic, Cornelia Cincilei, Natalia Sofiy, Gerda Sula, Tatanya Vonta, Ulvyia Mikailova, Dawn Tankersley, Bob Stake, Larry Bremner, Linda Lee, and many more. In Bangladesh I worked with and learned from Faith Lamb-Parker, Mahmuda Akhtar, Fahmida Tofail, Nishat Rahman, Golam Kibria, Shanti Chakma, and Muhammad Wahedi, to name a few. In Russia, I partnered with a great team led by the brilliant and heroic Lena Lenskaya and including Elena Cherkashina, Elena Yudina, Elena Kozhevnikova, and Tigran Shmis, among others.

Among my wonderful friends and colleagues in The Gambia were Elizabeth Ndebe Joof, Lisong Bah, and Herve Akinocho.

Open Society Foundations-funded projects in several southern African countries gave me the opportunity to work with Justine Ngulube, Patrick Makokoro, Lynette Okengo, and others.

I thoroughly enjoyed working in the Republic of Georgia on a UNICEF-funded project to develop a national curriculum with Nato Panchulidze, Ana Janelidze, Tamuna Bakradze, Tsira Barkaia, Nutsa Pruidze, and so many more.

I have always had great support from close friends and family, particularly Sunny Cohen, Jonah Saifer, Debbie Read, Lilia Doni, Felicia Doni, and Laurentiu Doni.

Finally, I am extremely grateful to the team at Redleaf Press for publishing this book, for all their support over more than a quarter of a century, and for accepting my next book for publication, currently titled *Higher-Order Thinking (HOT) Skills for Young Learners Pre-K through 2nd Grade*. I want to acknowledge in particular Eileen Nelson, David Heath, Laurie Hermann, Kara Lomen, and the many expert editors and reviewers.

Introduction

The purpose of this book is to make your job easier by helping you be more efficient and effective. I hope this book will give you skills and confidence to do what you know is necessary and right so your classroom is a fabulous place for children—and for you and your coworkers—to be nurtured, to learn, and to grow.

Know and follow the policies and procedures your program has in place. If some of those policies and procedures limit your ability to help the children and their families thrive, work toward amending them in a helpful and positive way. Use this book as a resource and be open and clear with your supervisor and coworkers about what you want to change and why. If you work in a facility licensed by your state, you must abide by the state's regulations—even if they are more stringent than the recommendations in this book.

This book approaches issues from the perspective of problems, but I think that it is optimistic. You will find that there are potentially many positive solutions to even the trickiest of problems. We will never eliminate all the problems in early childhood education. That's not my goal. Instead, I hope to help you reduce and manage them so your work with young children and families will be overwhelmingly positive. When things are going well, no job on earth is more fun, more rewarding, and more important to society than teaching and caring for young children.

I have tried to make this book helpful to all early childhood teachers wherever they work. I have tried to be relevant to all programs no matter their funding source (public, private, religious affiliated, and so on), their structure (full-day, half-day, or other), the curriculum they use (such as Montessori, Creative Curriculum, Reggio Emilia, or High/Scope), where they take place (whether in a center, school, church, home, or under a tree), or whether they are called child care, day care, preschool, nursery school, school, Head Start, pre-K, or kindergarten. In reality, excellent programs for young children have many more similarities than differences. In every one of the categories listed above, there are examples of superb teaching, very low-quality teaching, and everything in between. All good teachers are similar in many ways—they are intentional, creative, reflective, responsive; they individualize and have caring, positive relationships with children—but they all use different emphases, styles, strengths, and talents in their work. This book helps you solve problems while encouraging you to cultivate and assert your own style.

I wrote this book for both experienced and new teachers, for teachers with formal education and for teachers without. I assume that all my readers are intelligent, capable, quick learners and people who care deeply. For the new or not formally trained teacher, I have strived to be clear, concise, and free of jargon. I have focused on the basic, most vital advice and information, which is based on my forty years of experience in the field and on current and respected theory and research. You can learn more about every topic from the resources and the references listed at the end of the book. Because the Internet has put a world of information at our fingertips, the primary skills we need now in order to learn something new has shifted from finding information to sorting the good information from the bad and the useful from the useless. So I have tried to find a few key web-based resources that are good (accurate, insightful, and thorough), useful (relevant to our work and with practical implications), and, in many cases, enjoyable, particularly the blogs. There is a brief description of each website and they are organized into broad categories alphabetically by topic, from advocacy to testing.

One book cannot address all possible problems, and many good solutions are undoubtedly missing from this book. I hope the suggestions included here will serve to stimulate your own ideas. Carefully read the "Anticipating and Preventing Problems" section in each chapter because the best solutions are the ones you never have to use! A positive, nurturing, well-organized, and engaging classroom leaves little room for problems to spring up. It's like planting a field with beautiful wildflowers—they will crowd out the weeds.

Planting flowers reminds me of one of my favorite children's books, *Miss Rumphius* by Barbara Cooney. When she is a young girl, Alice Rumphius's grandfather instills in her the obligation to do something to make the world more beautiful. Toward the end of an adventurous life, the aging and ailing Miss Rumphius finally figures out how to do this. She spreads lupine seeds wherever she goes and from that time on becomes known as the Lupine Lady. Miss Rumphius passes down that same obligation to her great-niece, the story's narrator, who wonders, as Alice Rumphius once did, how she will do this someday.

As often as possible, do something with or for your children that makes the world a little more beautiful. And have fun while you do it.

HOW TO BE THE "PRO" IN PROBLEM-SOLVER

Choose the Problems You Like to Solve

Perhaps the main task of our lives is to solve problems, big and small. Solving one problem often leads to the "gift" of solving deeper, more complex, and, if we are lucky, more interesting problems. I think that people who are successful in their jobs have chosen a field and position that deals with the type of problems they like to work on, because a main function of any job is to solve problems, and problems never go away. If you care about children but prefer to struggle with balancing a budget rather than with balancing the needs of children, you should consider an administrative job in the field. However, if you prefer playing with boards rather than meeting with them, then please be a teacher, or perhaps an adventure playground designer! I have been in meetings with engineers and physicists who are quite impressed when I say that I can help a parent or teacher deal with an angry three-year-old who bites. They quickly agree that this is much harder than rocket science . . . for them. However, I think that the main difference between us is that I like the challenge of solving human problems and they like the challenge of solving physical or theoretical problems.

Have an Effective Approach to Solving Problems in General

Here is a five-part approach called the "10 Ates": Anticipate, Accommodate, Mediate (de-escalate, validate, collaborate, negotiate, and educate), Investigate, and Update.

- **Anticipate** problems that might occur and prepare for them.

- **Accommodate** needs.

- **Mediate** the problem directly. With conflicts and highly emotional issues, it is often necessary to first **de-escalate** tensions and to **validate** the feelings and needs of everyone involved. Then **collaborate** and **negotiate** a solution. Use the problem as an opportunity to **educate** yourself and others about ways to solve conflicts and other problems in positive ways that address the immediate problem *and* lead to a permanent solution in the longer term.

- **Investigate** to try to determine the cause(s) of the problem.
- **Update** your strategies and conditions in response to the results of the mediation and the investigation to better solve the problem and prevent it from happening again.

This approach is described in detail in regard to dealing with problematic behaviors starting on page 173. However, it can be applied to nearly any and every problem. The order of the five main strategies will vary and often overlap. They may even happen simultaneously.

Take Time If You Can

For less immediate problems, take as much time as you can. Solutions—or at least good ideas for possible solutions—often come after letting the problem "simmer" in your mind over several days. And they often come when you are not thinking about the problem directly. However, do not let problems go. Most problems will get worse and cause more problems if not addressed.

All You Can Do Is Good Enough . . . If You Have the Tools

Know your limitations. Ask for help when you need it from someone whom you respect and trust, and get information from a book, journal, video, or trustworthy Internet source. Sometimes implementing the best solution is impossible because of limitations of staff, funds, time, or other reasons. Knowing the best ways to fully solve the problem is still helpful. Then try partial or limited solutions, because they are more realistic. You may be able to implement a fuller and deeper response to the problem at a later point. As the expression goes, "Don't allow perfect to be the enemy of good." This book offers a variety of solutions to each problem for that reason.

To fix a wide variety of problems, you need to have many "tools" (strategies) in your "toolbox." The right tool for the job will usually fix the problem quickly and thoroughly, if not permanently. If you needed to pound a wood stake into the ground but only had a small hammer made for driving in tacks, you would be very frustrated and ineffective. If you had to use a sledgehammer to drive in a tack, you would probably put a hole in the wall and create more problems without solving any.

Sometimes it takes a particular tool to deal with a problem in the early stages and a different tool when things are beginning to improve. For example, to move a child from one activity to another, you may at first have to assist the child with verbal and gentle physical guidance, which is a very blunt tool. However, after a few weeks, you may be able to just use a verbal reminder, which is a more refined tool.

There are more workers and tools that are more powerful and specialized at a big construction site than at a home remodel. The same principle applies to solving problems. Larger and more complex problems require solutions that take more time and effort. In such cases you will likely have to use several approaches, more sophisticated approaches, involve more people who can help, and be persistent and patient.

How Is Criticism Like a Mosquito Bite?

Find an analogy to the problem. For example, think about how dealing with critical coworkers or bosses is like dealing with something else that is very annoying, such as mosquitoes. We keep mosquitoes at bay with a window screen, which still allows us to see outside and for air to flow. In a similar way, we can put up a "mental screen" that blocks out negativity but allows neutral and positive messages to flow through. We also avoid going where there a lot of mosquitoes, such as swampy areas or outside in the evening when they are most active. Likewise, we can avoid as much as possible being in the same place at the same time as a person who is critical. Mosquito bites can hurt, but the pain and itchiness do not last long. The same is true of criticism. Mosquitoes are annoying, but we don't let them ruin our summer fun. So, we should not let a critical person ruin the good things and enjoyment we get from our work.

There May Be a Good Reason for Being Unreasonable

Take the perspective of the person involved in the problem. If you were that person, why might you do what he did? Why would I, like one particular father I used to know, drop my child off in the morning at the front door and not walk him into the classroom, despite being repeatedly asked to do so? Perhaps because I'm always late for work? Because my child doesn't want me to walk with him into the classroom? Because my child separates from me more easily this way? Because for some reason I feel uncomfortable in the classroom or with the teachers? Because of a conflict with another parent who may be there? All of the above?

Look for positive aspects of the problem or problematic behavior. I once had to figure out how to get a child to take a nap or at least lie quietly on her cot. Nothing seemed to work and she disrupted other children from their naps. I thought that the positive aspect of the behavior may be that she did not want to miss anything. But what could she miss? All the other children were sleeping, or trying to. However, I finally realized that all the staff members were walking around doing various tasks and she liked to interact with adults more than with other children. The problem was solved when we decided that we would all lie down beside the children for the first fifteen minutes or so of naptime. The hard part was trying not to fall asleep!

Rules Rule

Good rules or norms that are fair and reasonable and mutually agreed upon can prevent and solve many problems. No society can function without rules (laws), no family or group can function without norms, and neither can a classroom. Nearly every chapter suggests establishing rules for that particular activity, in addition to general classroom rules. The essential element of nearly all the rules is to foster mutual respect. There are various ways to express respect in rules, such as "Use your hands and words to help, not hurt" or "Put a toy back in its box and back on the shelf when you are done." As much as possible, specific rules should be developed through discussions and by consensus with the children. Start the discussion by asking them what they don't like other children to do in the block area, during imaginary play, at lunch time, and so on. When a rule is agreed upon, help them rephrase it to state what to do, rather than what not to do. Rules should be revisited regularly, or as needed, and changed, eliminated, or added to. The core message of classroom rules is actually similar to most workplace and community rules for adults: respect each other and the environment.

Is There a Solution to Every Problem?

Apparently, believing that there is a solution to every problem is a particularly American trait, related to how much we value a "can-do, never-give-up" attitude. Whether true or not, and in spite of how naive it may be, I do think it is a helpful belief, particularly when dealing with difficult, complex problems. It spurs us to persevere. While I am a typical, overly optimistic American, I think it is realistic to believe that *most* problems have solutions and that every problem can be at least mitigated and better managed. I can't recall a time when I have not been able to offer a teacher at least *some* useful ideas for dealing with classroom problems more effectively. Admittedly, it probably has as much to do with being a neutral, outside observer as it does with having expertise, but please don't tell that to anyone.

Perhaps it is less naive to believe there *is* a solution to every problem if there is the will to solve it and it is given sufficient effort, resources, and time. I often think of my father, a scientist and political activist who died in 1995, whenever there is a new political development, social change, or advancement in science or technology that solves a problem he was concerned about during his life. So, perhaps it is more accurate to say that there is a solution to every problem . . . if you live long enough!

This book addresses many different specific problems organized into nine sections: daily dilemmas, classroom concerns, children with challenges, children coping with change, helping children with problematic behaviors (the largest section of the book), partnering with parents and families, dealing with the problematic behaviors of coworkers and supervisors, attending to your own needs, and being a professional. The final chapter goes into depth about the long-running problems in our profession that we have not been able to solve: low wages and status and implementing a child-centered, play- and exploration-based curriculum. We still have too many young children in low-quality programs that their parents can barely afford to pay for and that their teachers can barely afford to work for.

WHAT'S NEW TO THIS EDITION?

This third edition incorporates much of the new knowledge and many of the new issues, trends, and challenges that have impacted the early childhood field in the years since the second edition. Every chapter has been updated to reflect both the most recent thinking and research in the field and new technology. While still primarily focused on programs for children three to five, it is more inclusive of kindergarten programs. I made changes to certain terms that were outdated or needed to be more accurate. I updated the resources and references as well. In addition, I developed a website with direct links to all the web addresses and additional resources found in this edition. I will publish a bi-weekly blog post and host discussion forums there, too. The address is http://practical-solutions.net. I hope you'll visit!

New Knowledge

Essential Life Skills

We now know the importance of helping children develop a particular set of abilities, commonly referred to as essential life skills, that highly correlate with being successful in school and in life (Galinsky 2010): critical thinking, self-regulation (the ability to focus and have self-control), perspective taking, communicating effectively, making connections, taking on challenges, and being a self-directed and engaged learner. These abilities are rarely measured by IQ tests or school readiness tests.

Higher-Order Thinking Skills

The essential life skills of critical thinking, perspective taking, and making connections are all higher-order thinking skills. However, higher-order thinking also includes the ability to imagine, evaluate, make judgments and decisions, infer, generate ideas, and more. Even babies are capable of some of these thinking skills, at a basic level, when parents and caregivers elicit them and nurture their development (Bloom 2010; Saifer 2016).

Brain Development

Because of new technology and research, we know even more now about how the human brain develops and functions, about the capabilities of infants' brains, and about the impact of experiences in the first five years of life in shaping the actual structure of the brain. Cleverly designed studies of preverbal babies show they can make prosocial moral judgments, have preferences for others who are similar to them, and have negative feelings for those who are not. They are even able to make inferences about other people's intentions (Bloom 2013; Hamlin, Newman and Wynn 2009; Hamlin, Wynn, and Bloom 2007).

Praise Effort, Not Ability

Carol Dweck's (2015) research on motivation revealed the surprising finding that praising children's abilities has a negative impact on their motivation to learn. For example, saying, "You're really good at math!" has a negative effect on the child's motivation to learn math, which eventually affects her performance in math. Apparently, children come to view math ability (or any ability that is praised in this way) as an inborn talent, as part of their identity, and not in their control. Having to put effort into learning more difficult math conflicts with this self-image, so they avoid it. However, praise for their efforts such as, "You really worked long and hard to figure out the answer to that tricky math problem," conveys the message that ability is the result of effort, which motivates children to continue to work hard. In this way, they feel in control of their math ability and have greater confidence that their efforts to learn more difficult math will be successful.

Consequences Are Not Effective

Previous versions of this book included the use of logical consequences as an alternative to rewards and punishments for dealing with problematic behaviors. However, we now know that consequences do not eliminate, deter, or improve problematic behaviors (Lewis 2015). This is true particularly for young children who, in many cases, cannot make the connection between the cause (their behavior) and the effect (the consequence). They are just beginning to grasp the concept that a *cause* may have an *effect* that is not immediate or direct. Even when they can make the connection, it is difficult for most young children to use that information to stop themselves from repeating the behavior at a later time. Practically, consequences have little or no deterrent effect. From the perspective of the child, a consequence is no different from a punishment.

The Value of Social Imaginary Play

Social imaginary play—also called dramatic play, socio-dramatic play, make-believe play, and pretend play—involves two or more children imagining they are in a particular place, taking on roles related to the place, and acting out what they imagine happens there. It seems that the more we learn about the importance of play for children's healthy development, particularly social imaginary play, the more it is being eliminated from classrooms. This is especially true for kindergarten classrooms. There are few activities as complex as pretend play for young children. They use their imaginations, interact socially with several children at once, use language to direct the course of the play, negotiate roles and scenarios, take on the persona of a different person, create a story line, use props in unique ways, move physically, and more. Based on Vygotsky's theories, Elena Bodrova, Carrie Germeroth, and Deborah Leong (2013) have made a compelling argument that pretend play is one of the most effective ways to help children develop self-regulation, among other benefits.

Cultural Responsiveness

The United States is a more diverse country than it was when the last edition of this book was published, and it will be even more so in the future. Immigrant families, most of whom do not speak English at home, now live in every state and in nearly every county of every state, urban and rural. We have come far from the days when we thought that the best response to diversity was to see everyone as equal and treat all children just the same. Rather than ignoring cultural differences, we now strive to understand, appreciate, and celebrate the diverse cultures in our classrooms. We try to be responsive to the many different culture-based beliefs, values, and practices of children and their families, as well as to the significant differences among individual families within every culture. Although it's not possible to include a discussion of cultural differences for every issue and for every culture, there are "Cultural Awareness Alert" boxes throughout the book with examples of ways that the beliefs and behaviors of children and families from non-mainstream U.S. cultures and ethnic groups tend to differ from the norms and expectations in most of our classrooms. Even if there is not much cultural, racial, or ethnic diversity among your group of children, it is helpful to understand that many beliefs and practices we think of as "normal" and applicable to every child and family actually vary a great deal across cultures. This is particularly true about child-rearing practices. In addition, it is important for a homogeneous group of children to experience and appreciate diversity.

Intentional Teaching

Teaching with intention involves thoughtful planning based on children's needs and interests; using teaching and learning strategies that are responsive to the learning styles, abilities, and cultures of all children in the class; making adjustments during planned activities to be more responsive and effective; recognizing and using "teachable moments"; and critically reflecting on one's own teaching. In a nutshell, it's knowing what you are doing, why you are doing it, and how you might do it better! It's not so much a new concept as one that has been more recently recognized as a key attribute of quality teaching. (See Epstein 2007 and Barnes 2012 in the references on p. 309 for more information about intentional teaching.)

Globalization: New (and Continuing) Inspirations from Europe and Oceania

It should be no surprise that given our increasingly shrinking world (our global village), influences from other countries that have better systems of early childhood education and care would reach the United States. The Reggio Emilia approach, while well known and highly touted here since 1987 when the first exhibit appeared in the United States, has continued to strongly influence practices in early childhood programs. These influences include the use of "loose parts" and items from nature, spending time outside, classroom environments that are well organized and aesthetically beautiful, inquiry- and project-based learning, strong connections between early childhood programs and communities, and the thoughtful documentation of children's work.

The Netherlands has led the way in the development of a comprehensive, sensible, and effective relationship/sexuality education program, called "Spring Fever," that starts with four-year-olds and extends through high school (Melker 2015). Norway and other Nordic countries have given us Outdoor Preschools, also called Forest Kindergartens. Culturally responsive curriculum done deeply and with beauty and compassion comes to us from New Zealand and is called "Te Whāriki" (New Zealand Ministry of Education 1996). In Australia, intentional teaching and environmentally sustainable practices for early childhood programs are fully embraced and widely practiced, providing us with many creative ideas and concrete examples of how to teach with intention and engage children in caring for our planet. These are just a few examples of innovative and effective education programs from outside of the United States that can inspire us to do our best for our children.

New Issues, Trends, and Challenges

Preschool Expulsions and Suspensions

In 2005, Researcher Walter Gilliam found that children in preschool programs are expelled at three times the rate of children in K–12 schools. More recent research from the U.S. Department of Education Office for Civil Rights (2014) found that "Black children make up 18% of preschool enrollment, but 48% of preschool children suspended more than once, and boys receive more than three out of four out-of-school preschool suspensions" (p. 3). There is widespread agreement that the problem results from a combination of more children with more intense emotional needs, teachers who have not received adequate training to meet the needs of boys, black children, and children with problematic behaviors, and a lack of access to mental health specialists with expertise in young children. While this book is no substitute for a mental health expert or for training sessions, it will help you respond more effectively to the more serious problem behaviors (the ones that may lead to a child being expelled). It can be a good complementary resource to go with training and help from a specialist. There are children whose emotional needs are so great and behaviors so violent that they really do need to be in a different type of program where trained mental health specialists can provide intensive, individualized help to the child and the family, at least for a time. In these rare cases, the children need to be referred and helped, not expelled.

Sustainability and Environmental Issues

The need to instill in children an appreciation of nature and the disposition and skills to reduce waste and to reuse and recycle materials is greater than ever. When adults consistently model and promote these behaviors, children will internalize them. It's much like helping children develop good health habits. To instill the habit of tooth-brushing, we brush with the children, do it every day, and help them do it properly. To instill habits of sustainability, we model reusing and recycling paper, plastic, and glass; we remind children and help them reuse and recycle; and we do it many times each day, every day.

Technology Everywhere!

The ubiquity of smartphones and tablets is a mixed blessing. They distract teachers and parents from attending to children, but they also give teachers and parents amazing tools to make their jobs easier, more enjoyable, and more productive. Their potential for positive use with and for young children is unlimited and has barely been tapped. The expansion of the Internet in scope and power has given us access to many more resources, much of it free, particularly videos. It was not very long ago that videos meant for professional development—whether self-made or professionally done—were expensive and sparingly used training tools.

The Quantification of Early Childhood Programs

Outside of our field, there has been a major shift in how others view the purpose of early childhood programs. While we see ourselves primarily as nurturers of children's overall development and partners with parents to create happy childhoods, some—such as policy makers, economists, business leaders, and politicians—see us primarily as producers of outcomes, that is, of children who are school ready, score high on tests, and save taxpayers money because they will be less likely in the future to need special education, drop out, go to jail, or be unemployed. They see early childhood programs as only having value as an investment. And to show that early childhood programs are a "good" investment because they achieve those outcomes requires quantifiable data: Are children who attend preschool more school ready than those who do not attend? Do they score higher on tests? Are their scores average or above? Do some teachers and programs get better outcomes than others and, if so, which ones and why? The result of gathering all this data is that children, teachers, and programs are being scrutinized, evaluated, tested, and judged like never before. We are all feeling stressed by these pressures. This is what I mean by the "quantification" of early childhood programs.

Common Core State Standards (CCSS)

Another contributing factor to the quantification of early education are the Common Core State Standards. While the intentions of the CCSS are good—to improve the quality of K–12 education—the actual standards and their implementation are very flawed. This is particularly true of the standards for kindergarten, the earliest grade level for which standards exist. They were developed, in large part, to create uniformity so that the same tests can be given to students in schools across the country and, therefore, schools, districts, and even states can be compared and ranked, and rewarded and punished. Behind this is a political goal to hold public schools more accountable for the achievement, or lack of achievement, of their students.

To do this requires collecting a good deal of comparable data, which means that students now take too many high-stakes tests. Even if the tests were excellent—actually they have been widely criticized (Chicago Teachers Union, 2014; Greene, 2015)—they do not help teachers individualize better and teach more effectively because the school year is nearly over by the time teachers see the results. The tests are generally given in April and May and the results are not available for several weeks after that (Smarter Balanced Assessment Consortium, no date). The tests are high stakes because the results are used to make important decisions about funding, setting district boundaries, opening and closing schools, and hiring and firing teachers, principals, and administrators. However, the main impact is that it increases everyone's anxiety and stress because of the pressure for good test scores. These are not the conditions that optimize children's learning and development.

Early Learning and Development Standards (ELDS)

Yet another contributor to the quantification of early childhood education is the Early Learning and Development Standards (ELDS). Every state has developed its own set of ELDS that describe what four-year-olds should know and be able to do. (Many ELDS include standards for younger children as well.) The ELDS in a number of states include standards that are problematic because they were developed to align with K–12 standards, making them too heavily focused on a narrow set of superficial skills. While a set of standards can be helpful by communicating a shared belief of what is important for children's optimal development, they can also be harmful if they are too specific and prescriptive. Nonetheless, all standards are problematic by their nature because they create expectations for performing, put teachers in an evaluation mind-set, and have biases. Their biases are reflected most strongly by what is included and what is left out. To make my point, it's not all that difficult to develop standards that will favor urban children over rural children and vice versa, or favor bilingual children over monolingual children and vice versa. Standards are particularly troubling when applied to young children. Early development is characterized by its unevenness and by large differences among children in their rates and patterns of development. The main impact of the ELDS is similar to that of the CCSS tests: too much stress and pressure caused by too much assessing that too often leads to shortsighted educational decisions and ineffective, if not harmful, teaching and learning practices.

The Score: Superficial Skills = 1; Exploration, Understanding, Play = 0

Among these stress-induced negative decisions and practices are inappropriate curriculum content and methods pushed down to younger and younger children. The kindergarten curriculum is what the first-grade curriculum was twenty years ago, although children's developmental milestones have not changed in the last one hundred years (Gesell Institute of Child Development 2012). And now, early childhood programs are expected to prepare children for the rigors of kindergarten! This downward pressure is transmitted to early childhood teachers and administrators from parents, community leaders, K–12 educators, politicians, and so on who want the children who are growing up with challenges—including poverty, family language that is not English, and few intellectually enriching experiences—to be "ready for school" and the children who are growing up with ample resources to be ready to be "top [test] performers." They want every child to be well prepared for the intense pressure they will face at school—a humane reason, at least, but the wrong strategy—and because students' performance has high-stakes consequences for schools. All this pressure too often results in early childhood teachers teaching the curriculum, rather than the children. The curriculum is too narrowly focused on discrete, superficial math and literacy skills. In too many classrooms, time and space for deep learning across all areas of development is limited or nonexistent. Sustained imaginary play, creative expression, and big physical play are quickly becoming extinct.

Terminology

New Terms

Work-play time has replaced the term "free choice time." The reason for the change is that, unlike the names for all the other daily activities, free choice describes the format of the activity, not what happens during the activity. Other terms commonly used for free choice—free play, center time, learning center time, activity time, work time, play time—are also problematic for various reasons. I realize that creating a new term may cause confusion, especially because it is an invented term. But I hope it will catch on, because I think it accurately captures much of what children do and conveys the idea that for young children, play and work are often one and the same. In the saying "Play is the work of the child" (attributed to Maria Montessori), the meaning of "work" is ambiguous. It could mean "effort," in that children work hard at playing, but it more likely means "the main task" or "primary job." However, in practice, we use the word "work" quite often with young children, almost always to mean "effort" or to do a chore. Is a child who spends a long time completing a challenging puzzle working or playing? Perhaps the child is doing both—work-playing! Are children who clean up the block area by pretending to be forklift operators playing, working, or work-playing? Our language reinforces the notion that work means effort and play means leisure. So, only by combining the two can we communicate the idea that children simultaneously work and play or quickly change from one to the other.

Problematic behaviors has replaced the term *challenging behaviors*. I was never fully comfortable with the term *challenging behaviors*. From the child's perspective, her behaviors are not challenging. The term focuses on the teacher's perception and needs rather than the child's needs or on the dynamics of the interaction between a child and a teacher. Also, there are behaviors that need attending to but are not particularly challenging for most teachers to deal with.

Imaginary play has replaced the term *dramatic play*. The reason for this change is to use a term that describes the most important aspect of this type of play. The full term is actually *social imaginary play* because it usually involves several children, but it is shortened for easier use. Also, the word *dramatic* brings to mind theater, scripts, and performances. Children do take on roles, but there is no script and no audience . . . except for the teacher and his camera.

Family language other than English (FLOE) has replaced the term *English language learner (ELL)* and *dual language learner (DLL)*. Other terms have been used, and some are still being used, such as *English as a second language (ESL)*, *language other than English (LOTE)*, *English as a foreign language (EFL)*, *English as an additional language (EAL)*, and *English for speakers of other languages (ESOL)*. The use of ELL and other terms shifted to DLL because all those other terms are inaccurate. However, DLL is also inaccurate, as there are children who are learning to speak more than two languages (as did my own children) and a dual language learner can be a child whose primary family language is English. The children who we are concerned about, who we need to give specialized assistance to, are those children who live in homes where little or no English is spoken. In keeping with the tone of all the previous terms and borrowing from them, I rephrased this concept to "(children whose) family language is other than English (FLOEs)." I think it is more accurate and easier to remember than other terms and it "floes" nicely off the tongue!

Clarification of Terms

Preschool, school, child care, pre-K, kindergarten, and early childhood programs. All of these terms are used in various places throughout the book. If discussing an issue specific to full-day programs for working parents, the term *child care* is used. *Preschool* is used to refer to any program that serves children from older toddlers on up to kindergarten. The term *kindergarten* is used only when specifically referring to the grade before first grade (generally five-year-olds). However, *early childhood education and development (ECED) programs* is the term used most often as it encompasses all of these.

Teachers. This term refers to everyone and anyone who is responsible for the ongoing care and education of a group of children, even if the group consists of three-year-olds and even if it does not happen in an elementary school building. I realize that in some places, it is a legal term for someone who has a particular college degree and a state-issued teaching license (the term *educator* is sometimes used to get around this), but in common usage, *teacher* has a broader meaning. There have been many attempts to come up with a term that combines caregiving and teaching, but none of them have stuck to date.

Children. This term is used to describe human beings between one day and thirteen years of age, although this book focuses on those humans between about two and a half and six and a half years of age. In some settings they may be called kids, pupils, or students, but in this book they are almost always called "children."

Classrooms, centers, schools, and programs. These are also used throughout the book and are usually interchangeable terms. Although targeted to teachers working in center-based programs, this book has helpful ideas for early childhood teachers in any setting, including family child care homes, hospitals, shopping malls, cruise ships, resorts, and conferences. I apologize to all the talented and hardworking teachers in those settings for not specifically referring to your place of work beyond this paragraph.

Parents and families. These terms are used interchangeably and refer to the primary caretakers of the children in your class, including grandparents, foster parents, stepparents, relatives, or others. The child's legal guardians must also be included in all communications, if they are not the primary caregivers.

1

Daily Dilemmas

THIS PART OF THE BOOK deals with some very difficult situations for children. Separating from a parent, eating and sleeping somewhere other than home, wanting to be liked, and making and keeping friends are just some of the psychologically fraught issues that our very young children face daily. It's no surprise then why problems arise, particularly during these stress-inducing times of the day. There is a great deal for a "beginner at life" to feel anxious and insecure about, and for those children who already carry significant anxieties, these challenges can feel overwhelming. For some children, "acting out" is an effective way to cover up fears and push down anxieties. It is a stronger impulse than the fear of any negative consequences for the behavior. So, the teacher's role is to see things from the children's perspective, create an empathetic and safe emotional climate, and give children the skills and support they need to successfully negotiate these challenges.

1. RIGHT FROM THE START

The tone for the day for you and the children is often set within the first minutes of entering the classroom. Children arrive at the center or school in many different moods and with very different experiences from the previous night and the early morning, including the amount of sleep they had. If you recognize and respond positively to the moods and needs of individual children right from the start of the day, the children will be much more likely to have a "good" day—which means you will too!

Anticipating and Preventing Problems Related to Starting the Day

- Greet each child and parent individually as they enter. Look them in the eye and use their names.

- If you and the child feel comfortable, make physical contact with a gentle hug or by touching the child on the arm or shoulder. This lets the child know that she is fully acknowledged and appreciated and an important member of the class.

- Give positive attention to children as soon as they arrive, particularly for the children who need more emotional support. They usually come with their emotional "gas tanks" nearly on empty, and you must fill those tanks with the "fuel" of attention or they will get the fuel they need through negative, disruptive behaviors.

- Arrange for children (and adults) to wash their hands soon after arriving. Invite parents who bring their children to school to help guide their child's hand washing. This will help stop the spread of germs from home and greatly limit illnesses in your program. Make it fun by singing or by talking with them about why we wash and how soap works to clean our hands.

- If children enter in a large group all at once, have them go directly to the circle area or have them choose from a variety of activities that can be cleaned up quickly. Working puzzles, drawing with colored pencils or markers, playing simple board games, and browsing books are all quiet activities that can be quickly put away. Use this time to chat briefly with each child individually.

- Establish a regular, consistent, and simple start-of-the-day routine. This can involve children finding their name cards, which have been scattered on a table, and placing them on an attendance chart or "signing in" once children begin to write their own names. Then they check the job board and try to solve the Morning Mystery.

- Give all the children many chances to do jobs vital to the running of the classroom. Create a job chart where children's names are displayed next to the names and pictures of their jobs. Rotate the names daily. Examples of jobs are listed in the box on this page. Create as many jobs as possible. Try to have one job for each child every day.
  - ‣ Zookeeper 1—Feed the fish.
  - ‣ Zookeeper 2—Feed the guinea pig.
  - ‣ Waiter—Set the table.
  - ‣ Weather reporter or meteorologist—Draw or place a symbol of the day's weather on the calendar.

- Dentist—Lead the tooth brushing and collect the toothbrushes.
- Environmentalist—Turn off the lights each time the class leaves the room; collect litter off the playground; recycle paper rather than throwing it out.
- Teacher—Decide what song the class will sing; lead the song; dismiss the children from the circle.
- Custodian—Wipe the tables and sweep the floor.
- Librarian—Choose a book to read, distribute books for book browsing, collect and account for all books.
- Mathematician—Count the number of days since school began; count the number of children present and absent.

- For Morning Mystery, which changes daily in most cases, ask children questions or give them tasks such as the following: Find two things in the room that are similar but not the same. Find someone else who ate the same thing for breakfast that you did. Find something in the room that was not there yesterday. Find three things that are all different shades of the same color. Find someone in the class who is older than you and someone who is younger. Find something that is missing from the room today that was here yesterday. For many of these tasks, children can work in pairs or teams of three or four of mixed ages or abilities. Adjust the mystery's level of difficulty so that most children are challenged but can still understand the task and not feel too frustrated. Keep making it more challenging as the year progresses and the children become more adept.

- Set work-play time early in your schedule, as children get anxious and restless waiting for the period of time they like the best. Being surrounded by enticing materials, activities, and friends and not being able to interact with them is difficult for young children. They may refuse to comply, act silly, or misbehave. Scheduling work-play time early in the day for at least forty-five minutes will prevent problem behaviors from occurring.

- Time your first meal or snack to make it work for your own group of children. Experiment with the timing so that as many children as possible are getting fed when they are hungry, but not when they are too hungry. If they are eating the food quickly and voraciously, are irritable, or do not listen well before the meal, then you are scheduling the meal too late. If many children pick at their food and are sleepy during the meal, then the meal is coming too early. Kitchen staff can usually be more flexible with breakfast. If necessary, make it yourself with the children. Hungry children tend to be moody, and overfed children tend to be lethargic.

Solving Problems Related to Starting the Day

Children who have a hard time separating from their parents

- Encourage parents to spend five or ten relaxed minutes when dropping off and picking up their children. Invite parents to chat with staff and play with their children for a few minutes during this time. This helps ease the transitions to and from the center. However, encourage parents to leave quickly and smoothly once they have given their child a good-bye kiss. Both rushing in and out and lingering too long can add to the anxiety of separating.

- If a child is still anxious when the parent needs to leave, hold the child's hand or put your arm around his shoulders and say something like "I'm glad you're here. Now it's time for parents to go to work and children to go to school. You'll see Mom again when she comes to pick you up. Let's go see what there is to do today."

- As a way to ease the transition, give the child something to hold that symbolizes the parent. This may be a picture of her parent(s) or an item from Mom's purse or Dad's pocket. Something like an extra house key works well because the child knows the parent must return to get it. Fear that a parent won't return is often the cause of the separation anxiety.

Children who are fussy at the start of the day

You may have children in your class who are highly active, lethargic, very grouchy, or defiant in the morning but who improve as the day progresses. Parents may know the cause, or the problem may be due to one or more of the following reasons:

Allergies and Sensitivities. A child who is sensitive to particular fabrics may be grouchy in the morning because of sleeping on synthetic bedding. If this type of allergy runs in the child's family, she is probably affected also. Using only cotton and other natural fibers for bedding and clothing should relieve the symptoms. Food allergies and sensitivities can also cause behavior problems, and typical breakfast foods such as milk, eggs, and wheat are among the top foods that cause these problems. When a child is not feeling well or is having a mild allergic reaction, it's difficult for her to be at her best. Suggest to parents that they eliminate one category of food at a time to determine if the removal of this food improves the way their child feels. This is best done with the guidance of a knowledgeable pediatrician or allergist, and, perhaps, a nutritionist.

Lack of Food. Some children may arrive at school having had little or no dinner the previous night and little or no breakfast that morning. Securing food is your first priority, if the parents cannot. Teaching young children means meeting all their basic needs. Children who are hungry have trouble concentrating and controlling their emotions and behaviors. Many kindergartens provide a midmorning snack to the children, giving them the sustenance they need until lunchtime. Teachers who implement this often notice improved behaviors and a greater ability to focus and stay on task as the morning progresses. The children seem to do better too!

Lack of Sleep. Most young children need about nine to ten hours of sleep within each twenty-four-hour period. Help parents observe and take their cues from their children's behaviors and adjust the timing and amount of sleep accordingly. Children who share their bed and/or room with siblings or live in noisy neighborhoods may be sleep deprived. While problem solving with your families to find ways to increase the amount of sleep for these children, make a cot or space available for any tired child to take a short nap at any time during the day.

Stressful Mornings at Home. In many homes, particularly for single-parent and two-working-parent families with several children, morning is the most harried time of day. The attention and care that young children need, especially early in the day, is subsumed in the frenzy of getting everyone up, dressed, washed, fed, brushed, equipped for school and work, out the door, and on time. In some families, threats, yelling, crying, and worse characterize nearly every morning—not a good way to start the day! These are children who need their emotional "gas tanks" filled as soon as they arrive, as described earlier. If parents are open to suggestions, help them find ways to reduce the stress. One of the best ways to alleviate morning stress is to complete as many tasks as possible the night before. With adult help, the children can select their clothes and lay them out, make their lunches, pack their backpacks, choose their breakfast, and set the table.

Chaos: Too much going on at once

Parents want to talk to you, several children are demanding your attention, the director needs you, your assistant has a question, and two children are chasing each other through the room. This probably sounds familiar, because all teachers have had mornings like this.

- The children must always come first. Adults can wait. Greet and talk with parents briefly each day, if possible, but only after you have greeted their children. Make sure you can see all the children while you are talking or that another staff member is watching them.

- Keep a clipboard or a notepad on a bulletin board posted near the door for parents, visitors, or other staff to write messages to you. Post a sign above it that says: "I'm sorry I can't talk with you now. I'm working with the children. Please leave a message and include how and when I can get back to you. Thank you."

- Arrange the first routines or activities of the day so that children can get settled into them without much help. If the children cannot read their names, tape a picture of them or their own unique symbol in their cubbies. Have children help each other in the morning. "Ask three before you ask me" is a great classroom practice. The "three" refers to three other children. This will also foster a healthy interdependence and camaraderie among children.

- For some groups of children, playing soft, mellow classical music when children first enter the classroom can have a calming effect. For this to work well, play the same music each morning for at least three weeks before changing it and do not play the "morning music" at any other time during the day.

- Assign each adult, including yourself, some tasks to do each morning before the children arrive. Keep the written task list posted. To provide variety and the opportunity to learn new skills, swap the set of tasks among the adults about once a month. Make the task cards reusable by laminating them or covering them with clear, self-stick plastic. If you have volunteers or a new or substitute teacher, the details on the lists will give them the information they need to set things up independently. The lists, prepared ahead of time, might look like this:

Adult #1

- Mix paints and set up easel.
- Take out trikes, scooters, wagons, and helmets.
- Set out the following gross-motor equipment:
  - Equipment: large ball, Frisbee, bat and ball
  - Located: classroom closet near front door
  - Place it: bench next to porch
  - Equipment: plastic climber
  - Located: storage shed behind building
  - Place it: grassy area in center of field

Adult #2

- Take chairs down from tables.
- Wipe off tables.
- Set out the following activities on tables:
  - Activity: "Cherry Picker" board game
  - Located: red storage shelf
  - Place it: round table
  - Activity: five puzzles
  - Located: puzzle rack on wood shelves
  - Place it: rectangular table by window

---

2. CIRCLE TIME AND GROUP TIME: ALL FOR ONE AND ONE FOR ALL

"Circle time" refers specifically to a gathering of all the children for the purpose of connecting and creating a sense of community within the group. The opening circle should occur very early in the schedule or when most of the children have arrived. The closing circle should occur late in the schedule and while the majority of children are still there. When done well, circle time develops early, basic feelings of commonality, belonging, and mutual caring and respect among the children. "Group time" also creates community because everyone has a common experience, but it does not develop it as directly or intentionally as circle time. Typically, group time activities include read-out-louds, singing and making music, movement/dance, group games, short discussions, problem-solving role plays, and the like.

Anticipating and Preventing Problems Related to Circle and Group Times

- Keep your circle and group times short! Most groups of three-year-olds or younger have a maximum attention span of ten to fifteen minutes. For most four- and five-year-olds, the maximum is fifteen to twenty minutes. Every group is different, so take your cues from the children's behaviors for how long they can sit and pay attention. Start the year with circle/group times lasting just a few minutes and gradually increase the time throughout the first weeks and months.

- As a guideline to help children sit appropriately, give each one a rug-sample square. These can usually be purchased cheaply from carpet stores. As an alternative, you can laminate pieces of cardboard with children's names or a picture or symbol on them. Gluing a Velcro fastener (the loop side) to the back of the squares helps them stay in place on a carpeted surface. Some groups of children, particularly older preschoolers and kindergartners, attend better when sitting on chairs placed around the circle. All of these solutions provide individual spaces so children will not get into conflicts with each other.

Cultural Awareness Alert

The suggestion above helps avoid conflicts because most North American children do not like other children to encroach on their personal space (about eighteen inches from their bodies), let alone to be touched. The exceptions to this are children who are close friends. In nearly all of the countries that our families have more recently emigrated from, personal space is much closer. For many of these children, not being able to touch their friends and constantly being far away from people makes them feel that the classroom is a very cold and impersonal place. Allow children from the same cultural group, or any children who prefer to be close to other children, to sit the way that feels "right" to them.

- Hold circle/group activities away from toy shelves and other attractive places in the room. Ensure that there is enough room to seat all the children comfortably.

- Establish one or two simple rules and remind children of them at the start of the circle/group session. They might be "Keep your arms near you and your legs under you" and "Talk only when no one else is talking."

- Avoid using circle and group times for teaching specific skills. This is best done in small groups or individually. Keep it light, fun, and moving along.

- Plan circle and group activities that are not too difficult and are highly interesting to your particular group. Prepare well. Know your material well enough that you can stray from your plans, answer unexpected questions, and easily get back on track. Start with an active but not a boisterous game that requires the children to focus and attend. You might use the game "Follow the Rhythm." With everyone sitting around the circle, tap or clap a simple rhythm and then invite the children to repeat it. Make the rhythm a little harder each time you tap. Give a few children the chance to lead the game. After playing for a minute or two, end with a soft, slow rhythm and then begin your circle activity. This type of starting activity will also draw children to the circle who have not yet made the transition.

- If your planned activity does not hold the children's interest, have alternative activities ready or move on to the next activity.

- Place another adult (teacher, assistant, or volunteer) behind the circle of children. There she can see the whole group and move quickly to an area where children are having a hard time. Sometimes just sitting behind them or gently touching their backs will settle them.

- If possible, involve all adults in the group activity. An assistant or volunteer who is doing other things within sight or sound of the children will be distracting. Adults who participate act as good role models for the children.

- For group time activities, occasionally provide an alternative to sitting in a circle. For example, have the children sit in two rows facing each other. Do a variety of activities that involve the partners interacting with each other verbally and physically.

Solving Problems Related to Circle and Group Times

Hitting, arguing, or talking with others

Boredom during circle/group times is the most common cause of hitting, arguing, or talking with others. Boredom is caused by activities that are, well, boring or have gone on longer than the children's ability to attend. Follow the suggestions in "Anticipating and Preventing Problems" above to make the circle/group time short and stimulating. If this problem continues after trying the ideas in this chapter, and in spite of your best efforts, divide the group in half and have two groups meet as far away from each other as possible or in separate rooms. This assumes there is at least one other capable adult who can effectively run the other group. Change the composition of the groups regularly so that every child can connect with every other child in the class. For circle time especially, dividing the children into groups should be a temporary solution until you are able to make adjustments to the activities and manage the whole group more effectively. The main objective of circle time—to create a sense of community where everyone belongs and everyone is connected—cannot be fully achieved if the whole class is not together.

- Keep the children who "set each other off" away from each other. If necessary, assign seats.

- Begin your activity without waiting for everyone to join or be entirely quiet. Start with a louder voice to get the children's attention and quickly tone down your voice when the talking or moving has stopped. Alternate this with starting with a very quiet voice and slowly raising it to a normal level. This will get the children's attention because it is unexpected.

- At the start of your activity, remind the children that they will have an opportunity to talk right after you have finished.

- Use a nonverbal cue to get the children's attention, such as placing your thumb and index finger in the shape of an L and putting it by your ear (American Sign Language for "listen"). Use this cue to remind children that this is a time to listen. Quickly go back to your activity.

- Focus your attention and encouragement on the children who are behaving appropriately. Say things like "Thank you, Sam, for looking right at me. It lets me know that you're listening."

- Give no or little attention to problematic behaviors, but if they continue or escalate, then intervene.

- Remind the children again of rules.

- During group games, give children opportunities to be the "teacher" and decide what the group should do. For example, a child can decide which body part everyone should shake during "Hokey Pokey."

- Whenever possible, give children opportunities to talk and move in appropriate ways. Involve them actively during the circle. For example, invite the children to take turns holding the book being read. For well-known stories, leave off the ends of some sentences for the children to finish. Ask questions occasionally to give children opportunities to talk.

Can't sit still

- For a variety of reasons, some children cannot sit still for more than a few seconds. For these children, provide an alternative quiet activity, such as doing puzzles or drawing at a nearby table, where they will not distract the circle but will be able to see and hear the circle time activities. They are always free to rejoin the circle at any time. This is not a punishment or a reward, but recognition of the different needs of the children. If they were able to exercise control, they would. If other children want to do this other activity also, explain that the child is choosing another activity because sitting quietly is difficult for her at this time, although she will get better at it. Tell the children who can sit still that they are able to sit and listen well and that you appreciate their participation in circle/group.

- For some active children, sitting on an adult's lap during circle will provide the comfort and physical boundaries influence they need to be calm.

- Let the children who cannot sit still start the circle with the others, but when they are close to reaching their limit, give them the choice of listening a little longer or doing alternative quiet activities. The time they are able to stay in the circle should gradually increase if you are also working on the root cause of the problem. (See "Perpetual(ly in) Motion" on pp. 191–94 for more suggestions about children who are active and distracted/attracted.)

- If a child is still disruptive to the group, even while involved in another activity, then another adult (who is not leading the circle/group) should calmly guide him to a place where he can be involved in a quiet activity. The adult should stay with him but give him minimal attention. Tell the child that he can return to the activity or the circle when he is ready to listen. Give the child lots of encouragement when he does return and is calm for even a few seconds. Say something like the following: "I can tell that you're really listening because you're quiet. That's very kind because now everyone can hear."

Interruptions directed to the teacher

- Ignore the first interruption (unless the child needs to use the toilet or has some other urgent need). If the child interrupts again, he will likely keep interrupting until you respond. Act on the second interruption. (Usually it will be a request like "Will you tie my shoe?" or "Can I get a drink of water?") Tell the child that you are very interested in what he has to say but that he must wait until the end of circle/group time. If the child interrupts again, signal by nodding your head to another adult to help the child with his needs. Go back to the activity quickly.

- Keep a mental note of the nature of the distraction. At a later time, talk with the child about what he may be able to do differently the next time so as not to interrupt.

- Some interruptions are great learning opportunities. They should be allowed, and you should follow through on them. For example, if a child complains that another child hit him, use the conflict resolution strategies discussed in "Problematic Behaviors" that starts on page 173. All the children will be interested and will learn from the experience.

When "show-and-tell" does not go well

The purposes of show-and-tell are for children to make a connection between home and school, to practice speaking in front of a group and communicating clearly, and to share something personal to help everyone get to know each other better. There is, however, a tendency for show-and-tell to go on too long and to be a bit chaotic, in part because the children who are not sharing are disengaged from the activity. Sharing commercial toys creates a number of problems as well, so try to find alternatives to meet the goals of show-and-tell.

- Limit the number of children who share during show-and-tell by assigning some to share only on Monday, others on Tuesday, and so on. To keep the time appropriately short, consider doing show-and-tell in small groups or in two groups simultaneously.

- As an alternative to sharing a toy or object, suggest that children share family experiences using photographs from family trips or special events. They can also use photos to tell about their pets; bring in something that they or a family member have made at home or an interesting found object such as an unusual stone; or share a favorite book or song from home, or something similar. Sharing themselves rather than things helps children who have no item to share and makes for more personal, meaningful sharing.

- Involve all the children in this activity by making sure the child who is talking speaks to the other children, not to you. Encourage the other children to ask questions of the child who is sharing. Place yourself behind the child to facilitate this.

- A variation on show-and-tell is to have the children bring their items in bags so that the other children can try to guess what they are. They ask questions and get cues from the size and shape of the item in the bag. The child who is sharing can give hints, with adult help as needed. The hints can be physical, such as shaking the bag and tapping the object, or verbal such as "I found it on a beach" or "It fell from a tree" or "It has a picture of an elephant on the front."

3. WORK-PLAY TIME: MEANINGFUL PLAY, PLAYFUL WORK

This part of the schedule is sometimes called "free choice," "free play," "choice time," and other names. The rationale for calling it "work-play" is explained in the introduction on page 11. Work-play is the time children love the most. They get to decide what they want to do, how to do it, and for how long. Since young children learn best within complex play—play that is set up, guided, and mediated by skilled teachers—work-play time provides great opportunities for learning. The value of work-play depends on the quality of materials and equipment you have. It also depends on your ability to help children do what they choose at a higher level than they could do by themselves, to solve problems effectively, and to learn new skills. This all can happen when you listen and observe carefully and respond with suggestions, new materials, and probing questions. Among the choices children have during work-play is to work on a project or part of a project. Project ideas should emerge from children's interests and needs. (See "Curriculum Conundrums" on pp. 59–68 and the resources under "Curriculum and Project-Based Learning" on pp. 286–88 for more information about projects.)

Anticipating and Preventing Problems Related to Work-Play Time

- Schedule the first work-play time early in the day and for at least forty-five minutes.

- Rotate materials to reduce the boredom caused when children use the same toys and materials every day. Keep some in storage and then bring out this equipment after several months. When you do this, put some other equipment away.

- Change the imaginary play area fairly often. Have the children help you set up a post office for about three weeks, then a restaurant for several weeks, then a campground, and so on. Other ideas can come from common activities, the workplaces of the children's families, and popular places in the community. Have the children come up with their own ideas. If your room is large, have a permanent "house" area in addition to the rotating imaginary play area.

- Create boxes of imaginary play materials by theme. Store the ones that you are not using. Here are some examples: fire hats, pieces of garden hose, raincoats, and walkie-talkies for a fire-fighter theme; stethoscopes, crutches, bandages, scrubs, disposable gloves, and similar supplies for a hospital theme; stamps, envelopes, and paper of various sizes and types, pencils and markers, small boxes, tape, and mail bags for a post office theme.

- Set out a wide variety of activities to choose from, such as art materials, paint and easels, board games, puzzles, water play, sand play, and clay.

- If you have action figures in your class, use generic ones that cannot be identified with currently popular media characters. Also provide small plastic dinosaurs, lions, bears, and other scary animals with which children can safely play out fears and aggression, as well as small cars, trucks, fire engines, trains, buses, ambulances, tractors, and so on.

- Involve yourself with the children's activities and move around the room. Don't control the play or tell them what to do. Ask probing questions. Add supplies and equipment to expand and deepen their play. Help them solve problems and conflicts.

- Establish a system where children place name cards at the area they choose to use. This will help them plan and think ahead. Ideally, there should be no limit on the number of children in a given center; however, if necessary, you can limit the number of children by having a set number of hooks on which children can place their name cards. Such a system requires children to rotate in and out of centers after a reasonable period of time.

- Offer children the option to participate in projects, but ensure that all children can self-select activities for at least part of work-play time. Project ideas should come from children's interests and needs. To help them learn through play, ask questions about what they need and how they can obtain or make it; read information about the subject of their projects; and help them use tools and skills to measure, count, write, diagram, graph, and negotiate.

Solving Problems Related to Work-Play Time

The child who spends most of his time in one area

This is not necessarily a problem. A child who is less than three years old or who is a slow learner needs to spend time using materials over and over. This is particularly true early in the year when the materials and activities are new to the child. However, you should be concerned later in the year with children older than three if the behavior persists, because having children experience a wide variety of activities is an important educational goal. Below are some suggestions for expanding a child's experiences.

- Try to determine what the child is getting from playing in that area that is vitally important to him emotionally, cognitively, and/or physically. Could that same need be met in another area or during another activity? Often it can, but it may require some adaptations or the addition of different materials.

- Add some variety to the child's play. Introduce new materials or suggest different ways to play with the same materials. Bring materials from another area of the room to that area. For example, bring paper and markers into the block area and suggest that the child draw a picture of her block structure.

- Entice the child into other areas by providing challenging and fun art, cooking, or woodworking projects; water or sand play; or a new imaginary play center.

- If a child still uses an area too often, close it to all children for one or two days per week. This will give the child a chance to try new areas.

- If enticements do not work and closing the area brings shrieks of protest, back down and be patient. Let the child continue using that area for another week or two before trying again to promote a change.

The child who spends very little time in any one area

Work-play can be overstimulating to some children. They are so excited by all the activities and choices that they can't settle down or choose, and you see them move quickly from area to area. Here are some suggestions for helping overstimulated children focus:

- Cut down on the number of choices offered if this does not adversely affect your program. Gradually add more choices, one at a time. Start the year off with a limited number of choices and then add more as the year progresses.

- Before work-play time, ask the child to tell you what he will do and in which areas he will play. Encourage the child to stick to his plans. This will help the child who flits from one area to another to become organized. As most young children are developing self-regulation skills (focused attention, planning, and organizing), doing this with all your children is a good idea.

- Create a small, quiet area that is blocked off from most of the room, though make sure you can easily see into the area. Typically this is a library corner, but if you have enough room, create a second private place, containing a small table with one or two chairs. Encourage the child to play with building toys or other games in this area, perhaps with one friend. Stay with the child for a short time to help him focus on the activity. Ask questions, talk about what the child is doing, or do the activity with him.

- If the child finds it helpful and not restricting, make and place freestanding cardboard dividers (one and a half feet high) on the tabletop around the child's workspace to eliminate visual distractions.

- Use an empty large appliance box to make a private space for one child. Encourage the child to use this space when she feels overstimulated.

- Another reason a child may not stay in any area of the room very long is that the activities there are not challenging. Provide different levels of complexity for different activities and also within an activity. For example, make available a wide variety of art supplies, collage materials, and loose parts, so that a child can create a simple or very detailed project according to his interest and ability. Create math games that can be played at a variety of different levels.

Too loud, too boisterous

If children get too excited and active and the noise level rises to an intolerable level, try some of the following ideas:

- Establish or restate a classroom rule that only regular voices can be used inside the classroom. Demonstrate what a regular voice sounds like. Remind the children of the rule just before work-play. Let them know that they will be able to use loud voices when they are outside.

- If a particular child is responsible for the high noise level, remind her of the "regular voice rule" and the reason for it—so that everyone can hear each other and no one gets a headache. A child's raised voice can be the result of a hearing loss, either temporary, because of an ear infection, or permanent. The child is loud because she can't hear herself, like a person trying to talk while listening to music with headphones. Help her practice and get used to speaking with a quieter voice, regardless of the cause. Tell her that you will let her know if her voice is too loud with an agreed-upon, nonverbal signal or with two gentle taps on her arm. Every five to ten minutes, give her feedback if she is keeping her voice lower with a thumbs-up signal or by saying, "Thank you for making the effort to use a quieter voice. It really makes the room more pleasant."

- Provide more activities with more challenges to keep the children's interest high.

- Provide enough supplies to prevent arguments over toys. Purchase duplicates of popular toys, especially for the youngest children.

- Put number limits on the noisiest areas, at least temporarily.

- Encourage children who are behaving appropriately by saying something like: "Thank you for using a regular voice. It helps make the room a pleasant place for everyone to work and play."

- If there are two children who tend to "get each other going" when they play together, remind them before work-play time that they will need to work well together, resolve conflicts quickly, and use regular voices. Catch them just before things start escalating and provide more structure and direction to their play or help them resolve conflicts early, quickly, and more effectively. When they are playing well together, let them know: "It's great to see how much you respect each other and yourselves."

- Loud, boisterous play is very satisfying to many children, particularly some boys. Give them ample opportunities to play out exciting, action-oriented themes—pirates, firefighting, hunting for dinosaur bones, emergency medical team—when they are outside. Add play props and facilitate the play, as necessary, during outdoor playtime. Set up rules to avoid problems that can arise during boisterous play and to make sure that roles are rotated. Such rules might include the following: use only gentle contact, any child can call a time-out to leave the game, any child can ask another child to switch roles.

- Children can spend time, if they choose, during work-play making props and costumes for their outdoor play.

Too messy

Children may misuse the blocks, table games, the imaginary play area, or other areas, leaving materials in a mess or damaged.

- Remind the children of the rules, such as the following, before they use the area:
  - "Take blocks from the shelf as you need them to build."
  - "Put items back in their place when you are finished using them."
  - "Pick up anything from the floor that belongs on a table or shelf."
  - "Use all materials carefully so they don't break or hurt anyone."

- Make sure each item has a specific place that is clearly labeled for the children. Lead children back to an area they have left messy and have them straighten it up before moving on to another activity.

- Involve children in helping repair what they broke, even if it was accidental and unintentional. If the repair will require materials or tools that should not be used by children or near them (such as strong glue or a sharp knife), then just have the children use some tape and/or school glue to make a temporary repair. This way they will learn to take responsibility for mistakes.

- Observe the children's play carefully. If it starts to get out of control, which will lead to misuse of materials, suggest a different direction for the play, help them establish clear and complementary roles, add new props, briefly take a role in the play, or redirect them to different activities.

- Demonstrate and discuss the various ways different materials can and should be used appropriately. Ask the children for ideas and help them determine if their ideas reflect safe and careful use of the materials. This is especially important to do when a new imaginary play area is set up and when new materials are introduced.

Unimaginative imaginary play

Some children, particularly those who have few limits on the media they watch at home, want to engage in play that imitates what they see on television, videos, and video games. The resulting play is usually uncreative, repetitive, and low level. If they are imitating characters that are not from children's media, the play may also be violent, sexual, sexist, or inappropriate in other ways. However, sharing an interest in particular movies or shows from popular media is a common and effective way for children to connect with each other. Adults do the same. So rather than eliminate all such play, mediate it and put reasonable limits on it. Watch the popular shows and films most often viewed by your children to understand who the characters are and why they appeal to them.

- When children engage in derivative play, talk to them about how the show was written by a person who made it up. Explain that children have ideas just as good as the writers. Help the children rewrite the script, create new scripts based on the familiar characters, and create new characters to complement the existing ones. Suggest that the characters travel to different locations and be put in different situations than in the original script so that the children will need to think creatively.

- Ask questions and provide suggestions that help them get deeper insights into characters' personalities and motivations: "What might have made the bad guy bad? What special power can you use to change the bad guy in a nonviolent way? How can you use brainpower rather than physical power to stop the bad guy?"

- If necessary, explain to the children that school toys and activities are different from home toys and activities. The reason children come to school is to do different things than at home and to have different and more friends. Nonetheless, a few toys might be the same, such as Lego blocks, and toys from home for show-and-tell may be used for a short time.

War, gun, superhero, and violent play

Although play in which children act out violent scenes, including superhero play, may not involve direct acts of aggression against other children, many teachers find this kind of play disturbing. It glorifies aggression and often leads to children getting hurt, even if not intentional. Some teachers limit the play by allowing it only outside. Others are completely opposed to the play, believing that it is limiting and harmful to children's development. As mostly boys engage in this type of play, it reinforces stereotypical gender-based behaviors. However, this behavior reflects our culture more than it contributes to it. Male power is still strongly associated with physical prowess and dominance, and female power with attractiveness and social status. In addition, boys' development lags behind girls' development in most areas, so they struggle more with impulse control and other self-regulation skills.

Many young children, again mostly boys, have a strong need to work on issues related to good and evil (right and wrong) and power and powerlessness. They try to develop for themselves clear concepts of who are "good guys" and who are "bad guys," usually aligning themselves on the side of good. The bad guys must come to a bad end so that everything is right with the world and the children are safe. This type of play is important because it helps young children develop a sense of who they are in the world and how to control their own desires to be "bad." It gives them a chance to grapple with what is acceptable behavior and what is not, and to gain enough control to feel safe. The challenge for teachers is to give children opportunities to play out these themes and concepts while supporting play that is not aggressive or violent.

Violent or aggressive play often involves children pretending to use weapons. Because gun violence in the United States is a serious problem, it is important to send a strong, clear message to children that guns and other weapons are dangerous and hurt or kill people. One important way to do this is to ban toys or objects that look like weapons of any kind. If a child is pretending to use a gun, including the "thumb and index finger gun" and the "Lego gun," remind him of the classroom rule: "Use your hands and words to help, not hurt. Pretending to hurt also hurts." Redirect the play using these ideas.

- Use aggressive play as an opportunity to expand the children's understanding of issues of violence. For example, ask, "What is another way you can protect yourself from the bad guy? How can you use 'brainpower' instead of 'muscle power' or 'weapon power?'"

- Provide alternative scenarios that do not involve weapons yet give children power. For example, set up firefighting play, emergency rescue, or tracking down a wild animal to give it medicine or to be moved to a safer place. Move the evil or danger away from residing in another person to residing in something else—like fire or a dangerous animal.

- Redirect children into cooperative games that involve working together to complete a task, overcome an obstacle, or win against time.

- Read and make up stories that deal with issues of power and control by using cleverness, collaboration, and perseverance (brainpower). The characters defeat evil this way in many original or early versions of fairy tales, folk tales, and fables, such as in "Tom Thumb," "Hansel and Gretel," the "Musicians of Bremen," the "Lion and the Mouse," and "Jack and the Beanstalk." When the children become familiar with the stories, they can act them out.

4. SMALL-GROUP TIME: SMALL IS BEAUTIFUL (AND PRODUCTIVE)

If you are not already doing so, schedule a time during the day for about fifteen minutes for small-group learning. Ideally, have at least three small groups of children in three areas of the room (or at three tables) working on activities at the same time. If possible, plan for each group to do a different activity, and rotate the groups and activities each day so by the third day, every child will have done all three activities. For the remaining two days of the week, repeat the activities with slight variations to make them a bit more challenging. The activities can include art or craft projects, name-writing activities, making a book, science activities, lotto games, simple board games, math activities with manipulatives, memory games, role playing, social skill development activities, cooking projects, personal safety lessons, and so on.

With small groups, you can individualize learning more than you can when children are in a large group. You can provide information quickly and directly, answer questions, encourage problem solving, and give more feedback to individual children. Also, you can provide more challenging activities than children can do on their own during work-play. Finally, you are able to observe children better. You can more readily determine how they think, act, and feel, and what their strengths and weaknesses are. You can scaffold their learning, and you can then plan and adjust future activities accordingly.

Anticipating and Preventing Problems Related to Small-Group Time

- To get children to their places easily, name each group. Place a picture of that name on the table or the area where the children are to go. For example, the six children who are in the Tiger group will go to the table with the picture of the tiger placed in the center. Similarly, the children in the Bear group and those in the Elephant group will go to their tables. Give each child a picture tag that corresponds to her group. Within a few weeks, each child should know her group. Over the course of the year, change the pictures to symbols, then to letters, and then to words. Change the composition of the groups about once per month.

- Prepare all your materials and written instructions for the other adults ahead of time. Discuss the activities with them beforehand, so your expectations are clear. Tell them why the children are doing the activity and what you want the children to gain from it.

- Develop activities that allow the children to handle real objects and interact with each other. Avoid pencil and paper tasks and adults demonstrating something or lecturing.

- Divide children into mixed groups. Include within each group some slow learners and some quick learners, and some easygoing children and some with problematic behaviors. This allows children to learn from each other and to help each other.

- Individualize when you see the need. If a child is having difficulty, ask him to do only part of the activity, have him ask another child to help him, give him suggestions, provide a little physical assistance (only as much as is necessary), or offer different tools or a different way of doing it.

- Individualize according to abilities, but stretch children and challenge them a bit. For example, if your activity is making playdough, invite the child with poor small-motor coordination to pour liquids from the measuring cup into a large bowl. Encourage the child with good small-motor coordination to pour and measure a tablespoon of oil. Invite the child with reading skills to read the recipe for the group. Encourage the child with poor counting skills to count along with another child the number of tablespoons of salt added. Plan for this before the activity.

- Make sure activities are meaningful to children and have an emotional and/or experiential connection for them. For example, teach the math concept of half in the contexts of sharing cookies when there are fewer than the number of children; slicing a pizza; measuring half cup of water or flour when following a recipe; folding paper to make butterfly prints; or finding the halfway point between the front and back of the room using nonstandard measuring tools such as blocks.

- The focus of the activities should be less on learning skills or information than on understanding concepts. One way to do this is to show multiple ways that the concept you are teaching can be applied. The example above of teaching the concept of half involves five ways to demonstrate and explain it.

Solving Problems Related to Small-Group Time

Not enough staff

- Small-group time requires a capable adult for each group. If only two adults are available, you can have two groups led by adults and a third group involved in an activity the children can do well on their own, with some occasional checking. In any case, include no more than six children in a small group.

- As an alternative to this or if you are the only adult, extend your work-play time and involve five or six children in a small-group activity while the others are in work-play. When the first group is done, choose a different group of children to do the same activity, until all the children have participated. Select a different small-group activity each day, unless you are doing a task or teaching a game that will take several days to learn or to complete. The drawbacks to this system are that pulling children away from work-play activities is difficult, the continuity of their play is broken, and you cannot be actively involved in work-play while working with small groups.

- To compensate for these drawbacks, allow children to save whatever they have constructed during work-play time by making themselves a "Do not touch" sign or by placing their project in a special "saving" place. They can then pick up where they left off and not worry about others taking apart their work during the small-group activity.

Bored or resistant children

If the children clearly indicate that they would rather be doing something other than the small-group activity, try some of these ideas:

- Shorten each small-group activity so that children have to sit for only a few minutes. Gradually lengthen it.

- Plan activities that actively involve the children in movement or in handling real objects. Provide many chances for each child to talk and to do.

- Games, such as memory lotto, are a good way to engage all the children and to teach concepts.

- Use more activities that are creative, that allow children to express themselves, and that do not require one correct answer. Using sets of three wood scraps and glue to build various sculptures is more satisfying than circling the picture of three balloons on a work sheet. Yet the same information—the concept of three—can be taught in both activities and taught more effectively with the sculpture activity.

- Schedule very physical activities—such as outdoor or gym play—before and after your small-group time.

- Lead a short movement game (such as "Shake Your Sillies Out" or "Head, Shoulders, Knees, and Toes") just before and/or after the small-group activity.

5. MELLOW MEALTIMES: THE CURE FOR WHOLE-CLASS HEARTBURN

Mealtimes are opportunities to teach children healthy eating habits, a positive attitude toward food, and pleasant manners. It can be a time for quiet conversation. However, some children use mealtimes to engage you in a power struggle or to assert themselves in a negative way, particularly if they are "required" to eat. Some children have already developed poor eating habits just from not knowing any better. This is usually not difficult to correct with guidance and support. The key to pleasant mealtimes is to keep things calm in every way possible.

Cultural Awareness Alert

Food is very strongly related to culture as well as to religious beliefs. One culture's comfort food is another culture's poison. Children like the food they are familiar with, served the way they are used to. The same ingredients served as a salad may not get eaten but are gobbled up when rolled in a tortilla, put between two slices of bread, or stuffed into a pita pocket. Unfamiliar foods and serving styles take time to get used to. It took me quite a while to get to like sushi, having tried it for the first time as an adult. I even thought it a little repulsive at first, which is how children must feel when confronted with strange foods. On the other hand, one cannot get used to something without trying it . . . more than once.

Anticipating and Preventing Problems Related to Mealtimes

- Know about the food allergies or special dietary needs or restrictions that your children may have. Post the information in big letters near where the food is served and where it is prepared in the kitchen.

- Know the types of food that your children eat at home and the foods they like and don't like. When menus are planned, try to arrange for the favorite home foods of some children to be served, even if it can only happen occasionally.

- Arrange tables for eating so they are not too close together. This will help keep the noise level down. To avoid the need for you or the children to get up and down often, set the tables so that all food, utensils, and supplies are close at hand.

- Sit in small groups of no more than five children per adult, if possible. This allows for calm conversation during the meal. Extra adults can be recruited from office staff, kitchen staff, drivers, parents, and senior volunteers, among others.

- Because you are an important role model for good eating habits and manners, eat with the children and eat what they eat. Also, you can help ensure that children do not take too much or too little food when serving family style.

- Engage the children in low-key conversations during meals. Ask them about their families and about activities they did at home and school earlier in the day, discuss the food being eaten and where it came from, and share some things about yourself. This will set a calm tone, which is important for good digestion.

Cultural Awareness Alert

In some cultures, people do not talk during meals, so you may have a child who will not talk. Validate that child's behavior by saying, "I know that in your family it is important not to talk during meals. You can be silent here too. But in some families, it is important *to* talk during meals. Here we can choose to talk or not to talk."

- Avoid making children wait at the table to start eating or wait for others to finish at the end of the meal. This causes boredom, which leads to acting out. If they must sit for a short time, lead the children in a song, fingerplay, or simple thinking game to engage their interest.

- If everyone can begin the meal together without waiting, start with a short ritual, such as a short poem or a chant/song of thanks like "Thank you, Earth. Thank you, Sun. We won't forget what you have done" or "I like the moon. I like the trees. I like the food the earth brings me." This sets a quiet, contemplative tone to start the meal and gets all the children settled down and focused.

- To teach responsibility and manners, promote language skills, and reduce behavior problems, actively involve children during mealtimes. Before the meal, assign children to jobs such as "waiters" (set the tables) and "custodians" (wipe the tables, sweep the floor). Unless you are not permitted to do so for health reasons, serve food family style in bowls for children to pass around and serve themselves. When finished, allow all the children to clear their own places, scrape their plates, throw away paper trash, and put dirty silverware in a container.

- To prevent children from licking serving spoons during family-style service, put a piece of brightly colored tape on the upper part of the spoon handle. This way, the "signal" can be felt as well as seen. Remind children at the start of the meal that red-taped spoons, for example, are for serving and passing only. Explain that keeping the spoons away from their mouths keeps them clean and healthy for others to use. The greater the difference in size, look, and shape of the serving spoons from their own spoons, the easier it will be for the children to remember not to lick them. Remove the tape at the end of the meal so the spoon can be properly washed.

- If possible, provide choices among healthy foods or at least one alternative for the main protein dish at each meal. Often just providing this simple choice satisfies children's need for control regarding food. Similarly, when children can assemble their meals, they tend to eat it better than if it is presented fully prepared. For example, children can put together the ingredients for their own tacos, rather than being given ready-made ones.

- Encourage children to try at least a bite of all food served to them. One bite of everything served encourages children to try new foods and to get enough nutrition. However, a child can still decline to take a bite, because it is not a requirement or rule. In an environment with no pressure or tension, the child will likely come around to eating.

- If health regulations allow it, do frequent cooking projects with the children. The food can be prepared in the classroom and cooked in the kitchen. Have the children wash their hands before starting the activity and use food-service gloves when preparing the food. To increase their knowledge and appreciation of the food they eat, serve the food they made with their meals or as a snack.

- Avoid using food for art projects. Pudding paintings and vegetable prints teach children that playing with and wasting food is acceptable. Using food as art also makes reinforcing proper eating habits during meals more difficult. Fingerpaint and sponges work just as well as food for art projects.

- Visit the cook in the kitchen often. Ask her to demonstrate and explain to the children how to make some of their favorite dishes. Invite the cook to eat with your class so that he can see how the children respond to the food. Help the children send thank-you cards for especially good meals. This creates a positive attitude about the food served and the person cooking it.

Solving Problems Related to Mealtimes

The overzealous eater

This is a child who may grab the food from the table, take too much, eat very fast, or put too much food in her mouth. The child may have to do this at home to get her share of food, or she may be very hungry, have poor impulse control, or not be able to feel the sensation of being full.

- To start with, develop a clear system of serving the same amount of food to each child—one spoonful of vegetables, one slice of pizza, two ladles of soup, and so on. If leftovers remain for seconds, divide them up in equal portions. If everyone does not want seconds, give thirds to the children who want them. Before each meal, remind the overzealous eater of your system for equal sharing of food. After a few weeks of this routine, scarcity should not be an issue for any child.

- Expect and, as necessary, teach children to have a few simple manners. This also helps keep mealtimes calm. For example, children from about three years of age should be encouraged to say, "Please pass the crackers" instead of reaching across the table, and to say, "Thank you." They also should be helped to eat correctly with utensils, sit properly, and eat reasonably neatly and calmly.

- Sit next to the overzealous eater so you can help her slow down. Because she probably does the behavior out of habit, you will need to stop the child, show her how to chew slowly, talk her through the meal, and model good eating habits for several weeks. Tell the child that chewing food well is important. Explain that chewing helps her body take in all the food's goodness and makes her grow strong.

The messy eater

This child may have some fine-motor coordination difficulties or problems organizing himself. He likely also has trouble with puzzles and cutting with scissors. Getting slippery food from the plate to the mouth is not an easy task for any young child, but it is an exasperating one for the child with poor small-motor control.

- Help the child organize himself before he starts to eat. Help him place his glass where it won't be easily knocked over by a stray elbow or an unruly arm. Make sure he has pulled his chair close to the table and is sitting straight. Help him put his plate directly in front of and near to his body. Sticky putty (typically used for securing posters to walls) can be used to help hold a plate or bowl to the table, making it less likely to move or tip or to scoot off the table.

- Provide the child with a spoon for most foods, since it allows more control than a fork. A fork and a spoon together may provide even more control, since the child can push the food onto his fork with the spoon. If possible, use plates with high edges that prevent food from easily falling off and make it easier to corral.

- Help the child fill his glass and soup bowl less than halfway and then provide additional servings when he is done. Ensure that the child receives at least the minimum portion for his age as required by food programs, licensing standards, or nutritional guidelines. Smaller amounts are easier to handle, and if spills do occur, there is less waste, less to clean, and less frustration.

- Do not focus too much attention on the problem, as this may humiliate the child and make matters worse. Accept that the child has physical challenges. Provide him with many nonthreatening, playful opportunities to improve his small-motor skills through activities such as cutting with scissors, doing simple puzzles, building with Lego blocks or unit blocks, and drawing.

The picky eater

- Determine if the child eats different foods at home, has food allergies, or is picky for other tangible reasons. At first, it may be necessary for her to bring some food from home if possible, but the amount from home should be gradually reduced as she starts to eat the food served in the program. However, the food from home must meet the nutritional requirements of the program. Allowing one child to eat potato chips and cake while all others eat nutritious food is hypocritical and unfair.

- Some children have acute taste buds and are very sensitive to foods. Other children have allergies to certain foods and their bodies "tell" them not to eat those foods. If they eat foods their bodies cannot tolerate, these children may gag, vomit, have a skin reaction, or worse; they could have a full anaphylactic reaction. If the child has a note from a doctor stating that she is on a special diet, the program is obligated to meet her dietary needs.

- To begin with, provide the picky eater with small servings. Note that several small servings can feel less intimidating than one large serving of food.

- Do not force any child to eat. Set a pleasant and relaxing tone, model good eating habits, give children control wherever possible (serving themselves, starting, and finishing when they are ready), and follow the other suggestions in "Anticipating and Preventing Problems Related to Mealtimes" on pp. 31–33.

- Allow the child who is a picky eater the time and autonomy to develop better eating habits without pressure. You can say, "I see that you aren't ready to try it. Maybe the next time we have it, you will be ready to try a bite."

Unappealing food

Some children are picky eaters for good reason. They know, as do the adults who work there, that the food is not very good. Too many child care centers and schools serve substandard food. Food is a big budget item, so much money can be saved by serving lower-quality foods, and good cooks are hard to find at the wages that most early childhood programs can afford to pay. But good food is a key aspect of a quality early childhood program. Serving high-quality food makes an important statement about your respect for and care of children. This will not go unnoticed by parents. When children enjoy the food, problems at mealtimes are reduced. When children eat well, they are happier and better able to concentrate and learn.

- Educate the powers-that-be in your program about the importance of good food. Explain why the amount expended on good food is money well spent.

- Invite the director or principal to eat with the children often so she can see the impact of food on the children.

- Ask to have a nutritionist consult with the program to improve the menu. This specialist can often suggest ways to improve the food without adding much or any cost.

- To educate yourself about the issues, read about nutrition and cooking for children. Ask your director, cook, or nutritionist if you can suggest different meals or snacks that will be both healthier and more appetizing to the children.

Wasted food

- If many children leave a great deal of food on their plates, which then gets scraped into the trash, serve much smaller portions. If the children serve themselves, set clear limits on the amounts they can take to start with. Explain that they can have additional portions if they wish.

- Give feedback to the cook about how much food is actually consumed. The cook may be able to prepare much less and save the program a great deal of money, which can then be used for equipment, supplies, or salaries.

- Follow the suggestions provided previously in this chapter on food not being eaten because it is unappealing (see above) or because the atmosphere during meals is not calm (see "Too Much Noise" below).

- To aid in eating slowly, enjoying the food, and digesting it well, make mealtimes calm and relatively quiet. Before the meal starts, remind children to use quiet, pleasant voices during the meal and not to talk with food in their mouths. If the noise level rises too high, shut off some or all of the main lights. In a quiet voice, explain that you have turned down the lights to remind everyone to use soft voices when we eat.

- Use one signal consistently to get children to stop and be quiet. For example, you might use a special bell or chimes and the American Sign Language signal for "listen" as a visual cue for quiet, as described on page 20.

- To demonstrate acceptable behavior, converse with the children in quiet, pleasant tones. Have an adult strategically placed at each table to assist the children. Separate children who tend to be loud and boisterous when near each other.

Losing silverware in the trash

This is a surprisingly common problem in ECED programs. Giving children the responsibility of clearing their own places is an excellent idea, but it is unrealistic to expect them to do this perfectly every time. The consequence in this case is the expense of losing silverware.

- A simple solution is to assign a child the job of "environmentalist." Have this child stand by the trash, remind the other children not to drop their silverware in the trash, and watch for any silverware that may accidentally get put in. Most children enjoy this job because it makes them feel important, and they do it well. In programs where organic trash is separated from litter, the environmentalist can watch for correct separation of trash as well.

6. CREATIVE ART: MESS WITHOUT STRESS

Some mess during art time means that children are working hard and having fun. They're work-playing! Too much mess, however, results in valuable time being wasted while cleaning up, ruined equipment, soiled clothes (which makes parents unhappy), and frustration. The following suggestions will help you keep messes to a minimum while promoting creativity.

Anticipating and Preventing Problems Related to Art Activities

- Let parents know that the clothes their children wear to school will get messy. Although there are smocks or aprons to protect children's clothing, clothes inevitably will get stained if children are fully engaged in creative activities. If children do wear good clothes occasionally (often because they insist on it), at least parents are aware of what might (or is likely to) happen.

- For your own clothes, keep a bottle or a stick of stain remover handy to use in case of spills and stains.

- Have one apron or smock for each child in the room. Although you may never use that many, there will be an extra if one gets too soiled or torn. Old adult-size shirts with short sleeves or with long sleeves cut off halfway make excellent smocks and cost nothing if donated.

- Do art activities in small groups while the rest of the children are engaged in other activities during work-play. To avoid a big cleanup job at the end, help the children clean up some of the mess after each small group.

- Have a classroom rule that before moving on to another activity, children will clean up their own messes and put away any materials that will not be used by others.

- Before the start of a project, give a few clear, specific directions for using materials. Include a visual reminder. For example, limit fingerpaints to four tablespoons per large piece of paper to avoid paint flowing off the paper. Demonstrate putting four tablespoons of paint on the paper and put up a picture sign with four tablespoons drawn on it.

- Gather together all the materials you will need for an art project. Make the task easier by using a cart on wheels to hold and transport the materials.

- Keep collage art project items, such as scraps of paper, wood, and cloth, in separate, labeled containers. Organize them by color or type of item or both. This helps avoid the mess created by children rummaging through a large box filled with a variety of collage materials, and it encourages a more thoughtful approach to making a collage.

- Lay newspaper across the entire tabletop and tape the edges. Roll up the whole mess at the end of the project.

- Lay plastic sheeting or newspaper on the floor beneath your easel art table.

- Put adhesive-backed plastic paper over easels so paint can be wiped off easily.

- To catch drippy paint and spills quickly, place the art table and easels close to a sink. Add a small amount of liquid soap to paint. This will not change the quality of the paint, but removing spots from clothes will be easier.

- If it is not possible to be near a sink, keep a basin of soapy water with sponges and some towels nearby. Children can clean up on their own. Large auto or boat sponges make cleanup quick and easy.

- Keep a trash can and recycling box next to the art area. Both children and adults are more likely to use them if they are nearby.

- Provide a child-size broom and a regular-size dustpan. Many children enjoy sweeping, especially when two can do the activity together—one sweeps while the other holds the dustpan.

- Consider making the "abstract art" that results from messy art projects part of your classroom's aesthetic. An old table used only for art will look attractive with drips and spatters of colorful paint left on it. This frees children from worrying about being neat and from spending time cleaning.

Solving Problems Related to Art Activities

Drippy paint

- Add nontoxic liquid cornstarch to tempera paint to keep it thick. This produces less dripping and makes painting more satisfying to children by giving them more control over the paint.

- Make sure there is a brush for each container of paint.

- Give children specific directions, individually at the easel if necessary, to wipe both sides of the brush on the edge of the container before painting with it. Many reminders may be needed.

- Show children how to keep the different colors of paints from mixing in the containers and on the paper.

Paint spills and waste

- Paint containers that are short and wide are less likely to tip over. Use frozen juice containers that you have cut down, half-pint milk cartons, or commercially produced plastic no-spill containers.

- Use paintbrushes with short handles (about six inches). This gives children more control over the brush and eliminates the problem of the brush flipping out of the container or tipping it over. If the ends of brush handles are pointy, cut the end off and smooth it or cover it with a rubber tip.

- To avoid wasting paint due to drying up, pour unused paint back into a storage jar or cover the individual containers at the end of each day. Wash brushes thoroughly each day to keep the bristles soft and to make them last.

Gluing

White glue squeezed from a bottle is often a cause of conflict between teachers and children. Teachers admonish children to "just use a little," and children feel frustrated because either nothing comes out or too much does. Too often there are not enough bottles for each child to have one, the tops glue shut, and children become too involved in the fun of pouring, squeezing, and smearing. Although children need opportunities to pour, squeeze, and smear, they can do this better and more cheaply with paints and through water and sand play instead of with glue.

- As an alternative to the squeeze bottle, put a small amount of glue in a cup for each child and provide a small stick or brush, or a plastic eyedropper (with the hole widened) as an applicator. To save money, purchase the glue in a gallon size.

- An alternative to white glue is paste, which is less messy but will not work as well with certain materials such as wood. A few small containers of paste could be passed around or children can have individual squares of paper with some paste on them. Children can use sticks, brushes, or their fingers to apply the paste.

- Glue sticks work well for gluing paper to paper, but not much else.

7. MOVING MUSCLES: SAFE FUN OUTSIDE OR IN THE GYM

Large-motor (or gross-motor) play most often happens outside or in the gym. In this type of play, young children learn to coordinate their large muscles and increase their strength, agility, and understanding of how their bodies move. Developing these large-motor skills is as important to their overall healthy growth as developing cognitive skills and small-motor skills. Although it is tempting for teachers to use this time to "take a breather," your task is to provide children with many different and safe activities that allow them to practice balancing, jumping, running, climbing, hopping, ball handling, pushing, pulling, and more. Help them challenge themselves physically in many ways while staying safe.

Anticipating and Preventing Problems Related to Outside or Gym Play

- Schedule outdoor/gym time for at least thirty minutes each morning and thirty minutes each afternoon (for full-day or double-shift programs).

- Post a list of large-muscle activities that the children enjoy, as a reminder to yourself. Consider including the following on the list: hopscotch, hide-and-seek, playing gas station with riding toys as the cars, jumping rope, playing parachute games, tossing beanbags into buckets or at targets, dancing to music, "painting" the building with water and big brushes, pretending to be firefighters, hammering nails into a stump, making giant bubbles, and going through an obstacle course. Include a variety of cooperative group movement games.

- Refer to your list to provide a different activity for the children to do each day. A limited number of choices or the same choices every day does not provide for enough large-muscle growth and also leads to boredom. Accidents on the playground are often caused by unchallenged children taking dangerous chances.

- Before going outside, assign each staff person a different part of the playground to supervise. Make sure all children can be seen easily and reached quickly by an adult.

- Provide bicycle helmets to those using riding toys. This helps them establish good safety habits and reduces the possibility of a head injury. Make sure the helmets are adjusted to properly fit each child and are worn correctly.

- Most accidents on playgrounds are caused by swings. If you have a swing set, create a visible marker around the outside of the swing set area to signal children not to get too close. Clean railroad ties work well, as they are big enough that children will not trip on them, but not so big that they take up a great deal of space. They can usually be obtained inexpensively. A teacher should always be watching the swing area.

- Set a few firm playground/gym rules relating to your particular equipment. You might use the following:
    - "Go down the slide on your bottom."
    - "Swing only while seated and stop swinging before jumping off."
    - "Climb using two hands."

Solving Problems Related to Outside or Gym Play

Limited or unsafe play equipment

If you have very little in the way of usable play equipment such as swings, slides, and climbers, and there is not a park nearby, you can still provide a good large-motor program.

- Check your list of fun activities, as described in "Anticipating and Preventing Problems Related to Outside or Gym Play" on page 39, often. You will need to provide more structured activities if you have little usable equipment.

- Hang a tire swing from a tree.

- Create boxes of equipment to take outside that include balls, hoops, jump ropes, bubble blowing supplies, a parachute, balance beams, beanbags, shovels, pails, plastic discs, brushes, and so on.

- Fill boxes with props that relate to particular themes. For example, in a beach theme box, put shells, towels, sunglasses, empty plastic suntan lotion bottles, swim goggles, inflatable pool toys, and so on. Use a wagon to haul the boxes.

- Include among your materials soft rubber, plastic, or foam versions of sports equipment such as tennis balls, baseballs and bats, and soccer balls. These are inexpensive, safe, and easy for young children to use and easy for teachers to haul, and they can be used indoors or out. They have a short lifespan, however, so you will need to have the funds to replace them several times each school year. Supply dress-up clothes and art activities to add variety to outdoor play.

- Use large cardboard and wood boxes for a variety of creative play activities. Invite the children to use them to make houses, cars, ships, stages, and more. Also provide wood boards, bedsheets, and other loose parts.

- Put wheels on your water table so you can bring it outside on warm days.

- Make a large sandbox with wood boards. Supplied with shovels, funnels, pails, molds, and other creative sand toys, the sandbox will be a well-used and loved area of the playground. To keep out neighborhood pets, cover the sandbox when it is not in use with a large piece of wood or thick plastic tarp firmly tied down.

- If you have access to a gym but the equipment is designed for older children (high basketball hoops, tall volleyball nets), adapt to that equipment by using a large beach ball for a volleyball and a smaller rubber ball for a basketball.

- Check equipment at least weekly to determine if there are loose pieces, sharp edges or nails, splintered wood, or other problems. Children can help you find these problems and usually become aware of them before you do. At the first sign of an unsafe condition, keep children off the equipment until it can be fixed or replaced. Rope off the equipment or have a similar highly visible marker to prevent children from using it. The children can help fix equipment in some cases by sanding wood surfaces, hammering protruding nails, and painting. Close adult supervision will be needed.

Play areas with hard surfaces

- A hard surface under play equipment or where children run is extremely dangerous. Put mats, mattresses, or similar cushioning under and around any climbing equipment used in a gym. Surround outdoor structures with loose, nontoxic, and safe materials that will cushion falls. Some programs have been able to get these donated from suppliers, as they can be quite expensive. In the long run, loose materials can be more expensive than more permanent materials, but the cost to a program of one serious accident makes the price of essential safety equipment worth the expense.

No indoor gym space for when the weather is bad

If you live in a part of the country where children cannot go outside for very long for many months of the year, here are some ideas for providing an effective large-motor program.

- Unless the weather is severe, take your children outside for a short time every day. Start collecting a supply of extra boots, mittens, hats, and so on for children who do not come properly dressed for the weather. If heat is the problem, keep a supply of children's sunscreen and sun hats. Some fresh air and only ten minutes of running and playing will provide children with a satisfying experience. Afterward, they will be better able and more willing to engage in more restricted indoor play.

- If at all possible, move tables and shelves to provide room for children to move around within your room. Use CDs, audio files, or your own voice for movement games and exercises. Make sure the children have plenty of time to move on their own to music (creative dance), move freely to their own ideas ("Let's move like bees stuck in honey"), and be physical with each other (exercising with partners). Creative expression with their whole bodies can provide an emotional release for strong feelings or anxieties children may have. The hassle of moving furniture out of the way and then back will be worthwhile, as you will prevent problematic behaviors and meet children's needs for movement. With close supervision, children can help move some furniture.

8. NO MORE GNARLY NAPTIMES

Naptime can be either a stressful or a warm and relaxing time of day for both you and the children. Careful attention to the environment, to comforting routines, and to individual needs for rest and activity will help make naptimes peaceful. However, given the typical naptime conditions in early childhood programs, it's remarkable that any child ever sleeps. I realized this when I was in Eastern Europe and Russia and saw every six-year-old fast asleep in every classroom. (Children there do not typically start primary school until they are seven, or almost seven.) How does this happen? They sleep in actual beds under cozy quilts in rooms that are used only for sleeping. Most of these sleeping rooms have blackout curtains or shades, and the children sleep comfortably in their underwear.

Anticipating and Preventing Problems Related to Naptimes

- Schedule naptime late enough so that most children are tired.

- Darken the room as much as possible and allowable by your state's licensing rules.

- Leave at least three feet of space between each cot or mat, and place children who are near to each other head to toe. This prevents the spread of colds as well as minimizes talking.

- Start each naptime with "nap yoga." Lead the children in a group physical exercise while they are lying on their cots or mats. Talk them through lifting one leg, then the other; one arm, then the other; one leg and one arm together; then the other arm and leg; and so on. As the exercise progresses, use a quieter voice and slower movements. End by talking them through some breathing and muscle-relaxing exercises.

- After nap yoga, sing a quiet, soothing song or read a calming book. Use the same song each time to establish a comforting ritual. This is a good time to read a few pages of a simple chapter book each day, such as *Stuart Little* or *Charlotte's Web* by E. B. White. You could have a transition period when children can lie down and look quietly at books for about five minutes.

- Remind children of naptime rules such as "Stay quietly on your cot and rest if you cannot sleep." After thirty to forty minutes, allow children to get up if they are not sleeping.

- Reassure children new to your program that they are not going to sleep for the night but just for a few hours and that they will be picked up by their parents later in the day.

- Play soft, soothing music throughout naptime. Use the same music each day. There are many recordings of lullabies, classical music, and new age music designed to foster relaxation.

- Ask parents to bring in blankets, teddy bears, and other sleeping aids used at home. These should be kept in a closet or in cubbies and used only during naptime.

- Gently rub their backs or foreheads or just place your hand on their backs or arms.

- As children want to do what adults do, lie down yourself for a while, but do not fall asleep.

Solving Problems Related to Naptimes

Squirmers

Some children need to squirm for about a half hour before they can relax enough to sleep. These are the children who do not settle down or relax when you rub their backs or foreheads. Let them get their wiggles out before trying to help them sleep.

Non-nappers

Some children are just not nappers. However, they still need a rest period in full-day programs. After non-nappers have rested for about thirty to forty minutes, arrange for them to play in a different room or outside with an adult supervising, or allow them to do quiet activities in the room.

Noisemakers

Children who are deliberately loud and wake others up are usually either bored or enjoy the attention their disturbance brings. Try the prevention ideas and non-napper ideas listed on page 42 to prevent boredom and to encourage napping. Usually lying next to the child for a while and rubbing his back or putting your hand on his back or arm will eliminate the behavior.

Socializers

Some children have a difficult time not talking and playing with their friends who are lying nearby. Place the cots or mats of such children behind screens, shelves, or other furniture so they can't see their buddies. Strategically place short room dividers and rearrange the room to create as many private sleeping areas as possible, while ensuring that you will be able to see all the children.

No rewards necessary

Tell the children who have followed the rules that they have done well: "Thank you for resting quietly; naptime was peaceful and all the children were able to sleep." Do not reward children for sleeping, as it is not something children can control. But making the effort to stay quietly on the cot is worthy of appreciation.

9. TECHNOLOGY CENTER: KEEPING THE CONNECTION TO CREATIVE PLAY

There are three main issues to consider for an effective technology center: managing it for crowd control; keeping the computer from breaking or crashing; and making sure the children are using it for good purposes. It is not enough that children are busy and happy tapping away at a computer game or that it engages them for a long time—so do cartoons on television. Nor is it enough that they are learning computer skills like moving the mouse. They should be using the computer to create and learn in ways that no other tool or equipment in your classroom can do as effectively. Think of a computer as being more like a box of markers than a television. The computer should support and add depth to your curriculum and your goals for children, rather than be an add-on.

Most children's software are of the drill-and-practice variety—just electronic worksheets—or are mindless games. There are a few excellent programs, however, that allow children to be more creative and efficient than non-electronic materials allow, which is the same reason that adults use computers. These programs allow children to easily create, edit, erase, re-create, and save work; store and organize photos and videos; have easy access to a great deal of information (pictures and text) through the Internet; do animations; create and play music; make professional-looking storybooks; and more.

Insist that any computer and printer purchased for classroom use be as sturdy as possible. The upfront costs of higher-quality products are worth the expense in the long run. A computer in an early childhood classroom is bound to take a bit of abuse. Also purchase a keyboard specifically for children, which will be more durable than a regular keyboard. It should have the standard keyboard layout, but with larger keys and many fewer specialized keys.

Anticipating and Preventing Problems Related to Using Technology

- Treat the technology center just like other centers in the classroom, using a sign-up sheet for taking turns if necessary, making sure all who want a turn get one. Encourage children who are not drawn to it to try it out. Make it one choice among many during your work-play time.

- Create a few clear rules about the use of the computer and post them with images and words next to or on the computer. These may include the following: "Touch only the keyboard or the screen and only with clean hands," "Press gently," and "Ask for help as soon as there is a problem."

- If a particular child or children are skilled at using the computer and use it carefully, make them the class IT (information technology) specialist. Have them help other children when asked and direct other children with technology questions to them.

- Use special computer programs or settings that prevent the children from accessing any parts of the computer system other than the software you have selected for them and that prevents them from accidentally accessing inappropriate websites.

- Make each computer an activity center for two children and help them collaborate. This will also ease the problem of many children wanting to use the computer at the same time. They will often remind each other of the rules. It will add a social dimension to the activity and there will be conversation and negotiation. There are some software programs designed specifically for two children to use, although the quality of content varies. Ensure that children use the computer equally or collaboratively and one is not just watching the other use it.

- Find child-oriented websites or videos that relate to your theme or to a field trip. Put links to these sites on the desktop so that children can easily access them.

- Limit the software to two types: interactive high-quality children's books (fiction and nonfiction) and open-ended programs that allow children to draw and create stories. Using these will require some instruction at first.

- Learn to use a simple website creator (many are free) and make a class website. This will allow you to document, display, keep, and update children's work, class projects, field trips, and so on. Make a separate web page for each child in the class. Give parents access to the website, but protect the children and prevent any misuse of the site by requiring a password to access it. The site can be set up so that you are the "gatekeeper" allowing access only to specified people. Use the computer as a tool when working on projects. For example, a project to make a dinosaur could obtain information about dinosaurs from the Internet or software. Document the project's progress with photos and videos and display them on the website.

- Use a tablet computer or smartphone to record photos and videos of children's activities (for those whose parents have given permission to photograph). These can be used for discussing and reviewing the activities with the children, for displays, for children's and teachers' portfolios, and to post on your website.

- Use e-mail to communicate with families. A webcam can allow parents to visually drop in on your classroom at their convenience and see the great things you are doing as they happen, creating much goodwill with parents.

- If needed, take the time and effort to get some training on using computers and other technology. Learn how to troubleshoot problems, optimize drives, update drivers, kill viruses, and perform routine maintenance. You will ultimately save time because the computer will run faster, you will keyboard more quickly, computer glitches will be minimized, and you will be able to fix minor problems, reducing "downtime."

- Make sure you have access to someone who really knows how to keep the computer running well, fix computer glitches, and make repairs. Buy an extended warranty. Your computer will inevitably break down, crash, and need repair, even if it does not get heavy use, which it will in an ECED classroom.

- Make sure that children sit at the computer in an ergonomically correct way, such as keeping eyes level with the screen. Limit time on the computer to no more than fifteen minutes at a sitting. This should eliminate most concerns about improper use or potential harm to children.

Solving Problems Related to Using Technology

Children who do not use the computer correctly or carefully

- Remind children of the rules. Make sure they understand and can follow the rules. Help them fully understand what they did wrong and what they need to do to use the computer correctly. Sit with them and help them use it appropriately, giving as much guidance as necessary. Remind them about what they need to do just before they use it again.

- Children who continue to misuse the computer may not be ready for this type of activity. Show them other ways they can get their needs and interests met with more concrete, hands-on, sensory materials.

Too many users

- Avoid limiting the computer time for each child to a very short time (such as five minutes) so that more children can use it each day, as this will result in very unsatisfying experiences. Instead limit the number of children using it each day and have a rotating schedule so that half the children use it one day and the other half the next, or something similar.

- Add less expensive technologies to your collection, such as tablets and digital cameras. This expands the hardware available to children and the opportunities to learn to use them effectively.

- Sometimes the popularity of the computer is due to its entertainment value because of the software chosen. Use programs as described previously. Help children use one or two open-ended programs in increasingly sophisticated ways and go back and edit work they previously saved.

Children who do not want to use the computer

This is a similar problem to children who avoid other types of activities. Because it is important for children to have many kinds of experiences and gain skills in many areas, using the computer should be as widely enjoyed as listening to stories. Computer literacy is as vital to being fully literate as print literacy, so all children must become comfortable and capable using a computer, particularly those who do not have a computer at home or who are not allowed to use it.

- Girls tend to receive less encouragement and support for using technology than boys, resulting in unequal knowledge and skills starting in early childhood. Pay particular attention to any (unconscious) biases on your part or other staff. Pairing up girls adds a social dimension to the activity that many girls enjoy. Software that includes elements appealing to girls, or that are at least gender neutral, will also help. These may include female characters or voice-overs and the ability to use it for communicating and interacting with others.

- Using the rotating schedule described previously will provide opportunities for each child to use the computer. Do not allow children to cede their time to others; instead, find out why they are reluctant to use the computer and what will engage them. They may need to learn some specific skills and practice them without fear of criticism or failure. They may need to try a different software program or be given a sense of purpose for using the computer, such as "Let's make a story about the restaurant you created in the imaginary play today. Then we can print it out and you can take it home to show your family."

Pressure to eliminate computers, to have more computers, or to use age-inappropriate software

- It is important to have a balanced program with a broad array of activities and materials available for children. Access to one computer for about every ten children is sufficient and allows for ample time to work and play in other areas.

- Having no computers is a perfectly acceptable choice for many ECED classrooms, but it should be an informed, deliberate choice. This choice may unnecessarily limit the learning opportunities for your children, particularly for those who do not have computers at home. Many early childhood experts feel strongly that computers have no place in early childhood classrooms. My view is that computers do have a place in your classroom, particularly if your program serves children from low-income families. But they have, at best, a limited place in any early childhood classroom. For older children and adults, most computer activities involve being sedentary, staring at a screen, reading what is on the screen, and keyboarding letters and symbols to interact with the screen. All of these are actions that young children either cannot do or should not do very much of. Computer time should be one choice among many and should not replace any other activity. And the software programs need to be open-ended as described above.

- If you do work in a program that serves low-income families, having a computer in your classroom is particularly important. It helps provide experiences with a tool that is common to children from wealthier families. This unequal access to technology has been called the "digital divide," and ECED programs have an important role in closing that divide.

- Write a clear, one-page philosophy and approach statement about computers to give to parents, supervisors, evaluators, and others who may be critical of their inclusion in your program. Include the importance of variety and balance in the curriculum in your statement and draw on the resources at the end of the book under "Technology and Media Literacy" on pp. 296–97. Include a rationale for using a limited number of open-ended and reference software as being in line with developmentally appropriate practices.

10. TROUBLE-FREE TRANSITIONS: GETTING FROM HERE TO THERE WITHOUT GETTING LOST

Transitions are those periods of time when the children are moving from one activity to the next. Transitions can be a problem because waiting, with no directions from the teacher, is difficult for young children. Even a few minutes seems like a long time to children. The usual result is that children will wander, run around, or do things they are not supposed to do. Dealing with those behaviors further delays the next activity. Making children wait, intentionally or otherwise, does not help children develop self-regulation skills. However, teaching children ways to productively pass the time while waiting does develop self-regulation skills. Short, smooth transitions mean that more time will be spent in meaningful activities.

Anticipating and Preventing Problems Related to Transitions

- Develop a consistent daily schedule with as few transitions as possible. Plan in advance what each adult will do during transition times.

- Tell the children when a transition is about to occur and explain exactly what they are to do: "When you go inside the classroom, hang up your coat and then sit on the rug for a story."

- Structure staff time and duties so that as children move from one activity to another, something engaging is already happening at the next place.

- Have materials prepared for the next activity so the transition will be short.

- Begin the next activity as soon as even one child is ready. The other children will be attracted by what is going on and will join in quickly.

- Keep a list handy of favorite fingerplays, short songs, and simple activities to use during transitions. Activities that involve the children using their hands, like fingerplays or songs that include simple American Sign Language are great because they allow them to be active and to use their hands in positive ways. Because the following simple games require no materials, consider using them for transitions. When the children are familiar with the game, give them opportunities to lead it.
    ‣ Describe what a child is wearing and have the children guess whom you are describing.
    ‣ Have one child mime an action (such as playing the piano, sweeping, or making a pizza) and the other children guess what it is.
    ‣ Name a list of objects and have the children guess what category they belong to (such as bracelets, necklaces, and earrings are jewelry).

- ▸ Tell the children that you are thinking of an object that everyone can see. Describe the object, one adjective at a time, until someone guesses correctly. More transition activity ideas can be found in the resource sections "Behavior Issues, Positive Guidance, Classroom Management, and Social/Emotional Development" on pp. 283–84 and "Curriculum and Project-Based Learning" on pp. 286–88.

- During longer work-play times, help children clean up after themselves while they are engaged in activities and before they move on to another activity. This "clean as you go" system helps eliminate long, tedious cleanup periods when work-play time is over.

Solving Problems Related to Transitions

Transition from eating

- As children finish, have them clear their places and move immediately to the next activity or an interim activity. Avoid making everyone wait until all are finished eating. If the next activity is not quite ready, let the children browse through books or draw while waiting. Provide a place where unfinished pictures can be stored to work on later.

- If there is more than one teacher, one should begin the next activity while another helps the children who are still eating. If appropriate, invite the children to set up the next activity.

- To eliminate several transitions, consider having a snack or a meal take place during work-play time. Put the food out and let children eat when they are hungry (over a limited time period), with adult supervision. Make sure that all of the children wash their hands before and after eating and help clean the table. If allowable, use sanitizing gel or moist towelettes to clean hands after eating to make the transition happen much faster.

Transition to outdoor time

- Dismiss children from the previous activity a few at a time. They could be dismissed by types of shoes, colors of shirts, or first letters of their names, and so on. If coats are needed, invite the children to help one another put them on and zip and button them before asking an adult for help.

- If at all possible, avoid lining up. This only produces boredom and tension, which often lead to pushing and hitting. Ideally, one teacher will go outside with the first children who are ready, and the other children will follow when they are ready. Another teacher or adult can bring out the children who move a little slower. Ensure that you maintain the proper adult-child ratios in the process. If there is only one teacher, involve the children in a song while helping get them ready. If it is not too cold, a teacher on her own can bring out all the children when they have their coats on. Zipping and helping with mittens and hats can be done outside so the children can begin to play as they are ready.

- To avoid a rush for coveted pieces of play equipment, arrange a schedule ahead of time. Use a clipboard and have a list of all the children's names to determine the order of turns. Each child can check off her name after her turn. Rotate from day to day who gets to use the equipment first. Use a kitchen timer to time the length of each turn.

Transition from outdoors or from work-play

- Use a small pleasant-sounding bell or chimes to get children's attention and to indicate that a transition is about to occur. You can have a child walk around the room to each individual or small group of children and quietly ring the bell or chimes and say, "Five more minutes." Use an analog clock as a visual cue for the children to gauge five minutes. Point to the numbers on the clock and say something like "The long hand is on the five; when it reaches the six, it will be time to stop."

- When the five-minute period ends, the child can ring the bell or chimes louder and say, "Time to clean up." When you have the children's attention, point to the clock again to show them that the long hand is on the six. Following these procedures consistently makes the children feel like this transition is an aspect of the daily schedule, not an arbitrary directive from you. This results in less disappointment at having to end play and more willingness to move on to the next activity.

Clean-up

- Label all shelves with names and pictures of materials for quick cleanups that require little adult assistance. Provide child-size mops and brooms and other cleanup materials where children can get them and put them back easily. However, use a regular-size dustpan and sponge. Teach the children how to use these tools.

- To make the task more fun, make a game out of cleanup. Pretend that everyone is a cleanup robot, or a construction worker, or a hungry cleanup monster. Singing songs or playing special cleanup music can also be effective ways to make the task more pleasant.

- Give generous encouragement to the children who are conscientious about cleaning up: "Thank you for working so hard to make our room neat for everyone."

Transition from nap

- Let children get up off their cots or mats when they awaken. Guide them to quiet activities (playdough, puzzles, and so on), while you are getting others up and helping them with shoes.

- Move gradually and quietly from naptime into another activity. Sit close to the children and talk with them. Ask them about their dreams. If the lights were off, gradually turn them back on a few at a time if possible. If shades were drawn, gradually raise them one at a time. If children are able to carry their own cots or mats, have them bring them to where they are stacked or stored. (For the transition to nap, see "No More Gnarly Naptimes" on pp. 41–43.)

Transition to going home

- After a closing circle time, many programs end the day by having the children choose from a variety of activities that do not require extensive cleanup and/or in outdoor play. Parents can then pick up their children with minimal disruption. This makes for a smooth transition and makes chatting with parents a little easier. Before they go home, encourage children to put away what they have been using, with their parents' support and assistance if needed.

- If children leave as a group, end with a closing circle time. If there is still time after the closing circle, invite them to look at books, listen to music, or draw pictures. Dismiss them a few at a time when the bus is ready or when parents arrive. As they leave, encourage children to get their papers and artwork to take home from cubbies or from a teacher.

- End the day by giving a hug, a handshake, or a gentle touch on the arm to each child as the child leaves. Look directly at each child and say something, using his name, such as: "Good-bye, Carlos. Have fun with your grandma this weekend and I will see you on Monday, in just two days."

- While children are playing, try to talk with parents about the day's events, describe interesting or funny things that happened, and offer other positive comments.

11. SUCCESSFUL SCHEDULING: A DAY IN THE LIFE

The key to a successful daily schedule is alternating long active periods with short quiet periods and alternating short teacher-led activities with long child-initiated activities. Young children are naturally active and learn best by exploring and discovering for themselves. Imposing long periods of quiet, sedentary activities on children is stressful for them and will often lead to problem behaviors. It also reduces the time they spend engaged in vital learning activities.

The following samples give ideas for developing a workable schedule for your classroom. Make changes to fit your particular program's goals, equipment, meal schedule, outdoor schedule, space constraints, and the needs of your particular children.

Many half-day programs run less than four hours, so make adjustments to the following schedule as necessary. However, try not to shorten the time for work-play and for outdoor/gym play. Shorten other parts of the schedule if necessary.

Half-Day Toddler Program (2.5 to 3.5 years)

8:30–8:45	Children choose from a variety of activities that do not require extensive cleanup, such as puzzles, drawing, looking at books, and table games
8:45–8:50	Circle Time
8:50–9:00	Hand Washing and Toileting
9:00–9:20	Breakfast
9:20–10:25	Work-Play (includes teacher-prepared art and individual attention)
10:25–10:35	Cleanup
10:35–10:40	Story
10:40–11:40	Outside/Gym (includes creative movement/dance)
11:40–11:45	Book Browse
11:45–11:50	Music
11:50–12:00	Hand Washing and Toileting
12:00–12:20	Lunch
12:20–12:25	Toothbrushing
12:25–12:30	Closing Circle and Dismissal

Full-Day Toddler Program (2.5 to 3.5 years)

7:00–8:35	Children choose from a variety of activities that do not require extensive cleanup, such as puzzles, drawing, looking at books, and table games
8:35–8:45	Cleanup
8:45–8:50	Circle Time
8:50–9:00	Hand Washing and Toileting
9:00–9:20	Breakfast
9:20–10:25	Outside/Gym (includes creative movement/dance)
10:25–10:35	Story
10:35–11:40	Work-Play (includes teacher-prepared art and individual attention)
11:40–11:45	Music
11:45–11:50	Book Browse
11:50–12:00	Hand Washing and Toileting
12:00–12:20	Lunch
12:20–12:25	Toothbrushing
12:25–12:30	Story
12:30–2:30	Naptime
2:30–2:50	Snack
2:50–4:00	Work-Play (includes teacher-prepared activities and individual attention)
4:00–4:05	Creative Drama or Story
4:05–5:00	Outside/Gym (includes creative movement/dance)
5:00–5:10	Closing Circle
5:10–5:20	Music/Rhythm
5:20–6:00	Children choose from a variety of activities that do not require extensive cleanup, such as puzzles, drawing, looking at books, and table games

Half-Day Preschool (3.5 to 5.5 years)

8:30–8:45	Children choose from a variety of activities that do not require extensive cleanup, such as puzzles, drawing, looking at books, and table games
8:45–9:00	Circle Time
9:00–10:00	Work-Play Time
10:00–10:15	Cleanup, Hand Washing, and Toileting
10:15–10:30	Snack
10:30–10:50	Small Group
10:50–11:40	Outside/Gym
11:40–11:55	Group Time (read-aloud, music, discussions)
11:55–12:20	Work-Play Time and Cleanup
12:20–12:30	Closing Circle and Dismissal

Full-Day Preschool (3.5 to 5.5 years)

7:00–8:35	Work-Play Time (children choose from a wide variety of activities)
8:35–8:45	Cleanup
8:45–9:00	Circle Time
9:00–9:05	Hand Washing and Toileting
9:05–9:25	Breakfast
9:25–10:15	Outside/Gym (may include creative movement/dance)
10:15–10:25	Group Time (read-aloud, music, discussions)
10:25–11:30	Work-Play Time (including projects)
11:30–11:40	Cleanup
11:40–12:00	Small-Group Time
12:00–12:05	Hand Washing and Toileting
12:05–12:25	Lunch
12:25–12:30	Toothbrushing
12:30–12:45	Group Time (movement game, followed by a story or singing)
12:45–1:00	Nap Yoga/Story (on cots/mats)
1:00–3:00	Naptime
3:00–3:15	Group Time
3:15–3:30	Snack
3:30–4:15	Outside/Gym
4:15–5:00	Work-Play Time
5:00–5:15	Closing Circle
5:15–6:00	Work-Play Time and Cleanup

Half-Day Kindergarten (5.5 to 6.5 years)

8:30–8:45	Children choose from a variety of activities that do not require extensive cleanup, such as puzzles, drawing, looking at books, and table games
8:45–9:05	Circle Time
9:05–10:00	Work-Play Time (including in-depth projects)
10:00–10:15	Cleanup, Hand Washing, and Toileting
10:15–10:30	Snack
10:30–11:00	Small-Group Time
11:00–11:30	Outside/Gym (includes group games)
11:30–11:50	Group Time (read-aloud, music, discussions)
11:50–12:20	Work-Play Time and Cleanup
12:20–12:30	Closing Circle

Full-Day Kindergarten (5.5 to 6.5 years)

7:00–8:35	Work-Play Time
8:35–8:45	Cleanup
8:45–9:05	Circle Time
9:05–9:10	Hand Washing and Toileting
9:10–9:30	Breakfast
9:30–9:50	Group Time (read-aloud, music, discussion)
9:50–10:15	Outside/Gym (includes creative movement/dance)
10:15–10:25	Group Time (read-aloud, music, discussions)
10:25–11:45	Work-Play Time (including in-depth projects; snacks are available)
11:45–11:55	Cleanup
11:55–12:20	Small-Group Time
12:20–12:30	Hand Washing and Toileting
12:30–12:50	Lunch
12:50–1:00	Toothbrushing
1:00-1:20	Group Time (movement game, followed by a story or singing)
1:20–1:35	Nap Yoga/Story (on cots/mats)
1:35–2:30	Nap/Rest
3:00–3:20	Group Time
3:20–3:35	Snack
3:35–4:15	Outside/Gym
4:15–5:00	Work-Play Time
5:00–5:15	Closing Circle
5:15–6:00	Work-Play Time and Cleanup

School-Day Kindergarten (5.5 to 6.5 years)

8:00–8:25	Circle Time
8:25–9:25	Work-Play Time (including in-depth projects)
9:25–9:35	Cleanup
9:35–10:00	Small-Group Time
10:00–10:20	Outside/Gym
10:20–10:45	Group Time (read-aloud, music, discussions)
10:45–10:55	Hand Washing and Toileting
10:55–11:10	Snack
11:10–11:35	Small-Group Time
11:35–12:35	Work-Play Time
12:35–12:50	Cleanup, Hand Washing, and Toileting
12:50–1:15	Lunch
1:15–1:35	Rest and/or Book Browsing
1:35–2:00	Outside/Gym
2:00–2:20	Small-Group Time
2:20–2:30	Closing Circle

Classroom Concerns: In Control but Not Controlling

THIS SECTION OF THE BOOK covers issues from the mundane, like missing puzzle pieces, to the complex, like coping with an imposed and inappropriate curriculum. The concept of "control" is what unites all of the issues in this section. Teachers who have control over how they teach—even if they have little or no control over what they teach—are more motivated, have greater job satisfaction, stay in the profession longer, and are more effective than teachers who do not have such autonomy (Parker 2015). Unfortunately, the trend seems to be in giving teachers less and less autonomy.

Maintaining control without being controlling is a key early childhood teaching skill. It can be seen in the way a teacher individualizes by giving the minimum amount of help a child needs to solve a problem, while teaching her problem-solving skills in the process. Or it may be evident in the way a teacher responds to problematic behaviors firmly but compassionately, quickly but calmly.

1. THE ENVIRONMENT: EFFICIENT, EFFECTIVE, AND AESTHETIC

How you organize and decorate the classroom environment and the kind of furniture, equipment, and materials you place in it affect children's learning and behavior. Children who are bored by a dull environment, overstimulated by a "way too busy" environment, or confused by a poorly planned environment will make the teacher's job more difficult than it has to be. A well-organized and attractive environment will encourage positive behaviors and full engagement in meaningful activities. So, take control over the physical environment and make sure it reflects your beliefs about what children should experience and the goals you have for them. Make it work for you and your unique group of children. Make it a beautiful place to spend the day.

Anticipating and Preventing Problems Related to the Physical Environment

- To avoid arguments, have several duplicates of toys, especially for toddlers and three-year-olds. Include both push and pull toys, items that can be put in and taken out of containers, trucks to fill, and low vehicles to ride. Make sure that all toy parts are too big for the children to choke on.

- For all children, provide toys and games with a wide skill range so the more able children will be challenged but the less able or younger children will not be frustrated. Also, as children develop throughout the year, they can move on to more challenging tasks as soon as they are ready. For example, have four-piece, ten-piece, and twenty-five-piece puzzles; puzzles that can be completed in different ways depending on the child's skill level; and many open-ended materials and loose parts.

- Arrange the furniture so you have no long corridors that may invite running. Place quiet areas (library, table toys) away from noisy areas (blocks, dramatic play).

- Rotate supplies and toys to avoid boredom. Provide many toys and activities that children can use without help from adults. Walls painted in pastel colors and posters that are soothing to look at create a calm atmosphere. Consider hanging up reproductions of famous works of art or scenes from nature. Purchasing art or nature calendars when they go on sale in early January is an inexpensive option. Avoid very busy, brightly colored rooms, which please adults but can overstimulate children.

- Change the imaginary play area regularly. Set up a post office for two to three weeks, then a restaurant for several weeks, then a campground. If you have a large room, keep a permanent "home" imaginary play area and have a second imaginary play area that changes. Encourage the children to come up with ideas for themes and imaginary play scenarios.

- Label all shelves and counters with words and pictures so children will be able to put materials in their proper places without adult help.

- If you have a small room, an oddly shaped room, or other challenges to your physical space, you may need to limit the number of children in certain small areas to avoid arguments and ensure safety. A small water table or a woodworking table may need to be limited to two or three children. To indicate the number, put up picture signs that children can understand, or have just a few hooks by the center on which children can hang their name cards.

- Make popular areas of the room, such as imaginary play and blocks, as large as possible to accommodate many children. Avoid putting number limits in these areas (unless the areas are very small) because children will feel frustrated if they are kept out. Setting number limits in these areas may cause more problems than it will solve.

- Balance the hardness in the room (chairs, tables, floors, walls) with things that are soft. For example, use beanbag chairs, large floor pillows (but not for toddlers or younger), rugs that can be cleaned easily, wall hangings, and fabric draped from the ceiling.

- Create at least one private space where a child can choose to be away from others. For example, cut a door in an appliance box, paint it, and put cushions inside.

- Establish a place to store unfinished artwork and other projects to be completed later. Provide individual, personal storage areas where children can keep projects, notes, extra clothes, and stuffed animals from home.

Solving Problems Related to the Physical Environment

Small spaces

- If you have a small center or house with a number of small rooms, you can designate each room for certain activities. All groups of children then share all rooms on a rotating basis. One room can be for art, another for dramatic play, a third for group times, and so on. Several teachers could then share such spaces by coordinating schedules and assigning themselves to a room to supervise, rather than supervising only their own groups of children.

- To increase usable space and make a creative and fun room, install a loft. Caution: ceilings must be high enough, and enough money must be allocated to build a sturdy and safe loft. It may be necessary to obtain a building permit, have an architectural drawing, and gain approval by several licensing authorities.

- Put sliders or wheels under the legs of shelves, tables, and other heavy furniture and equipment. Use the kind of wheels that have a "toe lock" so they won't move once in place. This will give you greater flexibility in the use of your space and make it easy to move aside furniture to create sufficient space for circle time, movement activities, and so on.

Not enough storage space

- Build shelves high up on the walls to provide valuable extra storage space for supplies, portfolios, teachers' personal items, and classroom materials that you are saving for upcoming activities and themes. Ensure that the shelves are securely attached to the walls near the top to prevent them from tipping. If closed cabinets are too expensive, consider covering open shelves with fabric to make the room look neater. This also helps solve the problem of children being attracted to the items on the shelves.

- Store large items or boxes of materials that will not be used for a month or more in a garage, basement, or similar storage space. If you do not have such a space available, a friend, colleague, or family member may have one. You also may be able to find a local business or organization that has extra space and is willing to help you out. Give the person who agrees to the favor a small gift of appreciation, such as a gift certificate.

- Keep a list of every item in storage. When items are brought back to the program, cross them off the list. Add newly stored items to the list. It is a good idea to have a written and signed agreement with the person who is storing the items that indicates acceptance of the arrangement and acknowledgment that the items are the property of the program.

High ceilings and large open spaces

- Lower the ceiling by draping fabric or a parachute or similar items. Hang these very securely and away from light fixtures or heat sources, to avoid any fire danger. Before doing this, check with your local fire official to be sure it doesn't violate fire regulations and with the agency that licenses your program.

- Because a large space tends to get noisy and invite running and boisterous behavior, partition it. The partitions should be about four feet high, so adults can easily see over them, and be secured so they won't easily tip or create a tripping hazard. Stringing fabric between posts or walls to make a type of curtain can also work. Perhaps the unused area can be set aside for an indoor gym.

- Create several cozy spaces by draping attractive fabric between sets of bookshelves or cabinets. You can also cut doors and windows in cardboard appliance boxes and cover or paint them. Put some cushions inside.

Little money for supplies or equipment

- Teacher-made games are often the most used and best-liked materials in the classroom. Look in equipment catalogs and toy stores to find ideas for games and materials that you can make easily and for much less money. You can often adapt these so they are more culturally responsive, developmentally appropriate, and meaningful for your particular group of children. Laminate or cover the material with clear adhesive paper to make them durable.

- Ask parents and staff to help you collect reusable materials to make games, such as cardboard, paper, cereal boxes, paper towel tubes, egg cartons, juice containers, disposable trays from fresh food packages, cloth, ribbon, magazines, postcards, greeting cards, or playing cards.

- Host a party for parents during which they help make these games. Serve snacks and allow plenty of time to chat. Allow parents to make a game or two for home use as well.

- Check with manufacturers in your area. They may give you useful scrap materials, such as paper, wood pieces, plastic containers, and cloth.

- You can save hundreds of dollars a year on paper supplies by using paper that would otherwise be recycled because it has print on one side or is otherwise unsuitable for some uses. You can often obtain donated paper from local companies (particularly printing shops and recyclers) and from parents' workplaces.

- A local carpenter or a skilled parent or friend may be able to make classroom furniture and shelves very similar to the equipment sold in catalogs for much less money.

- Check garage sales, used furniture stores, and charity shops for usable items. These used items may only need minor repairs, fresh paint, or a few screws. However, check the manufacturer's website in case the item has been recalled for safety hazards or other reasons.

Sharing your classroom, sharing control

- To avoid problems, meet at least monthly with the teachers who share your room. Discuss expectations for use of materials and cleanliness. Define exactly what materials can be shared and what needs to be put away or locked up. Having a supervisor at your meeting to mediate can help avoid an impasse and help determine what constitutes reasonable expectations. When you find the room left in good condition, leave a note thanking the other teacher.

- If you have to move furniture and put away supplies at the end of each day or each week, make your job easier by putting wheels or sliders on the bottom of all your furniture. Hinged shelving units that fold together and can be locked are very handy.

- As the end of the day approaches, enlist the help of the other staff and the children to gradually put things away and clean up. This avoids the need for you to put in extra hours of hard work after class, when you are already tired and eager to leave.

2. CURRICULUM CONUNDRUMS

A good curriculum is the single most important and most effective strategy for preventing a whole host of problems, from children's problematic behaviors to complaints from parents. What is a good curriculum? It is one that reflects best practices in the field—our most current, research-based understanding of how to optimize the development and learning of young children—and is a good match with the cultural and social values and needs of the community, the families, and the children.

Curricula can be understood as falling somewhere within four possible categories. The four categories are created by two intersecting lines that form a matrix. One line represents *responsiveness to children's needs and interests* and the other line represents the amount of *agency* children are given. For a young child, agency means being able to make age-appropriate choices and decisions, pursue interests, use a wide range of materials, and express and act upon his creativity, individuality, feelings, and ideas. Each line is a continuum ranging from more to less. See figure 2.1. The four quadrants created by this matrix are the four curricula categories: Quadrant A (upper left) includes curricula designed to optimize children's development.

Quadrant B (upper right) includes curricula designed to promote children's general development so they will be developmentally (more) on par with peers who have had more privilege. Quadrant C (lower left) includes curricula designed to promote children's specific development and meet the particular developmental needs of individual children. Such a curriculum, usually for children with special needs, includes tutoring plans and individual educational plans (IEPs). Ideally, the curriculum activities should focus on the skills, knowledge, and/or dispositions children need to function successfully in a typical classroom. Finally, quadrant D (lower right) includes curricula designed to serve the needs of a school system for children to meet their kindergarten and first-grade standards in preparation to meet the standards in subsequent grades. They also serve the needs of certain early childhood programs for the cost efficiencies and "quality" control that uniformity and consistency provide. Links to the websites of a range of curricula can be found in the resources section under "Curriculum and Project-Based Learning" on pp. 286–88.

Children Have More Agency

A Inquiry- and project-based learning are the main teaching strategies and are primarily derived from children's interests and needs. Addresses all areas of development. Goals for children are primarily focused on dispositions, such as to develop understanding, creative self-expression, self-efficacy, and learning for its own sake, among others. **Examples:** Reggio Emilia approach, Emergent Curriculum, national curricula from Finland, Australia, and New Zealand.	**B** Some or all activities are developed by the curriculum writers. Any project-based learning is through "studies" or "investigations" of prescribed topics. Addresses all areas of development, but some have a main focus such as self-regulation or cognitive development. Many are designed for programs that serve poor and minority children. Goal for children is to boost overall development. **Examples:** Creative Curriculum, High/Scope, Tools of the Mind, Montessori.
C Activities are child-specific in response to needs, which are usually determined by formal assessment. Activities, delineated on an individualized plan, are provided through one-on-one or small-group instruction, classroom-based adaptations and assistance, or "embedded learning opportunities." Addresses one or a few areas of development. Goal for children is to boost development in targeted areas. **Examples:** Tutoring curricula and some curricula used by therapeutic ECED programs, as well as some developed by specialists individualized for children who are gifted or talented or who have a disability.	**D** Themes, activities, and sequence are developed by the curriculum writers. Most require purchasing specific classroom materials tied to the curriculum. Focus is on gaining specific knowledge and skills. Goals for children are to accept authority, learn specific discrete skills and behaviors, be "ready for school," and/or do well on assessments. **Examples:** Some are content specific: Building Blocks math curriculum, Waterford Early Learning (computer-based reading, math, science), Second Step (social skills). Some are general and comprehensive: Waldorf, Frog Street Pre-K, Scholastic's Big Day for Pre-K.

More Responsive to Children's Needs and Interests (left axis)

Less Responsive to Children's Needs and Interests (right axis)

Children Have Less Agency

Figure 2.1: Curriculum Continuum Matrix

Most teachers have no control over the curriculum they use. However, I have observed both great classrooms and very-far-from-great classrooms—often within the same center—that use the same curriculum by teachers who have received the same training. I have seen this occur with every curriculum, including Montessori, Waldorf, Creative Curriculum, High/Scope, Tools of the Mind, the Reggio Emilia approach, and several others. Along with using other strategies, great teachers confidently assert their unique teaching style and adapt aspects of the curriculum to better meet their children's needs and interests and to better reflect their community's and families' cultures. They do this while staying true to the goals and intentions of the curriculum if the curriculum reflects what our field agrees is good practice. Nonetheless, curriculum is important. If a curriculum encourages teachers to be responsive and there is a good match between the curriculum's philosophy and the teacher's philosophy, she will implement the curriculum well and the curriculum will be effective. If there is a good match between the curriculum's goals and practices and the families' values, hopes, and dreams for their children, parents will be happy and supportive. When there is good match in both cases, children will thrive.

However, a poor match in either or both cases is a definite problem that needs to be addressed. If a teacher believes that social imaginary play is an important part of an ECED curriculum, then teaching in a Montessori program might not be for her. A Tools of the Mind program, on the other hand, just might be. If a family primarily wants their child to learn specific, measurable "school-readiness" skills, then a program that uses the Reggio Emilia approach might not be for them, while a program that uses a curriculum with school readiness as a main goal *and* is child-centered, such as Creative Curriculum, just might be.

Cultural Awareness Alert

There are cultural and class differences regarding these issues. In the United States, many poor working-class and immigrant families tend to have goals for their children that they believe are realistic and practical. They want their children to be at least as "ready" and as successful in school as their peers from wealthier, more highly educated families. Lacking community resources, unstressed free time, "inside" knowledge of how schools work, and prior positive experiences in school (and perhaps not being a native English speaker) make it very difficult to provide the home learning supports that children from wealthier families receive. Therefore, they rely on schools to do this, and assume they will. The challenge for teachers who serve such families is to meet these parental expectations and the educational needs of the children using child-centered, meaningful, active, and interactive teaching and learning strategies.

An even bigger challenge—a serious conundrum—for teachers is being required to teach a programmed curriculum with preset themes in a particular order using prescribed or scripted activities. These are the curricula in quadrant D on the matrix above. These curricula make it very hard to be a flexible, responsive teacher. This chapter includes ideas for dealing with these issues.

It is good to know a little about some of the major curricula used in early childhood programs in the United States and throughout the world. This will give you a perspective on your own curriculum. More information about these curricula can be found on their websites, which are listed in the resources section under "Curriculum and Project-Based Learning" on pp. 286–88.

Anticipating and Preventing Problems Related to Curriculum

- Try to find work in a program that uses a child-centered, flexible curriculum that you can feel good about implementing. This type of curriculum will eliminate a large number of potential problems, as children will express few problematic behaviors. Also, without the stress of trying to circumvent the curriculum, you can focus your time and energy on developing meaningful activities and engaging in positive interactions with children.

- Know a few talking points about curriculum that you can express clearly and succinctly when necessary. They could sound something like this: "Young children learn through experiences in which they actively explore what is meaningful and interesting to them. This is also a definition of play. Their learning is enhanced when teachers challenge them just above their current ability level. Because every group of children is different and within every group there is a range of experiences, interests, and ability levels, curriculum activities have to be responsive and individualized. They also have to integrate all the subject areas within these meaningful experiences, because young children do not distinguish among categories of knowledge such as science, math, or literacy. Projects are an effective way to do this."

- Be confident in your ability to implement an emergent, responsive, child-centered curriculum and facilitate projects. If you are not, then take some relevant courses or workshops, read some books, watch some videos, and observe some classrooms.

- If your program will be adopting a new curriculum, volunteer to be part of the working group that selects the curriculum.

- If you are starting a new job with a new curriculum, make sure your supervisor understands that you cannot implement it fully, or as intended, without receiving thorough training on the curriculum and without access to all the necessary materials.

Solving Problems Related to Curriculum

The curriculum is changing

You have just been informed that your program has purchased a "great new curriculum" that everybody will be implementing. Here are some important things to know:

- What is the reason for the change? What are the goals of the curriculum for children? Where does it fit on the curriculum continuum matrix on page 60? If it is a programmed curriculum, what aspects of it, if any, are flexible? Will teachers be trained by the developers or by a third party? Will the training be conducted for the full amount of time and on the schedule that the developers recommend? Will teachers receive coaching or support in the classroom after the training? How long is the implementation period, and when will teachers be expected to have it fully implemented? What information have families received about it?

- Read about the curriculum from as many different angles as possible. Try to find objective reviews about it. Look online for videos of it in action. Observe classrooms in a program that has been using the curriculum for at least two years. Ask the teachers and administrators about its strengths, weaknesses, challenges, benefits, and what they like and dislike.

A prescription for programmed, predetermined curricula

- This curricula approach is the opposite of what is considered best practice in our field, which is based on decades of research on how young children develop and learn. There are many readily available resources, targeted to different audiences (parents, teachers, administrators, policy makers, and so on), that you can access to support an argument against it. See the resources under "Advocacy, Public Policy, and Research" on p. 282, "Child Development" on pp. 284–85, and "Curriculum and Project-Based Learning" on pp. 286–88.

- Understand the reason(s) why this type of curriculum is used in your program. This will help you figure out the best ways to respond. Here are some possible reasons:

    1. The person(s) who developed or selected it did not know about its shortcomings or better alternatives.

    2. It was the only option for some reason, or it was provided for free or as part of a grant, or it was adopted for a similar non-intentional reason.

    3. It is viewed as something that parents can understand and appreciate.

    4. Teachers are considered incapable of effectively creating their own themes and activities.

    5. Teachers and/or administrators view it as time-saving and easy to implement compared to more child-centered, responsive curricula.

    6. It creates uniform themes and activities across sites and classrooms.

    7. After careful and thorough review of many types of curricula, the person(s) who developed or selected it sincerely believed that it is the best curriculum for children and that its goals and practices align well with the program's goals, beliefs, and values.

    8. Some combination of reasons 1–7.

    Reasons 1 and 2 above lack intention so there may be a good chance that the curriculum can be changed, either in part or in whole. Reasons 3, 4, and 5 are intentional, but they are not very strong reasons to justify using this type of curriculum. Reason 6 is intentional and structural so it would be difficult to make changes unless the cost and time efficiencies that uniformity provides can be achieved another way. And reason 7 is highly intentional and therefore hard to refute and change, unless the person(s) who developed or selected it is no longer involved in the program or has adopted different views.

- Suggest small, incremental changes that will likely be acceptable to everyone. For example, once per year, teachers collaborate to decide on a theme that is not included in the curriculum. Then they share activity ideas and help each other plan. After implementing it, they discuss the children's responses, what worked well, and what they wish they had done differently. Then the teachers decide whether to make the theme and activities a permanent part of the curriculum.

- If none of the solutions suggested above can be used, or if they fail to work, there are still several things you can do:

- Supplement the programmed themes and activities with ones that are more responsive. This may require moving through the prescribed activities quickly.
- Alter themes and activities slightly to be more responsive. For example, the preset theme is "Community Helpers," but if one of the children's mother is a police officer, most of the activities for this theme could be focused on this one type of community helper.
- Some of the most important things that children need are not addressed directly in most curricula. These include feeling valued, cared for, and cared about; receiving the right balance of support and challenge; being able to make choices and experiencing consistent routines and expectations; having opportunities to connect with peers; hearing many high-quality children's books and stories; and being outdoors in nature whenever possible.

Thinking up thoughtful themes

Themes, or units, are probably the most common curriculum structure found in ECED classrooms. A theme typically lasts two to four weeks and provides the basis to integrate art, math, science, literature, language, field trips, and other activities. Most major curricula use a theme-based structure. Developing a theme that is meaningful to children and easily leads to a variety of active, engaging activities solves nearly every curriculum problem. One of the best ways to do this is by using an emergent project-based curriculum in which the themes primarily come from the children's interests and needs. Some examples of such themes are listed below. It is interesting that they all have to do with issues of power, strength, or control . . . or all three. And they all involve things that are scary and dangerous, even to the point of "life or death." These are issues that are very compelling to young children and they often choose to "play them out" when given the freedom to generate their own play themes.

- "The Wildness of Animals," from a program that is very near a zoo, emerged from teachers' carefully observing children's play. This theme and its various activities and projects can be seen in the video from the Portland Children's Museum (no date), *Inquiry into Wild Animals*. http://shop.portlandcm.org/Inquiry-Wild-Animals-CTRIWA-5324/

- "Big, Tall, and Very High Up," from an urban program, also emerged from observing children's play. See the video from Harvest Resources (no date), *Thinking Big: Extending Emergent Curriculum Projects*. www.youtube.com/watch?v=G-y4gUEbuW8

- "The Sinking of the *Titanic*," from the same teachers featured in *Thinking Big*, emerged from the children's interest in the song "It Was Sad When the Great Ship Went Down," which was introduced to the class by one of the children. See the video from Harvest Resources, *Setting Sail: An Emergent Curriculum Project*. www.ecetrainers.com/content/setting-sail-emergent-curriculum-project

Theme topics can also develop from what we know about children's age-related developmental tasks. For four-year-olds, for example, these tasks include what it means to be good or bad, how to feel safe and secure, and how to deal with strong emotions. Themes can also be based on important community events (both good events, like festivals, and bad events, like a house fire), experiences that most or all of the families engage in (such as family road trips, camping and fishing in rural areas, or going to museums in urban areas), and experiences that are compelling to nearly all young children (such as going to the doctor, house and building construction, and air travel and flying). Theme topics should easily lead to activities that are dynamic and active and that can be played out in imaginary play scenarios. Themes that are nouns, such as spring, colors, rocks, trees, do not typically lead to such activity. The exception are places where there is a good deal of action and people in many different roles, such as airports, markets, and construction sites. Some of the best themes deal with issues that affect all children and are deeply important to them. These address developmental tasks discussed above. Although the themes are abstract and complex concepts, there are many ways to make them concrete through active and meaningful activities. Consider the following themes, which include a few activity ideas as examples.

Separations. To grow, all people must separate from others and from situations. Children deal with separations every day and will deal with them for the rest of their lives. To develop a theme on separations, provide concrete activities that show children the difficulty and pain of separating, but also show the positive things that usually result from the separation, especially when proper nurturing and support is provided.

> **Science:** Transplant shoots from a mature spider fern to show how they separate. Focus on the special care needed to help the shoot survive and grow. Chart the growth of the new shoots. Transplant several with different variables; for example, no water, a little water, and a lot of water. Observe and chart what happens to the transplants.

> **Cooking:** Separate eggs and make one dish with the whites and a different one with the yolks. Point out how one thing separated into parts can result in each part having very different but very wonderful qualities.

> **Literature:** Read books about separations. "Hansel and Gretel" and many other fairy tales deal with separation. Read *I Love You All Day Long* by Francesca Rusackas and *The Kissing Hand* by Audrey Penn. Make books about events involving separations that happened to you or to the children, such as getting lost but learning how to ask for help in the process.

> **Project idea—bridges:** Start with brainstorming and charting all the ways that separations can be "bridged" literally, figuratively, and virtually. From there, the project can take form in a variety of ways depending on children's interests. It could involve investigating and creating different types of bridges. It could involve connecting with a classroom of children who are far away (separated by distance and perhaps an ocean or two) and investigating, using, and documenting the many tools and strategies used for bridging the separation. Or it could involve exploring the different jobs that parents do, where they work, and the reasons that children can't be at their parents' workplaces, which is why parents and children are separated.

Fairness. Almost all children feel strongly that everyone should be treated equitably. They feel deeply hurt if they do not get their "fair share."

Math and science: Strengthen math skills by having the children vote often. They can vote for things such as which book to have read or song to sing; whether a particular rule should be kept, changed, or eliminated; what to name a classroom pet; and which project idea to pursue. To vote, have the children stand in different areas to indicate their choice. For example, all the children who vote "yes" stand on the right side of the circle, and all the children who vote "no" stand on the left side of the circle. In some cases, there could be a third spot for the undecided voters, such as in the middle of the circle. This method eliminates the common problem of children voting for more than one choice. Make a graph to compare how many children voted for a particular choice (or were undecided).

To ensure that each child will get the same amount of an item, demonstrate weighing and measuring using a scale, ruler, plastic interlocking bricks or cubes, or a length of string. Show and explain fractions and simple division when food, drinks, and toys are divided up.

Social/cognitive: Discuss various ways of creating a list to determine the order in which children will take turns using a popular toy. Use some of the following ideas: alphabetical by first initial, picking names out of a hat, youngest first, tallest first, or rolling a die with the highest number going first. Ask children for their ideas. Vote on which idea is fairest and use the method that gets the most votes. Try the other ideas over the next few days. Vote again after the children have seen all ideas in action.

Project idea—good luck/bad luck: Sometimes you win, sometimes you lose: This project, which consists of activities best suited for children five years old or older, directly deals with feelings related to winning and losing—but mostly losing. It can be made more simple by using just the initial activities and expanding on them. The first activity is to show children that over time good luck (winning) and bad luck (losing) evens out over time. In pairs, children do a coin toss in which one child always chooses heads and the other always chooses tails. Each pair does twenty coin tosses and tallies the number of times heads wins (heads was lucky and tails was unlucky) and the number of times tails wins (tails was lucky and heads was unlucky). Then combine the tallies from all the pairs. The results should show an almost equal amount of good luck and bad luck for each side of the coin. Then the children play a more complex but common game that also primarily involves luck. Play it many times with many children, and tally who wins and who loses each time. Graph this as well so that it is visually evident that, over time, the wins and losses are about equal. The project then entails examining every game that children play and have played and determining if winning and losing is mostly by chance (being lucky or unlucky), mostly by skill and strategy (little to do with luck), or an almost equal combination of the two. Create a chart that puts each game into one of the three categories. Then carefully examine games that involve about equal amounts of skill and luck. Determine all the aspects of each game that involves luck (which card is drawn, the roll of the dice, and so on) as well as the skills that are involved (such as choosing a strategy and sticking with it, thinking fast, being patient, or trying to figure out what your opponent(s) will do next). Examine some games that involve mostly skill to determine the specific skills needed to do well and ideas for improving those skills. Help the children change the rules of some games so that luck plays either a greater or lesser role in winning and losing. Then discuss and vote on which version they like best. Finally, help children create a new game based on the elements of games they like the best, including how much luck, if any, should be involved in determining the outcome.

Changes. Change is part of living and growing. Although it can be painful, changing means growing up. Examples of change are everywhere.

Cooking: List the qualities of uncooked eggs. Ask children to predict what they will look like when cooked various ways (such as fried or boiled). Cook them and observe how they change as a result of heating. Eat them. Cook other foods that change when heated and compare them. Note that although eggs get harder when heated, vegetables get softer. Find out why.

Science: Show how water changes among its three states: solid (ice), liquid (water), and gas (steam). Talk about the unique and helpful properties at each state. Observe weather and track changes over a one-month period and record morning, midday, and afternoon temperatures each day. Discuss why these changes occur and the benefits and problems of the changes. Do not include unusual changes like metamorphoses—caterpillars to butterflies—as they are difficult for children, or even for adults, to understand and explain. Also avoid long-term changes (such as seasons and trees) that are difficult to directly observe.

Literature: Read *Changes, Changes,* by Pat Hutchins; *Love You Forever,* by Robert Munsch; and *Lifetimes,* by Bryan Mellonie.

Art: Let children experiment with mixing and changing colors. Provide a small plastic pitcher of water, clear plastic cups, eyedroppers, food coloring, and a basin to dump out cloudy water. Offer paper towels or watercolor paper to see how the colors change when dripped on the paper.

Project idea—stories of family changes: This is an exploration of the changes that the children's families have experienced. With the help of family members, the children identify one significant change that the family has experienced. Examples include immigrating to the United States, the birth or adoption of a new sibling, moving to a new house, getting a pet, going on a unique family trip, the loss of a family member or beloved pet, or a major event such as a rescue or winning a prize. One product of this project is a large wall chart categorizing the changes using photos. The chart has a column for each category, such as Moving, New Baby, New Pet, Loss of a Pet, or Loss of a Family Member. Within each column, are the children's names and photos of the pet, baby, house, and so on. From the chart a bar graph is made showing the number of children with a change in each category. Then children are helped to make a book about their family's change. These should be detailed and include the impact the change has had on the family. From these books, a class book is made in which each child has one page about her family's change. All the items are digitized and posted on the class's secure website. Two or three stories are selected to create short plays that the children act out. They practice the plays, make props and costumes, and prepare to perform them for parents when the project is showcased. If the children prefer, the plays can be videotaped and shown to parents rather than performed live. Some children may volunteer to read their stories at the parent event. Parents may also tell stories, sing songs, and the like.

Consider other themes such as "Choosing and Making Decisions," "Feeling Scared/Feeling Safe," and "I'm So Angry!" Once the ideas and activities in a theme have become familiar to the children, revisit or review the themes at various times during the year when related issues arise in children's lives. For example, the children can use the skills gained during the Fairness theme to solve daily conflicts. If there is an unexpected event that is of high interest to the children—such as the start of a nearby construction project or an impending storm—cut short or delay the current theme to focus on that issue.

3. "OF COURSE I TEACH CHILDREN TO READ": PRESSURE TO TEACH READING AND TO TEACH IT INAPPROPRIATELY

This pressure—for example, to use direct instruction to get children to memorize the names of letters and their sounds—used to come primarily from parents who just wanted their children to do well, if not excel, in school and beyond. But now it comes down from school systems, administrators of government education agencies, politicians, media, toy companies, and more. The goal has shifted from *wanting* children to do well or excel in school to *needing* children to get good test scores. Parents feel this new and increased pressure and pass it down to early childhood teachers. But it's hard to fault parents when they are so worried that their children will be ill-prepared for the rigors of kindergarten!

The pressure comes in the form of increased (and unrealistic) expectations for children and the following misinformed, wrongheaded beliefs:

- Young children learn the same way that older children learn;

- Rote memorization is the same thing as learning and understanding; and

- Decoding words is the same thing as reading.

Anticipating and Preventing Problems Related to the Pressure to Teach Reading Inappropriately

- Assure parents that the children are learning to read in these ways:
    - ▸ being exposed to good literature and a great deal of print in many forms for a variety of purposes
    - ▸ learning that print carries meaning and is a form of communication
    - ▸ having many opportunities to write, and being challenged to write better
    - ▸ using writing in play—taking orders at the restaurant, writing a prescription at the clinic—whether scribbling, making letterlike symbols, or using invented spelling
    - ▸ being encouraged to recognize and write their own names and those of the other children
    - ▸ learning letter sounds and how to form letters, to the extent they are able and interested, starting with their names

> ► dictating stories that are written down by adults and then read to them or by them

>> ► seeing the pictures they draw captioned by the teacher

>> ► becoming good at rhyming

>> ► hearing and using new words every day

- Explain that this is teaching reading to young children in an appropriate way. It is not just pre-reading or reading readiness. Develop a written statement about this issue to give to parents and others who are looking at your program or who are new to the program. Make this part of a parent handbook (either for your class or for the whole program). Post the statement in the classroom and online.

- Ask new parents for their opinions on teaching reading to determine if your philosophy and theirs mesh.

- Save examples of children's work, such as stories they have dictated to you, signs they have made, their attempts at writing, pictures they have made that are labeled, and similar items, to show to new parents as examples of reading and writing development in your class.

Solving Problems Related to the Pressure to Teach Reading Inappropriately

You can respond to the pressure by assuring everyone that you do teach children to read, and every child will learn to read to the fullest extent of his ability and readiness. For many who create this pressure, reading means being able to decode letter symbols to sound out words. For them, teaching reading entails first teaching the alphabet, then the sounds of the letters, and then how to blend letter sounds to form words. But being able to read means being able to get meaning from print. Print is a form of communication, documentation, expression, and, with literature, art. Does getting meaning from print entail decoding? Absolutely. But decoding alone is not reading. So teaching reading means also arranging for children to experience the various ways that print communicates and carries meaning, from name tags, to shopping lists, to traffic signs, to captions under field-trip photos, to the poignant messages from the authors of *Miss Rumphius, Where the Wild Things Are,* and *Knuffle Bunny.* It means having the vocabulary to understand what is being read, which requires providing lots of language-rich experiences for children.

- For those children, regardless of their age, who are ready and interested in learning to decode letter sounds, it is important to help them do so. Start with the child's name and expand to the names of family members, pets, and friends.

- Scaffolded writing, developed by Bodrova and Leong (1998), is a strategy in which children as young as three write meaningful messages on paper by representing words with lines. They gradually add letters as they learn their sounds and how to make them, but they always write a complete message and then read it aloud. This keeps the focus on the communication and meaning-making purposes of reading and writing.

- Reading aloud stories that children enjoy is one of the best ways to ensure that they will become readers in the future. Do this often (at least once a day in half-day programs and twice in full-day programs) and let parents know you are doing it. Select books carefully. Choose those that will hold the children's interest and will not be too difficult to follow. Use original versions of classic children's literature and avoid watered-down, cartoonish updates. If the children start to get restless, stop reading. Continue the book at a later time or choose a book they will be more interested in hearing. Read with enthusiasm and expression in your voice. Change your voice for each character. Read aloud to individuals or small groups of children at various times of the day, including during work-play time.

- Create a print-rich environment with signs around the room, names on cubbies and on charts, simple graphs, shelves for toys and materials labeled with pictures and words, and lots of wonderful books. Create a daily sign-in sheet for children to write their names when they arrive.

- Use turn-taking sheets so children can sign up to use a popular toy or area of the room and cross off their names and call the next child on the list when they are done.

- Display children's writing on the walls and bulletin boards. Create documentation displays with labeled photos of projects from their start to finish.

- Have a cozy book corner with soft pillows and many books displayed attractively.

- Provide markers, pencils, and blank sheets of paper in the block area, imaginary play area, and art area.

- Make available alphabet games, letter puzzles, magnetic letters, sandpaper letters, cookie cutter letters, and so on.

- Write and post children's names in many places around the room: on job charts, on birthday charts, on cubbies, and more.

- Set up imaginary play areas, such as an office, hospital, post office, or library, so children can imitate the reading and writing that adults do in those places.

- Individualize. Most children are interested and ready to read between six and seven years of age. But for children who are younger than this and ready and interested, or who are already starting to read, provide additional assistance. Supply some enjoyable, easy-to-read books such as those by Dr. Seuss. For many children, *Hop on Pop* or *Green Eggs and Ham* are the first books they read independently.

- Good language skills and a good vocabulary are the foundations of good reading and writing skills. Speak clearly yourself, encourage children to use language as much and as well as they are able, and expose them to many new words and phrases.

- Use mealtimes as an opportunity for children to use language to get food passed, milk poured, and so on.

- Teach many songs and read stories that contain new words. Explain the meaning of the words.

- Set up board games and imaginary play areas where the children need to talk to each other in order to work out roles, ideas, turns, and rules.

- Recite fingerplays and poems and sing songs that involve rhyming. Leave off words on occasion so children can "catch" the rhyme and say it on their own.

- Be aware of potential reading problems. Children with poor language skills (making many grammatical errors, using only a few words in a sentence, having a limited vocabulary) are a cause for concern. Make a referral to a speech and language specialist for testing and evaluation. Catching the problem early can be very helpful in preventing later reading problems.

Cultural Awareness Alert

Early childhood programs that serve children from families living in poverty need to be rigorous in regard to literacy development. Children from very low-income families often hear far fewer words and less rich language than children from wealthier families, resulting in an "achievement gap" (a "word gap" is more accurate) even at three years of age (Hart and Risley 2003). However, being rigorous does not mean resorting to direct instruction and rote learning or putting children under stress with unrealistic expectations for what they can learn, how quickly they can learn, and how long they can sit and pay attention. Being responsive means being very intentional and thorough by providing an abundance of language-rich materials and experiences that actively involve children in enjoyable activities.

---

4. TESTING WITHOUT TEARS . . . EXCEPT FOR THE TEACHER'S

This chapter deals with problems related to the direct assessment of young children. The larger issues of tests and testing—their overuse and misuse—are addressed in more detail in " 'E' Is for Egregious" on pp. 273–78.

The purpose of assessing young children is to know them well so that you can individualize effectively, ensure that curriculum activities are responsive to their needs and interests, and successfully partner with parents to optimize their children's development. It is difficult to accurately assess young children. Their development is rapid, uneven, and sometimes not even linear. We have all seen children "regress," because of an illness or a traumatic event, and then eventually bounce back. If the test directions are too complicated or the questions phrased in a way that is unfamiliar to the children, which is not at all unusual, the results will have nothing to do with measuring children's actual knowledge or abilities. The best way to get something that is close to an accurate assessment of young children is by intentionally observing them in a variety of typical daily activities and routines over an extended period of time and at home as well as at the center or school. Information about children's behaviors and abilities at home should be obtained from parents and from any direct observation done during home visits. Using a well-constructed observation checklist or rating form is helpful because it guides you to observe the same things with all children and to observe all areas of development thoroughly. Recordings of what children actually say and do—written, photographed, videotaped—and collections of their drawings and writings, are necessary to document your observations and complement the checklist or rating form.

You may, however, be required to administer other types of tests, tests that give children scores based on how their results compare with those of a sample of children of the same age. These norm-referenced tests are not designed to improve teaching and learning directly, but are for purposes such as screening for possible disabilities and measuring achievement or "school readiness." Screening tests determine if a child should be referred to a specialist for more thorough and technical testing and, ultimately, if the child should receive special education services. Screening children is very important so that problems are identified and children can get help as early in their lives as possible.

Achievement tests, usually given to children at the start and then again at the end of a program (and sometimes once or twice in between), determine if a child's skills and knowledge are lower than, the same as, or better than average for children of the same age or grade. The group of children whose scores are used to determine the average score is called the "normed sample." They are usually selected to reflect the general U.S. population in terms of gender, race, ethnicity, and income. However, the children in the sample may be very different from the children in your classroom. The amount and rate of progress children make, which is their achievement, is the difference between the first test scores and the last. This achievement score is compared to the average achievement score made by the children in the normed sample. The ultimate purpose of achievement testing is to be able to evaluate and judge children, teachers, programs, schools, school systems, and so forth on factors such as making sufficient progress, and to help bridge the achievement gap between children from low-income families and higher-income families and among various racial and ethnic groups.

> ### Cultural Awareness Alert
>
> All tests have a cultural bias—they reflect a particular culture, its knowledge base, and its values. Children should not be viewed as incapable because they lack the experiences of the culture reflected in a test. For example, four-year-old children in the inner city may not know what a "lake" is, while rural children may not know what a "curb" is. Children whose families have recently immigrated may not know either term in English, but they may know both terms in several other languages.

Anticipating and Preventing Problems Related to Testing

- Anticipate some of the problems that may arise with testing. For example, you probably know which children are likely to find the testing situation stressful or may even be "untestable," particularly if the test is being administered by someone the children are not familiar with. You also know which children are not likely to do well on the test. In collaboration with parents, develop some strategies to help these children. For example, allow them to bring a comforting object from home, permit a parent to be in the room during the testing, schedule the test at an optimal time of day for each child, and explain to children what is going to happen.

- Help children become familiar with the types of questions that will be asked on the test, without using the actual test items. Occasionally but regularly phrase questions during games, group discussions, story time, and similar activities as they typically are on tests: "Which one is different from the others?" "Is there something missing?" "What just happened?" "What do you think will happen next?" "Who has the most and who has the least?"

- At the start of the testing session, tell the child some things that she can do to control the situation, such as asking for more time, asking for the question to be repeated, or requesting water or a break.

- Prepare the testing space in advance. Make it comfortable and inviting, if it is a separate space from the classroom. Set up the room or space with a cup of fresh water for the child and for yourself, a timer, and a few toys or materials, which will not be visible to children, for those who may need a short break.

- Know the test well. Read about it on the company's website and from independent reviews. Know its strengths and limitations; all tests have both. Make sure that the test was designed for the purpose for which it will be used and for the age of your children. A screening test cannot be used as an achievement test or vice versa.

- Read the directions carefully to determine how much flexibility there is to be responsive to children. Can they have a second chance? Can you offer encouragement? How many errors are they allowed before you can stop? Can you break up the test and give parts of it to a child at different times or on different days?

- Ensure that the test, especially the language items, can be administered in the child's first, strongest language by a native speaker of that language (unless it is a test of a child's English language ability).

- Try to determine if the children used in the normed sample are comparable to the children in your class in terms of age, geographic location, culture, ethnicity, race, and income. This information is usually found in the test's user guide, technical manual, or on their website. If they are not comparable, request a different assessment or make a note of this whenever reporting or discussing the results. The skills and knowledge your children need to be successful in their particular life circumstances are unique and may be quite different from those of "average" children in the normed sample.

- Every test requires extensive training, ongoing support, access to a user's manual, and time to practice it in order to get accurate results and to ensure that it can be administered smoothly and with as little "waiting time" for the child as possible.

- Inform parents about any assessment you will be using with their children. Early in the year, share with parents the assessment tool and review some of the items. Tell them the purpose of the assessment and how the results will be used. Explain the rationale for not sharing results or, if results will be shared, how and when this will be done.

Solving Problems Related to Testing

It's not the right test or it's not a good test

- There are more reasons that a test can be problematic than those discussed above. If there are many children who can correctly answer every (or nearly every) test item and/or many children who are not able to answer any (or most) of the items, then the assessment does not span a broad enough age range and is clearly not the right test for your group. If children get a very high score on the initial test, then it is not possible to show what they have learned or determine their rate of achievement over the course of the year. If children cannot answer most or all of the questions, then the results will not provide information about what they do know and can do, and their rate of achievement may be exaggerated. Children might not be able to answer the test questions or the results may not be accurate if the child does not understand the language that the test is given in, the child does not comprehend the test directions, or the mechanics of the test are too difficult. For example, the test may require children to make small, accurate marks or lines with a pencil to indicate the answer. The child may know the answer but not have the ability to show it. Or, the child may not know the answer but accidentally mark the correct answer.

- Gather additional information about each child's skills and abilities that you believe are important but not measured by the test or not measured accurately. In your teaching, you spend a great deal of time promoting creative expression, problem-solving skills, kindness to others, respect for the environment, and appreciation of differences. However, very few assessment tools measure these. Even if your children will do well on an achievement test, their abilities and progress on many very important dispositions and skills will not be recognized, valued, and appreciated.

- If the test only asks for a number rating on items, write down some anecdotal information from your observations of the children related to the items (as well as to any additional items you think are important but are not on the assessment). This will give a more complete picture of the child and useful information for planning and for discussions about the test results.

- Minimize the importance of the assessment by showing evidence of learning and growth through a wide variety of ways. Over time, keep examples of children's artwork and writing, make audio and video recordings, take photos, document the things they say, and complete observation checklists. Include a wide range of abilities, knowledge, and dispositions, particular those not measured on the tests. Share this information when discussing the test results.

- As much as possible, assess items on the test naturally through observations during daily activities. However, it can be difficult to see certain behaviors or skills naturally. For example, some assessments ask if a child can seriate (put things in some order such as by shortest to tallest, largest to smallest, or lightest to heaviest). You can elicit this by finding or creating materials or simple games that involve seriating. You can cut cardboard paper towel tubes in various lengths and place them in a container that will hold them upright. Or put about twelve small stones of various sizes in an egg carton. If some children do not seriate on their own with these materials, you can provide some playful guidance through strategies such as asking, "I have put these rocks in a certain order; could you figure out what it is?

Can you put them in a different order and see if I can guess?" At first, they may need assistance seriating. Guiding them to start by separating and organizing the items and then arranging them from left to right will be very helpful to most children.

- Find one or more alternative tests that provide similar information but are more effective, accurate, and appropriate for your children. Request that one of these tests be used instead. Offer to assist in the process of making this change.

The child is not responding to the questions or is becoming stressed or discouraged

- After a few gentle attempts to engage a child who is not responding, stop the test. Write down exactly what happened in the test booklet, if possible, or on an attached sheet of paper. Indicate that the child is untestable and do not score the test. There should not be a score of zero because that would indicate that the child took the test and got all the items wrong, which is not the case.

- Sometimes children express their anxiety or discouragement by trying to distract you or by asking questions unrelated to the test. These behaviors may not look like anxiety or discouragement on the surface, but they often are. The children are just trying to "save face" or not disappoint you. Take these behaviors as seriously as you would more obvious stress behaviors.

- At the first signs of distress—whether overt or indirect as described above—stop the test. Tell the child that he can have a short break and set a timer for about three minutes. Do some stretching together and then give him a choice of two or three things he can do, such as look at a book, draw, or do a puzzle. At the end of the break, remind the child of the ways that he can have more control. If the child is not ready to go back to the test or is still anxious when it begins, end the session. Write down what happened in detail in the test booklet or on an attached paper.

The child misinterprets questions or the directions

- If nearly all children are having these difficulties, then it is the wrong test for these children. See the suggestions above related to this issue.

- If just a few children are having these difficulties and it is not related to language differences, restate the directions, according to the test manual. Although the test questions usually cannot be altered, every test is different in terms of what the test-giver is allowed to say.

- If it is clear that the child knows the answer or can do the task but is not able to show it, for whatever reason, make a note of this. Include in the note how you know that the child knows the answer or can do the task. Add more detail to the note after the testing session is over and make a copy of it (digital, hard copy, or both). If possible and allowable, leave the item unscored and, if there is no space for comments on the score sheet, attach the note to it and keep the copy in a folder with other comments, information, critiques, concerns, and resources related to the test. Even if it is not clear that the child knows the answer or can do the task, but it is clear that the lack of a response or the wrong response is due to the child not understanding the question or the directions, write a note to this effect as described above.

Sharing test results with parents and others—the good news and the not-such-good news

- Parents or others may ask you about how well their children are doing compared to others in your group or to the norms. This drive to compare and rank is fueled daily by the media. Because these scores are not useful or helpful to you in any way, have a supervisor, a researcher, or an online system calculate the scores. Then you can honestly say that you do not know the score and do not want to know the score. Offer instead to provide information about how the children responded to the test and the items and the areas that were challenging to them or that they were particularly adept at. Include information about the purposes and limitations of the test, issues related to administering it, and the supplemental details about the children that you have collected through observations and documentation. Giving parents a rich story about their children that includes examples of their progress in all areas of development greatly diminishes their desire to compare their children to other children.

- Parents do, of course, have the right to full access to any assessment information on their children, but it is to everyone's benefit if the results from norm-referenced tests are given to parents by a supervisor, a researcher, or an evaluation specialist, moving it away from the classroom level and your important relationships with families.

Pressure to teach to the test

- This pressure is understandable wherever it comes from, including from within yourself. After all, if a test item asks children to stand on one foot for thirty seconds, why wouldn't you have children practice this? We all want our children to do well and to score high, so practicing only seems positive and logical. However, there are two reasons not to practice test items or teach to the test. One is that this strategy is surprisingly ineffective in improving the skill and therefore the score. The ability to perform these skills has more to do with age and development than with experience. Of course, experience is important too. However, children may be able to do this task without the experience, but they could never do it without the capability. The other reason not to practice is that doing so is bad pedagogy. It makes your curriculum more programmed and less responsive. See the previous chapter on curriculum for more information about this.

- Many test items, particularly those on screening tests, are indicators of abilities and are not necessarily important in and of themselves. For example, a test item may ask children to copy a simple diagram or to stack small blocks. These items are assessing small-motor and eye-hand coordination skills. Such skills are best developed when children are engaged in similar activities that have meaning for them, where they have some choice (in play situations), and as part of everyday routines (pouring juice, for example). This way they are motivated to learn and are not put under pressure to perform. If you teach to a high level and provide engaging, challenging, and complex activities, especially through projects based on children's interests, children will have an easy time with these basic skills without direct instruction or practice.

5. INDIVIDUALIZING: DIFFERENTIATED INSTRUCTION GOES TO PRESCHOOL

Individualizing means the same thing as differentiated instruction, but it is a better term for early childhood programs, as we facilitate development and learning more than we "instruct."

One of the characteristics shared by all great teachers, whether teaching toddlers or teenagers, is an ability to individualize, even with large groups of children. Why is individualizing so important? Because it makes children feel valued and cared for, it makes activities more engaging and meaningful for them, and it is one of the most effective ways to promote learning and development. The more you individualize, the smoother your classroom will run. Problematic behaviors will be minimized and the amount of positive, productive activity will increase.

Individualizing means that your schedule meets children's needs for action and rest. It means that the equipment, materials, and layout of your classroom enhance the growth of every child and that the activities you choose are good ones for each child. It also means that the way you present the activities makes every child feel successful but challenged. Is this possible? Well, probably not for every child at all times, but most teachers can do a great deal more individualizing than they do currently, often with little or no additional effort. In many cases, it is just a matter of doing things a bit differently. Individualizing should happen on at least three levels: for individual children, for particular subgroups of children, and for the whole class of children. A subgroup consists of children with similar needs and other commonalities. Subgroups may include the children who are among the youngest or the oldest, or those who speak the same language at home that is different from the language used in class. Each class may include several language-based subgroups if there are more than two languages spoken by the families. There are also gender-based subgroups: girls, girls who identify as boys, boys, and boys who identify as girls. It is helpful to consider ways to meet the needs of these children through particular supports, curriculum activities and materials, assistance connecting with

Cultural Awareness Alert

There are great differences among cultures regarding the importance of a person as an individual as compared to a person as a member of a group or groups, particularly the family group. At one extreme, mainstream U.S. culture is very individualistic. The rights and needs of individuals are highly valued and individual achievement is glorified, while family and community ties are weak. It is very common for adult children to live far from their parents and the community in which they grew up. In most other cultures, children are raised to see themselves as a group member first and an individual second. At the other extreme to U.S. culture are certain non-Western cultures in which a person's group identity greatly supersedes any individual identity to the point that a personal identity hardly exists. However, individualizing is not directly related to individualism. While individualizing does value and focus on the unique needs and interests of individuals, the primary purpose and goal of individualizing is to effectively help children be successful, contributing, and responsible members of a group. Now the group is the ECED class and family, later it is the school class, and, as adults, it is the workplace, their own family and community, and society at large.

children outside of their subgroup, and protection from the biases of other children and adults. Because these subgroups of children often separate themselves from the rest of the group, it is important to help them integrate fully into the classroom community. Individualizing at the whole class level is important because every group of children seems to have its own strengths, challenges, and unique "personality." For example, it's common for your group of children to "click" one year—they get along well, enjoy each other, have fun together with little effort— but the following year they seem to be constantly arguing, complaining about each other, and generally grumpy.

Anticipating and Preventing Problems Related to Individualizing

- Know as much as you can about your children's lives. How many brothers and sisters do they have and how old are they? What are each family's beliefs and values about child rearing and education? What does each family do for fun?

- Conduct home visits for each child, if at all possible. This will give you great insight into their lives. Alternatively, meet with families at a park or a similar place, other than the center/school, but where children can play independently and be active while you are talking with the adult family members.

- Ask each parent these essential questions: "What do I, as your child's teacher, need to know about your child? What are your hopes and dreams for your child five years from now? When she grows up?"

- Know the children's abilities well through careful observation. Jot down notes about each child's strengths and challenges, and keep your observations in secure files. Refer to the file regularly to refresh your memory about particular children, especially when you are planning. This will help you maintain realistic expectations about what each child can and cannot do.

- For children with special needs, ask family members and specialists who work with the children for suggestions on specific ways to individualize during each type of daily activity.

- Prepare for the children to respond to activities in a wide range of ways. Assume that any given activity might not be successful for all or some children, and plan some alternative ways of doing it or a back-up activity.

- Do all you can to get good volunteer help from the community, from families, or wherever possible. Individualizing can be done much more effectively in small groups or one on one. Spend time informing your volunteers of what they can expect from particular children and train these volunteers to work effectively with those children.

- If you cannot get extra help, do activities in small groups while the rest of the children are engaged in work-play activities. If you have only one assistant, divide the large group of children into two smaller groups. Each child can have much more individual attention and many more chances to talk in smaller groups.

- Individualize during work-play, which should last at least an hour. Move around the classroom and observe each child or group of children to determine what interests them, problems they are working on, challenges they have, and abilities they bring to the activity. Ask questions or begin a conversation that will extend children's thinking and creativity. Help them do the activity at a more advanced level with the least amount of direct help as possible, if it will not interfere with their activities. You might say: "Tell me about the picture you are painting." "Can you think of some ways that you could reach the book if I wasn't here to help you?" "I suggest that you stop for a minute, talk with each other, and make a plan." "How can you get Sara to give you a turn using the toy without grabbing it from her?"

- Provide equipment and materials for a range of skill levels. Have some simple five-piece puzzles as well as a range of more difficult ones. Have some easy-to-ride trikes as well as two-wheel scooters or small bikes, some with training wheels. Have markers, pens, fat pencils, and regular pencils. Have easy board games and more challenging ones.

- Offer many different kinds of open-ended materials and sets of loose parts—a variety of small shells; bottle caps of various colors and sizes; stones that vary in shape, size, and color; and so on. The possibilities for individualizing with these materials are limitless.

- Arrange the physical environment so that it is flexible and uses the principles of "universal design" to the greatest extent possible. This means the environment will work for all children with no, or very few, accommodations necessary. (See "In the Mix" on pp. 116–22 for more on this concept.)

Solving Problems Related to Individualizing

Is it really possible to plan for the whole group, subgroups, and every individual child too?

- When you are planning, meet with as many members of your teaching team as possible, including volunteers. By doing this, everyone can contribute individualizing ideas and the team will have a shared understanding of what to do as well as a shared sense of responsibility for individualizing.

- Develop a systematic method for planning for individual needs. One way to do this is to plan an activity, or to modify an activity, that is designed to be responsive to the needs and interests of at least one or two specific children each day. In this way you will provide an individualized activity for each child in your group once or twice per month. Create a chart with the names of each child in the first column and the names of the months across the top row. Under each child's name, write a brief version of a goal for that child. When an individualized activity has been planned and carried out, write the date that it happened and a very brief description of what happened in the box under the current month and to the right of the child's name. This will ensure that each child receives at least one such activity every month and will document what was done and when. Some teachers are able to individualize more often, particularly for children who need more support and assistance than others. In addition, when you individualize for a child or group of children spontaneously (unplanned), add a short note about it on the lesson plan form.

- Review the activities of the previous week before you plan. Determine what was successful, what was not, and why. Pay particular attention to the children who have special needs and review what worked well for them and what did not.

- Here's an example of planning an activity for a small group of children as well as for individual children. You have developed a game that will be played during small-group time. As part of the game, children will give and follow verbal directions, such as, "Please put a red block underneath the chair." You know that there are several children who will find this very easy and at least one child who will find it challenging. So you add two alternative directions to this part of the game: "Please put a blue block on the arm of the chair and a yellow block behind the chair," and "Please put a block on the chair." Planning ways to individualize is helpful because thinking of good alternative directions in the middle of the game can be difficult and because you can now gather any additional materials you might need prior to the activity.

- Individual goals should address all areas of development, including social, emotional, and dispositions. For example, while planning the game described above, you know that one or two children will have trouble waiting for a turn. Think of and write down several possible strategies to help them, such as the following:

  - Allow them to have their turns early and then to move on to another activity shortly after their turns.
  - Do the activity twice with half of the small group at a time and do it a bit quicker. This way the time between turns will be very short.
  - Actively involve all the children more by modifying the game so that children team up and work together in pairs.
  - Make the activity more physically active. Add or change some of the directions, such as "Please hop to the chair and put the red block on it."

In spite of careful planning, the activity still does not meet the needs of some children

- No matter how thoughtfully and thoroughly you plan, the activity will always bring some surprises. You will have to observe carefully and be ready to make changes spontaneously. This, by the way, is an important attribute of intentional teaching. If many of the children are restless or bored, change the activity. Make it simpler or quicker, or involve the children more actively. If necessary, move on to an activity that has worked well in the past. Afterward, you may be able to go back to the planned activity.

- If a child is having a difficult time accomplishing the activity you planned, modify it for him or give extra help, without calling attention to the child's struggles. For example, during a cooking activity, a child who has weak muscle tone in his arms is having trouble pouring water from a large pitcher into a measuring cup. First ask the child if he wants help and, if so, give him some choices: "Pouring water from a heavy pitcher into a cup is difficult. Would you like to pour from a smaller pitcher, or wait until there is less water in the pitcher, or ask a friend to help you?"

- Avoid highlighting a child's problem. If a child with gross-motor difficulties or who is overweight cannot do jumping jacks as well as the other children, ignore the differences, appreciate that the child is trying, and provide help at a later time when you can be with the child privately. This will prevent him from feeling different and less able than other children. It also will enable you to provide direct and more effective help.

- If a child can do your planned activity quickly and easily, add a challenge to the activity. For example, you discover during the same cooking project that a child knows how to measure half a cup. For the next ingredient have her measure out one-fourth of a cup. If necessary, talk her through this process. "One quarter is half of a half. Can you find the line on the cup that is halfway between the bottom and the half-cup line?"

- An important way to individualize on the spot during an activity is to include something specific and unique about each child. This could simply mean making short statements such as, "It's Rafael's turn and he has been waiting very patiently," or "Sierra, your mother is coming home from her trip tonight. You must be very excited," or "Look at Diego's picture. It has so much detail and such bright colors," or "I don't know how to tell the difference between a seal and a sea lion, so let's ask Kelly, and if she doesn't know she can ask her dad, who is a marine biologist."

If children are "out of sorts" much of the day, it may be the schedule

- You may need to revise your schedule to meet the unique needs of your particular group of children. The most important aspects of the daily schedule are that there is consistency from day to day, there is variety within each day, and it is responsive to children's needs, interests, and cultures. If a number of the children tire easily or have short attention spans, you may need to shorten group times, lengthen work-play time, and perhaps add another short rest time. For children with advanced cognitive abilities for their age or who have particular talents, use the increased work-play time to provide challenging activities. If they are not tired during the additional rest time, offer them quiet reading, writing, drawing, or other activities of interest to them.

- You will likely need to revise your schedule one or more times during the year as the children change and mature and as their behaviors and sleeping and eating patterns are affected by the seasons.

- If you have two shifts of children attending a part-day preschool or kindergarten program, the primary criterion for deciding which group to place a child in is the child's daily rhythms. Children who usually nap in the afternoon and/or are early risers should be in the morning session.

6. MULTIAGE GROUPS: MULTIPLE BENEFITS, MANY CHALLENGES, MUCH SATISFACTION

It is becoming increasingly common for early childhood educators to teach and care for a group of children whose ages range several years. Sometimes this is done just for expediency, but it is a good approach with many benefits for children and teachers. However, there are some challenges, particularly if you have not previously worked with younger or older children. But, after an adjustment period, most teachers find it so rewarding that they are reluctant to teach single-age groups again. Among the rewards are being with children over an extended period and helping them grow from being the "babies" of the group to leaders whom the "babies" look up to. Siblings can be together, in some cases, adding to more of a family atmosphere. Not having to teach classroom rules and expectations to an entirely new group of children at the beginning of each year saves a great deal of time and effort. Younger children gain advantages by engaging in more complex play and activities than they would if they were only with their age-mates. Research shows that older children are not disadvantaged in any way by being with younger children and that younger children do better than those in single-age group classrooms. Compared to children in single-age group classrooms, children in multiage classrooms are more empathetic, have more advanced social skills, and have a more positive attitude about school, other children, and even themselves (Saqlain 2015; University of Toronto Childcare Resource and Research Unit 2014).

Anticipating and Preventing Problems Related to Multiage Groups

- The age range should not be too large. Infants and toddlers do not mix well with preschoolers. There are basic safety concerns and it is too difficult to meet the needs of children across such a range. They need different types of materials and equipment, management strategies, and schedules.

- Ask for the support you need to be effective with a multiage group, especially if you have not taught in such a classroom before or have not worked much with the younger or the older age group. This support may include training, purchasing new materials and equipment, extra planning time, time to observe an experienced teacher with a multiage group, and being observed and getting feedback from a knowledgeable coach.

- Make the differences in abilities and skills among children work for you. Encourage children to help each other—ask older children to assist younger ones and younger ones to ask for assistance from older children. Have older children "read" to younger ones.

- Have an efficient, workable system for observing, assessing, and planning, as the range of needs will be great. Your observational checklist or rating scale needs to apply to a very wide age range, or you may need to use more than one such tool.

Solving Problems Related to Multiage Groups

Issues with the older children

- Some older children enjoy helping younger ones too much. They will speak for them and do things for them that the younger children could do on their own. Help older children assist younger children without doing too much. For example, you might say to an older child: "Point to where the puzzle piece goes and let Leah put it in," or "Let Omar try to carry the box but walk next to him to make sure he doesn't drop it or trip over something," or "Let's listen to what Isabel has to say, first."

- Some younger children can be unreasonably demanding of older children. If older children seem annoyed by this, suggest gentle strategies they can use to keep younger children from being too bothersome. They can say: "I can help you in a little bit, but not right now. Can you ask someone else?" or "I can play with you for just a few minutes because I want to finish my project too."

- Do not allow older children to exclude younger children from any activity. You might remind them of the rule "There's a role (or place) for everyone" or tell them, "Say, 'You can play.'" Teach older children some skills and strategies to include a younger child in imaginary play, games, and other activities that are acceptable to both. Often this involves suggesting a role that will enhance the play and will be meaningful and enjoyable for the younger child, such as the brother/sister, son/daughter, helper, assistant, patient, or customer. But while being the dog or the baby is a good initial strategy for a younger child to be involved in the play of older children, it is important that the younger children are not *always* in these passive, subservient roles and that they eventually "grow" out of them and move into more equal roles.

- Age bias is common among children, and older children sometimes tease or bully younger ones. One great benefit of multiage groupings is the potential to counteract such bias, but it does require effort and being proactive. Make it clear to children that age bias is unacceptable and act on it quickly and consistently. Place a strong classroomwide emphasis on being kind and helpful to others by modeling such behavior and teaching positive ways to get needs met. This will help reduce age bias a great deal. Treat age bias as you would any other aggressive behavior. Remind the older child of this rule: "Use your words and hands to help, not hurt." Specific strategies for dealing with a variety of aggressive behaviors can be found in "Problematic Behaviors" starting on page 173.

Issues with the younger children

- Assist younger children to seek help and companionship from a wide variety of classmates, not just one or two older children.

- Teach younger children to seek help or attention from older children appropriately: "Wait until Alma stops talking with Elena; you may need to wait for a while" or "Victor doesn't seem to like being tapped on his arm. To get his attention, look at him and say his name."

- Help younger children learn to enter and take a role in the more complex play of older children. They first need to watch and figure out the imaginary place, situation, and various roles being played. Then they can take on a role that will complement the play—"Can I be another customer?"—or ask what role they can play.

- Younger children may feel inadequate or intimidated by the behaviors of older children. They, therefore, may not participate at all or not participate fully in some activities, particularly those that are above their current skill or knowledge level. Many younger children who are not participating are watching carefully. For them, this is an effective strategy to become familiar with the activities and gain the confidence they need to participate. Others, however, will need your assistance to participate fully in all activities.

Meeting needs and individualizing across a wide age/developmental range

- Seek volunteer help from parents or community agencies.

- Obtain or create an ample number of toys, games, and materials that are both easier and more challenging.

- Rework your daily schedule. This may mean more or less time spent on a particular part of the day (large-motor, work-play, and so forth) or may just entail reordering the activities.

- Request or give yourself more time for planning in order to adequately prepare for the large age/developmental range of the group. Focus at first on the few children who seem to be having the most difficulty. See the previous chapter on individualizing for more ideas.

7. ARE WE HAVING FUN YET?: FACILITATING FIASCO-FREE FIELD TRIPS

Field trips are an important part of a program for young children. Although they can be costly and involve risk, they are worth the effort because children get to see, hear, smell, and touch firsthand the world around them (which is the way they learn best). For programs serving children from low-income families, field trips are essential because most of the families cannot afford the cost or time to provide these experiences. After taking my class on a field trip to a busy city harbor, without any prompting on my part, the children made elaborate ships and docks with blocks, drew pictures of boats, and acted out riding on a ship and loading and unloading cargo for several weeks.

A display or book of photographs from the trip, captioned with children's comments and memories, helps extend the educational value and enjoyment of the trip. Providing opportunities for children to see and experience something new, followed by time to re-create it through imaginary play and art, is a powerful way to help children learn and develop. If at all possible, plan about one field trip per month. A field trip does not have to be very elaborate or to an unusual place. You can simply show the children a new aspect of something familiar. A trip to a popular local restaurant where the children can see how the food is prepared and ask questions of the cook and staff can be very rewarding. This will provide the basis for some great social imaginary play, especially if you provide some playdough to "cook" with, paper and pens to make menus and take orders, trays, big pots and pans, wooden spoons, and other related supplies.

Anticipating and Preventing Problems Related to Field Trips

- Before a field trip, get parent permission forms signed and place large notices to remind parents of the trip.

- To allow time for preparation, arrange the field trip early in the week, but not the first day back after a weekend. Children are often more attentive early in the week. During the rest of the week, you can provide activities in which the children play, talk about, and draw what they experienced on their trip.

- Carefully scout out and plan your trip. Visit the place yourself before the trip so you will experience no unpleasant surprises with the children. Make sure there are things to see and do that will hold the children's attention and interest. Places such as art museums, which do not allow touching, may be frustrating for them. Request a host who knows about and has had experience with young children. Gather some basic information about the place you are visiting that will be of interest to your children to supplement the information provided by the host.

- Keep the trip short and simple. Avoid the temptation to visit several different places on the same day because they are near each other. Even within one place, if it is large it is a good idea to limit what children see. For example, visit only two or three sections of the zoo. It is more educational and less tiring to get to know a few types of animals in depth than many types of animals superficially. If the field trip will be a long one, plan for an unstructured period (at least thirty minutes) when the children can freely play at a nearby park or playground, perhaps after a picnic lunch.

- Before the trip, tell the children a little of what they can expect to see. If possible, show some pictures of the place. Read a book and sing songs related to the trip. For example, you might sing "Johnny Works with One Hammer" and read *In Christina's Tool Box*, by Diana Homan, before a trip to a hardware store.

- Put a button or tag with the name and phone number of your center/school on each child in case a child gets lost. Consider dividing the class into two smaller groups for a field trip. If allowed, get extra help from responsible, well-known adults who can legally be alone with a group of children, such as management staff, parents, or volunteers. Assign four to six children to each adult. The adult will then be responsible for those children throughout the trip. Make sure that every adult has a working phone that is turned on and can be heard if it is noisy. Periodically ask for a head count from each adult to make sure all the children are accounted for. Each child should have a partner for the entire field trip.

- Set one or two rules for safety, such as "Walk at all times" and "Stay with the class and stay with your partner." Make sure that the children understand the rules. If necessary, practice following these rules by taking a short walk before the field trip. Set any special rules needed for a particular trip, such as "Stay back from the water" or "Keep your hands and feet behind the railing." Tell the children what they should do if they get lost or separated from the group. Make it as simple and clear as possible. For example: "Look for a person wearing a uniform or a mother with children. Say 'Please help me, I'm lost.' Show her your tag."

- Consider using a long rope with knots tied along it when walking on a field trip. Have each child hold onto a knot and one adult hold the front while another adult holds the back. Control the length of the rope, the spacing of the knots (so that children do not step on one another's heels), and the pace of the walk. This provides the group control you need for safety while giving children some responsibility and autonomy.

- Bring along snacks and plenty of water, especially on hot days. Build time into your field-trip schedule to allow for food and drink breaks, as well as bathroom breaks. The children will be tired from walking during the trip, so if they are also hungry and thirsty . . . well, let's just not let that happen!

- Document your field trips with photos and make a book of each trip. Write text based on the children's descriptions and memories. Post a digital version of it on the class website. Before an upcoming field trip, review one or two of these field-trip books with the children. Ask them what went well and what did not and what they enjoyed most and least. Then discuss how these lessons can be used to make the upcoming field trip more successful and enjoyable.

- Plan for the possibility that the field trip will not work out. Is there an alternative place to go near the location of the field trip, such as a park or playground? What arrangements can you make in case you need to cut the trip short and return to the center or school early?

- Have a back-up lesson plan for the day in case you are not able to leave for the trip because the bus needs repairs, the public transportation that you planned to use is out of service, a key assistant called in sick, or other such problems develop.

- Take along a first-aid kit and emergency numbers for each child, as well as tissues and some extra clothes . . . just in case!

- In hot weather take sunscreen and ensure that children have hats and in cold weather that they have warm enough jackets, hats, and mittens, and appropriate shoes. Rain coats and boots may be necessities any time of the year, particularly if you are in Portland or Seattle! Jackets and hats can always be put on or taken off if the weather changes during the day. Give the children drawstring backpacks to hold their jackets and hats and any other small necessities. These can be pre-printed with the name of your program or school and the address and phone number, solving two problems at once (in addition to providing some free advertising).

- Start the year out with short, simple, nearby field trips. Get as many adults as possible to help. As the children gain skills and learn rules for field trips, increase the length and complexity of the trips.

Solving Problems Related to Field Trips

The group is overly excited, not following rules, or not listening to directions

- There are many reasons why children might get "out of hand" and become difficult to manage on a field trip, in spite of your best efforts to prevent such behavior. The usual reasons are that the place they are visiting is overstimulating or is not a good match for their needs, interests, or developmental level. If possible, change your plans and go to a nearby park or playground or for a walk. (Parent permission forms for all field trips should include a statement that it may be necessary to do this.) Make sure that your administrators know where you are as well as anyone else who needs to know. Another option is to cut the trip short and go back to the center or school.

- If only one particular child typically makes your trips unpleasant and difficult, assign an adult to be with that child and no more than one other child during the trip. As a last resort, consider leaving this child with another class for the day or making a similar arrangement (if allowed by state regulations). In any case, don't deprive the majority of your children the value of field trips because of one child.

No transportation or funds for field trips

- There are likely many places near you that you could visit for free and that would make for great field trips—stores, businesses, public services, organizations, and agencies—even if they are familiar to the children. The special attention the children receive from an owner or a worker during a field trip and the behind-the-scenes look provide a very different experience from the one they get when they go to these same places with their parents as customers. Visit some of the following places for your neighborhood trips: library, post office, fire station, police station, telephone or cable company, newspaper publisher, train station, theater, hospital, clinic, doctor's office, veterinarian's office, dentist's office, optometrist's office, animal shelter, schools, lumberyard, florist, hardware store, auto dealership, auto repair shop, photographer's or artist's studio, carpenter's shop, hair salon, radio station, recycling center, hotel, restaurant, construction site, bank, supermarket, pet store, computer store, bakery, and so on.

- Any field trip will be enhanced when you make it intentional and focused. One effective way to do this is to have children record their observations on a sheet of paper attached to a clipboard. Make inexpensive clipboards by stapling or gluing paper to a stiff piece of cardboard. The paper and clipboards should be half the size of a sheet of 8 ½ inches x 11 inches (letter-size) paper, so they will be manageable for small hands. Glue one side of a small piece of Velcro to a pencil and the complementary side to the top or side of the cardboard.

- The paper on each child's clipboard can have small photos or drawings on it to match to things they will see, or most likely see, on the trip. Encourage them to check off the picture when they see the real thing. They will feel grown-up and important carrying clipboards, pencils, and checklists, and you will give them focus and a sense of purpose while on the trip. Have children work together in pairs to enhance their social and language skills. Select a range of things to find: some that are familiar and fairly common, some that are familiar but not very common, and some that are unfamiliar to most of the children. However, most of the items should be unique to the place you are visiting. These ideas can help make a familiar trip a unique experience.

- Another option is to take a walk around the neighborhood or to a nearby park. As you walk through different areas—inside a big building, near a busy street, by a bus, in a park, near a school playground, in a market, near a body of water, under a bridge or overpass—challenge children to notice things that are out of the ordinary, such as the unique soundscapes and color palettes of each area. A walk can also have a particular focus and can lead to a great deal of spontaneous learning. Give the children a small sack and ask them to collect as many different types and colors of leaves or kinds of seed pods that they find on the ground. However, they should only collect one or two items of each type. The clipboard checklist can work well for neighborhood walks when looking for items that cannot be collected, such as types of trees and flowers or categories of shops. As children gain skills, you can make this activity more challenging by having them identify things that are a bit more abstract, such as smells: sweet smells (blossoms, some flowers), polluting or foul smells (cigarette smoke, auto exhaust), strong smells (fertilizer), and various types of food smells (deli, bakery, coffee shop, pizza shop). When you are back in the classroom, discuss, sort, and graph what the children saw, listed, or collected.

8. TOYS FROM HOME: CONFISCATE, TOLERATE, OR REGULATE?

Although most teachers have a rule that toys from home are not allowed in school, children still bring them in. They crave the security of a link from home and they enjoy showing off what they own. Children often use toys from home as a way to make friends by connecting with other children with similar interests. Accommodate these needs in your classroom to a degree. Completely stifling them will only lead to devious behaviors and frustration, which may then lead to other problematic behaviors. This chapter presents a variety of ways to allow toys from home in the classroom while preventing the problems that are usually caused by them.

Anticipating and Preventing Problems Related to Toys from Home

- At least once a week, give children an opportunity to share their toys. You might do this through a show-and-tell session. To prevent show-and-tell from lasting too long, have some children share every Monday, others on Tuesday, and so on. Put reasonable bans on certain toys, such as those that look like weapons of any kind or have weapons as part of the toy, action figures, and Barbie dolls. Encourage children to share things that they have made or something that is not a commercial toy. Other ideas for making show-and-tell engaging can be found in the chapter on circle and group times under "When 'Show-and-Tell' Does Not Go Well" on page 22.

- Allow the children who bring their toys from home for show-and-tell to invite other children to play with the toys with them for the first ten minutes of work-play time.

- Provide many opportunities for children to make friends and engage with each other physically and socially. Find ways to incorporate interests from home into the classroom that are not related to commercial objects. For example, develop imaginary play or interest centers around the occupations or avocations, or hobbies, of their parents. Use some materials that are borrowed from the families. Even just adding a single item from children's homes to an area can have a big impact. This may be a tortilla press in the kitchen area or a favorite book in the library.

- Instead of toys, suggest that children bring photos—of parents, pets, homes, or favorite places to play. These will meet similar needs that motivate children to bring toys from home.

- Have a clearly written policy about toys from home for parents to read when they enroll their children and have it posted on a parent bulletin board. Include an explanation of the specific limits you have set.

Solving Problems Related to Toys from Home

Owning a coveted toy gives the owner status and power in the eyes of his peers. It's all too tempting to use and abuse that status and power. Typical ways for children to abuse their power is to allow some children to use the toy but not others and to grab it away arbitrarily from a child who is using it. Some of the prevention strategies above should make this less likely to occur.

- If the child still abuses his owner status as described above, then mediate the situation as you would if the child had grabbed a classroom toy from another child or had acted mean or biased for any other reason. Help the children negotiate a turn-taking process or another solution. Explain that if toys from home are used in the classroom, then they have the same rules as classroom toys. Give the child the option to put the toy in his cubby or another safe place until it is time to go home. Help the child make and keep friends in kinder and more effective ways.

- Check the toys that children bring to school soon after they arrive. If a toy is inappropriate for any reason, remind the children of the rules regarding toys from home: "You can bring any toy that does not look like a weapon, is not an action figure, and is not a Barbie doll." Then help the child find something else she can use for show-and-tell. Perhaps she can tell about something special she is wearing, a story about something she did with her family or about a family member, or something from the classroom that she particularly likes.

- If a child has "sneaked" in a toy from home, and it is an appropriate toy, invite the child to show it to the whole group and talk about it at the next group time. If it is an inappropriate toy, explain the reason it is inappropriate and offer him a choice: "Would you like me to keep it safe for you until you can take it home at the end of the day, or would you like to keep it safe in your cubby until then?" Help her figure out what acceptable toy or item from home she could bring to school the next day.

- If problems persist with a number of children, put a hold on allowing toys from home and try it again in about a month.

9. DISAPPEARING DINOSAURS, LOST LEGOS, MISSING MITTENS, AND OTHER MYSTERIES

Clothing and toys (or parts of toys) are the two most common items that get lost or go missing in early childhood programs. In either case, the loss is very frustrating because clothing and toys are expensive and time consuming to replace, and the loss was probably preventable. When there are many lost items, it is usually symptomatic of a disorganized program. Although lost or missing items will always be a reality for groups of busy adults and active young children, losses can be minimized by using some of the ideas in this chapter.

Anticipating and Preventing Problems Related to Missing Items

Missing clothes

- In your parent handbook and during new parent orientation, request that all clothing be labeled with the child's name. Also state that in spite of all the care you take, clothing will occasionally get lost or be taken home unintentionally by another child and may never be seen again. This creates a realistic expectation that if the child attends the ECED program for more than a few months, there is a good chance that some item will get lost. Ask the parents to please check all clothing their children bring home to make sure it actually does belong to them. Remind them that many children have clothing that looks similar to those of other children.

- When outside, bring a box or have a very specific place designated where children are required to put any jackets, sweaters, or other clothing that they remove.

- Make sure each child has her own cubby or box where she can keep her personal belongings. Be very consistent about requiring the child to put in her cubby any clothing she removes when inside.

- Do a quick check of cubbies before the children go home each day. Also check before leaving any area—a field-trip site, the playground, the gym—where children may have removed jackets, sweaters, and so on.

- Keep a lost-and-found box in a place where it can be seen by staff most of the time. Also, keep a supply of clean, new, or gently used children's clothing that has been donated or purchased cheaply from secondhand stores or charity shops. If you can replace an item of lost clothing with a reasonable facsimile, you may be able to diminish parents' unhappiness.

Missing toys or toy parts

- Put the name of your class on any item that may be used in another classroom but that belongs in your room. Write the name of your school on any item that is shared with various programs or sites. Make an inventory. List every item in your class so you will know if anything is missing. Update this list whenever something new is added or something is removed.

- Most cardboard toy boxes or game covers will not hold up very long under constant use in an ECED classroom. Falling out of a flimsy box is a common way for pieces to get lost. Start to build a collection of sturdy plastic containers (the clear ones are best, as they make it easier to find a particular item). Get a variety of sizes and shapes, but ensure that a particular game or construction set will fit fully and easily into its container with plenty of room to spare so pieces will not easily fall out. These containers can often be found at charity shops and they regularly go on sale at discount stores.

- Keep a list of websites, physical addresses, and phone numbers of toy companies listed on the boxes or wrappers of items you purchased. If the item has a model number, note that on your list. You can order replacements of most missing pieces of games or toys for a small fee. However, you may have to wait a number of weeks before you receive the part. Many companies offer this service online and by phone.

- Label all your shelves and containers. Always require that children return toys and games to the spot where they belong as soon as they are finished playing with them.

- Code your puzzles and all the pieces. For example, on the back of a puzzle box, write the number 1 with a permanent marker and write the same number on the back of each piece of that puzzle. Code your next puzzle number 2, the next 3, and so on. If pieces from various puzzles get mixed together (not uncommon in ECED classrooms), you can separate them easily by finding the code number.

Solving Problems Related to Missing Items

When clothing is missing

- Enlist the help of the children and other staff in tracking down the item. Form a "search party" and make a game out of it.

- As you know, clothing is a major expense to parents, and so the loss of any clothing is upsetting. Explain to the parents again the program's policy about missing clothing and show it to them in writing. Describe what you have done to locate the item. Assure them that you will continue to look for it. Send a note home to all parents in case the missing item mistakenly went home with another child. Place a note on your parent bulletin board about the missing item. Knowing that you are concerned, that you take the problem seriously, and that you are trying your best to find it will usually satisfy most parents. (See "Beyond Feedback" on pp. 228–31 for ideas on dealing with parents who are irate about lost clothing.)

When a toy or toy part is missing

- Check your shelves at the end of work-play time to make sure all items are back where they belong. Check puzzles and games to make sure all the pieces are still there. If any pieces are missing, take the time to have every child look for the missing piece before the class does anything else. In looking for the piece, move shelves, tables, chairs, rugs, and other furnishings as necessary. Check in the trash cans and recycling boxes, and sort through all the toy containers. Ask all the children to check their pockets and cubbies. If a child has put a small toy in his pocket, assume that it was not intentional. If you know or suspect it was intentional, see "Stealing" on pp. 214–15 for ideas on how to deal with the problem.

- Do this all-out search for a number of reasons: First, the longer you wait, the less likely you are to find a missing toy or toy part. Second, you are teaching the children that the supplies are valuable and must be taken care of. They will be much more diligent about not losing pieces after one or two such searches.

- If the item is still not found, ask the janitor (if you have one) to look for it when cleaning. If it does not show up in a day or two, contact the company for a replacement as described previously. If possible, show the children how you order or have ordered a replacement so they can appreciate the process. When the package with the replacement part arrives, open it with the children during a group time.

- If the missing item or piece is something that can be or needs to be made rather than purchased, involve the children in the process, if possible. Puzzle pieces can be made from wood scraps with a band saw or jigsaw, from "plastic wood," or from thick cardboard, which is laminated upon completion.

10. ACCIDENTS AND INJURIES: REDUCE RISKS AND OFFER FIRST-AID FAST

Nothing is more frightening than a hurt child. Not only are you concerned about the health of the child, but you are worried about responding to anxious parents and perhaps an upset boss. You can do many things to prevent problems, but accidents will occasionally happen even in the best program. Although preventing and avoiding injuries is one of your most important tasks, children need to take risks in order to fully develop physically and emotionally. Balancing prevention with the need for risk taking is difficult. While every insurance company wishes that centers or schools did not have playgrounds, the benefits to children's development far outweigh the risks.

Some of the anxiety of coping with the inevitable injury can be lessened when you feel secure about your knowledge of first-aid and emergency procedures, have quick access to a full set of first-aid supplies, and are able to quickly get help from a medical professional.

Anticipating and Preventing Accidents and Injuries

- Before a child enrolls in your classroom, obtain from her parents an emergency release form. This includes the name and phone number of the child's doctor, insurance information, and permission to take their child to the nearest hospital in case of an emergency. Update the form at least every six months and make a copy of it. Put the original in the child's file. Put the copies for all the children together in a binder to take on field trips.

- Role-play with the children what you will do and what they should do when a child gets hurt outside, on a field trip, and inside the classroom.

- Set a few inside and a few outside rules related to safety. You might include the following:
  - "Always walk inside the classroom."
  - "Pick toys up from the floor after you have finished playing with them."
  - "Swing only when seated."
  - "Go down the slide on your bottom."
  - "Climb using two hands."
  - "Wear a helmet when riding a bike."

- Enforce these rules consistently. Focus your energy and attention on the children when they are following the rules and give them information about their behavior: "I'm glad to see that you're wearing a helmet and keeping yourself safe." Practice the rules by role-playing in small groups.

- Keep your first-aid and CPR cards current. First-aid training is available through most Red Cross chapters. However, it is important to request and receive first-aid training that directly relates to young children and to the types of injuries common to ECED programs.

- Have a first-aid kit, a blood spill kit, and a box of sterile disposable gloves available where you can get to them quickly. Keep the kits well-stocked and replace items that have been used within twenty-four hours. Check with your local health department for recommended additions to your kit. Take the kit with you when outside and on field trips. For children who are highly allergic to certain foods or insect bites, the first-aid kit will need to contain injectable epinephrine. Ideally, every large center or school should also have an AED (automated external defibrillator) device with an additional set of cables especially designed for use with children between the ages of one year and eight years.

- Have readily accessible an up-to-date book of first-aid procedures for children. Also install the American Red Cross First Aid app on your smartphone and/or other electronic device. Get familiar with the app so you can quickly find information when there is an accident.

- Keep several ice packs in the freezer for minor head injuries and sprains. Bags of frozen peas also work well because they are pliable and inexpensive. However, the plastic bags they come in tend to be thin, so they need to be placed inside another sturdy plastic bag. Before using the bag of frozen vegetables, wrap a thin, clean tea towel or cloth around it.

- To prevent choking, do not give popcorn, peanuts, or whole grapes to children under three years old, or peanuts to children under four years old. Do not give balloons to any child.

- Keep any poisonous or dangerous substance in a locked cabinet with a "Mr. Yuk" sticker on it. Tell the children what the sticker means. Show them examples and explain that there are things that look like food or beverages but are for cleaning, and they will become sick if they eat or drink them.

- Cover all electrical outlets with childproof safety covers. Check with your local child care licensing agency or rule book to determine which type of outlet covers to use and to learn about other injury prevention suggestions. These will be helpful for all early childhood programs, not only child care centers.

- Remove, from both outside the building and inside the classroom, any plants and shrubs that are toxic. Replace them with nontoxic plants.

- Provide plenty of water for the children to drink, particularly outside on hot days. If there is no water fountain outside, take a thermos of water and paper cups outside with you. Each child should have his own bottle of sunscreen, specifically made for children, provided by his family.

- After you have established safety rules and the children understand them well, provide opportunities for the children to take physical risks while minimizing the possibility of injury as described below. Most children love to challenge themselves, which is one reason they disobey safety rules. If they know they will have many opportunities to take risks, they are more likely to obey the established rules.

- Know what equipment and activities have the potential to cause injuries. Many injuries happen on playground or gym equipment. (For safety ideas, see the chapter "Moving Muscles: Safe Fun Outside or in the Gym" on pp. 38–41.)

Solving Problems Related to Accidents and Injuries

When a child wants to do or does something dangerous or risky

- The activity may be either potentially dangerous (risky) or actually dangerous. Of course, if it is only potentially dangerous, then it can be made safe by managing the risks. However, an actually dangerous activity, such as jumping from a very high place or throwing rocks, has to be prevented or stopped. Try to determine the reason the activity is enticing to the child—what need it seems to address— and find or create an activity that meets that need but is safe or whose risks can be managed.

- Here is an example of what you can do if children are taking potentially dangerous risks on a climbing structure: Bring out mats to put under the climbing structure. Be the "spotter" to make sure the children do not fall awkwardly or too hard. One at a time, allow children to do their risky actions but provide guidance and support so they will learn to stay within their abilities. Teach them other challenging actions (depending on your equipment and their skill levels), such as hanging from a bar, using a swinging motion to grab the next bar and the next, or sliding down a pole. Teach them to break their falls with bent knees. If needed, add additional safety equipment, such as more mats, knee pads, and bike helmets. Allow only one child on the equipment at a time and put a short time limit on each turn, if necessary.

- Provide the same guidance and support in introducing other activities, such as basic gymnastics, tumbling games, jumping from reasonable heights, and swinging on a rope.

- Invite an older child who is a good skateboarder or skater, or who is good at another street sport, to visit your class. Before this older child demonstrates her skills, have her talk about all the safety equipment she wears and why she wears it. Encourage her to talk about the hours of practice it takes and other ways that she manages the risks involved.

If a child is injured

- While it is not possible to cover every possible injury or provide a first-aid course in this chapter, there are some general guidelines that apply to nearly all injuries.
  - ‣ Act quickly and calmly.
  - ‣ Call another adult or adults for help, trying to express urgency without sounding panicky. Have him get the first-aid kit, if you are not able to grab it quickly.
  - ‣ Do not move an injured child until you know what is wrong.
  - ‣ If the child is not moving or conscious, follow the ABCD first-aid guidelines: A = Assess the scene, alert EMS, airway open. B = Breathing—begin rescue breathing if necessary. C = Circulation—check circulation and, if necessary, begin chest compressions. D = Defibrillation—if rescue breathing and chest compressions are not working, use an automated external defibrillator (AED), if available.
  - ‣ If the child is conscious, reassure her that she will be fine and that you will take care of her.
  - ‣ If you are not sure what to do or if it is an unusual type of injury, have the other adult call 911 and check the first-aid book or app for what to do, while you calm the injured child.

- After an injury has occurred, write a note (or fill in a preprinted form) to give to parents, explaining what happened and describing the treatment you gave. Sign the note yourself and have the parent sign it. Make a copy for your own records. This will keep all information clear and straight and will protect you and the parents from liability.

- At the end of each month and year, review the records to determine the most common injuries. Set a goal to reduce those injuries by making specific changes, such as fixing or removing certain equipment, setting some new classroom rules, rearranging furniture or materials, or starting a fundraising campaign for a new playground surface.

If a child eats or drinks something poisonous

- Call 911 if the child has collapsed or is not breathing. If the child is awake and alert, call 1-800-222-1222 and be prepared to tell the poison control specialist the child's age, approximate weight, what the child ate or drank, and when he ingested it. Listen carefully to the instructions.

11. EMERGENCY AND DISASTER PREPAREDNESS: PREPARE FOR WHAT YOU CAN'T PREVENT

This is an increasingly important issue, even if you are located in a place that is not prone to floods, earthquakes, or other natural disasters. How many times have you heard people say on the news just after a disaster, "We never thought this would happen here!"? There is no doubt that climate change is causing more severe, unusual, and unpredictable weather events everywhere. Emergency preparedness is also necessary in case of a fire, power outage, roof collapse, chemical spill, bomb threat, dangerous animal nearby, shooter or person with a gun in the area, or another terrible possibility.

Anticipating and Preventing Problems Related to Emergencies and Disasters

- The most important steps in emergency preparedness is to have the following in place:
    - ▸ a good multi-hazard emergency plan
    - ▸ all key staff trained on emergency preparedness in general and on the center or school plan specifically
    - ▸ adequate food, water, and other emergency supplies for all children and staff for several days
    - ▸ regular evacuation drills occurring at various times of the day and days of the week

- Once or twice a year, check the websites of several federal agencies or national organizations and your state emergency management agency for updates on their preparedness resources that are specifically for schools and early childhood programs (most use the term "child care"). The recommendations change as new information is gathered, new techniques are developed, and new technologies become available. Among the federal agencies and national organizations that have such resources—including sample plans, toolkits, guidelines, and checklists— are Federal Emergency Management Agency (FEMA), which also has an entire course on the topic, General Services Administration (GSA), Centers for Disease Control (CDC), National Association of Child Care Resource and Referral Agencies (NACCRRA), and the American National Red Cross.

- Learn what to look for or test for when inspecting safety devices to ensure they are in good working order or to determine if they need to be upgraded or replaced. Each quarter check your fire extinguishers, smoke detectors, carbon monoxide detectors, AED, and other devices. Twice a year, have an expert check the sprinkler and alarm systems, observe the evacuation drill, review the emergency plan, and provide feedback.

- Practice an evacuation drill at least once a month. Early in the year, before the first actual drill, slowly walk the children through the process several times. Talk to them about what they are doing and why. Tell them about the loud bell (or other alarm sound) and what to expect. Make sure each adult knows his specific assignment during evacuation drills.

- Have children practice "stop, drop, and roll" in case their clothes catch on fire. Unless you are in an area that has a very low probability of an earthquake, have children practice "drop, cover, hold on."

- If you are in a tornado-prone area, conduct periodic tornado drills. Help children practice moving quickly to an area of the building on the lowest floor that is away from windows and glass and is as close to the innermost center of the building as possible. Children then practice crouching on their knees and covering their heads with their arms.

- Demonstrate these techniques first and/or show a video of children doing them. If you plan to do more than one type of drill, do them at least three weeks apart so that children will not be confused.

Solving Problems Related to Emergencies and Disasters

Noisy, disorganized, or slow evacuation drills

- The problem may be caused by children not getting the message that these drills are unique, important events that need to be taken seriously. If your center or school does not have a formal alarm bell for evacuation drills or one that is distinct from the bell used for other, non-emergency purposes, use a loud and distinct whistle, gong, or large metal handbell instead. It must not be used for any other purpose. The sound should convey urgency, so if you are using a whistle, for example, make a series of quick, short, and loud blows. In order for the children to respond quickly, they must associate this sound with evacuating the building and with nothing else. If you also hold other types of drills that do not involve evacuating, such as earthquake drills, use a different device with a different sound pattern, although it should still sound urgent.

- To ensure that the seriousness of your message is conveyed, make good use of your body language. Keep a straight back and concerned facial expression, and make sure your voice tone conveys a sense of urgency, yet maintain very clear and steady enunciation.

- At the start of the drill, shut off the room lights (if it will not be too dark) and remind the children of the evacuation rules. Using the body language and voice tone described above, remind them to "Walk quickly and silently," "Stay close to the person in front of you," and "Follow the teacher's directions."

- Also remind children where they will be ending up, such as "You will stop along the fence behind the big climber."

- Enlist all administrative and support staff to be with the children so that there are adults at short intervals all along the line of children. Then, any child who is not focused or moving along can quickly be assisted.

- Take your class attendance list with you and account for each child once you all arrive at the outside destination. Doing this in a formal way by calling each child's name also communicates that the drill is something to take seriously.

- Time the evacuation from your room with a stopwatch. Set a goal with the children for reducing the time they need to evacuate the room safely and work together toward this goal.

- When the children and adults are safely outside, briefly discuss how much time the evacuation took, what went well, and what can be improved. Then, later in the day or the next day, do a practice walk-through evacuation drill again with your children.

- Hold evacuation drills at various times of the day, including when children are outside, as they will still need to go to a specific location.

- When the children are proficient at the drill, change an aspect of it. For example, block one of the exits or doorways, and use another route to go outside. In a real emergency, your quickest exits may be blocked by rubble, fire, smoke, or a locked door.

12. CHILDREN WHO ARE ILL AND OTHER HEALTH CONCERNS: STIFLE THE SNEEZE, COVER THE COUGH, SNUFF THE SNIFFLE

Are children in early childhood programs sick more frequently and with more serious illnesses than other children? Of course, in any indoor environment where a large number of people are close together for an extended period, there will be more illnesses. And there are more illnesses among groups of young children than adults because they get sick more often (building up immunities is a work in progress) and they are not yet adept at preventative hygiene practices. However, in programs where reasonable health precautions are taken and teachers are aware of the causes of common illnesses and ways to prevent them, the frequency and severity of illnesses are the same, or only slightly higher, than for children who are not in group care. Also, children in group care develop resistances and immunities to more types of viruses because they are exposed to more of them.

Anticipating and Preventing Illnesses

- Stay home when you are sick. Because you may get little sick leave and substitutes are hard to find, you probably feel obligated to be at work unless you are practically dying! If you do this, however, you will likely infect some children, who will infect other children, who will then infect you again. This "sick cycle" is well known to early childhood teachers.

- Help ensure that all children are fully immunized. You can obtain information about immunization schedules from your local and state health departments. Most states require all children in group care settings and schools to be up to date on their immunization schedule.

- Before children enroll, they should receive a physical examination from a physician, who can provide a note clearing them to participate fully in all activities or explaining any limitations. The note should also indicate any special needs or issues, such as allergies, food restrictions, and medical conditions like asthma or diabetes.

- Request that parents fill out a health and medical history form. This can be very helpful if, for example, you notice spots on a child that look like chicken pox. The form will tell you if the child has already had chicken pox or has been vaccinated. This will help determine the nature of the spots. If the program keeps these files in a central location, make sure you know how to find them for the children in your class and that you see the form for each child entering the program.

- At enrollment, provide parents with the school's or center's illness policies, particularly in regard to the illnesses for which children will need to stay home or be picked up early. Include information about head lice, how serious contagious diseases will be handled, and the dispensing of medication.

- Contact your local health department for information on identifying and treating common contagious illnesses and for suggested policies for your center. This type of information is also available from the websites of Healthy Child Care America from the American Academy of Pediatrics (www.healthychildcare.org) and the National Resource Center for Health and Safety in Child Care and Early Education (http://cfoc.nrckids.org).

- For the most common illnesses, have preprinted information flyers that list the symptoms, suggested courses of action, and when children are allowed to return to the school or center.

- Many programs require children to be free of fever, diarrhea, coughs, and other symptoms for twenty-four hours and to feel well enough to fully participate in activities before they return.

- Teach children to sneeze and cough into the inside crook of their elbow if a tissue is not available. Model it yourself. This reduces the spread of germs much better than using your hand to cover the coughs and sneezes. Keep plenty of tissues around.

- Wash your hands thoroughly with warm water and disinfectant soap. Along with ensuring that children wash their hands often and well, this is the single most important thing a teacher can do to prevent a wide variety of illnesses. Wash your hands after diapering, using the toilet yourself, helping a child with toileting, helping a child blow his nose, blowing your own nose, and before serving and/or eating food. Always carry a small plastic bottle of hand sanitizer for when you and the children cannot get to a sink quickly, and then wash with soap and running water as soon as possible.

- Supervise children's hand washing carefully. Make sure they thoroughly wash when first arriving at school, after toileting, after blowing their noses, before meals and snacks (and after them if the food is messy or sticky), and after playing with dirt, sand, paint, and so on.

- Keep spray bottles of diluted bleach water handy but well out of children's reach. Most state health agencies recommend one tablespoon of bleach to one quart of water for general use, and one part bleach to ten parts water for blood spills. Use this bleach-water solution to wipe off toilets and sinks at least once during the day or whenever necessary. As it has an unpleasant, unappetizing odor, use it sparingly and only when necessary to clean surfaces where food is served.

- Wash toys regularly in the water-play table with warm, soapy water. Most children enjoy doing this. In programs for toddlers, toys need to be cleaned daily and put through a kitchen sanitizer/dishwasher at least once per week.

- Use sterile disposable gloves when treating wounds and serving food.

- Keep trash, especially used tissues, in a container with a secure lid. Keep the container covered. Empty the trash at least daily in half-day programs and at least twice a day in full-day programs.

- Provide at least three feet of space between beds, cots, or mats. Place children head to toe so their faces are not close to each other during naptime.

- If toothbrushing is permitted, see that each child has her own toothbrush. The sample schedules given earlier include a toothbrushing time. Store the brushes in such a way that the bristles are not touching anything else, especially other brushes, by using plastic travel covers, hooks in individual cubbies, a rack with separators between each brush, or something similar. Do not let children touch any brush but their own. Sterilize toothbrushes frequently with mild bleach water (and then thoroughly rinse) or in a dishwasher. Check them carefully at least weekly and replace any that show signs of wear.

- Provide a "get well" space where children can lie down on a small bed or comfortable cot if they are not feeling well. Set up this space away from other children but within eyesight of an adult. Have any ill children who are waiting to be picked up by parents use this area.

- Establish an approach for promoting good health in general, and encourage and assist families to do the same. Programs such as Let's Move! Child Care (https://healthykidshealthyfuture.org) suggest a five-way approach that focuses on good nutrition, healthy beverages, physical activity, encouraging and supporting breast-feeding, and limiting screen time.

Solving Problems Related to Illnesses

Children who come to school sick or become sick during the day

- Do a quick, nonintrusive "health check" on all children when they arrive or soon after. Look at their exposed skin—face, neck, arms, hands, and legs—for obvious rashes or bruises. Look at their facial skin tone for any change from their usual tone. Flushed cheeks or paleness can be signs of a fever. Look at the way they are walking and their carriage; are they lethargic, walking stiffly, slumping, or limping in a way they have not done before? Are they scratching themselves excessively? Do any have a "runny nose" with thick mucus that is either yellow or green? Ask your nurse or an administrator to look at any children whom you are concerned about to collaboratively make decisions, call parents, and give treatment and to help ensure established protocols are followed. In the meantime, keep the child comfortable and away from other children as best you can.

- As a general rule, children who have a fever or show signs of an infectious or contagious illness should stay home so they can get the bed rest and medical care they need and not infect other children. Some infectious diseases are not contagious, such as ear infections and Lyme disease. However, many infectious diseases are communicable (can spread from one person to another), such as conjunctivitis (pinkeye) and the common cold, or are contagious (can *easily* spread from one person to another), such as the flu and E. coli. Head lice is not infectious, but it is contagious. A child may not have a fever but still have an infectious illness and/or be contagious, so take cues from the child's behavior, appearance, and other symptoms.

- If a child becomes ill while in school, notify parents (or the emergency contact person the parents have designated if they cannot be reached) to pick him up.

- Give an information flyer about the suspected illness to the parent when he comes to pick up his child. If it could be one of several illnesses give a flyer for each one. Make it clear that you do not know what illness the child has, but his symptoms seem to match those listed on the flyer(s).

- If a child has or develops a serious contagious disease, she has to be separated from other children immediately, picked up by her parents, and given medical care as soon as possible. All parents need to be notified and given complete and accurate information about the disease as well as updates on the child's condition. Your local or state health department also needs to be notified and will guide and oversee the actions that need to be taken. Health departments usually require reporting cases of certain illnesses, including Lyme disease, measles, rubella, giardia, hepatitis, and whooping cough.

Children who are extremely allergic

- Know what symptoms to look for and what to do if a child has a severe allergic reaction, especially an anaphylaxis reaction, which is life-threatening. Signs of anaphylaxis include a rapid, weak pulse, trouble breathing, a skin rash, sweating, and nausea and vomiting. It can cause a child to go into shock. Anaphylaxis requires an injection of epinephrine, an antihistamine, and a trip to the emergency room.

- The most common causes of anaphylaxis are reactions to bee stings, latex, and particular foods. Some children are so allergic to certain foods that it is necessary to ban the food from the center or school completely. Peanuts are the most common food that can cause such a severe reaction among children. Eight foods account for about 90 percent of all food allergies in children: milk, eggs, peanuts, tree nuts, wheat, soy, fish, and shellfish.

- Each child with a serious allergy should have her own written allergy action plan (developed by the child's allergist and parents) that is kept in her file—and taken on field trips—describing potential triggers, what to do in case of an attack, and other pertinent information.

- If you have a child in your program who is extremely allergic, it is necessary to have and know how to use an anaphylaxis kit. The kit will contain an epinephrine auto-injector and an antihistamine. Take the kit outside and on field trips. Make sure several other staff members know how to access information about what to do if a child has an allergic reaction, in case it happens when you are absent or away.

- For children who are allergic to dust, dander, or various animals, you may need to remove any class pets and reduce the number of pillows and the amount of carpeting. If any linens and blankets are used, these should be washed weekly in hot water.

- For children who are allergic to certain chemicals found in cleaning products, paints, perfumes, and similar substances, there are natural, or at least nontoxic, products available for just about every possible purpose.

- The air quality in your classroom is an important consideration for every child and yourself, but especially for children with allergies. Daily dusting (damp rag) and vacuuming of any carpeting with a professional machine that has a high-quality filter will be very helpful to children with allergies. Filters in the heating and air-conditioning system should be very high quality and be replaced or cleaned at least monthly. If there is dampness, additional air purifiers and dehumidifiers are needed to keep mold spores from forming.

Head lice: A "lousy" problem, but not a health threat

Head lice are very tiny wingless insects that live only on human scalps. Our blood is their food source and our hair is their "nest." They crawl very quickly, which is why they spread so readily from sharing hats, combs, hair brushes, etc. One louse lays about six eggs a day, called nits, which it firmly attaches to strands of hair close to the scalp. These little white oval-shaped nits are hard to remove and they hatch in about a week. For some reason, the problem is much more common among children under ten than any other age group (Nichols 2016). These conditions make head lice a persistent problem in ECED programs. Fortunately, they do not spread disease, although they are itchy and annoying. The presence of head lice is not related to poor personal hygiene or a dirty environment . . . it only feels that way!

- There is much you can do to stop the spread of lice. Do not let children share hats, combs, pillows, hair ties, and similar items. As soon as you see a child scratching his head, check for lice using an approved method (see the websites listed below).

- Children with head lice do not have to be picked up early and do not have to stay home the following day or days as long as effective treatment has been started.

- New treatments for head lice come on the market regularly and recommendations from health experts keep evolving. It may be best to consult certain websites when head lice "come to visit" your program, to determine the best treatment to recommend to parents and to implement at your school or center. Here are a few of the many sites that have information on head lice: Centers for Disease Control and Prevention (www.cdc.gov), Mayo Clinic (www.mayoclinic.org), Medical News Today (www.medicalnewstoday.com), and the National Health Service (www.nhs.uk). For all these sites, just enter "head lice" in the search box.

Children with asthma

- Asthma is one of the most common chronic health problems among children, and the number of affected children continues to rise. Rates of asthma are higher among children than adults, among children from low-income families than upper-income families, and among black children than white or Latino children. When a child has an asthma attack, she has trouble breathing due to swelling of the air passages in the lungs and a buildup of mucus. It can be triggered by a common illness, too much strenuous activity, or an allergic reaction (see above). Most children with asthma can participate normally in activities, but some cautions and restrictions may be necessary, such as having more rests and breaks than other children.

- Most children with asthma will have some medication, typically in the form of an inhaler, that is either taken regularly or when an attack occurs. You and the child's parents must ensure that the child takes his medication with him wherever he goes. As with all medications, make sure you have clear directions on its dosage and use.

- As with allergies and other serious health issues, each child with asthma should have her own written plan that is kept in her file (and taken on field trips) describing potential triggers, what to do in case of an attack, and other pertinent information. As the child's teacher, you should know this and not have to rely on looking in the file. Know how the child needs to use her inhaler, nebulizer, or other equipment. If a child has an attack, help keep her calm by being calm yourself and talking in a soothing voice. Have her sit upright and rub or gently tap her back as you implement the treatment plan and get any necessary help. Make sure several other staff members know what to do if the child has an asthma attack, in case it happens when you are absent or away.

Children who need to take medication during school hours

This often causes problems for teachers, as they sometimes have to remember to give medication to several different children at different times during the day. A missed dose may harm the child and will undoubtedly be of great concern to parents. This also causes stress because teachers worry that they might make a mistake with the medication or the child might have an adverse reaction.

- Always request that parents ask their child's doctor to prescribe a form of medication, if available, that entails two or fewer dosages per day so it can be administered entirely at home. This can be done with many drugs and usually can be arranged over the phone with the doctor or pharmacist.

- Keep the medications locked and out of reach of children.

- Use an electronic "pill reminder" alarm. They are very small and relatively cheap. A parent may be willing to purchase or lend you one if it means not missing a dose of medicine. Have a different one for each child and label them with the children's names. There are also smartphone "pill reminder" apps for this purpose.

- Administer only prescription medications with written orders from the doctor and the parent's signature. This will limit the number of medicines given out. Don't give over-the-counter medications to children at the request of parents. Insist on permission from a doctor.

- If a parent works or lives nearby, request that he come to the class and administer the medicine. This may have to be a requirement if the child is resistant to taking the medicine or if the administration of it involves anything more technical than the child swallowing a measured dose of liquid from a spoon. The only exception is for children with chronic medical conditions such as asthma.

- Ask for brief written information about the medicine that describes precautions and possible side effects. You need to know if the medicine should not be taken with certain foods or other medications and if it may make the child sleepy or overly active.

- Ask the parents to have the pharmacist provide a small, extra, labeled bottle to use at preschool. This will eliminate the hassle for parents of picking up and bringing in the medicine daily and relieve you from having to return it to them at the end of each day.

- Post a log sheet near where the medicine is locked and write down each dose of medication you give. This will help you remember if and when you gave it. Prepare a separate sheet for each child.

Children who are excessively dirty

Cultural Awareness Alert

To a point, standards of cleanliness are personal and cultural. Some people and some cultures accept body odor more and have more relaxed or different standards of bodily and clothing cleanliness than mainstream U.S. culture. The reason a child has dirty clothes and/or a dirty body may be related to culture or it may be because of the limited availability of clean running water, soap, towels, washing machines, and dryers, due to poverty or other circumstances.

In one case, after following up on a child whose clothes were dirty and smelled of urine, I learned that her parents were both developmentally delayed. The child was not developmentally delayed and at the time of enrollment she had been living with her grandparents but was now living with her parents. I told them that I was concerned about their child because other children were avoiding playing with her only because her clothes were dirty and smelly. I asked if there was anything I could do to help them so their daughter could have clean clothes. The parents reacted positively to my concern for their daughter and seemed to appreciate my help. I received their permission to talk with the grandparents, who gave them the help they needed.

For children to be healthy and socially accepted by others, a reasonable amount of cleanliness is necessary. In places like centers and schools, a relatively high standard of cleanliness is necessary because of how easily illnesses can spread. If the lack of cleanliness creates a problem for a child in your class, consider the following:

- Meet with the parents, preferably for a home visit, to determine the issues regarding cleanliness. Let them know objective reasons for your concern: the child is not making friends, a cut became or could become infected, the child is physically uncomfortable, and so on. Explain that in the classroom setting a higher standard of cleanliness is needed for a child to stay healthy because so many children are close together for long periods. If necessary, help them find resources or easy methods for cleaning clothes and children and ask if it is something they would like your help with.

- A family's standard of cleanliness is only of concern if it is a direct threat to a child's health. If this is the case, refer the family to your local social service agency. Follow your program's policies on referrals. Usually a supervisor will make the call. (See "Save the Children" on pp. 237–39 about parents who may be abusive or neglectful.) Typically, the agency will provide the family with a home health worker who is trained to help with these matters.

- Help the child clean himself at school soon after he arrives. He should clean all exposed skin, especially his hands and face. Assist with this, if necessary. If the child's clothes are very dirty and have a strong offensive odor, offer the child a clean set of clothes to wear (donated or secondhand) if he desires. Do this discreetly to avoid embarrassing the child. Most children who do this prefer to change back into their clothes from home before they leave school at the end of the day.

- Help the other children maintain respect and consideration for the child. Remind them of the rule about being kind and respectful. Model kind regard for the child and point out his positive attributes.

Children who are overweight or obese

While rates of obesity among two- to five-year-olds appear to have declined in recent years it is still much higher than it was prior to the 1980s. The decline seems to be due to a combination of public education campaigns, changes to school lunch menus, improvements to school-based and after-school physical education programs, help for families to access healthier foods, and efforts to integrate more physical activity into daily routines (Robert Wood Johnson Foundation 2016). There are several issues of concern regarding obesity: the child's health, self-image, and treatment by other children. (See "Diversity, Difference, and Democracy" on pp. 122–28 for a discussion on biased behaviors.) While genetics and family income are factors in obesity, lifestyle is still a major factor and one of the few that can be changed. Partner with families. The food/nutrition program and physical activity at the center or school is not enough to make a significant difference for the child. There also has to be lifestyle changes at home.

- Help the child increase her stamina during physical activities by gradually raising expectations for the types of activities in which she participates, the number of activities, and the amount of time she engages in them.

- Find out the types of physical activities she enjoys or sports that she likes. Most children will spend more time in activities that interest them. If she likes basketball, for example, set up a low basket and provide a small ball so she can feel successful. Then gradually increase the challenge of the activity by raising the basket. Teach the children a simple version of "Horse" or another basketball game to promote social interaction between the child and the other children.

- Talk with families about how important it is for children to maintain the appropriate weight for their height, for both physical and emotional health. Overweight and obese children, as compared to other children, have more problematic behaviors, learning difficulties, and rates of depression. They are more prone to illnesses and diseases, particularly asthma and type 2 diabetes (Mayo Clinic 2015). In 2015, an obese three-year-old in Texas became the youngest child to be diagnosed with type 2 diabetes (Knapton 2015).

- Help families access a physician and/or nutritionist who can develop a healthy diet and exercise plan with them. Take an active role in implementing the plan at school and in supporting the child and family. Provide ideas for alternative activities to screen time. Create a list of inexpensive or easy-to-make games for the child's family. Suggest good books and active games that the whole family can play. Suggest apps, videos, and websites that encourage physical activity and healthy eating.

13. BABIES, BREASTS, BOTTOMS, AND BOUNDARIES: TALKING WITH CHILDREN ABOUT BODIES, RELATIONSHIPS, AND PERSONAL SAFETY

Many teachers of young children feel unsure of themselves when talking about or dealing with issues related to sex, sexuality, and genitals with children. There is great fear of being misunderstood by parents or others who may mistake a healthy openness about bodies and sexuality with perversion, particularly for male teachers. We live in a society that is intensely ambivalent about sex. The rudest, most offensive word in the English language is a slang term for sex. We have difficulty disassociating the naked human body from sex, and sex from pornography. Overt sexuality is pervasive in the media, but frank, straightforward talk about bodies and sex is rare and very uncomfortable when it does occur. This makes it difficult to foster children's healthy sexual development. In addition, people in the United States perceive child sexual abuse as occurring much more frequently than it actually does. The rate of abuse of young children (which includes sexual abuse) actually declined 64 percent between 1992 and 2014 (Finkelhor et al. 2014, 2015). Eighty-four percent of sexual abuse of young children occurs in the home of the child or the perpetrator, and 50 percent of perpetrators are family members (Townsend and Rheingold 2013).

Cultural Awareness Alert

There are great differences across cultures about what one can say in public; about when, where, and for whom nudity is appropriate (or if it is ever appropriate); and about all issues related to bodies, bodily functions, and sex. Views range from very conservative in predominately Muslim countries and communities to very liberal in most Western European countries. In sub-Saharan African countries, women's breasts have no or very little sexual connotation; they are a food source. Of course within each country, particularly in the United States, there is also a great range among families' beliefs and practices based, in large part, on their religious affiliation or lack of; the culture, state, and community in which they live; personal beliefs; and other factors. Try to understand the norms related to these issues for your families. One way is to ask families at intake to list the words that their families use for urinating, defecating, and for male and female genitals.

Many families want sex education to happen only at home (which often means no sex education at all), but it's impossible to avoid it in early childhood programs. Children make comments and ask questions that teachers must respond to honestly and directly. Children need help with toileting and sometimes changing clothes. Most early childhood programs talk with children about personal safety and "private parts."

One day I was doing an activity with the children in my class in which each child says something they like about another child. Travis said, "I like Sabastian's penis." Of course, I was quite surprised and more than a bit tongue-tied. I said, "Thank you, Travis. Okay. Amelia, what do you like about Maria?" A bit later, I started to worry about the comment. I wanted to make sure that nothing inappropriate was going on and I was concerned that Sabastian might tell his parents, "Travis said that he likes my penis." Also, other children might talk about it in a way that may cause their parents to misconstrue what was said and why. At that point, I realized I needed to talk with both Travis's and Sabastian's parents and describe what happened. But first I talked with Travis. In our conversation, Travis told me that he sees Sabastian's penis in the bathroom and it's different from his. Our program was in a church and we used regular adult bathrooms. The men's bathroom had urinals and so the boys could readily see each other peeing. Travis was circumcised and Sabastian was not, which I knew because I supervised them in the bathroom. When I told their parents the story, we all had a good laugh. Phew!

Healthy sexual development for young children means that they feel good about their bodies, they can use the correct words for body parts and bodily functions and don't think of them as "dirty" words, they have a healthy curiosity about bodies, and they have internalized the social boundaries for appropriate behavior regarding these issues.

The Dutch school system uses a comprehensive relationship and sex education program called *Spring Fever* (Melker 2015; Rutgers, no date). They never separate sex from relationships and feelings. It's a coordinated curriculum that starts with four- and five-year-olds and extends through the last year of high school. They believe that it's necessary to start early if students are to feel comfortable talking about sex when they are in middle and high school. For the youngest students, there are five modules: *Who Am I?*, *What Do I Feel?*, *Being Naked* (about when it's appropriate to be naked and when it's not, and using the correct terms for body parts), *At Home*, and *We Are Friends*. The Dutch have the lowest rates of teen pregnancy and sexually transmitted diseases in the world. (See the resources under "Sexual Development, Sex Roles, and Gender Identity" on pp. 295–96.)

Anticipating and Preventing Problems Related to Talking about Bodies, Relationships, and Personal Safety

- Have in your classroom several different types of children's books that deal with the human body and personal safety. (Some are listed in the resources under "Sexual Development, Sex Roles, and Gender Identity" on pp. 295–96.)

- Include among your dolls anatomically correct boy and girl dolls.

- Neither avoid nor go out of your way to talk about body parts, bodily functions, babies, and so on. Use the correct terminology. This may involve using terms that children do not typically hear: urethra, uterus, womb, testicles, clitoris, and anus, among others. The only exceptions to this are the terms "peeing" and "pooping," which have become socially acceptable terms. Now the more "correct" terms— urinating and defecating—seem way too formal.

- If your school or program does not already have an approach or curriculum to promote children's healthy sexual development, then borrow from the Dutch approach described previously. If it does have an approach or curriculum, make certain that it is a good one according to the ideas in this chapter.

- Talk with children about good and bad touches and personal safety. There are curricula you can purchase and use, but this may not be necessary. While the onus is on responsible adults to protect children from exploitation and abuse, children can learn a few basic skills to protect themselves. Unfortunately, this is necessary because in nearly all cases of abuse, children know the perpetrator and in many cases they are relatives. All parents should be given information about what will be discussed with children. Pictures, simple story scenarios, short role plays for practice, demonstrations, questions, and discussions teach children the following:
  - "Always ask." If someone wants to give them something, such as a toy or sweets or to take them somewhere, they may not do so until they ask permission from the person who is taking care of them—their teacher, mother, father, older sibling, and so on.
  - There are good touches and bad touches. Good touches make them feel loved and cared for. Bad touches hurt them or make them feel uncomfortable and scared. They should always say "no!" to touches they do not want.
  - A bigger person should never touch their private body parts except their parents, a doctor, or a nurse. And even a doctor or nurse can only touch their private body parts when their mother, father, or family member is in the same room.
  - They should never keep a secret about bad touches. They should keep telling grown-ups about it until someone helps them.

Solving Problems Related to Talking about Bodies, Relationships, and Personal Safety

Inappropriate words

- Supply the correct term to use when children use a slang term. However, do this without directly correcting the child. For example, if the child says, "I hurt my wee-wee," you can reply by saying, "I am so sorry that your penis got hurt. Sit down and rest for a bit until you feel better." Do the same for bodily functions and fluids. Babies grow in the mother's uterus, not stomach. Asses are bottoms or butts, and the hole is an anus. Boobs or tits are breasts. Balls or nuts are testicles. A boy or man has a penis and testicles. A girl or woman has a vagina and clitoris. (Although the vagina is an internal organ and the correct term is vulva, vagina has become the commonly used term.) Both sexes have two nipples.

Questions about sex

- Most questions about sex reflect a healthy curiosity about how babies are made, about relationships between men and women, and about the human body. Give honest, short, straightforward answers to these questions. However, make sure that you fully understand what the child actually wants to know. For example, if a child asks how a baby is made, he may really want to know about the birth process, not about the sex act. Also, ask him how *he* thinks a baby is made. This will reveal the nature of the child's question and level of understanding, to which you can effectively respond.

- Most children under eight years old cannot understand sexual intercourse and conception. The abstract concepts involved—ovulation, sperm cells, eggs cells, insemination, fertilization—are even more confusing and difficult to understand. Actually, most adults do not have an accurate understanding of exactly how it all works. Therefore, answers to children's questions need to be simple, straightforward, but truthful. Avoid metaphors like "planting a seed" because young children will take it literally, not metaphorically.

- Here is one example of an appropriate explanation: "Most babies are made when a mommy and daddy love each other very much and decide it's time to have a child . . . or another child. The daddy and mommy hug each other very close and together create a tiny embryo inside the mommy's body in her uterus. It doesn't look anything like a baby yet. But it lives there for a long time, slowly growing arms and legs, hands and feet, fingers and toes, and all the parts of the body and soon starts looking very much like a baby. When the baby is big enough and strong enough, he or she comes out from inside the mommy through her vagina. Now, you can ask me any questions that you have."

- It is not necessary to explain all the exceptions to this explanation—artificial insemination and cesarean section, for example—unless it is directly relevant to any of the children's family circumstances or to the question that was asked. These exceptions and additional information can be given at a later time or when and if children ask further questions.

Mutual exploration

- If you see children exploring each other's genitals and they are both mutually involved and interested (there doesn't appear to be any manipulation), tell them, "It is important to keep your clothes on outside of the bathroom, and it's never okay to touch another person's penis or vagina. This is because they are very delicate and can easily get hurt or sore. The parts of your body that are covered by your bathing suit are private and not shared with anyone but your parents, a doctor, or a nurse. I see that you want to know about penises and vaginas, so let's read this book together." If parents ask you about this issue, help them understand that the goal is to ensure personal safety while supporting children's healthy curiosity and encouraging them to feel good about their bodies. One way to do this is to be open about nudity and bodies at home, especially when children are under about ten years old, while being firm (but calm) about not touching private body parts.

Children with Challenges: Abilities, Disabilities, and Vulnerabilities

THIS SECTION OF THE BOOK focuses on those children who require something "extra." They need particular supports to get their needs met, to be fully included in all activities, and to be an equal member of the classroom community. However, everyone benefits from the inclusion of children with challenges in the classroom. The classroom reflects the pluralistic society that we live in and in this setting all children learn democratic skills and dispositions: acceptance and appreciation of differences, fairness, empathy, and helpfulness.

Some of the challenges these children face are extreme versions of common feelings such as fear or shyness. Other challenges do not lie within the child but in the child's circumstances, such as being the only child in the class whose family does not speak English or the child who is cognitively more advanced (gifted) than all her classmates.

The something "extra" that these children need can range from verbal support, attention, and encouragement to a full-time professional aide for children with complex disabilities. It may require sophisticated, customized equipment, such as a mobile stander (a wheelchair that supports the child in an upright position) and a computerized communication device, or simple low-tech devices, such as pointers, page turners, and pencil grips. In some cases children with challenges are already competent and do not perceive themselves as deficient or needy, but they still need protection and assistance in responding to the biased attitudes and behaviors of other children (and sometimes adults).

1. IS THE CHILD JUST IMMATURE OR IS THERE REALLY SOMETHING WRONG?

As you are the first teacher for most of your children, you will come in contact with some who may have a disability or special need that has not been previously detected. These are the children who stand out in some way, whose behaviors are not typical of their peers. It may be a child whose speech is hard to understand, who is unusually clumsy and runs awkwardly, who doesn't connect with other children, or who generally acts and seems to be younger than his actual age. Sometimes these issues are not identified because no one has yet realized that a problem exists, but sometimes parents deny that their child has a problem or the family physician says the child will grow out of it.

How do you know if a child has an actual disability? Observe the child carefully and systematically, review a list of developmental milestones for her age, read information about the behaviors or issues you are concerned about, talk with her parents, and help them arrange for a developmental screening test. Based on this information, if you still have concerns or are just uncertain, make a referral. If your program does not have a referral process in place, give parents information and the phone number and website address for your state and/or local Child Find and early intervention service provider. (See the helpful resources under "Disabilities, Inclusion, and Children with Special Needs" on pp. 288–89.)

Anticipating and Preventing Problems Related to Identifying Children with Special Needs

- Observe *all* children. Most programs will screen *all* children. This avoids the problem of singling some children out from others, which may upset parents or make those children feel different. Some screening tests—for hearing and speech—require special equipment and licensed professionals to administer.

- Observe and screen early in the year or soon after any new children enter your class, but give yourself enough time to get to know the children well and for them to feel comfortable with you. Children must feel supported and relaxed when being tested to get accurate results. Don't wait too long, however. Share your concerns about a child and make a referral as quickly as possible. Getting an appointment with a specialist and starting a treatment program often takes months.

- Give all parents a written policy on observing, screening, and referring children to specialists. Ask them to sign permission forms for this when they enroll their children. They will not be surprised then when the time comes to discuss the results of the screening and observation with them. Include the following in your written policy: the reason for observation and screening; specific information about the observation process and screening test(s) you use; where and to whom referrals are made; a few stories about how children and families have been helped by the observation, screening, and referral process; and an assurance of confidentiality.

- Use a screening test that requires or allows input from parents. Some have a separate form for parents to complete that complements the form completed by a teacher. These naturally facilitate connections and communication between you and family members.

- Schedule regular conference times with parents at least twice a year. Hold the first one soon after the child is enrolled and screened. Hold the second one toward the end of the program year. This creates a situation where meeting with parents is a given. If there is a concern about the child, a special meeting will not have to be arranged. Asking parents to attend a special meeting may cause them great anxiety and they may refuse to come or just not show up.

- If at all possible, do home visits with all your families. This will give you great insight into each child and family. You may see very different behaviors at home than at school. Use the home visit as a time to form a bond and strengthen your relationship with each family, especially during the first visit. Don't have a set agenda or specific educational goals in mind. Build trust and observe for the purpose of getting to know and understand the child and family more thoroughly and deeply.

Solving Problems Related to Identifying Children with Special Needs

Observing every child and still finding time to be a teacher

It's possible to observe every child and have plenty of time to be a teacher, but only if you have the right tools, are well organized and systematic, and have had some practice and experience.

- One of the tools you need is a good, simple observation checklist. Its main purpose is to help ensure that you observe the key behaviors in all areas of development and have the same information for every child. Items on the checklist should reflect behaviors and actions that can be readily seen during typical activities and routines: "Child runs, jumps, and climbs with agility and only occasionally trips or falls" (rather than, "Child stands on one foot for thirty seconds"). You can rate this item for every child during one or two outside periods while doing your usual teaching duties. Hopefully, the items also align with your state's early learning standards.

- Another tool you need is a simple strategy for recording focused observations of the behaviors of children for whom you have concerns. One such strategy is to keep a running record of the behaviors over a period of about a week. Write down, or record using your smartphone's voice recorder, exactly what the child does without interpreting it and without judgment. Here is an example for the first two days of a week:

    Monday
    - 8:44   Slipped and fell near door when entering class
    - 9:00   Kicked chair into the table when attempting to pull it out to sit on
    - 10:20   Bumped into shelf while running to circle; bruised knee
    - 11:43   Spilled some juice onto table when attempting to pour it into a glass
    - 3:10   Ran trike off the track and fell off

    Tuesday
    - 9:06   Knocked over milk glass with elbow
    - 11:52   Dropped bowl of pasta
    - 2:55   Tried to ride scooter several times. Fell off one time, stepped off quickly other two times. Left the scooter and got on a tricycle
    - 4:18   Bumped elbow on doorknob when entering room

- An objective running record like this is very helpful, especially to health professionals and early intervention specialists, as it shows the frequency and types of behaviors and may reveal patterns: Is the behavior more frequent or severe during certain times of the day or particular days of the week?

The screening test results are not good

- Screening tests will sometimes identify a child as needing further evaluation when the child really does not need it. Perhaps the child was uncomfortable during the testing, not feeling well, anxious, and unable to focus, or did not understand the directions, among many other possible reasons. These tests will also sometimes fail to identify a child who actually does need further evaluation, because the items or questions do not probe deep enough, there are no items or not enough items in a particular area of development, the child had a particularly "good day" and performed better than he typically would on most other days, or the child made some lucky guesses, among other reasons. To correct for these errors, screening test results need to be used alongside observations of children and parent input.

- A child who scores significantly lower than her age-mates in one or several areas of development, and the observations at school and at home correspond with the results, should be seen by a specialist. Typically, a referral is made using a process established by your program or school, or parents contact the agency that provides early intervention services. The specialist will then give the child in-depth diagnostic tests to determine the extent of the issue. The result, or the diagnosis, will determine if the child has "categorical disability" and is therefore eligible for special education services. An individual educational plan (IEP) or individualized family service plan (IFSP) will then be developed for the child and family, which will include where the child will receive services—a special education program, at home, in your classroom, or perhaps all three. If the child is to continue in your classroom, either fully or in part, you should be included in the planning process, ongoing assessment, and modifications to the plan and have access to support and assistance from the specialists involved.

Parents who deny there is a problem

- Some parents do not know enough about child development to recognize that their child has a problem, but when you give them objective, jargon-free information and specific examples of the problem in a caring way, they are glad for the help.

- Some parents may refuse to acknowledge that their child has a problem, even when they have the knowledge and the evidence. Usually they have good motives for doing this, such as not wanting their child labeled or considered not normal; not wanting to feel responsible for the problem or being overwhelmed by it; not wanting to admit their own similar weaknesses or problems; or being concerned that their child and family will be stigmatized. These are real and valid concerns. However, if the result is that the child does not get the services he needs at this critical time in his development, their protective instinct may do more harm than good.

- You and your program have a professional, ethical, and, in some states, a legal responsibility to do all you can to obtain the services that a child needs. Teachers have an obligation to do no harm, and by doing nothing, harm may be done. Use this information as motivation to help the child. Keep a diary of your communications and meetings to document your efforts to meet your ethical and legal responsibilities.

- Be very supportive, friendly, and helpful to parents. Ask questions and consider them the experts on their child. Try to understand their perspective on their child. When they feel you have their child's best interests at heart, they will be ready to listen to your concerns. During this time, continue to observe and gather information about the child and to read more about the particular disability you suspect.

- If parents avoid talking to you informally, set up a meeting with them. Tell them that the purpose of the meeting is to listen to them, answer any questions they have, and learn as much about their child as possible so you can be the best teacher possible. Spend this time just listening, asking questions, and discussing positive or typical things about their child. It is important not to invent things or paint a false rosy picture, however. Leave the door open for the parents to express their concerns. If they do, tell them that you will think about what they said, observe the child carefully, and meet with them again to discuss it. If a screening test was not done, ask for their written permission to arrange for one and inform them that the results of the screening may indicate that their child may need further diagnostic testing. Also remind them about your program's procedures for screening and referral.

- When you state your concerns, do so by telling the parents only what you have observed. Do not make judgments. Simply say something like "I have seen that Chris falls down and bumps into things quite a bit. Here are some specific examples from notes I took during the week of February 20." Include information from the screening test, if one was done. Share information about where the parents can get more information and assistance, usually from the state's or county's Child Find program or the local school district.

Health professionals who believe there is no problem

- Some physicians, pediatricians, or other health professionals will occasionally downplay or deny a child's problems. "The child will outgrow it" is a phrase you might hear. A health professional may do this because she thinks the problem is not that serious or that the child will be able to compensate for it, especially if the child is strong in other areas of development.

- If you have the opportunity, inform health professionals and parents that children's problems can be addressed in positive ways by caring and sensitive teachers and professionals who build on their strengths. When a child improves his skills and makes progress, he feels good about himself. Young children usually overcome problems more quickly and easily than older children, and there is less stigma at this time, particularly from peers. Many problems will get worse if left untreated. It makes little sense to ignore or downplay a problem when a child can be helped and still feel good about himself.

- There may be other reasons why a child is not provided with the services he needs. Too often these children are the ones who are emotionally fragile and volatile and whose behaviors are the most difficult and stressful for teachers to deal with. You can still do many things in the classroom to help such children, even when parents do not want their children to receive services. Doing those things is just part of individualizing, which all good teachers do. Read as much as you can about the child's particular issues and about ways to help. The next chapter has more ideas for helping children with challenges and disabilities in general, and "Problematic Behaviors," starting on page 173, has ideas for helping children with specific problematic behaviors.

Difficulty in finding or affording professional services

- If you work in a program that has no access or funding for the services of a health professional and the parents cannot afford the services, consider other options such as the following:
    - In most places, your local school district is responsible for identifying, evaluating, and providing services for children with disabilities no matter how young.
    - Information and assistance should also be available at the county and state levels. These include health departments, the state department of education, and social services departments.
    - Every state has a system in place, usually called "Child Find," in which multiple departments and agencies cooperate to identify children who may have a disability or other special need as early as possible and begin the process of getting services to those children who need it.
    - Numerous nonprofit organizations, professional associations, and service and charitable organizations can assist with accessing services or, in some cases, even help pay for them if necessary. Some key associations, organizations, and agencies are listed in the resources under "Disabilities, Inclusion, and Children with Special Needs" on pp. 288–89.

2. IN THE MIX: INCLUDING CHILDREN WITH DISABILITIES AND SPECIAL NEEDS

Many teachers worry about having a child with challenges and special needs in their class. They worry that they do not have the proper training or expertise to help the child or to deal with the child's problems. They worry that the child will take up so much extra time and energy that the rest of the class will suffer. These are real and valid concerns. However, most teachers find that when they actually have a child with a disability in their class, the joys far outweigh the problems, real or imagined. When this is not the result, the child was either misassigned (perhaps her needs were too complex to benefit from a regular classroom), did not get the adaptive equipment or other assistance she needed, and/or the teachers did not receive the information and support they needed.

If you are already using good early childhood practices (individualized, active, social, playful, child-centered curriculum) and applying principles of universal design, you will not have difficulty caring for and teaching a child with a disability. You will have to stretch some of the things you already do, but your basic approach and routines will not have to change. For example, many children with developmental delays or who are emotionally fragile have short attention spans and experience difficulty focusing in group situations. Undoubtedly you already have a few children who fit this description, but not to the same degree. Lower your expectations slightly for this child, including the rate at which you expect him to develop or improve behaviors. Use the same techniques you already use—small groups, short group times, alternative quiet activities for some children during group times, seating the child next to you, involving all children actively—but employ these techniques sooner, more often, and more consistently.

After an initial stage of trepidation, mixed with curiosity and concern, young children are usually accepting of other children who have disabilities, even very complex disabilities. You will quickly find that children with disabilities are children, first and foremost. The similarities between them and typical children are far greater than the differences.

Anticipating and Preventing Problems Related to Inclusion

- Read articles or books about the particular disability of the child in your class. Every distinct disability has its own set of support organizations and associations of professionals and parents with helpful information and many resources on their websites.

- If possible, prepare your children in advance for including a new child with a disability. One way to do this is to share with them books and films about children with a variety of challenges and disabilities. The best ones do not make the disability the central focus but include the children as part of a good story. Use these to talk about individual differences and similarities.

- Take a proactive approach to giving children positive and factual information about people with disabilities. Do this through concrete activities such as the following:
  - Invite to your class people with a variety of disabilities who will talk openly and who are able to connect with young children. Ideally, this should include older children and teens. If possible, take a field trip to places where adults with disabilities work.
  - Correct misconceptions as soon as you hear children say them.
  - Show specific examples (through films, books, and on field trips) of people with disabilities functioning in a variety of self-sufficient ways and situations.

- Request to be a member of the team who meets to determine and periodically review the child's goals and services. In the early intervention system for a child with a categorical disability, this is usually called the interdisciplinary or multidisciplinary team and the goals and services are written in an IEP or IFSP. If the team has already formed, request the parents' permission to become part of future team meetings and to read the plan. Ask questions to make sure you fully understand the plan.

- If you are already part of the planning team, suggest educational goals or objectives that can be easily met in your active, child-centered classroom. An objective such as "Angie will stack six blocks with 80 percent accuracy" implies direct teaching, boring repetition, discrete skill development, and no joy for Angie. A goal such as "Angie will use blocks daily for creative play and stack them on the storage shelf when done" develops the same skills as the first objective but in a natural and enjoyable way. It integrates the skills into play and routines and promotes Angie's sense of self-efficacy.

- If possible, meet individually with all team members, which may include the parents, a physical therapist, an occupational therapist, a speech pathologist, and/or other health professionals, before the child enters your class. Discuss their goals for the child, their expectations of you, your concerns, and how the team members can help you. Make sure that the logistics of when and how they will provide therapy to the child are specified and that these logistics will not cause problems for your schedule or routines. Request that services be provided in the classroom, to the greatest extent possible. Get the phone numbers of the team members so you can contact them quickly, if necessary.

- Set up a regular system for communicating with therapists and health providers to discuss the objectives they are working on and how you can help the child meet those objectives in the classroom.

- For children with complex disabilities, reach a clear understanding that you would welcome the child to your class on a trial basis. Set up in advance a meeting date (about one month after the child starts) to discuss any problems and concerns, as well as successes. Be honest and forthright, but reasonable, about what you need to help the child and about what the child needs in order to be successful and fully integrated into your class. If those needs cannot be met, then suggest that child might be better off in a different placement.

- To the greatest extent possible, apply the principles of universal design. The idea behind universal design is to create a physical environment and use teaching strategies that are responsive to all children. Examples of this in public environments are ramps instead of or in addition to stairs, curb cuts on sidewalk corners, accessible bathrooms, and braille numbers on elevator buttons. All of these design elements have either no impact or a positive impact on the people who do not need them, but they are essential for the people who do need them. Ramps and curb cuts are a great help for people pushing babies in strollers, pulling wheeled suitcases, and riding skateboards. Universal design does not entirely eliminate the need to make accommodations—we still have to reserve parking spots for drivers with mobility challenges—but it certainly reduces the need. This is important because accommodations can be costly and not as effective as universal design. For example, retrofitting a bathroom to accommodate a wheelchair can cost as much or more than building a barrier-free bathroom from scratch and it will likely not be as easy to use.

- An example of universal design in teaching is to read a large-format book to children clearly, slowly, and with expression, while checking for understanding and pointing to the words as they are read. This helps ensure that the story is engaging and meaningful to all children including, among others, children with vision and hearing impairments, children whose family language is other than English, children with short attention spans (for whatever reason), and children who are beginning to read.

- Provide a wide variety of equipment and materials that span a broad range of skill levels. For example, have five-piece, ten-piece, fifteen-piece, and twenty-five-piece puzzles.

- Make any final adjustments necessary to the room, furniture, equipment, and materials before the child enters your class, if possible. If the class has already started, enlist the help of the children and explain what you are doing and why. Show them a photo of the child and tell them all you know about her, not just about her disability. Establish relevant classroom rules that do not allow children to exclude others, such as "Everyone's included, everybody plays."

- Maintain daily communication with parents, or do so as often as possible. Meet regularly to discuss the child's needs and progress.

Solving Problems Related to Inclusion

Questions from children that may be hurtful or difficult to answer

- If the question is impolite, respond to that aspect of the question. A question such as "Why is his face like that?" warrants a response such as "We will answer your question, but let me help you ask it in a way that doesn't hurt Michael's feelings. You can say to Michael, 'Michael, you don't look like anyone else I have seen before. Could you please tell me why?'"

- If the child with the disability is physically and emotionally able to respond, have him respond directly to questions from other children. If necessary, help the child with the disability respond to such questions honestly and simply. For example, "I was born with cerebral palsy. It's hard to control the muscles in my face and body. Inside, I'm just like you and everyone else."

- If you have to respond to the questions, give direct, simple, and factual answers. If you are unsure or don't know the answer, say so, and seek the answer together from reliable Internet sources. If a child asks, "Why can't Michael walk?" you might say, "When he was born, his legs didn't work. So instead of learning to walk, like you did when you were little, he learned to use a wheelchair." Many children are not just curious but are worried that this disability might happen to them or that they will "catch it." They need some reassurance that the disability is not contagious.

Conflicts with special educators, therapists, or other specialists

Conflict between teachers and others who serve the special needs of a child with a disability often arise because each views the child from a different angle. Early childhood teachers tend to see the whole child, including her strengths and abilities, whereas a specialist might be more focused on fixing what is "wrong" with the child. They also have been trained very differently and even use different jargon. Miscommunication can easily happen.

- Find areas of commonality. You both want to help the child learn and grow, your ultimate goals for the child are usually the same, and you likely agree on the child's strengths and challenges. Build on those commonalities and discuss ways in which you can collaborate to help the child. For example, the specialist can sit with the child during a math game and help him count the dots on the dice, track when his turn is about to come up, and record his progress.

- Be patient and understand that the special education or therapeutic approach is designed to be precise, clinical, and scientific. The therapist was trained in this approach, which comes from good intentions to help the child. This approach often gets good short-term results and children with complex and serious disabilities benefit greatly from it. However, continue to use and to advocate for your child-centered approach, as children with mild to moderate disabilities benefit greatly from developing self-initiative, especially for their long-term growth. They are young children first and foremost and, like all young children, they learn best through play-based, active, hands-on, integrated activities.

- If a special educator suggests using rewards and punishments as part of the child's plan, demonstrate the effectiveness of managing children's behavior by creating a stimulating environment, providing an active schedule, encouraging and teaching positive behaviors, giving children many chances to be successful, providing individualized assistance, giving positive helpful feedback, scaffolding skills, having children help each other, and more.

- Some ECED programs have set policies stating that rewards, especially food and tokens, are not allowed. This frees a teacher to reject the use of a reinforcement system without having to defend his position.

The overly involved parent

Parents of children with disabilities care deeply about their children, are very concerned about their growth and development, and tend to be very involved in their lives. Some parents might want to spend a great deal of time in your classroom. While this can be extremely helpful, it can also create problems. The child might not get enough time to be independent and the parent may at times be more of a hindrance than a help.

- Meet with the parent, preferably before the child enters the classroom, to discuss potential problems, to explain your approach, and to make expectations clear. Agree to a regular schedule of volunteer hours. Make it clear that you may need to reduce the hours.

- Meet regularly, at least monthly, to discuss any concerns and to make plans for improvements. Give informal feedback more frequently. Clarify your roles and do quick informational sessions about your methods.

- Ask the parent to work with other children to give his child time to be independent.

- Provide very specific, factual information about problems: "This morning you started to cut Julia's food for her. I then asked you to help her cut it for herself. A few minutes later you were cutting it for her again. Tell me what happened and let's figure out how we can help Julia learn to be more independent."

- Express your appreciation. Give specific, positive feedback about what the parent does well.

The child with a disability who does not play with others

For many children with disabilities, playing with other children does not come naturally. This could be due to weak language skills, unclear speech, or other communication challenges, or they might have had fewer opportunities to practice their social skills. Most young children with disabilities can learn to play with others, and vice versa, particularly if a caring teacher helps. Usually the teacher has to provide direct and specific assistance to both the child with a disability and the other children.

- Involve the child as fully as possible in all group games and activities. Physically guide a child with a developmental delay through all the actions in a group movement game. See that the child has a turn just like everyone else.

- Teach the child how to pretend, starting with common actions like eating and drinking or talking on a phone. Help her connect with other children to pretend together, eventually pulling yourself out of the game.

- Teach the child the right words and actions to use to join children in play. You may need to say them for her and show her how, until the child can do it on her own. Often the best method of joining play is to start by copying what the other children are doing and then take on a role that fits and complements the scenario, such as another brother or sister, or another customer.

- Mediate a play situation. When the child with a disability is playing alongside another child and they are using the same materials, encourage them to play together by suggesting a slight variation or by introducing a new item: "Sara is building a road and so are you. You can hook your roads together to make a big, long road. There are more cars on the shelf behind you."

- Set out play materials that are of particular interest to the child with a disability.

- Encourage another child to play with a child with a disability by providing a special game or unique toy that only two can use and that will play to the strengths of the child with a disability.

- Adapt toys and equipment to make them easier for the child with the disability to use. For example, add straps to the pedals of a trike to make it possible for a child with a mild physical disability to use it. He can then be part of the active outdoor play along with the other children.

- Help him expand his play skills by imitating what he does and then doing something slightly different. For example, if the child is stacking small blocks, do the same thing until you have his attention, and then stack the blocks by alternating big and little ones. Assist him as necessary.

The child who requires too much time and effort

A child with a disability often requires more time and work than other children. If the situation becomes too much, however, then you are not getting the support you need. Many children with disabilities need an aide (at least part-time), and often the local school district or early intervention program will provide one. This can be a great help to you and the child, especially if the aide is capable, flexible, and hardworking. If you have an aide who is not, and she is not responding to your requests and needs, make sure you provide objective information about this to her supervisors. A year in the life of a young child is too important for him to receive less-than-excellent services.

- Enlist the assistance of other children to help the child with a disability. Most will be eager to help if the task is reasonable. Children can push a wheelchair, help the child clean up, assist with completing a puzzle, zip a jacket, button a sweater, tie a shoe, or even teach a simple skill. This will also encourage responsibility and altruism, while freeing time for you. However, make sure they do not do things for a child with a disability that she can do for herself. Children with disabilities need to develop independence to the greatest extent possible.

- Part of the problem may be that you are not getting the information, support, and/ or the equipment you need to be effective. You must have access to a competent professional, who can observe you and the child in the classroom and recommend methods or materials to use that will save time, increase efficiency, and allow the child to be more independent. This person is usually one of the health professionals on the child's team, but he could be a specialist from a hospital, social service agency, or university.

- If all the suggested strategies are not effective in reducing the amount of time and effort required to include a child with special needs to a manageable level, then request to meet with the multidisciplinary team to discuss solutions such as increasing supports, reducing the amount of time the child is in your classroom, or placing the child in another ECED setting.

3. DIVERSITY, DIFFERENCE, AND DEMOCRACY: CULTURAL RESPONSIVENESS

Culture is how we live our lives. It is what we eat, when we eat, how we eat, how we dress, what we believe in, how we talk, what we hope for, the music we listen to, how we raise our children, and so much more. Everyone is part of a culture—many cultures, actually. Seeing culture broadly is important in order to create a truly supportive classroom and to counter biases. Our society has numerous cultures. A culture of poverty, a culture of wealth, a male culture, a female culture, gay and lesbian cultures, urban and rural cultures, racial and ethnic cultures, regional cultures based on one's ancestral country or the part of the United States where one grew up, cultures of childhood, adolescence, and adulthood, and many more.

A child whose culture, race, or ethnicity is different from all the other children in your classroom may need support and assistance to be fully included as a member of the classroom community. This is true whether the child is the only (or almost only) black child in a predominantly white classroom, white child in a predominantly Latino classroom, girl among boys, or a child from a poor family among children from upper-middle-class families. Similarly, a group of children who are all different from the predominant culture around them (for example, a class of all Syrian children whose families recently immigrated) will need teaching and learning activities and methods that address their particular needs. Children in more homogenous classrooms, where all the children are from the predominant culture, need to learn about other cultures and people who are different from them. This broadens their view of the world and its incredible diversity and teaches them to appreciate the similarities and differences of others. All children receive great benefit from learning to actively counteract stereotypes and to move beyond judgments based on superficial attributes.

In most early childhood classrooms, the biases and prejudices of some children toward others are more likely to be based on differences in appearance, age, or gender than on racial or ethnic differences. Physically attractive children are liked more by their peers than other children and are viewed as smarter and more competent based on appearance alone. The opposite view is imposed on children who are perceived as physically unattractive. Girls and boys tend to stick with children of their own gender. Older children tend to exclude younger children, or worse. These biases are a good place to start to help children develop tolerance and compassion for others and to help children who may be victims of bias stand up for themselves. They are immediate and real problems to confront.

The early childhood classroom is a place to counter stereotypes and the more harmful aspects of popular culture. It may be the *only* place. Classrooms need to be free from commercialism and the kinds of toys and activities that children experience many times a day at home, at the homes of friends and neighbors, and in the community. They are alternative communities in which competition is minimized and mediated; cooperation and collaboration are maximized; creativity and imagination are valued more than following directions; and the process is as important as the product. There are no cliques, factions, in-groups, or out-groups. Everyone is included.

Teachers need to employ a wide variety of methods to help children change misguided beliefs and to prevent the development of those beliefs. This chapter discusses concrete ways to replace stereotypes and prejudices with knowledge and compassion.

Anticipating and Preventing Problems Related to Biases and Diversity

- Establish a clear, simple policy about these issues and share it with families. For example, "This classroom embraces and celebrates diversity of all kinds. Children are taught the values of respect, understanding, and appreciation. A child who acts in a biased way is helped to change her behaviors to reflect these values. Stereotypes and misinformation about groups of people will be corrected. Here, children learn the dispositions and practices of a democratic society: understanding, fairness, inclusion, consensus, and negotiation."

- Families should also know your specific policies and procedures related to celebrating cultural diversity, your approach to holidays, and your methods of counteracting bias. This should be in writing in a parent handbook.

- Meet with all parents to understand their cultures. Ask open-ended questions such as, "Please tell me about what is important in your family." "What is unique about your family?" "What are the key values and character traits that you want your child to have?" and "What are your hopes and dreams for your child?"

- Establish a classroom rule: "Use your hands and words to help, not hurt." Discuss with children some of the types of words and actions that hurt, including teasing, name-calling, and excluding others.

- Provide books, puzzles, pictures, and artwork that reflect a variety of cultures and show people of different races, ethnic groups, physical attributes, and abilities. Also show women and men in nontraditional jobs.

- Invite to your class or visit people who have jobs that defy stereotypes. For instance, when doing a health unit, invite to the classroom a male nurse and/or a Latina dentist. Invite a female firefighter when doing a unit on community workers.

- Invite people from the community or from among your families to share their cultural traditions—stories, songs, dance, dress, and food. Make sure the children understand the differences between costumes or historical dress and daily dress, and between rituals or ceremonies and everyday activities.

- Show children how holidays are celebrated in other countries or cultures, rather than repeating the same activities that they will likely do at home and in the community, or instead of doing nothing at all. Draw ideas from the diversity among the families within your class. If there is not any diversity, read up on other traditions and use one that you find interesting and will be engaging to the children. For example, during Halloween, tell children how it is celebrated in other countries. Role-play some of these traditions. Invite the children to tell you a joke for an apple or a nickel as the children in Scotland do on Halloween. Scotland also celebrates Halloween with bonfires on almost every street corner, so gather the children in a darkened room around a pretend bonfire made from pieces of wood piled up on top of flashlights and decorated with paper flames. Tell (not very) scary stories. Share your own traditions with the children. You can also do activities, including science activities, related to celebrations in many countries, cultures, and religions through a unifying theme such as "Lighting Up the Dark" in December and "New Beginnings" in April.

- Use holiday celebrations as a basis for counteracting stereotypes. Around Thanksgiving, focus your activities on Native Americans rather than on Pilgrims. Read up on the real history behind holidays and develop age-appropriate activities that reflect aspects of what really happened. Show examples of Native American stereotypes (readily found at Thanksgiving time) and explain in simple terms why they are not accurate. For example, "Native Americans, or American Indians, wear the same kinds of clothes that most people wear. They dress up in the kinds of clothes they wore a long time ago just for holidays and celebrations."

- Use a bicultural and bilingual (if appropriate) curriculum with a class consisting of all or many children who are culturally and linguistically different from the predominant society. Alternatively, obtain as many classroom materials as possible that are in the children's family language, or are bilingual, and reflect the children's culture and the way they look. In this approach children learn the values, language, and customs of their own culture as well as those of the predominant one. The goal is to help them be biculturally, or multiculturally, competent.

- Include themes that explore issues of diversity such as "Hats, Clothes, and Shoes," which investigates the range, similarities, and differences, and the reasons and purposes that people in different countries wear their particular types of hats, clothes, and shoes. Include U.S. mainstream culture too. Why do so many men in the United States wear baseball-style hats? Children's books by Ann Morris have lovely photographs to support this theme including *Hats, Hats, Hats* and *Shoes, Shoes, Shoes*.

Solving Problems Related to Biases and Diversity

Questions from children about differences

- As described previously, if a question is impolite, help the child ask it in a different, kinder way.

- Some questions will catch you off guard. Don't feel compelled to respond immediately if you are not sure how best to answer it. You can say, "Ana, I need to think about your question. I will answer it a little bit later."

- Have resources and information available to help you respond to difficult questions such as, "Why is his skin so black or so white?" or "Why are your eyes like that?" or "Why does she always wear a scarf on her head?" There are numerous children's books on these topics, including *All the Colors We Are* by Katie Kissinger. It is also a bilingual book. (For more ideas, see the resources under "Cultural Responsiveness and Diversity" on p. 285.)

Responding to biased behaviors

Children will not change their misguided beliefs about differences (learned from parents and/ or absorbed from media and society in general) simply by seeing and hearing positive images of different cultures or by celebrating culturally specific holidays such as Martin Luther King Jr.'s birthday, Hanukkah, Kwanzaa, Chinese New Year, and Cinco de Mayo. To change their beliefs or to minimize the likelihood that they will develop harmful beliefs, it is necessary to address the biased behaviors proactively and directly.

- Give children correct information as soon as they hear stereotypical statements (whether from other children or adults) or experience biased behaviors. Say something like "It hurts deeply inside to be told you can't play because of the color of your skin (or how much you weigh, what type of clothes you wear, and so on). This goes against our class rule of using words that help, not hurt. People have to get to know each other before they can really tell if they like or don't like each other. Let me help you play together and get to know each other." This will likely entail being involved in their play at the start to get things going.

- Support the child who gets ridiculed and say something like "Matthew is a kind person and a good friend. I think that is much more important than the way that a person looks."

- Help the offended child stand up for himself. Support his hurt feelings and then help him say such words as "I'm proud of my skin color, and I can play wherever I want to." Don't try to force friendships or deny a child's feelings of trepidation or displeasure. The feelings usually stem from a fear of what is different or unknown, or from biased messages from family members. Set up many opportunities for friendships to develop through play, projects, and mutual interests.

- Develop activities that intentionally counteract the stereotype that was acted upon. Write stories with the children about classroom events in which biases were overcome (such as two culturally different children who didn't like each other at first but then became good friends). Use puppets and role plays to tell stories about incidents of bias and how children can deal with them effectively.

- When you or the children notice examples of prejudice, show them ways to do something about it. For example, on a field trip to the zoo, you realize that the train platform has many steps and is not wheelchair accessible. Ask the children, "Can every person get up these steps? Which people can't? How can they get on the train? How would you feel if you couldn't go to the train? What can be done about it?" If they have trouble developing solutions, suggest some, such as talking to the person in charge of the station or the train system or writing a letter. Follow through on the idea as a class and share the response. Sometimes you can get dramatic and satisfying results. Your actions may result in the installation of an elevator! If this happens, take several trips to watch the elevator being built.

- Meet with the parents of the child who often expresses bias. Explain how you are dealing with this behavior in the classroom and discuss your views on it. Listen carefully to their views and develop a plan together. If they disagree with you and support their child's biases, make it clear that in your class you still will not allow the voicing or acting out of biases and will counter it. Have a meeting with all the parents and discuss these issues. You will likely gain good support this way, and the parents who disagree with your approach will get the message that they are "outliers." They may in the end choose a different center or school.

Cultural differences in learning styles and priorities

Different cultures emphasize certain values and abilities over others. While some cultures strongly value education, others value hard work and physical labor. Some cultures value promptness, and others value relationships and "being in the moment" over promptness. The visual sense is very important in some cultures (colorful art and clothing), while other cultures place more emphasis on the auditory sense (music, discussion, and literature). These are generalizations about cultures and, of course, there is great diversity of beliefs and practices among families within any one culture. Seeing the strength of what each culture values and recognizing how it may be different from those in your classroom is important. A clash between a child's own culture and the culture of the school will result in the child feeling less capable than she actually is, confused, and unwelcomed, and therefore less amenable to participating.

- Once you have recognized the differences between your values and the values of a family, help the child by being flexible about your values and by supporting his. For example, in the culture of the urban poor in United States, many families view time as very flexible and flowing. The family may have no set mealtimes, bedtimes, bath schedules, and so on. When the child enters your class, he confronts a set schedule with specific times for everything. This is very different from what he has always experienced and has internalized as the meaning of time. It would be helpful to this child if you regularly review the schedule with all the children and give frequent reminders about what happens and when. Give ample warnings before the next activity on the schedule and allow children to finish projects or save them to finish later. Allow plenty of time for children to play and to choose from a wide selection of activities. Occasionally alter your schedule as needed. This universal design approach helps all children develop a sense of time and order (which is highly valued in mainstream U.S. society) while supporting the child whose culture views time differently. Apply a similar approach to other cultural issues.

Multiracial and multicultural children

The numbers of children of mixed race, ethnicity, or culture are increasing faster than the numbers of single-race children. You may even have such a child in your class and not realize it. They have different needs than children of one race, ethnicity, or culture (whether a minority race or white). As these needs are complex and vary from child to child, they often get overlooked, even by teachers who use culturally responsive practices (Baxly 2008; Dotson-Renta 2015).

- Every multiracial/multiethnic child has a different situation, and one set of mixed-race parents may view their children's race or ethnicity very differently from another set of mixed-race parents. Have conversations with parents about how they view their child. Some feel strongly that their child should identify with one particular race, while others feel that their child should identify with both equally or as a unique biracial person. Still others may feel strongly that they should have no firm identification with any race or that the child should eventually choose. Also find out how they combine their cultures. Do they celebrate all holidays associated with both (or all) cultures, or do they celebrate none or only some? Are most of the family's friends and relatives of one particular race or are they diverse?

- Most families want—and most children need—to have their particular combination of identities recognized and appreciated. When talking about winter holidays, for example, you might say, "In Paula's house they celebrate Christmas and Hanukkah." Or during a meal, "Ken eats with chopsticks sometimes and a fork at other times in his house." Or around Martin Luther King Jr.'s birthday and St. Patrick's Day, "Kylie is proud of both her African heritage and her Irish heritage."

- Many multiracial/multiethnic adults talk about how, as children, they felt that they belonged to no group, that they were always "in between" two cultures. They also report being teased a great deal and feeling ashamed. This is of great concern, as a clear sense of identity is important to growing up healthy. You can do many things to help multiracial/multiethnic children feel visible and valued. There are some excellent picture books for children to help you as well. (See the resources under "Cultural Responsiveness and Diversity" on p. 285.)

- Although doing many things to celebrate the diversity around us is an important part of this effort, it is not enough. It is also vital to talk about the diversity within the group. Most of your children (as well as teachers and staff) have mixed heritages in some way. Every person also has different characteristics, some of which are more like their fathers and some more like their mothers. Ask parents about their heritages and characteristics, and discuss them with the children. Make class books with and for the children, with titles such as "Everyone Is Bi-something!" or "I Have My Daddy's Skin and My Mommy's Eyes."

- You may have single-race children in your class who have been adopted into families of different races. Their needs are similar in that they usually have multiple racial or ethnic identities and should feel proud of all of them. However, they have the additional needs of children who have been adopted.

- Ask for training and resources. Almost all communities have a sensitive, knowledgeable person who can provide insight into the particular needs of multiracial/multiethnic children and how teachers can help meet them. Read more on the issue. Good information on this topic can be found in the resources under "Cultural Responsiveness and Diversity" on page 285.

4. A DIFFERENT KIND OF SPECIAL NEED: GIFTED AND TALENTED CHILDREN

About five percent of all children, regardless of family income, age, or race, are gifted or talented. If not nurtured, their abilities will not be fully realized and they may develop problematic behaviors from boredom and frustration. In fact, a child in your class with problematic behaviors may be a gifted child who is unchallenged. By identifying gifted children and providing for their needs, you will help them as well as yourself.

Although a small percentage of children have unique, above-ordinary abilities, which we call gifts or talents, all children have strengths, interests, and proclivities. An important job of teachers and parents is to recognize these in each child and provide active support, resources, and guidance to help them fully develop. As with other children with special needs, providing a good program for gifted children is not hard if you already have an active, child-centered, individualized classroom. You will just need to provide some additional challenges and opportunities within your current curriculum and routines.

You will find that the suggestions in this chapter can work well with almost all children, not just the gifted. However, for their basic needs to be met, gifted children *require* these approaches.

Anticipating and Preventing Problems Related to Gifted and Talented Children

- Provide many opportunities for all children to be creative through open-ended art activities, music, creative dance and movement, and making up and acting out stories. A talented child will be excited to participate in her area of interest and strength.

- Make available a wide variety of creative materials, which any child can use for any purpose (within reasonable limits) during work-play. Include many different kinds of blank paper, streamers, pieces of foam, different sizes of cups and containers, wood scraps, cotton balls, cloth, buttons, foil, colored chalk, pens, colored pencils, glue, paste, staplers, scissors, tape, and so on. Keep these items well organized in separate boxes.

- Know the interests of the children in your class. Give them many opportunities to talk about and pursue their interests. Although some gifted children are very capable across all areas of development, most have one or two specific areas of talent and interest and are "typical" in other areas. By giving all children opportunities to pursue interests, you will be able to determine which children are gifted and talented and will need to be challenged and supported.

- Ask the parents when they enroll their child if he has any particular talents, skills, interests, or strengths. Parents are usually good judges of their child's abilities and can easily identify them, particularly if they have a checklist to use, such as the one that follows. As with any child with special needs, frequent communication with parents is necessary to avoid problems and provide the best possible services.

- Understanding the eight different intelligences (Gardner 2006) can help you see and nurture a broad range of gifts and talents. These are linguistic intelligence ("word smart"), logical-mathematical intelligence ("number/reasoning smart"), spatial intelligence ("picture smart"), bodily-kinesthetic intelligence ("body smart"), musical intelligence ("music smart"), interpersonal intelligence ("people smart"), intrapersonal intelligence ("self-smart"), and naturalist intelligence ("nature smart"). Value them equally and provide many opportunities in your classroom for all of them to be expressed and developed.

- Become familiar with the common attributes of gifted and talented children, so you will recognize such children among your group. The following is a list of characteristics of young children who are gifted and/or talented. Most gifted children have a number of these characteristics but not all.

  - has a very good memory, especially long-term memory
  - has a very good vocabulary for her age
  - can concentrate for long periods
  - retains information easily
  - observes keenly and is very curious
  - has strong interests
  - shows early empathy for others
  - is concerned and worried about big problems like climate change, poverty, and war
  - is interested in books
  - exhibits a high energy level
  - is very insistent (aka "stubborn")
  - is often a perfectionist
  - is very persistent
  - prefers to play with older children or to be with adults
  - does simple math problems easily and enjoys them
  - has an advanced sense of humor
  - uses common items in uncommon ways
  - shows a strong interest in any or in several of the arts
  - has a particular advanced skill or ability more typical of much older children or adults
  - is very sensitive

- As most children have at least one area of strength, take a wide view of giftedness and talent. Look beyond usual areas such as music, art, reading, and math. A child may be gifted in the area of social skills and leadership (could he be a future politician?), large-motor skills (a future athlete?), empathy toward others (a future psychologist?), small-motor skills (a future carpenter or surgeon?), or verbal skills such as persuasion and negotiation (a future lawyer?).

Solving Problems Related to Gifted and Talented Children

Teachers and parents have a critical role in helping gifted and talented children reach their full potential. Although such children have within themselves these abilities, the adults in the children's lives will need to work hard to ensure that the abilities are fully realized. We all know someone who has great talent and ability that was not pursued and is not being used. The adults need to provide gifted and talented children with a good balance of healthy activities (time for active play and to be with friends) and emotional support, and they need to be careful not to overlook the needs and challenges of these children. The adults also need to access the high-quality teachers these children require and deserve to nurture their talents. For example, a child who is artistically talented will need to have instruction from a specialized art teacher, usually from an art school. However, finding the right art teacher is important and difficult. The teacher should understand the developmental needs of young children, challenge the child without putting too much pressure on her, and nurture the particular, unique strengths of the child.

- When planning your activities, devise ways to make them more challenging for gifted children. If, for example, you will be playing a memory game during small-group time, plan to add items when your gifted child has a turn. For instance, for most children you would place four items on a tray, cover the items so they can't see which one is removed, and take one away. Then you would invite a child to guess which item is gone. For gifted children you might place six items and take two away. Plan this ahead of time so the activity will run smoothly. For all the children, including gifted children, increase the difficulty of the activity slightly once they can do it with little effort. However, start and end with activities that are not too difficult, so that all the children will feel competent and successful.

- Provide alternative activities, if necessary. If a gifted child is bored during a story that the other children are enjoying, let him choose to look at another book by himself.

- Ask gifted children for their suggestions about changing aspects of an activity and follow through on reasonable ideas. This will stretch their thinking skills and provide valuable feedback about the way they think and perceive their own needs.

- Give gifted children many opportunities to make real choices and to be leaders: "You can dismiss the children from circle. How would you like to do it—by first initials, by the types of shoes they are wearing, or in some other way?"

- Allow gifted children to pursue their own interests and unique abilities as far as they can go. Encourage them by providing books and materials related to their interests. Many gifted children are particularly attracted to computers, because they enable them to stretch their skills and knowledge beyond what they can do on their own or with any other tool. Computers also have challenges inherent in them; there are always new things to do on the computer and more sophisticated ways of doing them. (See "Technology Center" on pp. 43–46 for more ideas.)

- Ask gifted children about how they came up with a particular response. Although some children will not be able to tell you, others will. For example, if a child says to you, "I think that sign says 'Open,'" ask her how she knows this. Her response will give you insight into how her mind works and help you understand and plan for her needs. She might say, "I see it every time we go into the store" or "My mother read it to me yesterday" or "I sounded out the letters." The first response indicates that she is a very receptive, quick, and self-directed learner; the second indicates a good visual and auditory memory; and the third reveals a high level of analytical thinking skills.

- Because most gifted children are very active and have broad interests, provide a wide variety of choices, including challenging games, puzzles, imaginary play situations, and table toys.

- Give gifted children many opportunities to generate ideas through brainstorming or problem solving. Ask them for ideas about new themes and activities. Ask them to come up with different and better ways of doing things.

- Include many nonfiction books on a wide range of topics in your book collection.

- Give gifted and talented children regular opportunities to use and "show off" their skills. Encourage the other children to be appreciative and proud of their classmate.

Lack of access to supports and resources

This is a problem for all teachers and parents of gifted children, but it is particularly true for families with low incomes and those in rural areas.

- Maintain a list of good teachers and resources in the community related to specific talents; add new names as you become aware of them. When resources are limited, some compromises may be necessary. For example, a child with musical ability who wants to play the piano may be better off learning to play the violin (at least to start) because the best music teacher in town teaches violin, not piano.

- Some teachers and professional and service organizations will offer scholarships to talented children from low-income families. Every city has an association of music teachers, art teachers, and so on. Help parents access these resources. Larger cities will usually have a chapter of the National Association for Gifted Children (www.nagc.org), various support groups for parents, and gatherings/events for gifted children.

- Some communities have music centers or programs that assist with the cost of renting or purchasing a musical instrument. Also, in many communities, you will find clubs for various interests—astronomy, computers, photography, dance, theater, or drawing, for example—that have adults who really enjoy nurturing the development of young children with similar interests.

- Help find a mentor for the child. This can be an older child or teen with similar talents who will help the child—emotionally as well as with skills—by taking a strong interest in him.

Problematic behaviors of some gifted children

Because of their uniqueness, some gifted children have a tendency toward certain behaviors that can cause problems for themselves and the people around them. Use the suggestions in the table below to minimize these problems.

Behavior	Possible Solution
Bored, acts silly, acts out	Provide more stimulating and challenging activities. Give the child opportunities and ample time to pursue her own interests at her own pace.
Invents his own methods or systems of doing things that conflict with yours or the way things need to be done	Provide many opportunities for the child to do things his own way when it will not cause a problem. When something must be done your way, be firm about the need to do it your way, but explain your reasons clearly. Ask the child for the reasons he needs to do something a certain way. If he is able to respond, it will give you an insight into his needs and may give you ideas for negotiating an agreement. Invite the child to generate ideas for slight variations that will not be a problem for you after you explain the parts that are nonnegotiable.
Gullible, easily fooled, and swayed	Appreciate the child's sense of wonder, trust, and curiosity that causes her to be gullible. Respect her by not teasing her about it or taking advantage of it. Point out calmly the truth of the situation. Support and validate her feelings so she will continue to be open and trusting. Don't let other children or adults tease her or take advantage of her.
Perfectionist, discouraged, critical of self and others	Continue to encourage the child's attempts: "You feel that you can do better and I'm sure you will. You tried hard and worked hard, which is something to be proud of" or "Look how much better you did this time than last time." Tell the child specifically what he does well and why it is good. Support and validate his feelings of frustration at his own shortcomings and that of others: "Some children find things more difficult than you, but everyone has some things they do very well. Let's appreciate how much people try rather than what they can or cannot do. Do the same for yourself."
Gets impatient or angry at interruptions	Allow plenty of time for the child to work on things of her own choosing. Give plenty of warning before she has to finish an activity. Have a way and a place for her to save her work to finish at another time. Ensure that she can keep the work safe in this place.
Dislikes repetitious activities or games	When the child is bored with an activity, offer him an alternative. Help him express his discomfort in a socially appropriate way: "When you are restless, ask me to help you find something else to do."
Resists directions	Give the child many opportunities to have control over her time and routines. Explain thoroughly the reasons for your directions. Give her plenty of advanced warning before changes.
Very active and energetic, talks too much, and dominates discussions	Provide long work-play times with a wide variety of active choices. Redirect the child's energy into activities that are creative and constructive. Limit the amount of time any child can talk in a group setting. Use a "talking stick" to make it clear who can talk and when. When he wants too much of your time, tell him that you will listen to him for one more minute now (set a timer) and that you will listen again at a specific time such as, "As soon as we go outside."
Overlooks details and skips routines; impatient with things that are not important to her	Give the child some slack by not putting too much emphasis on formalities and routines. Remind her when she needs to do something for health or safety reasons, and explain why: "Tie your shoes so that you don't trip over your laces." You will have to do this often but say it calmly. The child is usually not forgetful, simply disinterested.

5. IS IT INTROVERSION, INSECURITY, OR SOMETHING ELSE?: SHY, QUIET, AND SOLITARY CHILDREN

In the United States, extroverts "rule." This makes us worry for the children who are shy with meek little voices . . . that is, when they speak at all. But, as surface behaviors can be deceiving, it's important to determine if the behavior is a personality trait (introversion), an emotional obstacle (insecurity), or something else. Introverts prefer to be alone or, perhaps, with one other child on occasion. They may or may not have the social skills to join the group or be a leader, but what is key is that they would prefer not to. You are not going to change an introvert into an extrovert and attempts to do so will only make a child feel bad about himself. Instead, view your task as helping introverted children cope and be successful in an extrovert's world.

Then there are children who would prefer to join the group and have many friends (naturally extroverted) but are not able to because of a situational insecurity, due to circumstances such as being the "new kid" or a recent divorce or other major life change. For some children their insecurity is more serious. It is chronic or consistent across situations and groups and over time. Some of these children are also "clingy," preferring to hang on to you rather than play with other children. But what about the "something else"? There could be many other reasons as well. In one case, a child in my care was withdrawn because she was afraid of another child in the class, who was manipulative and mean to her in the neighborhood. Some children are not very good at picking up on social cues and have just never figured out effective ways to connect with other children. This behavior can also be a way to avoid doing something difficult for a child, such as engaging in imaginary play with other children.

All of the children who appear shy, but are not introverts, need your assistance to join the group. The children with chronic insecurities need more intensive and sustained help than the others. The clingy child needs to be more independent and to play with other children. The solution to relieving their insecurities is to help them have success at making friends and becoming part of the classroom community.

Tessa was a child in my class who definitely fit the description of a chronically insecure child. She looked longingly at others playing but strongly resisted all our attempts to get her to join their play and activities. The odd thing was, we never saw her being rejected and there was never any indication that other children did not want to play with her. An important insight that her mother provided was that when she was a child, she was exactly like Tessa and that her childhood memories were mostly painful. This actually spurred me to take stronger action rather than think this must be genetic and therefore there was nothing I could do! The spur to action was about not wanting Tessa to someday look back on an unhappy childhood and, more important, I wanted her to be happy *now*. I felt emboldened by knowing that she wanted to part of the group, that the group would likely not reject her, and that her happiness and well-being were at stake. Over several days I took Tessa by the hand and we joined the play for long periods. I was quite directive at first to make sure that the play could work for Tessa and she would be included. I gave her choices like "Do you want to be a baby squirrel or a mama squirrel?" The other children were quite happy to have more squirrels in the family (of any kind) and even tolerated the very large baby squirrel with the beard (me). Once she felt certain that she would not be rejected and she could just play along to fit in, Tessa was a changed child. While still a bit insecure—a little clingy and hesitant to speak up—on the playground and in the imaginary play center, she was able to be her true self, a not-very-extroverted extrovert. But more important, she was "one of the gang."

Extreme shyness is a debilitating condition called "social phobia," for which a child needs intensive help from a mental health professional. (See "Little Volcanoes" on pp. 185–89 for ideas on dealing with extreme behaviors.)

Anticipating and Preventing Problems Related to Shy, Quiet, and Solitary Children

- Make all children feel important, appreciated, and respected.

- Rotate assignments and classroom jobs, and provide opportunities for the children to make choices and decisions and be leaders in a way that is optimal for each child. A shy child may blossom when given formal opportunities to be a leader (for example, the opportunity to choose children to leave the circle time area based on the colors of their clothes).

- Provide a wide variety of challenging activities that involve different numbers of children. See that some activities are only for one (a puzzle), some for two (a board game), some for three (a lotto game), and so on.

- Accept and appreciate every child's feelings, ideas, and statements, even if these are just attempts at vocalizing.

- Do most of your group activities in small groups, because shy children tend to be less shy around fewer children.

- Give some one-on-one attention to each child at some point during the day.

- Teach all children the skills needed for making and keeping friends. Do not allow children to exclude other children from playing with them. Observe children's play carefully so that you can assist children to effectively play with others.

Solving Problems Related to Shy, Quiet, and Solitary Children

- Accept a reasonable level of shyness as a normal individual difference. Intervene only if shyness causes the child to have problems making friends, playing, and being involved in activities that he really wants to be involved in.

- Don't push the shy child. Respect his need to stay back and move slowly. Continue to offer opportunities and suggestions for participation, however.

- Learn as much as you can about the shy child. Do a home visit so you can see if the child is shy at home. Many shy children are more talkative, even boisterous, at home. The shyness is still something to be concerned about and dealt with, but less so if the child does not act shy at home. Find out about the child's interests, strengths, family, pets, and neighborhood friends. Use this information to connect with the child during class time and to help him connect with other children with similar interests.

- If the child is facing temporary stressful changes in his life, give him extra attention and affection for a while. When you give attention before it is asked for, you reduce the need for him to get attention through inappropriate behavior. Ask him to request this attention in acceptable ways, such as by asking or signaling you.

- At first, incorporate the introverted child into play activities without making him change his behavior too much. For example, if you have involved a group of children in acting out the *Three Little Pigs,* acknowledge the shy child's important role as a watcher and listener: "Thank you for being an attentive audience member. Plays aren't much fun without an audience." As the child feels more comfortable, try to incorporate him even more in the activity by suggesting that he take the role of a tree or a guard or other passive, nonverbal role. Again show appreciation for his important role. Continue to encourage him to take more and more of an active part in the play (Chenfeld 2006).

- Give the shy child several options for participating. For example, if he refuses to join a movement game, ask him if he would like to lead the game or keep track of who had a turn. Provide other options, such as being the "audience" or having the last turn (there is security in first seeing how everyone else participates).

- Limit the amount of time the child spends in a private, quiet area in the room. Tell him that other children want opportunities for quiet also and that it is important to do a variety of activities. Help him get started on a different activity.

- For a child who uses a very quiet voice, stop him quickly and encourage him by saying, "Let's hear your big five-year-old voice. It's beautiful to listen to!" Avoid saying, "Speak up, we can't hear you," as this further embarrasses the child.

- Suggest to the child's parents that they arrange to have him spend time with another child in the class outside of school. This can often cement friendships that provide more play opportunities back at school.

- Encourage the shy child to bring items from home, as "transitional objects," to make the connection between home and class or as a way to help him form friendships. Put some limits on the use of these toys, as discussed in "Toys from Home" on pp. 88–89.

Too clingy

- Put a limit on the amount of time the child can spend by your side. Set a timer and say, "In two minutes I will give you a hug and you can find a place to play or I can help you find a place to play."

- Create a simple system for taking turns for children who would like to sit next to you at a meal or during a circle time. Post a list of the children's names (have them write their own if they are able) and have them cross off their names when they have had a turn. This is a concrete way for those children to know that they will get to be near you, to see when that will be, and to know that the system is equitable.

- Don't reinforce the child's dependency by hugging or holding her too much. Give her very little attention when she is clinging, and physically guide her to an area in which she can play.

- If the child interrupts your interactions with others often, tell her that she can wait or find something to do and you will come to her when you are finished. If she chooses to wait, place your hand gently on her arm while you are talking (so that she will know you have not forgotten her) and tell her that when you remove your hand and turn around, you will be ready to talk to her, but not before. If you do this consistently, she will learn not to interrupt, as she will feel secure that she will get your attention.

- Engage her in a game or a more social, positive interaction with you. Tell the clingy child, "Sit (or stand) across from me. That way I can see your sweet face and hear you better." Play with construction toys, puzzles, or a board game together. Move away when other children join or when she is happily playing on her own.

- Try to connect the child with one other child who would make a good playmate. Find a common interest between them and help them start playing together. Remove yourself when you see they are playing on their own.

- Guide her and another child to an activity that is specifically designed for two, such as a board game.

- Actively teach the child specific social skills and ways to enter play with other children. The fear of involving herself in play with others may come from failed attempts to do so. Help her say the words and do the actions needed to join others: Watch the play and figure out what they are doing and what the roles are; take a complementary role, not a leading role; fit in and go along with the scenario at first. Gradually do less for the child as she develops these skills.

6. MODERN FAMILY: CHILDREN IN NONTRADITIONAL FAMILIES

These families include single-parent families (especially single fathers), same-sex couples, foster care families, children who have been adopted, children being raised by their grandparents, and more. They also include families whose composition may be traditional but their beliefs and practices are outside of the mainstream. For young children, their families' circumstances and practices are all they know and therefore are "normal" to them. However, by about age five or six, children in nontraditional families are starting to realize that their families are different from most others, in large part because their family type is "invisible." They are not reflected in children's books, films, television shows, and other media.

Anticipating and Preventing Problems Related to Children in Nontraditional Families

- Know your families. Know not only their composition and beliefs and practices, but how they want themselves to be viewed by others. Some are very open and will actively help you meet their child's needs and talk about their family with the class. Others are more circumspect and want no special attention focused on their families.

- When reading books and discussing families, include a wide range of families as a matter of course. Even if you have no children from nontraditional families in your class, all children benefit from knowing that families come in a wide variety of "flavors." They also need to know that no two families are exactly alike in their beliefs and practices. In some families children do not watch television at all, in other families children can watch a little television and only a few shows, and in still other families children can watch a lot of television of any type. Children do not celebrate their birthdays with parties in some families, in other families they have small parties with just family members, and in still other families children have big parties with many other children.

Solving Problems Related to Children in Nontraditional Families

Same-sex parents

This is a growing population, as birth technologies improve and as more gay and lesbian couples, and other nontraditional partners, are able to adopt children. There is strong and consistent research evidence that children of gay and lesbian parents are no different from, or are slightly better off than, children of heterosexual couples in regard to all aspects of development, including their mental health and sexual orientation as adults (Patterson 2009). However, there is as much diversity in beliefs and practices among same-sex parents as there is among heterosexual parents.

- The simplest and most appropriate way of talking about sexual orientation with young children is not to deal with the issue of sex at all, but focus on what is visible: some families have two mommies, some have two daddies, and some have a mommy or a daddy.

- Display pictures and read children's books that show male couples and female couples with children. This is important in helping the children of same-sex parents feel that their families are valid. These children are vulnerable, primarily because they will undoubtedly be subjected to bias from other children and adults. They will likely need a bit more support, assurance, protection, and self-esteem building than other children. Make sure you intervene if you see any biased behaviors from others by using the strategies discussed previously.

Children who have been adopted

It is now common practice for children who are adopted to be told so by their parents, but many parents still do not tell their children. While it is true that if the child does not know he was adopted, you probably don't know either, it is important not to assume that if you know, the child knows. Telling a child he has been adopted is a delicate matter that should only be done by parents. If parents are unsure about what and when to tell their child that he is adopted, refer them to some of the resources under "Cultural Responsiveness and Diversity" on p. 285.

- Include adoption whenever talking about birth, babies, and families.

- When discussing adoption, as with all complex issues, give a modest amount of information at a level young children can understand. Focus on the joy of being "chosen" and bringing happiness into the lives of the new parents. The child, after all, makes the family.

Children in foster families

Unfortunately, most children in foster families have experienced abuse or trauma early in life and are likely to have lived in at least one other foster family prior to their current one. So, these children are very vulnerable and many are angry, depressed, despondent, and/or generally insecure. They need lots of encouragement and emotional support. (See the ideas related to specific problematic behaviors in "Problematic Behaviors" starting on page 173.)

- Talk about foster families along with all other types of families. Here are some examples of simple and clear information about children living in foster families: Foster children are cared for by adults who are not their parents because their parents cannot take care of them. Some children live with their foster parents for a short time, for a few days, but other children live with them for a long time. There are many reasons that some parents can't take care of their children. Usually it is because they are very sick and they don't have anyone to help them. If their parents start getting better, then the children living with foster families can *visit* with their parents. If their parents recover (that means they get completely better), then the children can *live* with their parents again.

- It is important to have regular contact and good communication with the child's foster parent(s) and her case worker/social worker. Because most case workers are overwhelmed with too many cases, the child might also have a volunteer court-appointed special advocate (CASA), who may be the most knowledgeable and available person in the child's life. Contact this person to share and request information about the child's situation, behavior, and progress, to the extent that is possible and legal.

- Familiarize yourself with the issue of children in foster care and how the foster care system operates in your state and city. Know about the weaknesses of the system: after experiencing trauma, a child has to then adjust to the major change of living in a different home with strangers; too many children are abused in foster care homes; and other problems occur in these settings. Also know its strengths: a child can be immediately taken out of danger and live in a home rather than an institution; the vast majority of foster parents are kind, caring people greatly skilled at helping an emotionally fragile child feel more secure.

Families with nontraditional beliefs and practices

Some families are part of a religious or cultural minority and have beliefs and practices that are very different from other families and from typical classroom practices. Most, but not all, of these parents will send their children to schools or child care centers that also follow the same beliefs and practices. Make sure every family knows your approach to celebrating holidays and birthdays when they enroll. Meet with such parents to negotiate any alterations of your approach that is acceptable to both of you. This may involve, for example, a Jewish parent showing the children how Hanukkah is celebrated or a Muslim parent explaining why girls wear head scarves. Some cultures require girls to wear skirts or dresses, though many parents allow their daughters to wear pants or thick tights under the dress. If there are unusual dietary restrictions or requirements that involve only one or two families, parents should supply food for their child. If a fair compromise cannot be worked out, the parents may feel more comfortable placing their child in a program affiliated with their particular religion or belief system.

- Help parents recognize that many religious holidays have secular aspects to them. Dyeing eggs and egg hunts at Easter and Santa Claus and trees at Christmas have become secular U.S. cultural symbols and events. Although these practices are affiliated with a specific religion, most of them began as pagan rituals and symbols, related to seasonal changes and fertility. Almost all children know about and enjoy these activities and traditions. However, limit the amount of time you spend celebrating traditional holidays in typical ways because the children get exposed to them from many other sources. Expand children's cultural understanding and awareness by presenting a wide array of holidays and traditions from many different cultures and countries, as described in "Diversity, Difference, and Democracy" on pp. 122–39.

- Use children's excitement about holidays to foster learning and growth in all areas of development. Invite the children to classify and match Easter eggs of various patterns or make books for holiday or birthday presents. Make your classroom a place where all children's interests and families' beliefs and practices are supported and then deepened and expanded.

7. GOING WITH THE FLOE: CHILDREN WHOSE FAMILY LANGUAGE IS OTHER THAN ENGLISH (FLOES)

The term FLOEs has not been commonly used for these children. (See "New Terms" on pp. 11–12 in the introduction for an explanation of this terminology.) The number of FLOE children has increased rapidly in recent years and will continue to do so in all parts of the United States. Among the challenges you'll face are helping them understand basic rules of the classroom, to communicate with other children and make friends, and to be equal members of the classroom community. Communicating with their parents is another challenge.

Your general, long-term goal is to help these children become bicultural and bilingual (or multicultural and multilingual). That means putting a high value on home language and culture while supporting new skills and abilities related to learning English and U.S. culture. It is challenging to help children learn a new set of behaviors—some of which may be in opposition to those learned and valued at home—and to do this while not diminishing the importance of the home culture. But it is achievable and necessary to help these children be successful. For example, in mainstream U.S. culture, looking directly in the speaker's eyes is considered respectful. However, in many cultures, looking down while an adult or higher-status person is talking is a sign of respect. If this happens, you can tell the child that you appreciate that he is being respectful, that it is good to do this at home, but most adults want you to look directly at them when they talk to you. This "teaching" mode is a good strategy for helping children learn to be bicultural, while being supportive of their home cultures. Many adults who once learned English in U.S. classrooms talk about how "different" and "inferior" they felt at the time. They also report that their teachers often did things that contributed to these feelings, rather than to help make life easier for them. Of course, there also are many positive stories of supportive, caring teachers. This chapter includes ideas for helping these children negotiate the daily transitions among home culture, community culture, and school culture.

My own stepdaughter (now an adult) came to the United States when she was four years old. Her native, home language was Romanian. At first, she joined the children's play at preschool by taking the role of the dog. Her barking skills were superb and, of course, "bark" is a universal language. She had a wonderful teacher who recognized that, for her at this time, taking this role was a positive action, not something to worry about. The next year, she attended kindergarten at a French immersion school. This was not as crazy as it sounds, as her mother and older brother spoke French and her brother was at this same school. However, this teacher was concerned that my daughter was spending "quite a lot of time being a dog." When I said, "I know, she's been like this ever since she was a puppy!" she didn't laugh. That's when I began thinking that this was not the right school for her. So, for first grade we sent her to the neighborhood public school, which had a Spanish immersion program! Now, at twenty-three, she can get by in Spanish and French and is fluent in Romanian, English, and German. And it all started with a bark.

Anticipating and Preventing Problems Related to FLOEs

- Become aware of what constitutes U.S. middle-class cultural practices and values, which operate in most schools and programs, and how they are distinct from other cultures. This will help you see where children and families may differ. Teachers in most U.S. classrooms foster individualism and independence ("do your own work"). Children from many other cultures often mistake this for coldness, a lack of personal connectedness, and an uncaring teacher.

- Learn some basic words and phrases in the child's language, especially those that may comfort her in times of stress. Also learn some phrases that will help you communicate with parents. Do this while continuing to learn as much of their language as you can.

- The most important and strongest parts of communication are nonverbal. Creative teachers find many ways to support and connect with children with whom they do not share a language by being emotionally responsive and sensitive. Smiles, hugs, encouraging nods, gestures, observing for needs, and helping them meet those needs all go a long way toward supporting children without knowing their home language.

- If you have a number of children in your group who speak the same language and the rest speak English, strive toward a bilingual classroom if you or an assistant can speak both languages. This puts equal value on English and the other language and helps the English-speaking children by introducing them to a new language. Start with teaching everyone songs, fingerplays, and "functional dialogue"—such as words and phrases used during mealtimes—in the second language and then expand from there.

- Find ways to communicate with families, such as having notes translated. Assist families in linking with resources in the community that help immigrant families and in finding classes that teach English to adults. If families feel connected and valued by the school or center, they will be supportive of you and their child's growth and development.

- Identify some of the unique aspects of the children's cultures, including styles of communication, popular foods, beliefs, routines, songs, dances, games, and folktales. Use this information to add to your curriculum and obtain materials that support their home culture in the classroom. This will also help other children by deepening their cultural understanding and appreciation of diversity.

- If you have a diverse group of multiple-language learners who speak a number of different languages, find some commonalties among them to connect them with one another. In one child care class in a diverse community of many different immigrant groups, the teacher found that imaginary play around a restaurant theme was very successful because many of the children's families were involved in the restaurant business. Common items and activities vary slightly across different cultures and countries, such as the tools we use to eat, types of bread we eat, kinds of clothes we wear, and the way we carry things.

Solving Problems Related to FLOEs

Subgroups of children who speak the same language

It is fairly common to have a number of children in the same class who speak the same (non-English) language. Some of these children may even be related, typically as cousins. They tend to stick together and form a tight-knit group. The problem with this behavior is that it sets the children apart socially from the rest of the children and can delay their process of learning English and U.S. culture. Using the bilingual approach described previously can help. Take steps to bring children in the subgroup into the main group.

- Connect other children with them through their mutual interests or skills; for example, block building, cars/trucks, drawing/painting, music/singing, or science.

- Provide specific help to all children to get them to play and interact with each other.

- Teach both groups of children some basic words and phrases in each other's language, as well as gestures, and social cues (eye contact, gentle touching) and help the children use them.

Problems with a bilingual assistant

Many times the assistant teacher or aide speaks both the language of a number of the children in the class and English. He is expected to help children who are monolingual or just beginning to learn English to understand what is happening and to assist you, as the teacher, to speak to them. However, in some cases the bilingual aide may not have much education or professional experience in early childhood education and this may result in some clashes between you and him.

- Try to prevent such clashes by giving him a thorough orientation and rationale to your teaching approach. Also, as much as possible, explain as you go along why you are doing what you do.

- Advocate for training opportunities for him from your school or agency.

- Enlist his help and support in pursuing the goal of bicultural and bilingual competence for all children. This will help avoid a common problem where the assistant speaks his native language to those children who understand it, almost all the time and nearly exclusively.

- Sort out which of the assistant's behaviors that concern you are culturally related and which are due to lack of training. You may need to ask some questions and have a discussion with him to determine the differences. For example, you might say, "I want to understand your approach. Tell me about your discussion with Carlito this morning." Do this when he does good things as well as things that concern you. You might also need to ask other people of the same cultural group about the behaviors to determine what is cultural and what is just practice. Be flexible with the culturally related behaviors and use the other behaviors as opportunities to teach the assistant new skills.

- Choose your battles carefully. If you are instructing and correcting too often, you will undermine your relationship. Start by working on one specific concern that is likely to meet with success. Tell him what he does particularly well so not all your feedback is negative.

The child who won't speak at all

The "silent stage" is a common phase in the course of learning a new language. Most people (of any age) who are newly immersed in a foreign language environment go through it. During this stage, the person is learning by listening intently and is waiting to feel more confident before speaking publicly. In young children, it typically lasts one or two months but can last longer, especially for children who are shy. If it goes on for much longer, seek the help of a speech and language pathologist (with parent permission) who knows about children who are learning a new language. Often, such children will first communicate with a particular person with whom they feel safe, usually another child or a teacher. Typically these first communications will be in a very soft, quiet voice. Support and assist them, but don't push them to speak. Provide some alternative ways for them to communicate—like pointing, gesturing, or using sign language and picture boards—but not to the extent that it becomes an easy way out of speaking. Seek ideas from the children's parents and use some of the strategies recommended for children who are shy under "Is It Introversion, Insecurity, or Something Else?" on pp. 133–36.

8. EVERY DAY IS LIKE HALLOWEEN . . . WITHOUT THE CANDY: CHILDREN WITH EXTREME FEARS

Most young children have common fears, such as a fear of spiders, strangers, the dark, or being left alone. These fears are healthy if some possibility of danger or harm really exists. Extremely fearful children are obsessed by their fears. They will talk about them and have anxiety about them often and at times when little or no cause is apparent.

Fears develop because young children have active imaginations and are becoming aware of cause-and-effect relationships: "If it is dark, then dangers can't be seen, and if they can't be seen, then I can't protect myself." They have an increasing awareness of how many ways they can be hurt, and they have conflicts within themselves over being independent but still needing adult protection. Fears of monsters can represent children's anxieties about not being able to control their own anger or aggressive impulses. For toddlers or developmentally delayed children, some fears develop because to them the world is still an unsure place: "Is my brother with a mask on still my brother or is he somebody else?"

Some gifted children develop extreme fears of events like hurricanes, airplane crashes, earthquakes, fires, or epidemics. They are aware of these events from the news and they understand them and their awful consequences, but they lack the ability to comprehend that they are unlikely to experience them or be hurt by them.

Extreme fears can develop as a result of the factors discussed above and the added experience of a trauma. In most cases, extreme fears are linked directly to a troubling experience, such as fear of fires after seeing a neighbor's house burn or fear of water after a near drowning. In other cases, the connection is less clear. For example, a child who has witnessed a violent act may become extremely fearful of the dark even though darkness was not connected to the event. A neglected or an abused child may have a number of extreme fears, although none of the fears are necessarily related to her particular trauma.

Anticipating and Preventing Problems Related to Fears

- When families enroll their children, ask about any stressful events in the child's life and about any fears the child has.

- Maintain regular communication with parents so that they will inform you of any problems or traumatic events in their children's lives.

- Create a sense of security for all children by having a consistent daily schedule, comforting routines, child-centered curriculum, an attractive and well-organized physical environment, and a warm emotional climate. Give individual attention and positive regard to every child, but more to those who need it most. Whenever possible, make children aware of any and all changes before they take place. Children feel safer when they know what will happen next.

- Support and validate the feelings of all children, even if you can't support the behaviors. For example, "I can hear that you are very angry. I would be angry, too, if someone teased me. Let me help you talk to him about it."

- Provide many opportunities for children to safely express and deal with their strong feelings and fears through a wide variety of methods. Children can talk about fears during a sharing session that is carefully mediated by the teacher. They can also draw pictures; make up stories that adults can write down for them; use dress-up clothes and props for dramatic play about escaping from or outwitting monsters, "bad guys," and other scary things; and play out scary scenarios with small figures of people and animals, including a few scary ones like lions, gorillas, and dinosaurs.

- Read a wide variety of stories to children about fearful events that children overcome. While there are helpful children's books that deal directly with fears, original fairy tales do this better than most other forms of children's literature. Stories such as the "Wolf and the Seven Little Kids" and "Hansel and Gretel" put children or young animals in extremely dangerous circumstances, but through their own abilities they come out of these adventures alive and even better off. These stories are very comforting and can even be healing for children who have experienced trauma, particularly when they act out the stories.

Solving Problems Related to Fears

- Children with extreme fears usually need help from a professional counselor. Recommend this and with the parents' permission, ask the counselor for advice about helping the child in the classroom. Counseling will be of most benefit if the whole family is involved. Provide suggestions for finding counselors who are skilled in working with young children.

- Support the child's feelings no matter how irrational they seem to you. Avoid the temptation to say anything like: "Come on, there's nothing to be afraid of." The fears are very real to the child. Do not make the child do something that she is terrified of. Support her by saying: "I know dogs are frightening to you. You can hold my hand, and you don't have to pet him. I will protect you."

- Join the child's fantasy about the fear and help her overcome it. For example, if a child is afraid to go into a closet for some art materials because there is a monster in it, go into the closet with her to get rid of the monster. Follow her lead by asking, "What can we do to get rid of the monster?" Perhaps you will both need to catch the monster, put it in a garbage bag, and throw it in the dumpster.

- Most counselors help people overcome their fears by very gradually introducing the fearful element and letting the person get used to it slowly. You can do the same. For example, you can help a child overcome a fear of water through the following steps, moving on to the next step only when she feels comfortable and in control:

  1. Have her play in a gentle sprinkler or hose aimed at her feet and hold her hand.
  2. Hold only one finger.
  3. Let go and have her play on her own.
  4. Gradually raise the level and intensity of the water.
  5. Have her stand in a small wading pool and hold her hand if needed.
  6. Have her stand in the wading pool on her own.
  7. Have her sit down in the wading pool while you hold her body.
  8. Have her sit while you hold her hand.
  9. Have her sit while you hold a finger.
  10. Have her sit on her own.
  11. If you have access to a larger pool, have her wade in the shallow end while you hold her body.
  12. Hold only her hand.
  13. Hold only a finger.
  14. Have her play on her own.
  15. Gradually have her go into deeper water.

- Some children can move through these steps more quickly than others or may be able to skip some steps and still be successful, while other children may need to take even smaller steps. Make sure the child controls the process: "If you need my hand back again, just tell me."

- If the child talks about her fears very often, give only minimal attention to her comments and limit them. Say something like this: "I'll listen carefully to you for one more minute (set a timer), and then you need to choose an activity." Respond so she will know you listened and then help her engage in active play with other children.

- Give the child many opportunities to be in control, such as by assigning her the job of the "environmentalist" who turns the lights off when leaving the room. Give the child appropriate but real choices as often as possible: "Would you like to sit in the red chair or green chair?" "Who do you want to be your field-trip buddy?" "Choose the book that you would like me to read to you."

- Make up stories or read books related to the child's particular fear. In the invented story, describe how a child or small animal overcame a fear that is similar but not the same as the child's fear.

- Provide specific, factual information about the object of the fear and ways to take control of fearful situations. For example, help a child who is very afraid of dogs by saying, "Only pet a dog if you know the dog's name and if the owner tells you it's okay. Most dogs will not chase you if you don't run. Most dogs will go away if you say 'go' in a loud, firm voice, stamp your foot, and point with an outstretched arm." Demonstrate this and have her practice.

- Talk with the child's parents. Find out if they know where the fear comes from. A child in my class had an intense fear of insects. One day, her mother came to pick her up and suddenly the mother started screaming and flailing her arms. Apparently an insect of some kind buzzed her. Although I now knew where the fear came from, there was not much I could do about it. The mother did not see her daughter's fear as a problem and had no desire to change her behavior.

- Reassure the parents that with support most children grow out of or overcome their fears, if they are not too extreme.

9. TOO MUCH TOO SOON: THE SEXUALLY PRECOCIOUS CHILD

This is the child who seems to know about sex, acts sexually or provocatively, or engages other children in games that simulate sexual activity or involve touching genitals. It goes beyond the typical behaviors of young children who are curious about what other people's bodies look like and occasionally want to "play doctor." This child wants to do these activities often and may manipulate other children in disturbingly sophisticated ways. The child who exhibits these behaviors may do so because of any or all of the following reasons:

- The child has been inappropriately exposed to sex acts and is imitating the behaviors he has seen from parents, older siblings, relatives, babysitters, or neighbors.

- The behaviors are an effective way to get attention, control others through manipulation, and feel "grown up" and in control.

- The child has been sexually abused and sees himself as having value in a relationship only because of his body. A sexually abused child can come to believe that sex play is the way to connect with others and a necessary part of a relationship.

Anticipating and Preventing Sexually Precocious Behavior

- In a natural, relaxed way, provide opportunities for children, who are all naturally curious about bodies, to see what bodies look like. Have children's books about bodies (see the resources under "Sexual Development, Sex Roles, and Gender Identity" on pp. 295–96) and have boys and girls share bathrooms. At about five years of age, some children begin to want privacy, and that should be respected. Give older preschoolers the option of sharing a bathroom or having privacy. Supervise the bathrooms carefully to make sure that no child is being manipulated by a sexually precocious child. A relaxed atmosphere about bodies will help children understand that the human body and its natural functions, such as elimination, is different from sexuality. This will also reduce the desire and need to explore bodies through playing doctor or other games.

- Have books that show bodies in natural, nonsexualized ways. This is usually done through tasteful drawings that are detailed and accurate and not cartoonlike. Often books that help children avoid unwanted touches have such illustrations. There are several such books listed among the resources under "Sexual Development, Sex Roles, and Gender Identity" on pp. 295–96.

- Make sure that all children can be seen by an adult at all times. Tell children that there are no private or secret hiding places at school, indoors or outside.

- Talk to children about protecting themselves from sexual abuse and the importance of getting help if they are being sexually abused. (See "Babies, Breasts, Bottoms, and Boundaries" on pp. 106–9 for more information.)

- Give all children lots of attention for who they are and for appropriate things they say and do. Build the self-worth of all your children with this type of attention. Note that the absence of a great deal of positive attention from adults can create an atmosphere in which children seek attention from other children or accept attention from abusive or manipulative adults. When children seek attention from other children, the result is a classroom of children with behaviors that are difficult to manage, such as acting out, silliness, and the controlling of some children by others.

- Give minimal attention or praise for how children look or what they wear. If a child comes in with a new dress, screeching with delight, "Look what I'm wearing," respond by saying, "It's a lovely dress, but I like you no matter what you are wearing."

- Know your families. If a child starts exhibiting sexually precocious behaviors, you may already have an idea where the behaviors might be coming from based on what you know about the family. When this happened with a child in my class, I suspected that her older brother was abusing her, having seen him interacting with her and with his friends and having talked with him on several occasions. Of course I was not able to act on my suspicion as I had no evidence, but this somehow made me feel more empathetic and protective of the child. I took stronger action where I had some influence—the only place where I had any influence—which was in my interactions with the child while she was in my class. I gave her more emotional support, positive attention, and appropriate affection. In time, her manipulative behaviors became less frequent, but the surprising change was to her general personality. Her "hard" demeanor melted and a happier, nicer, more likeable child emerged.

Solving Problems Related to the Sexually Precocious Child

When a child manipulates other children

- In some cases, a child does not so much manipulate as initiate. The other children do not feel uncomfortable and may even enjoy the activity, but it's not something they would ever initiate themselves. However, sexually precocious children initiate it often and with many different children. Even mutual exploration is not appropriate behavior at school. (See "Mutual Exploration" in "Babies, Breasts, Bottoms, and Boundaries" on p. 109 for ideas on how to handle this.)

- Intervene calmly in the situation where a child is getting others to do what she wants. Remind them both about private parts. Help the child who is being controlled by the sexually precocious child to stand up for himself. Give him specific words he can use to assert his right not to be taken advantage of. He can say, "I don't have to do what you tell me to." Help both children come up with other, acceptable ways to play together. Tell the manipulative child that you will help her learn better ways to play. Give her positive feedback often when she interacts with others positively: "Thank you for playing fairly. It makes our classroom a fun and safe place for everyone." Watch the child very closely so you can intervene before she manipulates another child.

Grown-up play in the imaginary play area

- If a child spends a great deal of time in the imaginary play area acting out sexually advanced behavior, provide materials and a starting structure for the imaginary play area to be a restaurant, an office, a store, or another community place. This will be less conducive to the behavior than a house or a kitchen area. Spend time playing with the children in this area and redirect the play if it goes in a sexual direction by asking for ideas for other play scenarios, providing them if necessary, and introducing new and interesting props into the play.

- All children are bombarded with images of overt sexuality from movies, TV, and advertising. Tell the children that it is like driving a car. It is something that adults can do, but children cannot.

Appropriate affection

- Provide the sexually precocious child with a great deal of positive attention when she is acting appropriately. Give her hugs and safe physical affection (put your arm around her shoulder; hold her hand) so she will learn how normal relations between adults and children should and could be. Let her know that she is worthwhile and loved for who she is, not for what she does or doesn't do.

Determining if the child is being sexually abused

- Teach children about personal safety as described under "Anticipating and Preventing Problems" in "Babies, Breasts, Bottoms, and Boundaries" on pp. 107–8. There have been many cases where a child has told his teacher that he is being abused after hearing the teacher say, "If someone is touching your private parts, tell an adult. If that adult does not believe you or doesn't stop the bad touches, keep telling adults until someone believes you and helps you."

- Provide opportunities for children to draw pictures and dictate stories about their fears and concerns.

- Create some safe one-to-one time for the two of you to talk casually about a variety of things. This will give the child opportunities to talk about any abuse that may be happening. If it is happening, tell her that you will help her make it stop. Follow your state's rules and your program's procedures for reporting abuse. If a social service agency is involved with the family, ask someone in the agency if he has knowledge that sexual abuse has occurred recently. Ask any of the social service or health professionals involved for advice about how to help the child. (See "Save the Children" on pp. 237–39 for information about indicators of sexual abuse.)

10. EQUAL PLAY FOR EQUAL WORTH: GENDER IDENTITY, GENDER EQUITY, AND SEX-ROLE ISSUES

In a typical class, you will have children with a range of sex-role and gender perceptions about themselves and others. Most boys and girls take their own gender in stride and happily engage in a wide variety of activities with other children of either sex. However, some boys will act very masculine and some girls very feminine, expressing exaggerated and stereotypical sex-role behaviors. They rarely play with children of the other sex and may act biased to other children who do not behave the same way. These behaviors can be a reflection of what children see from older siblings, parents, and the media, or they can be masks to hide insecurities, or both. The behaviors are problematic because they restrict children's options, do not align with current social reality, are rigid rather than flexible, and are usually not genuine.

Some boys have a clear and consistent preference for toys and activities more associated with girls, and some girls prefer traditional boy toys and activities. They usually prefer playing with children of the other sex. Ideally, there shouldn't be any gender-assigned toys and activities for young children, but a look down the toy aisle of a store or through the rack of Halloween costumes makes it clear that we are far from this ideal. These children who may, even at four years old, identify as being of the other sex, are a minority with behaviors that many adults (but very few children) view as problematic, if not unnatural and pathological, especially among boys. All this occurs in spite of recent significant progress toward ensuring the equal rights of gay men and women. This is why these children need support and acceptance and may even need protection from bias.

The goal in regard to gender identity and sex roles is to ensure that both boys and girls experience a wide variety of activities and roles and feel comfortable in them. When this happens, and when children are valued and accepted for who they are, not for how they act, the exaggerated gender-based behaviors will diminish and there will be much mixed-gender play.

Anticipating and Preventing Problems Related to Gender Issues

The following ideas are designed to help you create a classroom atmosphere where a broad range of sex-role behavior will be accepted and supported. To support healthy sex-role and gender identity development, implement these ideas even if you do not currently have a child in your class who identifies with the other sex or one who exhibits exaggerated sex-role behavior.

- Eliminate or avoid any activity or routine that unnecessarily distinguishes children based on their sex. For example, avoid forming a boys' line and a girls' line or counting the number of boys and the number of girls in attendance.

- Avoid complimenting children for their clothes. Compliment all children for *appropriate* dress: "Those jeans will be perfect for playing and climbing outside."

- Teach children the only actual difference between the sexes. Boys and men have a penis and testicles. Girls and women have a vagina and clitoris. Differences between girls and boys are basically physical ones and are not related to ability and skill. In her 2013 HBO special *We Are Miracles*, the comedian Sarah Silverman said, "Stop telling girls they can be anything they want when they grow up. Not because it's wrong, but because it would've never occurred to them they couldn't." So, tell the children that both girls and boys can do and be anything they want. Show and display pictures of girls/women and boys/men in a wide variety of jobs, hobbies, and roles, such as female construction workers and men taking care of babies.

- Actively encourage boys and girls to play with each other, form friendships, and accept a wide range of behaviors from each other. When pairing children for an activity or to be field-trip partners, use a system in which children are paired randomly each time this happens. This can be done by selecting name tags from a box.

- Include in the imaginary play area male- and female-associated materials and clothing, such as plastic tools, ties, sport jackets, and men's and women's shoes and hats (along with the typical dresses). Let children know that they can dress up in any of the clothes they choose.

- If the imaginary play area tends to attract mostly girls and the block area tends to attract mostly boys, arrange the room so that these areas are right next to each other to encourage play between them.

- Read stories that include strong female characters and nurturing males. Avoid stories that reinforce stereotypes or leave out female characters. Read stories that specifically counter sex-role stereotypes and that feature children who identify with the other sex. (See the list of children's books in the resources under "Sexual Development, Sex Roles, and Gender Identity" on pp. 295–96.)

- Include females in songs and fingerplays. For example, each finger during "Where Is Thumbkin?" can be "ma'am" as easily as "sir." It also can be a gender-neutral "friend." In the same way, the monkeys jumping on the bed can be female as easily as male, and the doctor who is called when they fall off the bed can be a woman.

- Assure parents that you enjoy and care about all children regardless of individual differences in behavior or appearance. Tell them that all children are unique— they all have strengths and weaknesses. The nature of their character and their well-being is much more important than their preferences for playmates, toys, or dress. Let parents know that you will not tolerate teasing and meanness in your class and that children will be taught to appreciate differences and to be supportive and positive toward others.

Solving Problems Related to Gender Issues

Teasing

- Intervene when another child rejects, laughs at, or teases the child who identifies with the other sex. Help him verbally stand up for himself with statements such as, "I can play whatever I want. I can be whoever I want." Have him practice saying this. Tell the child who is doing the teasing that "We use words that help, not hurt." Assure her that you would help her if she were being teased. As soon as possible, shine a positive light on the child being teased specifically for the behaviors he's being teased about. For example, invite him to show off his cheerleading skills to the other children or select him to play Goldilocks. (See "Mean Girls, the Prequel" on pp. 204–6 for more information about intervening when one child is mean to another.)

Exaggerated sex-role behaviors

- Deal with exaggerated sex-role behavior by limiting the time the child spends in such activities (as you would any uncreative, repetitive activity) and redirecting him into a more creative and varied but similar activity. You can also extend and deepen the activity by adding variety and challenge. Cheerleaders, male or female, can learn new tumbles and movements. They work hard at stretching and exercising. The routines are often complicated.

- Children who engage in exaggerated sex-role behavior, particularly boys who act "macho" and girls who act "sexy," need to know that it is acceptable to be the child they are. For some children, encouraging them to be the "baby" in imaginary play meets an emotional need and reduces the amount of adultlike behaviors. Also do many other things to build a children's self-efficacy: support strengths, give positive feedback for appropriate behaviors, engage in playful interactions, and give them verbal affection and physical affection if they enjoy it.

Helping parents

Almost all parents of a child who identifies with the other sex know this about their child. Many, however, are in denial about it or believe that it's just a phase. Some will want to know how they can best help and support their child. Parents of girls may be more accepting because "tomboy" behavior is socially acceptable. Parents of boys may have a harder time because society is less willing to tolerate effeminate behavior in males. Girls can wear pants or a skirt, socks or tights, and play with just about any toy. The term "sissy" has a much more negative connotation than "tomboy."

- Talk with and write notes to the parents often about the positive aspects of their child: "He has a great attention span." "She loves books." "He's a champ at putting together puzzles." Let parents know that you are willing and able to help and are available to talk whenever they have any questions or concerns.

- Share resources, such as children's books, with parents who are ready and interested in supporting their children and/or in helping their children understand and appreciate gender diversity.

11. REVERSED ROLES: CHILDREN WHO ARE TOO RESPONSIBLE

These children do not show problematic behavior in the typical way, and therefore, you can easily overlook them. They are the children who take care of others' needs beyond what is expected or reasonable for young children. They may focus on other children whom they see as weak and vulnerable and "parent" them. They may focus on adults and show unusual concern for their feelings and needs. On the surface, these behaviors are altruistic and positive. However, when children behave this way too often and too consistently, when others don't want or need the help, and when they put their own needs last, the behaviors are problematic and of concern. By and large, these are children who are denied the opportunity to grow up free of adult responsibilities and to be taken care of by adults, which is the right of every child.

In many cases, overly responsible children are growing up in homes where roles are reversed. The children are taking care of their parents, psychologically if not actually. Whether the parents are not functioning well because of alcohol or drugs (most common), poor health, emotional problems, mental illness, developmental delay, or other reasons, the effect on children is similar. They learn to take on the parent role in the household for their own survival. Often, these children are the oldest child in the family or have no siblings. Children who feel they are worthless because of years of negative feedback also can exhibit these behaviors. They have found that they can get positive feedback and satisfaction from doing something that comes easy to them—putting themselves last. Most often, these children are girls, because these behaviors are more socially acceptable in females, more expected of females, and generally modeled more by females. If this pattern of behavior continues, it can have a profound effect on the children's lives. They will continue to deny their own needs and may develop destructive behaviors as adults, such as being overly passive, allowing themselves to be victimized, living with poor health, or abusing drugs or alcohol.

Anticipating and Preventing Problems Related to Children Who Are Too Responsible

- Make the development of self-efficacy a vital part of your curriculum and integrate it throughout all parts of the day. During lunch, discuss the children's accomplishments that day. Help them evaluate themselves in positive ways by asking what they have done that makes them proud of themselves. One of the best strategies for building self-efficacy is to challenge children cognitively and physically without pushing or pressuring them. This sends the message "I believe you are smart and capable."

- Help children switch roles or create new, more equal roles in imaginary play situations. This will reduce the amount of time some children dominate others or some children spend in inferior roles, such as the "baby" or the "dog."

- Inform the children through books, puppets, and plays about the appropriate roles of adults and children. Show situations where children are told to do unacceptable things, such as a five-year-old being told to care for younger siblings for several hours. Ask them for ideas on ways they can refuse. Give them ideas if necessary. Tell them that if they find themselves in a situation that feels uncomfortable or scary, they need to find another adult and ask that person for help and keep asking until someone helps them.

- Serve as a role model of an appropriately responsible adult. Explain how some responsibilities in the classroom belong to the children (using toys correctly), some to the teacher (providing safe toys), and some to both the children and the teacher (developing a new imaginary play area).

- Show children how to be helpful without completely doing things for others. For example, explain that they can help another child with a puzzle by doing one or two pieces and then letting her finish, or by showing her how to match the color of a puzzle piece to the color on the puzzle frame.

- Meet with parents regularly and do home visits if at all possible. This will give you great insight into family situations, values, and challenges.

Solving Problems Related to Children Who Are Too Responsible

- Intervene when you see overly responsible behaviors. Tell the child that you appreciate her helpfulness (these are usually children who are emotionally fragile just below the surface) but that she needs to play with the other children. Redirect her into an activity and spend a few minutes making sure she is on the right track.

- Help the child who is the focus of the caretaking behaviors by giving him the words he needs to assert his independence: "I can do it myself, thank you." The child may also need to learn to negotiate imaginary play roles to be more equal: "Let's both be doctors, and the doll can be the patient."

- Set up games that involve children taking turns and participating in equal relationships. Board games or lotto games, store bought or teacher made, are good for this. Make sure the games are easy enough for children to do on their own but challenging enough to make them engaging. Guide the overly responsible child to these games and try to have her play with a child who will stand up to her but not dominate her.

- Work on the root cause of the problem. If you discover, for example, that the child lives with an alcoholic or drug-abusing parent, seek help from local agencies that deal with helping people in these circumstances. In almost all cases, these agencies will suggest ways to assist the family and the child without violating trust or scaring them off.

- Find quiet time to spend with the child in an area that is not too near other children. Read a book or make up a story related to (but not specifically about) her problem. Establish rapport and be open, empathetic, and ready to listen so she will talk about her situation. This will take much time and patience, as most young children have difficulty knowing that they have a problem and they assume everybody lives the same way.

12. ADULTS' PROBLEMS, CHILDREN'S TROUBLES: CHILDREN WHO EXPERIENCE TRAUMA

Children who have witnessed or experienced violence or tragedy firsthand will need a long time to heal and will almost always need an initial period of intensive support from a mental health professional who specializes in helping young children cope with trauma. Whether they witnessed or experienced the trauma, children's responses to such tragic events will vary. But all of them need firm and consistent reassurance that they are safe, that adults are protecting them from harm, that the world is predictable, and that people are basically good. Although in reality we cannot guarantee 100 percent protection for our children, they need to feel safe and secure to grow up healthy.

Anticipating and Preventing Problems Related to the Impacts of Trauma

- Create an emotionally supportive climate. These children need to be told and shown often that they are cared about and important. Establish a clear expectation that children will care for and about each other. Actively teach the skills of caring—negotiating, turn-taking, asking for what you need, asking about others' needs, being respectful, offering help to others, and comforting each other.

- Keep pop culture and commercialism out of your classroom and greatly limit the pop culture that children bring into the classroom. Make it a sanctuary from the commercial world. Display photographs (particularly of the children and their families) and art (particularly the children's work). Have plenty of high-quality children's literature available.

- Talk to parents about the importance of limiting all TV/video viewing and video games, especially those meant for adults, such as the news, scary movies, and violent games.

- When children are within earshot, do not discuss events or issues with other adults that are difficult for children to comprehend or that may frighten them. Talk to parents about the importance of limiting such discussion at home. Wait for the children to go to bed.

- Teach children some basic media literacy skills. (See "Child Advocacy" under "'A' Is for Advocacy" on pp. 266–67.)

Solving Problems Related to the Impacts of Trauma

- Give yourself ample time to sort out your own feelings about a trauma that a child has experienced or that everyone in the community has experienced, such as a natural disaster, shooting, bombing, or family lost in a house fire. Talk at length with empathetic people who can help you deal with feelings of outrage and sadness. Remain calm and informed in order to help children. They will pick up and mirror your emotional state more readily than the words you say.

- Keep your routines consistent and activities simple. Children find assurance in sameness during times of stress. This is not the time to make major changes or go on a field trip to an unfamiliar place.

- Increase the amount and variety of calming activities. Match the activities with particular children. Some will find music soothing; others enjoy being held; some need to talk; and others will want to listen to stories or look at beautiful picture books.

- Add more sensory activities and give children more time to engage in them. These include sand and water play and playdough and clay.

- Provide a wide variety of art materials and media. Encourage children to draw pictures about what they have seen and how they feel.

- Watch children carefully for how they are reacting to the event. Look for signs of stress and changes in behavior. Talk with and comfort children at the first sign of stress.

- Observe their spontaneous imaginary play to see how they may be "playing out" the event. If necessary, build on the play to include roles that offer help in emergency situations such as EMTs, firefighters, and police officers.

- Ask children what they know, have seen, or heard about the event. This will give you insight into what they are feeling and how they are thinking about it. Immediately clear up any misconceptions or wrong information they may have. Hearing their concerns and interpretations will help you know what to say and not say to them about the event.

- Validate and support their feelings. Tell them no more than they need to know in as simple terms as you can: "It was very scary, but now we are safe." "We all feel very sad and worried, but I, your parents, and many others will work hard to make sure that it doesn't happen again."

- In discussions with children, follow the advice of Fred Rogers (Mr. Rogers) and "focus on the helpers." Even in tragedies of epic proportions like the Holocaust, there were numerous (even if not nearly enough) helpers such as Oscar Schindler, Miep Gies, and the Danish people whose boat lift saved nearly all of Denmark's Jews. During most emergencies and disasters, firefighters, police, doctors, nurses, and neighbors are able to save many lives. This gives us hope and faith in others, which helps counteract the fear we have of perpetrators or of natural disasters.

- In response to children's questions, it may be necessary to say, "No one knows at this time" or "I don't know, but I will try to find out and tell you later." This will give you time to figure out the best way to answer them.

- Tell children, "Your parents and I will take care of you. We will protect you." Tell them this before they even ask for comfort as well as after. Tell them even if you have some doubts about your ability to do it.

- If a child makes a statement that generalizes blame for terrorist acts on a particular group or religion (usually repeating what she heard from adults), respond by saying that there are many, many more people from the same group who are very caring and peaceful. Many of these people are also working hard to stop the violent people in their group.

- Read stories to them about children (or small animals) who make it safely through scary and traumatic events. Some of the original versions of the Brothers Grimm's fairy tales do this better than most contemporary stories. These include "Hansel and Gretel," the "Wolf and the Seven Little Kids," "Tom Thumb," and "Rapunzel." Stick to the stories that have strong girls and children who are saved by their own cleverness and the help of an empathetic adult rather than merely saved by a stranger, as in "Little Red Riding Hood," or the Disney versions of "Snow White" and "Cinderella."

13. NO ONE LIKES ME!: CHILDREN WHO ARE SOCIAL OUTCASTS OR EASILY VICTIMIZED

These are the children that other children don't want to play with primarily because they are hard to relate to and like. These children tend to be targeted by mean and manipulative children, as their passiveness and vulnerability is evident. Although they may also be depressed and/or very insecure (as discussed in "Problematic Behaviors" starting on page 173), their main character traits are poor social skills, flat affect (showing very little emotional expression), lack of responsiveness, and odd behaviors. Odd behaviors include things like responding to a question with an answer that is not related to the question, taking a role in imaginary play unrelated to the scenario or to the other roles, making unusual sounds or muttering, or laughing at inappropriate times. Some of these children are very intelligent and are in their "own world," oblivious to social conventions; some are emotionally very needy; some have physical challenges such as speech and language delays; and some may be mildly autistic. All of them need the help and support of caring adults to be included more in the classroom community and to be less vulnerable to victimization.

Anticipating and Preventing Children from Becoming Social Outcasts or Easily Victimized

- Know as much as you can about your children, particularly when they enroll or enter your class as well as on an ongoing basis. However, avoid being intrusive when asking questions of children's families. If you are caring and concerned and have the child's best interest in mind, family members will know this and be willing to share information. Try to learn some of the following: What are the children's life circumstances and health and social histories? Are their behaviors consistent between home and school? Do they have any medical conditions and are they on medication? How are their relationships with siblings? What are their families' cultural values, beliefs, and practices in regard to children and child rearing?

- Observe interactions among children carefully to ensure that they are positive, reciprocal, and relatively equal. Mediate with any interaction that is not.

- Make it a priority to create an inclusive classroom and develop a strong sense of community among the children. Previous chapters include many ideas to make this happen.

Solving Problems Related to Children Who Are Social Outcasts or Easily Victimized

- Actively and consistently help these children. Because they do not cause disruptions, it may be tempting to ignore their behaviors. If a child has already reached the point of allowing himself to be victimized, it will be partly because he does not have a responsive adult in his life whom he can turn to for help. You have to be that adult, at least while the child is in your care. Also, it is important to assist these children now when they are young and their sense of self is still developing.

- Observe carefully to determine which traits or behaviors seem to be the primary reason that the child is rejected by other children. Is it the child's overall demeanor? Is it a lack of social skills, such as not responding to or initiating eye contact with other children? Is it something physical, such as being difficult to understand because of a speech impediment or delayed language development? Is it related to appearance, such as obesity or wearing dirty, smelly clothes? Is it due to an odd behavior as described previously?

- If there are several reasons for the problem, select just one to work on right away and intensely. Choose one that is most likely to bring positive results relatively quickly. For example, helping the child initiate and respond to eye contact would be a better choice than addressing a speech problem or obesity. Nonetheless, you can (and should) start the process of talking with parents about getting help for these other problems, such as making a referral for a speech and language assessment or nutritional counseling.

- Begin with the easiest skills to learn. For example, if you are helping a child initiate and respond to eye contact from other children, start with responding to eye contact, as it is a less complex skill than initiating eye contact. When another child tries to make eye contact, tell him what is happening and that he needs to return the gaze. Model it if necessary. As always, give as much help as necessary but no more. Provide less assistance as he begins to "get it." For example, move from verbal assistance to nonverbal cues.

- Help the other children understand and connect with the child who is (currently) a social outcast. Say something like "If Christopher does not respond when you look at him, say his name or tap his shoulder gently."

- Give the child who is or may be easily victimized the words to use to stand up for himself and to stop the child who is victimizing him. Show him how to make his voice sound strong and his face show anger. Help him with the words to say: "Stop! I don't like it" or "No! I won't do it." Suggest several strategies to use after defending himself verbally: "You can walk away and play with other children or ask for help from a teacher." Have him practice these behaviors. Of course, at the same time you will be working intensely with the child who is doing the victimizing to change her behavior, using the strategies discussed in "Problematic Behaviors" starting on page 173.

- If the child is allowing himself to be victimized because he is being physically hurt and threatened with more harm by the other child, then a more intensive and direct intervention is required. This will entail a greater focus on changing the behavior of the child who is doing the victimizing and protecting the child who is being victimized. To start, keep them apart from each other at all times while they are at school. At the same time, access assistance from a mental health specialist for yourself and, if possible, for the child and her family. (See "Little Volcanoes" on pp. 185–89 for more ideas.)

Big Burdens on Small Shoulders: Children Coping with Change

THE EXPRESSION "NOBODY likes change except a wet baby" isn't true. At least it wasn't for my kids when they were babies. I think they disliked being interrupted from their deep investigations into the meaning of the universe more than they disliked being wet. But whatever the reason, they, along with most of the human race, didn't like change. Period. Young children need consistency and reliability to feel secure and safe, so major changes are difficult at best and traumatic at worst. Typical major changes in a young child's life are moving, going to a new school, divorce, new baby, hospitalization, death of a loved one, and moving on to the next grade or the "big school." The resource section "Behavior Issues, Positive Guidance, Classroom Management, and Social/Emotional Development" includes a list of children's books on p. 283 that deal with the range of the changes we'll discuss. I tried to select books that have clear and accurate messages without being pedantic, that are good children's literature or at least have an interesting story, and that are beautifully illustrated. Unfortunately, very few "topic" books meet these criteria. While reading to children can help them cope, it is important to give them helpful information about different kinds of change and about separating through concrete experiences. (See "Thinking Up Thoughtful Themes" for ideas on implementing themes about separations, on p. 65, and changes, on pp. 67–68.)

1. NEW KID ON THE BLOCK

Almost all new children will have a hard time at first, especially with separating from parents at the start of the day. This is particularly difficult for the child who enters the class in the middle of the year. Usually this gets better within a few weeks when the child knows she will be picked up regularly and when she is familiar with the new surroundings and with you, her new teacher.

Anticipating and Preventing Problems Related to a Child Whose Family Has Recently Moved

- If at all possible, visit the child in her home. Bring one or two toys from the classroom that the child is not likely to have at home that she can play with during the visit. Don't have an agenda or do a screening test or ask the parents too many formal questions. The purpose is to establish a relationship. Before you leave, take a picture of you and the child for her to have.

- Invite the child and her parents to visit the class for about an hour before her first full day. Put no pressure on her to participate in any way. Respect her need to observe. If possible, have her visit several more times, gradually increasing the visiting times until her first full day.

- Request that a parent (or relative or friend) stay in the classroom the first few times the child attends, if at all possible. Ask the parent to sit quietly on the sidelines and not push the child into participating.

- Encourage the new child to bring in favorite toys from home to help her form friendships. Put limits on the use of these toys as discussed in the chapter "Toys from Home" on pp. 88–89.

- Make sure the parents have ample information about your program and class-room, so they can answer any questions their child may have before she begins. Provide a list of frequently asked questions (FAQs) and answers. Some FAQs may include "What do I call my teacher?" "What will I do all day?" "Will I eat at school?" "Do I take a nap?" "What can I bring from home?" and "What if no one wants to play with me?"

Solving Problems Related to a Child Whose Family Has Recently Moved

The child who is having a hard time adjusting

- Recommend to parents that they drop off and pick up their child at the same time each day. This will establish a clear routine, and routines create security.

- Encourage the parents to arrange for their child to spend time outside of school hours with another child who is in the class. This will help the child establish a special bond with a classmate and help her look forward to coming to school.

- Read children's books dealing with the issue of starting school and/or moving.

- The child who still has separation problems six weeks after being in the program with the same teacher(s) has a problem most likely due to causes other than being new. Ask yourself if the child is gaining anything by the behavior, such as extra attention. Can you change things so that the child will gain extra attention by separating easily and joining the activities quickly? (The attention can be in the form of encouraging remarks, smiles, and hugs.)

- Try to find time to observe the child carefully. Perhaps another child is being mean to her when you are busy with other children. Perhaps there is something in the room or some activity that makes her feel uncomfortable or frightened.

- Meet with the parents to discuss possible causes and brainstorm possible solutions together. Determine if the child has certain fears. For some children, a house in a new neighborhood and new school are too many changes at once. Ask about the child's situation prior to moving and about other major changes at home, such as a new sibling, a divorce, or a remarriage, so that you can help the child work through those issues.

- Consider the possibility and discuss with parents that the child might be happier in a different arrangement, such as attending fewer days or using a family child care program, or at least for now. (See "Right from the Start" on pp. 14–18 for additional ideas on helping children who are having trouble separating from their parents.)

The child who has recently moved

- If the child has recently relocated, read books about moving and provide many opportunities for her to talk about her move. Ask her to show pictures, if she has them, of her old house and her friends from her former neighborhood. Help her write letters or draw pictures for these old friends.

- Help the child's parents learn about activities and resources for families in the area. These can include fun parks and playgrounds, places to swim, short hiking trails, zoos, museums, libraries, campgrounds, amusement parks, skating rinks, restaurants that welcome children, community centers, health clinics or pediatricians, social service agencies that help families, and family-oriented organizations such as the YMCA, YWCA, Big Brothers, and Big Sisters.

- Provide all families with a list of other classmates and schoolmates with their e-mail addresses, home addresses, and phone numbers. Get permission from each family first to be included on the list, as some may want to keep their contact information private. Help new families locate neighbors on the list whom they can connect with to ask questions and possibly carpool. The children may want to spend time playing together outside of school.

MOMMY'S HOUSE, DADDY'S HOUSE: CHILDREN WHOSE PARENTS ARE DIVORCING

Although divorce has become an almost commonplace experience for children today, the emotional effect of divorce on a child is still devastating. When a child experiences a divorce, you will most likely see behavior changes, such as moodiness, defiance, a short temper, increased aggression, nervous habits, more toileting "accidents," shorter attention span, temper tantrums, whining, and crying. The stress is likely due as much to the tensions and arguments in the home as to the divorce itself. Children who fare best under this difficult situation are those whose parents remain civil and mature toward each other, do not play "tug of war" with their children or with their children's loyalties, speak well of the other parent to their children, keep in close contact with the children, and help them realize that they are not responsible for the divorce. As the child's teacher, you may not have a big role in influencing these factors, but you can give parents this information. You can also be a great support, a source of stability, and someone who clarifies information for the child. You can certainly help him realize that his parents' divorce is not his fault.

Anticipating and Preventing Problems Related to the Impact of a Divorce on Children

- The chances are good that at least one child in your class will experience divorce during the year, so discussing the topic any time will be helpful. Use children's books, stories, puppets, and videos.

- Provide information through books and pictures about many different kinds of families. Let the children know that children are loved and cared for in families with a wide variety of configurations: single moms, single dads, gay parents, joint custody, grandparents, foster parents, adoption, and so on. Discuss the different family arrangements of the children in your class. (See "Modern Family" on pp. 136–39 about children in nontraditional families.)

- Provide many outlets for the children to express their feelings and emotions. This includes drawing, painting, sand play, water play, working with clay and play-dough, creative movement, and making up stories.

- Set up places in your classroom where children can have semi-privacy and quiet, such as a decorated appliance box with a big cushy pillow inside.

- Provide many opportunities throughout the day for children to have control in appropriate ways. For example, allow them to make many choices and decisions regarding books to browse, activities to engage in, and materials to use. This will help ease one of the negative results of a major change in a child's life: the feeling of having no control.

- Make sure children know that your classroom is a safe place to express strong feelings, including anger. Teach them how to redirect their anger appropriately as described under "Little Volcanoes" on pp. 185–89. Help them learn how to calm themselves down and get comfort from others. Then, when a circumstance like divorce happens, they will have the tools they need to deal with their intense emotions.

Solving Problems Related to the Impact of a Divorce on Children

After their parents separate, many children go through a grieving process over the loss of their family and/or a parent who has left. Children in foster care go through this repeatedly. The stages in this process are the following:

Denial: They deny the divorce is really happening or happened.

Anger: They express their anger through a variety of problematic behaviors. They might be angry at themselves and believe that it was their fault.

Hope: They wish for or even try to bring their parents back together.

Sadness: They begin to accept the reality of the situation and express their feelings more appropriately.

Acceptance: The new situation, whether living without Mommy or Daddy, or shuffling between two houses, becomes the new "normal."

- Be aware of these stages so that you can help children move through them at their own pace. Accept their feelings but help the children express these feelings appropriately.

- Make it clear to the child that the divorce was not his fault and nothing he could have done or not done would have prevented it. Use books and stories to reinforce this message.

- Give the child many ways to express his feelings through open, creative activities. Ask him if he would like to write a story with you about a bunny who is sad. Using animal characters helps give the child some distance from the issue, allowing him to risk expressing his feelings. Ask him what made the bunny sad and begin to create the story. Move the story along by asking questions such as, "What did the bunny say to his daddy?" "What did he say to his mommy?" "What can the bunny do to not feel so sad?" Ask the child to draw pictures for the story. Help him see a positive side of the divorce: "Your parents will be happier if they are not fighting so much. If they are happier, then it will be more fun to be with them." Do not deny the pain and the negative feelings the child is experiencing, but present another perspective.

- Avoid overprotecting or overindulging the child because of his pain. He will be better off with clearly defined, consistent limits and comforted by the usual routines and activities.

- Be empathetic but do not allow the child to become dependent on you. Make sure he spends most of his time engaged with other children and not clinging to you. If this happens, say something like "I'll give you one great big hug, and then you need to go play."

- All children and families undergoing this major change could benefit from professional counseling. Recommend this to parents as a way to ease the stress for everyone and to prevent future problems. Increasing lines of communication with parents by meeting and talking more often is crucial at this time.

3. ADORABLE BABY SISTER OR ALIEN SPACE INVADER: A NEW BABY IN THE FAMILY

Whether by birth, remarriage, or adoption, a new sibling in the family will mean major changes. Children who have good preparation for this will weather the changes more easily, minimizing the feelings of uncertainty, jealousy, and insecurity that can develop. You, the teacher, can be a great source of information and support.

Anticipating and Preventing Problems Related to a New Sibling

- Occasionally read children's books about babies and childbirth. (See the resources under "Sexual Development, Sex Roles, and Gender Identity" on pp. 295–96.) Some teachers, especially in rural areas, like to do this in the spring when farm animals are giving birth.

- Discuss the wide variety of family configurations, including adoption. Tell the children why people adopt children and how this process works.

- Use terms such as "uterus" or "womb" to explain where the baby grows. When children are told the baby is in Mommy's tummy, it gives them inaccurate information and unnecessarily confuses them.

- Make sure that the children understand that a long time passes before a baby grows old enough to be fun to play with. Explain that babies require a great deal of care and attention, so parents tend to fuss over babies and not give big brothers or sisters the attention they used to have. As the baby grows, things will (almost) go back to the way they were.

Solving Problems Related to a New Sibling

- The main need of a child who has a new sibling is attention. Parents are intensely focused on the needs of the baby and are exhausted. The child is no longer getting as much attention at home as she did before the baby came. You can help by increasing the amount of attention and affection you give the child. Do not wait until the child acts out for attention. Provide attention by talking and doing things with her based on her interests, rather than around her role as a big sister or discussing the baby.

- Give her specific ways to get attention without making others angry or annoyed. Help her practice questions she can ask her parents, such as, "Can you read to me when the baby is napping?" "Can you take me to the park while Daddy watches the baby?"

- Inform the parents that the more they involve their child in all aspects of the preparation, birth, and caregiving, the more the child will feel needed and important. This reduces feelings of being displaced and deprived of attention and prevents jealousy. Some families print out birth announcements that read: "Amy Rubin would like to announce the birth of her new baby brother, Angelo James, on July 26, 2017."

- Discuss the important jobs that a big brother or sister has, such as helping make sure the baby is safe and happy. The most important job of an older sibling is to teach by example by being helpful, caring, patient, and independent—at least to the extent that can be expected of a typical preschooler or kindergartner.

- Parents also need to know the importance of devoting special time to the older sibling. Although giving this time on a regular, scheduled basis is hard because new babies are so unpredictable, striving for this is wise. Suggest that parents could have a story time with the older child each time the baby naps.

- Over the course of the pregnancy, follow the progress of the fetus by showing the children pictures in a book depicting its growth, such as *In the Womb* by Peter Tallack (National Geographic 2006). Invite the mother and father to come to class, as often as they can, so that the other children can see the mother's expanding middle and ask questions about the pregnancy and birth. Give the child many opportunities to proudly share the progress of the baby's prenatal growth, birth, and care. Have the parents bring the baby into the class and teach the children about diapering and baby care. Let the older sibling take the lead, as much as she can, in showing how to care for the baby. Invite the child to make books about the new baby and her concerns as well as her good feelings. Have her illustrate the book with pictures or photos.

- Accept any feelings of jealousy and dislike that the child has toward the new baby. Soon after a new baby arrives, many children want to "give the baby back" because it's not at all what they expected. Encourage the child to talk about her feelings and frustrations about her sibling and about her needs that are not being met. Have her dictate to you a letter to her parents.

4. GET WELL SOON, BIG BABOON! WE MISS YOUR SMILE, CROCODILE!: HOSPITALIZATION

Presenting this topic is important even if you do not have a child in your class who is scheduled to enter a hospital. Young children often go to the hospital because of an emergency, and you may have a child in your class with a chronic condition that requires frequent hospital visits. A hospital experience can be traumatic to a young child because he may be in pain, the environment is so different from anywhere else (strange equipment, unusual smells, workers in masks and uniforms), the atmosphere is formal and rule-bound, and many hospitals are not as child-oriented as they should be.

Anticipating and Preventing Problems Related to Hospitalization

- Read books about going to the hospital such as *Franklin Goes to the Hospital* by Paulette Bourgeois (Kids Can Press 2011). Afterward, answer any questions the children have.

- Help children understand that illnesses that are treated in hospitals—appendectomy, having ear tubes put in, and so on—are not their fault.

- Visit a hospital. Prepare for the field trip well in advance and arrange for a tour from someone who relates well with young children. Have a paramedic visit the classroom with an ambulance the children can tour. Visit a doctor's office to give the children additional information about health care. (See "Are We Having Fun Yet?" on pp. 84–88 for more information on fiasco-free field trips.)

- Set up a hospital imaginary play area. Include cots, blankets, bandages, stethoscopes, pads of blank paper and pens, old X-rays, pictures of hospitals and doctors' offices, several toy doctor's kits, and crutches. Extend the play by having the children build an ambulance and role-play paramedics.

- Have small toy ambulances as part of your set of cars and trucks. Provide props that can be used with small figures of people to play out hospital scenes. Do this inexpensively by making small stretchers, beds, operating tables, surgical masks, and so on out of cardboard, craft sticks, and cloth.

Solving Problems Related to a Hospitalization

- If you find out that a child in your class will be hospitalized, do the activities described above unless you have done them within the past six weeks.

- Create opportunities for the child who will be hospitalized to talk about his concerns. Help him make books about his concerns and draw pictures. Meet with the child's parents to gain a full understanding of why, when, and for how long he will be hospitalized. Ask them what you can do to help their child.

- Provide parents with information, or at least access to information, about talking with children who are going to the hospital. Most hospitals have materials for parents, and the larger ones may have a specialist whose primary job is to help parents and children.

- Give parents ideas for activities the child can do while lying in a hospital bed.

- Make up a package for the child in the hospital. Include pictures of the class, a video and drawings made by the children, new markers, and a drawing pad. Present this package to the child in the hospital or just before he leaves for the hospital.

- For long stays, provide regular (weekly, if possible) packages to the child with pictures of what the other children did that week, materials to do an art project that was done in the class during the week (which may have to be modified for the hospital setting), some books, and pictures and letters from the class to the child.

- With permission from the child's parents, provide information to other parents so that they can take their children to visit the child in the hospital. Remind them to call the child's parents before visiting to make sure it won't be disruptive.

- Visit or call the child while he is in the hospital. If possible, call from the classroom so that all the children can talk with him. When a child returns to the classroom after a hospital stay or an emergency room visit, provide many chances for him to share his experiences with the other children. Set up a hospital imaginary play area if this was not done before the stay. In one classroom, a child's real experiences with a broken arm in the emergency room led to rich and exciting dramatic play, which led to investigating bones and skeletons, which then led to exploring organs and the inside of the body.

5. HEALING A HURTING HEART: DEATH OF A LOVED ONE

When I was a teacher, two siblings in my class, one just over three years old and the other almost five, lost both their parents in a car crash. They were a handsome couple in their late twenties, out for a romantic weekend, while the children were being cared for by various members of their large, extended family. It was their first road trip in their new sports car and, being a rare sunny day in the Northwest, they had the top down when the semi hit them. While the relatives were aware of the importance of keeping routines, the children didn't stay in my class very much longer because it was a parent co-op and none of the relatives lived nearby. It was the relatives' decision to not tell the children what happened, which was probably okay for the younger brother but not the older sister. Not telling her meant that she anticipated their return, yet she knew something was wrong because everybody's behavior had changed and her parents had never been away that long without calling. I could only say to the relatives that if they changed their minds, I could recommend some books and help them figure out what to say to the children. During the short time I had with the children, I could not give them what I felt was best for them, but I could give them one important thing they needed that no one else could give them: normality, routine, and consistency.

When a loved one dies—whether a parent, grandparent, or beloved pet—the child will typically go through a grieving process. How long it lasts depends on many factors, including the child's age and how important the person was in the child's life. Be aware of where the child is in the process so you can help in a meaningful way. Here are the steps in the grieving process:

Denial: The child believes the dead person (or pet) will come back.

Anger: The child expresses strong feelings of being abandoned and rejected by the person who has died. The child may express these feelings through a range of problematic behaviors.

Grief: The child mourns over the loss. She cries often and feels despondent.

Acceptance: Gradually the child returns to more typical behaviors and feelings, although when something reminds her of the loss, perhaps "grandparents night" or "bring your pet to school" events, the child will likely return to grieving for a time.

Anticipating and Preventing Problems Related to Coping with Death

- When a child finds a dead insect or small animal, use it as an opportunity to teach children what death means in concrete terms. Even very young children can understand that death means no movement, stiffness, silence, and no response.

- Read appropriate books about death to all the children occasionally. Allow time for children to process the ideas and to ask questions. In addition to reading nonfiction and storybooks on the topic, many original versions of fairy tales, such as "Cinderella," deal with the death of a parent and the healing that comes from grieving. More contemporary versions tend to leave out these important details.

- Read simple versions of tales and myths that deal with death from a variety of cultures and lands. Point out how different people believe different things about what happens to people when they die. Discuss the different ways that people cope with loss through rituals. A beautiful American Indian legend/dance is about a shrouded widow—the cocoon of a caterpillar—who mourns for a year. She then realizes all she is missing in life and removes her shroud to reveal the colorful butterfly underneath. In many cultures a grieving spouse wears black or drab clothes for one year, during which he is given the leeway and support to mourn.

- Many traditional children's songs are about death—"Blue," "Who Killed Cock Robin?" "Go Tell Aunt Rhody," "The Sinking of the Reuben James," "The Titanic (It Was Sad When the Great Ship Went Down)," and others. Sing these songs with the children so that death is not a taboo subject.

- Talk about famous people when they die. The children will usually be aware of the death from the news and adult conversation. Explain in simple terms what made them important or famous and how their deeds will live on after them.

Solving Problems Related to Coping with Death

- If a child in your class has experienced a recent death in her immediate family, do the activities described above. Ask the child's parents or guardians for ideas for helping the child in the classroom. Explain your approach and ask for their approval and ideas for changes. Negotiate any activities that they feel uncomfortable with or would like to see included. Assure them that young children are aware of death and greatly benefit from simple but factual information and opportunities to express their feelings in a variety of ways.

- Ask the child's permission before talking about the death of her parent or relative with the whole class. Take your cues from her about how much detail to go into. Have children direct questions to the child, unless she would prefer that you do the talking. Check each response you give with the child for accuracy and approval.

- All children and families who have recently experienced the loss of a loved one, particularly if the death was sudden and unexpected, could benefit from the help of a professional counselor. Recommend this to the family.

- Because young children often have trouble putting their feelings into words and because they usually act on their feelings, you will likely encounter problematic behaviors. Often a child will feel a mixture of sadness and anger. Help her express her feelings appropriately, such as by drawing. Provide her with safe outlets for venting her anger. Outside she can yell, cry, run, pound nails into a stump, or do whatever makes her feel better and won't hurt anyone.

- Help the child soothe and calm herself. She can generate her own ideas and/or you can suggest she listen to music, sing, look at a book, talk, draw, or play with sand or water.

- Help the child write a book about the person who died and the wonderful things the person did while alive. Use photos with the parent's consent and assistance. Be aware, however, that some children cannot or prefer not to talk about a recent death. They will need a bit more time and distance. Respect the child's feelings and instead write stories about young animals who suffer losses of various kinds. Start with the animal's loss of a friend. This will be less threatening and will be healing.

- Use the words "death" and "dead" instead of euphemisms such as "loss," "gone to sleep," or "passed away." If the death was due to an illness, assure children that ordinary illnesses almost never result in death, especially for children and young people.

- Help the child's parents see the importance of including the child in the funeral and in all aspects of the death and mourning. This is the only way they can know and benefit from the rituals and ceremonies our society has for death.

Questions about death

- Answer questions simply and honestly. If a child asks, "What happens to people when they die?" answer by saying, "No one knows for sure. Different people believe different things, and when you are older, you can learn about it and decide for yourself. We do know that their bodies become stiff and cold, and the person can never talk, play, laugh, or move again. This makes us very sad because we will miss them."

- Be aware that children who often and regularly ask questions about death are working through the issue and may have had a recent experience with death. In some cases, the questions reflect a general insecurity, anxiety, or fear related to other issues. As your best approach, provide loving reassurance to the child and try to determine the actual cause of the anxiety. If she asks, "When will I die?" respond with, "I hope you live a very long time because you bring joy to everyone and many people love you a lot." If the questions and concern continue for more than a few weeks, talk to the parents about getting help from a mental health professional who works with young children.

- The causes of death are of great interest to most children. This is natural, as they are trying hard to understand all aspects of the world around them. If they ask a blunt question to a grieving child about the cause of the death when the child is not yet ready to talk about it, help by saying (if you don't know the cause yourself), "Kim isn't ready to tell you now because it makes her very sad. Maybe in a few days, or whenever she feels ready, she will tell us." If you do know the cause, give a brief explanation if it is okay with the child: "Julia's father was in a car accident. He was a kind man and everyone, especially Julia, misses him."

Death of a classroom pet

- The death of a classroom pet provides an excellent opportunity to explore the subject of death with your children, so don't minimize the event. If the pet died very recently and is clean and whole, let the children hold the dead pet so they can learn concretely what death is. (Of course, any child can decline to do this for any reason.) Encourage them to feel the stiffness, coldness, and lack of response of the animal. Compare it to how the animal used to be. Help them wash their hands thoroughly afterward. Take plenty of time to read books about death, sing songs, and talk about feelings and beliefs. Have a ceremonious funeral and bury the pet outside under a marker. Invite each child who desires to do so to say something about the pet. Put together a book of remembrances. Plant something in memory of the pet.

6. GROWING UP AND MOVING ON: TRANSITIONING TO THE NEXT GRADE OR TO THE "BIG SCHOOL"

Helping children make a successful transition to the next grade or age level or to primary school ("big school") will be a great benefit to the children as well as the teachers. This preparation will help reduce any anxiety children may have and increase their confidence and their ability to adjust. Whether children are excited and feel big, or are worried and nervous, or have all of those feelings, moving to the next class is a big change for all children.

Your task as the teacher is also to help transition the children who will be entering into your class. Show care and interest in those children, if they are known to you. This will help them feel positive toward you and feel happy to be in your class, which will prevent many problematic behaviors from developing. Invite those children, two at a time, to spend time in your class during the last few weeks before the transition.

Many early childhood teachers are concerned that by following child-centered practices—giving children choices among active, hands-on experiences, encouraging exploration, collaborating in project-based learning—they are doing children a disservice. In the next grade, children will be required to sit at desks for long periods, take directions from the teacher, do paper and pencil tasks, work independently, and line up. While this may be true in many cases, it makes no sense to subject children to a program that does not meet their needs and will cause them stress, all because of what they may face in the next school year. Children who feel good about themselves, are self-motivated learners, and have good self-regulation skills will do better when faced with such challenges than children who do not possess these qualities. However, you can ease the transition by helping children know about and prepare for what they will encounter in the next grade.

Anticipating and Preventing Problems Related to Transitioning to the Next Grade or School

- Set up field trips to visit some of the classrooms your children will be attending. Invite teachers from the next grade to visit your classroom and talk with your children. Prepare the children to ask questions of the teachers. Invite several children who were in your class last year to talk to your current group about what it is like being in the next room, grade, or school.

- With the permission of parents, send information to the next teacher about the children in your class. Stress their strengths and abilities. Show their portfolios that document their progress and interests. Express any concerns objectively and cautiously. You do not want the new teacher to prejudge a child, as he might act differently in the new class or mature more by then. However, because you have information that will help the child and his teacher, sharing it is the ethical thing to do. You will have to make a judgment call if you think that, for whatever reason, sharing the information could do more harm than good.

- Talk to several teachers of the grade to understand their expectations for children. This does not mean you will change your curriculum to meet what may be inappropriate expectations. You may find, however, that the expectations are more appropriate than you anticipated. You may learn some helpful information, such as the style of handwriting used and taught in that grade. To ease the transition for your children, use this style when printing names, writing stories, and helping children write their names.

- Organize a few meetings during the year when all the teachers in your grade/age level meet with all the teachers in the next level. Exchange information, coordinate the content and timing of themes and activities, make plans to collaborate on a project or two, and clarify philosophies and goals.

- Read books and create stories about children who go to a new class.

- Develop an imaginary play area that includes the materials and equipment used in the next grade. Observe the spontaneous play that develops and correct misconceptions about what will happen in the next grade. Allow them to freely work through their concerns and their excitement.

- Near the end of the school year, practice some of the routines and rules that are used in the next school or class. This may include the "raise your hand to talk rule" and the "lining-up routine." Explain the reasons for the rules or routines: "It may not be fun, but it is necessary because the new school has many more children than our school and fewer teachers in each class." Help children find ways to deal with any stress the rules and routines may cause: "If you don't get called on, try raising your hand higher and looking at the teacher directly while smiling. But don't say anything or make noise" or "Let's think of things you can do while waiting quietly and still for a long time. I like to sing a song to myself inside my head."

- Toward the end of the school year, role-play situations that the children are likely to encounter in the next class. Help them learn the actions and words to use to get their needs met without causing problems. For example, if a child is given a math worksheet to complete, he can raise his hand and ask if he can use his crayons to figure out the problem. Children can also ask (politely) for additional materials to make projects more creative. They can bring their own blank notebook or pad for drawing and writing stories during transition times.

- If you have not already done so, give all the families (who want to be included) class lists with e-mail addresses, home addresses and phone numbers so that friendships can be maintained. Give all the children a class photo.

- Meet with parents to discuss the importance of helping their children move on to the next grade. Invite a teacher or the principal to meet with the parents and to answer questions they have about the new class or school. Request that the guest bring a copy of the report card used in the next grade, if there is one. Help parents with ways to deal with any different expectations and levels of involvement in the new school or class by providing specific information: "At Jefferson School, take your concerns directly to the teacher first. If you are unsatisfied with the teacher's response, go to the parent advisory committee before going to the principal. They will help you figure out the best way to move forward. Offer suggestions and make requests rather than simply complaining and making demands. Be assertive but polite in advocating for your child."

Solving Problems Related to Transitioning to the Next Grade or School

Children who are worried about moving to the next grade

For children who are expressing fears and concerns about going into the next grade or school, whether to you, their parents, or both, try the following ideas:

- Determine, if possible, who the teacher will be and talk with him about the child. Set a time for the child to visit the teacher and the classroom. If fear of the unknown is the greatest fear, then making things known for the child should greatly reduce his fears.
  - Set up a time when a child from the next class can talk to the child in your class about what he can expect.
  - Determine, if possible, the child's specific concerns. You may be able to clear up some misconceptions easily.
  - Role-play with the child situations he might encounter in the next grade. Having a chance to practice some new skills, before facing the real situation, always helps.
  - Help the child stay in touch with at least one friend from the current class. Talk with his parents to arrange a photo exchange and to share e-mail addresses, home addresses, and phone numbers. Encourage the parents to set up visits with the friend.

Conflicting styles and expectations among teachers in the next grade

If your children are going to a number of different classrooms with teachers who are all very different, helping children transition from your class to the next is more challenging.

- Perhaps the best approach is to role-play and discuss two or three (at the most) of these approaches, particularly those most different from your own. All children will benefit from learning that different teachers have different expectations and styles. Compare it to spending time at their grandparents' house. Children *can* do some things there that they *can't* do at home, and they *can't* do some things there that they *can* do at home.

- If, for example, a variety of handwriting styles are used, pick the one to use in your class that you believe is the most appropriate for young children. Base your decision on the ease children will have in writing and reading it. If you have no preference, choose the one that is most common.

Celebrations are child-centered, graduations are not

In many programs a great deal of time, energy, and money is spent on graduations. Most of these events are designed to meet the needs of the parents and may put the children under stress. The children often have to spend too much time sitting and they have to perform as a group. Young children do neither very well. However, parents consider graduation from preschool to be a major milestone in their children's lives and like to mark it in some way.

- Meet the needs of both the parents and children by having a less formal celebration. Prepare a special snack with the children and serve it to their parents at a short, early evening gathering. Make "graduation caps" with the children that they decorate. Present a short (ten-minute) video or slide show of some of the highlights of the year. Have the children sing a few favorite songs that they have been singing all year, and ask the parents to join in. Do some movement games that involve the children and the parents together.

- Plan your celebration with parents so they will understand your goal of involving the children in a meaningful, enjoyable occasion. Work out compromises and accept parents' good ideas. They will take more responsibility for organizing the event if some or most of the ideas come from them.

- Send a "diploma" to each child in the mail. Children love receiving mail and rarely get any, so sending the diploma will make it very special. Follow up to make sure every child received one.

PART

5

Problematic Behaviors: Helping Children Who Hurt

THE PHRASE "HELPING CHILDREN WHO HURT" can be read two ways and both ways apply to the information in this section of the book. Children who are hurting inside hurt others.

Dealing with children's problematic behaviors is the number one issue of concern for early childhood teachers, and it has been the number one concern for the entire forty years that I have worked in the field. Why? One reason is that most of the strategies teachers use to deal with problematic behaviors do not work. Consequences, punishments, rewards, time-outs, and similar strategies do nothing to eliminate or improve the behavior, and in many cases make it worse.

Another reason is that every child's temperament, personality, history, needs, and motivations are unique. Even if two children appear to have the same problematic behavior—grabbing toys, for example—the reasons for the behavior and the strategies that will solve the problem while helping the child change may be very different. So you need that entire toolbox of strategies discussed on page 3 in the introduction.

Because you have to know *how* to use the tools, especially the more sophisticated tools needed to solve complex problematic behaviors, this section gives you an in-depth understanding of children's behaviors and a general approach to addressing problematic behaviors. Following this are ideas to prevent, mediate, and change a long list of problematic behaviors, from the very problematic, such as biting, to the somewhat problematic but very common, such as acting way too silly. The main focus of this section, however, is on behaviors that are more serious and difficult to deal with.

UNDERSTANDING PROBLEMATIC BEHAVIORS

Why do some children act defiant, aggressive, mean, destructive, violent, manipulative, or in other seriously problematic ways? Because they *need* to and because the behavior *works*. They need to express their anger, hurt, outrage, sadness, frustration, and sense of powerlessness. These feelings are particularly intense for children who have been or are being abused or neglected. They need to get attention to fill the emotional emptiness inside and to validate their existence. And it is easier and quicker to get attention for a negative behavior than a positive one. For young children all this happens subconsciously, nearly instinctively.

Because the behavior works, it will continue or increase as long as it works, even if to a small degree or only occasionally. The behavior works because it gets the desired attention the child needs and because it feels powerful to make another child cry, control her, and make her afraid. It feels even more powerful to make an adult upset, angry, and frazzled. A young child who feels invisible and worthless has very few options to make an impact big enough to counter those intense feelings. Any punishment from adults for the behavior is just confirmation to the child of how much he was able to get "under their skin" and it is accepted by him as just part of what it takes to survive psychologically. Punishment may even be useful to the child as a way to establish and maintain an identity as the "bad kid," which is better than having no identity at all. So for these reasons and more, punishment does not deter or improve problematic behaviors. In fact, they almost always make them worse.

Of course, there are many other reasons for children's problematic behaviors, particularly the less serious ones. They include emulating what they see and experience at home, in the

Cultural Awareness Alert

Some problematic behaviors are the result of differences between a child's home/community cultural or religious values and practices and that of the school/center and teacher, whose values and practices usually reflect mainstream, middle-class U.S. culture. For example, a teacher may be concerned about a child who appears to be very shy and passive, who rarely speaks and is barely audible when she does. But in some cultures and belief systems, this is an expected and typical behavior for children, particularly for girls. However, the behavior *is* problematic because it is an ineffective behavior in U.S. culture, which will put the child at a disadvantage. We value extroverts, people who stand up for themselves, are proactive, and can "grab the bull by the horns." In this country, only "the squeaky wheel gets the oil." The implication of this saying is that if you don't assert yourself, you won't get anything you want or need. But is this behavior a cultural trait or personality trait? In many cultures, a child is expected to be demure in public but not in private. At home and with close relatives, this same "shy" child may be very talkative or even boisterous. In this case, the behavior is clearly a cultural trait. For the child to begin to be a bit more open and active in public situations, such as the classroom, she has to feel safe and secure but also encouraged to take more initiative, participate more, and be more vocal. She needs to be supported and respected for behavior that is culturally appropriate in her home culture and for the positive values it reflects—listening, being thoughtful, and respecting others—but at the same time helped to behave appropriately according to the mainstream culture.

community, and in the media. There could be physical reasons such as hunger, lack of sleep, poor vision or hearing, allergies, or illness. Or a child may just not know a different and better way of behaving. Understanding children with problematic behaviors will help you feel more empathetic and caring toward them. Feeling positive toward a child who is mean and manipulative may be the opposite of how you feel initially and what you believe the child deserves, but it may be the single most important thing you can do to reduce or eliminate the behaviors.

THE TEN "ATES" APPROACH FOR EFFECTIVELY DEALING WITH PROBLEMATIC BEHAVIORS

This section explains how to apply the Ten "Ates" approach to help a child with problematic behaviors. The Ten Ates approach (discussed in the introduction under "How to Be the 'Pro' in Problem-Solver" on pp. 2–5) includes five main strategies: **anticipate** problems to prevent them, **accommodate** the needs of the group and of individual children, **mediate** solutions to problematic behaviors when they occur, **investigate** causes and reasons for the behaviors, and **update** strategies to address the behaviors more effectively. Then there are five sub-strategies used in mediating behaviors, particularly when they involve conflicts: **de-escalate** emotions and tensions, **validate** feelings and needs, **educate** children about better ways to get their needs met and solve conflicts, and **collaborate** to **negotiate** a solution. The timing and/or order of the five main strategies will vary. They often overlap and sometimes happen simultaneously.

Anticipate Problems

Think ahead and consider some of the possible, but realistic, obstacles you may encounter and things that might go wrong. Taking these into account, plan and prepare for what you will do. If you are planning activities for children, carefully prepare the environment and materials ahead of time and have one or two alternative strategies and activities ready, just in case. Build flexibility into the activities for the range of abilities and needs of your particular group of children. Think about the child or children with problematic behaviors and special needs. At what point in the day or during which activities are they likely to have a hard time? Have a few ideas on ways to help and support these children before that point in the day or just before the activity, as well as some ideas for helping them during the activity.

Ideas might include telling the child what will happen next and what he needs to do, partnering him with a helper, getting the activity started for him, or giving him verbal encouragement. Of course, it's not possible to anticipate all problems or to always plan correctly, but expecting that there will be some problems will help you be flexible and responsive. A little pessimism is a good thing!

Accommodate Needs

There are two main types of needs to accommodate and be responsive to in order to prevent problematic behaviors: the needs of the group in general and the needs of individual children. "Needs" is a broad term that includes many things from the need for all young children to be active and to feel valued and secure to the need for a particular child to express her intense anger or for another child to make a friend. Accommodating needs proactively and thoroughly will dramatically reduce the number and intensity of problematic behaviors. It will prevent many problematic behaviors from emerging. Addressing the needs of the group in general entails caring interactions, engaging and meaningful activities, a balance of support and challenge, active play, and other child-centered practices. But addressing the needs of a child with problematic behaviors requires giving lots of positive attention and close guidance and support that is specific to the child's needs *before* the problematic behaviors happen. As stated in the introduction, the best solution to a problem is one you never have to use.

If you have many children with problematic behaviors, or seem to be dealing constantly with such behaviors, chances are that there is a problem with your program, not with the children. Their needs are not being met. You will have to change aspects of the program, which may include the physical environment of the classroom, the schedule, the curriculum, the emotional climate, and how you interact with the children and how children interact with each other. Listed below are a few of the main needs for all young children. Children with serious problematic behaviors are likely to have been deprived of some or many of these needs and therefore require a "double dose" or even a "triple dose" of emotional support, positive attention, and help from their early childhood teacher.

The need to be valued and cared for

- Children feel valued and cared for when they get individualized attention and support. This happens when adults look in their eyes, say their names, show interest in what they have to say, take them seriously, and speak with them warmly. They feel cared for when protected from harm; live in a predictable, safe, and child-centered environment; and have ample time and space to play and be a child.

The need to be respected

- Children feel respected when adults use a voice tone and words that convey respect for children. You can check if you are doing this by asking yourself if this is how you would talk to an adult friend. Expressions like "Use an indoor voice" or "You need to clean up now" are patronizing, while "Please speak more softly" and "Let's work together to pick up all the toys" are more respectful. The use of an exaggerated, overly sweet tone of voice condescends to children. When adults show respect for children, they get respect in return. Mutual respect will prevent and eliminate many potential problematic behaviors.

The need for positive regard

- Adults who make many more positive comments than admonishments or corrections, and make them at least as emphatically as the negative statements, show positive regard for children. They look for children's behaviors or actions that are positive—being kind to another child, staying focused in an activity for a long time, coming up with good ideas during imaginary play, solving a problem—and let them know that they are doing well. At the same time, they give them useful, specific information about their behavior, focusing on their efforts: "Thank you for working hard to put away the blocks; our room looks neat and it will be easy to find all the blocks tomorrow." Tell them how much you enjoy them, but only if you can be honest about this sentiment. Once a week or so at opening circle, I used to tell my children things like "I love seeing each of your sweet faces every morning. You are so much fun to be with; thank you for coming to school today."

The need to belong

- Creating a classroom community is discussed throughout "Daily Dilemmas," starting on page 13. Belonging is also promoted through engagement in many cooperative activities. In the absence of opportunities to collaborate, cooperate, and solve conflicts, aggression and competitiveness among children can flourish. The classroom rule "Ask three before you ask me" promotes cooperation by requiring children to seek help from and give assistance to their classmates before seeking adult help. Some children will need assistance to ask in a way that will get a positive response and to give help without doing everything for the other child.

- Cooperative games promote belonging. "Islands" is an example of one. The adult lays down about ten rug squares or pieces of cardboard in a large space, such as outside or in a gym. The children are told that the object of the game is for everyone to help each other get on the islands (rug squares) quickly and be safe. When the music plays, the children "swim" (walk with arm movements as if swimming) all around the islands, but when it stops they must get out of the water and onto an island quickly, or the fish will nibble their toes. Before the music starts again, two or three rug squares are removed. The game repeats until only one square is left and all the children try to get on it. It is the opposite of "musical chairs" because the squares are removed, not the children. This game has no winners and losers, but it offers a challenge and a great deal of fun (Schneider and Torbert 1993). To foster belonging, adults can modify existing games and equipment to make them more cooperative. For example, "Farmer in the Dell" can be played with two farmers and two of each character and more characters can be added if needed so that everyone can be in the circle by the end. Here the "cheeses" stand in the middle at the end and invite everyone else to make a circle around them. Everyone sings "The cheeses have lots of friends," instead of "The cheese stands alone," and the "cheeses" move around the circle shaking everyone's hands.

- Children feel like they belong when they engage with their classmates in imaginary play situations involving exciting adventures where everyone works together to meet a challenge. Fighting fires, conducting emergency rescue operations, and saving animals are examples. Adults teach children how to join play, make friends and keep friends, negotiate, and resolve conflicts.

The need for (some) control

- Young children have very little control over their lives. There are so many things that they cannot yet do. There are so many things that they can't understand. They have no control over when they have to wake up, when they get picked up from school, where they can and cannot go, and when they eat, how often they eat, and (usually) what they eat. The early childhood classroom is a place where they can be given more control over their lives than at home and in the community. This is done by giving them choices and opportunities to make decisions to the greatest extent possible. However, they must be real choices and decisions and appropriate for their age and abilities. Some examples are which song to sing, book to listen to, or movement game to play. They choose from among a variety of engaging activities during work-play time. Outside, they choose where, what, and with whom to play.

- Self-care and independence make children feel in control of themselves and competent. Children are given easy access to sponges and soapy water and child-size brooms and mops to clean up their messes, easy ways to put toys back where they belong when they are done playing with them, and simple methods to dress and take care of themselves. Even a two-year-old can put his own coat on by laying it flat on the ground with the front of the coat facing up, then, while standing behind the top of the coat, putting his arms in the sleeves and flipping it over his head. Encourage the children to help each other with buttoning or zipping jackets, putting on mittens, tying shoes, and so on.

The need to feel and to be competent

- Sensory activities are satisfying because children cannot fail at them; there is no right way or wrong way to do them. Children under five years old should have access to sand and water play daily with fun and interesting equipment in each, such as plastic bottles and containers of different sizes and shapes, funnels, tubing, and measuring cups. They need plenty of time to play. Children can repeat sand and water activities over and over with no costs or consequences, such as when they make a bridge in the sandbox that keeps collapsing or pour water into a plastic bottle until it overflows.

- To feel competent, children need to know what is happening at any given moment and understand what is being read to them and said to them. Voice tone and gestures communicate as much or more than words, particularly for children whose family language is not English. Pictures and graphics help children understand what is being said to them. Stories come to life when adults use a different voice for each character and for different emotions—fear, sadness, glee, suspense, surprise, relief.

- Treating the mistakes and errors that children make as a natural part of growing and learning is important for maintaining their feelings of competence. Rather than being admonished or punished for spilling juice, they need to hear, "It's all right. You can get the sponge and wipe it up. I'll help you if you need help." Adults are open about the mistakes they make. They apologize to children when they mess up.

- Children count on adults to ensure their success. Caring adults let children know exactly what they expect in advance. And when a child is not doing what she should be doing, they view it as a failure on their part, not on the part of the child. They also remove barriers that prevent children from being successful. They don't make a child who needs to move sit for a long time. In a (nearly) failure-free classroom, even very discouraged children will feel better about themselves. Then, with a fundamental sense of competence, children can take on the many risks and challenges that come their way or that they seek with the confidence they need to be successful.

The need to be nurtured, especially intellectually

- Children's physical, cognitive, emotional, and social growth and development all need to be nurtured by knowledgeable and caring adults. In too many early childhood programs, the nurturing of children's cognitive development is inadequate, more so than the other areas of development (Howes et al. 2008). Children need to be cognitively challenged with questions and activities that promote higher-order thinking. They need many opportunities to be creative and to use their imaginations. They need to be asked questions such as "What do you think will happen next?" "What can we do to make Gwen feel better?" and "Do you have other ideas for how to fix this?" And they need to be cognitively challenged with Morning Mystery questions. (See "Anticipating and Preventing Problems Related to Starting the Day" in "Right from the Start" on pp. 14–15.) Children need opportunities to experiment with cause-and-effect relationships by mixing colors, creating marble runs, or playing (with modified rules) commercial games like "Topple" (Pressman Toys) and "Jenga" (Hasbro). Adults should play many thinking games with them, such as "Categories," where they guess the category after hearing a list of items that fit the category. For example, shoes, pants, shirts, dresses, and socks are all clothes or things to wear; water, juice, milk, lemonade, and tea are all drinks or things to drink. Once children are familiar with the game and become competent at it, they can take turns listing items for the other children to name the category and they can be given more challenging lists of items, such as jewelry, parts of a car, things you use in a kitchen, and musical instruments. As this game requires no materials, it's ideal to play during transitions when waiting is unavoidable.

Accommodating the needs of a child with problematic behaviors

Feel positively toward the child with problematic behaviors. View him as a valuable gift, as he will provide you with an opportunity to learn a great deal. You may learn about the causes of behaviors, new approaches to helping, the nature of your own biases and fears, new skills, and the availability of community agencies and resources. He will provide you with a chance to help turn a life around for the better. A child with problematic behaviors also can help you improve your program. A highly active child may be the first one (or the only one) to let you know that your activity is boring. A child who cries often can tell you that you may not have enough inviting things to do (he probably has too much time to think about his unhappiness). Although you may feel that the child with many and serious problematic behaviors has come into your life just to make you miserable, he has not. He is behaving the only way he can.

Believe in yourself. You can help children improve and be happier, even a child who may require years of treatment with a professional counselor, a special education program, and/or a family intervention. If all you do is start the process of helping the child, by making a referral or having a frank conversation with the child's family, you will have done something important. Don't be tempted to pass a problem off as a phase. Although it might actually be a phase, such as toddlers who bite, you can still help improve the behavior. Don't shrug off the problem as being due to the child's "terrible" parents, over whom you have no control. Many children learn to behave positively at school while acting differently at home. They come to see themselves as worthwhile because of a caring, attentive teacher. It is important not to blame parents, but to help them in their very difficult task.

Don't ignore a child's problematic behavior, hoping that it will go away on its own, that the child will move, or that soon he will be the next teacher's problem. Too many children get passed on this way and never get the help they need. Often they grow up to be troubled teens and adults who cause serious problems for themselves and society. Changing problem behaviors when the child is young is much easier than waiting until later. Believe in the child's ability to change and in your ability to help him.

> ## Julia's Story (Part I)
>
> I used to teach a multiage group of three- to five-year-olds. When I planned, I thought about some of the things I believed are most important for my children: that everyone knows that I see, hear, and value them and that they treat each other with kindness and respect. So I anticipated problems in these areas by greeting each child by name and with a smile every morning. At opening circle, I reminded them of the rules we had developed together, including "Use your hands and words to help, not hurt." On one particular morning before the children arrived, I reviewed my plans and reminded myself to observe Julia closely and give her extra positive attention. Julia's behavior had become erratic lately, or perhaps I had just become aware of it. Although she seemed happy most of the time and enjoyed a wide variety of activities, she would suddenly get upset and be defiant for little or no apparent reason. During the past week, she had refused to put on her jacket to go outside and on another day she lay on the floor and cried because she wanted the "librarian" job, which had been assigned to Max.

Mediate Solutions

Deal with problematic behaviors by putting yourself in the role of a mediator. Mediators are calm and neutral but involved, attentive, and empathetic. The first step is to **de-escalate** emotions, starting with yourself, if necessary. It's almost always a mistake to act on your initial emotional reaction to problematic behaviors. That response is usually not helpful and sometimes makes the problem worse. Unless there is a health or safety issue, take a little time to calm yourself down and think about how to best respond. If you are calm, then you can calm children and make good decisions. Mediators also teach people conflict-prevention and conflict-resolution skills and only resolve it for them as a last resort. When there is a conflict between children, you may even consider observing what will happen without your mediation, but be ready to step in immediately if necessary. Observing first gives you insight into children's ability—or lack of ability—to resolve conflicts and solve problems.

It may be necessary to de-escalate children's emotions before you can mediate a solution. A soothing voice tone and caring expression can go a long way toward easing tensions. However, sometimes children are so upset that they can't listen, talk, or negotiate. An upset child may need your help to calm down first. Different children need different strategies to do this. Help children figure out which calming strategy will work best for them. These include taking a few deep, slow breaths, looking at a book, drawing a picture, listening to music or a story, lying down, walking, being held, holding an adult's hand, hugging a pillow or toy animal, or crying for a while.

In some situations, as when a child is trying to engage you in a power struggle or seeks your attention through negative behaviors, it's a good idea—and it may even be necessary—to wait about fifteen minutes and then talk with the child about the behavior and better ways to get her needs met or to resolve a conflict. This strategy allows you to disengage but still address the problematic behavior.

Validate the feelings, emotions, and needs of the child and, in a conflict situation, the needs of everyone involved. Feelings are always valid but beyond our control; how we act on those feelings is within our control. Even as adults we struggle to figure out the best way to act on our strong feelings, so for young children it is the beginning of a long process that requires the able guidance and patient support of adults. You can let children know that all emotions are acceptable by naming their emotions and empathizing with their feelings.

Your main task as a mediator is to **educate** children on how to deal with their feelings and act on them in productive, positive ways: how to behave appropriately in general, how to get their needs met in acceptable ways, and how to resolve conflicts civilly. Assume that the child does not know the correct behavior, even if you are quite sure that he does. Remind him of rules and teach the appropriate behavior, starting with ideas from the child (**collaborate**). Help the child think of an activity that is very similar to the one he is doing, that meets the same, or a very similar, need but is safe and/or kind. If the child has no ideas, suggest two options to choose from (**negotiate**). Part of educating children and giving them some control is letting them know that they can always make other, better choices. Then give the child only as much help as is necessary to act appropriately, get his needs met, or resolve a conflict. At first, this may mean providing a great deal of help. More persistent and serious problematic behaviors require more intensive teaching and support over a longer period of time.

When there are conflicts, require children to **collaborate** and **negotiate** a solution. For example: "You both want the same toy, so what can you do that will make you both happy?" Sit with them and repeat the ideas they generate. Ask them to think through the consequence of each idea: "What might happen next if you grab it? If you ask for it? If you ask me for help? If you wait for it?" Summarize and then ask the children to agree on a solution they both like. Help them negotiate an agreement rather than a compromise, if at all possible. In a compromise, both people get some of what they want, whereas in an agreement that is more collaborative, they get most of what they want.

With attention-getting behaviors, the dilemma is that you usually cannot ignore them even though this would be the best way to stop them. One strategy is to mediate, as just described, but to do so dispassionately, quickly, and minimally. If another child has been hurt physically or emotionally by the behaviors, give her more attention and comfort than the child who did the hurting. This way, the attention-getting behaviors will be less effective and the child will know that the behaviors are not acceptable. Another strategy is to say calmly and without

Julia's Story (Part II)

Previously, when Julia refused to put on her jacket to go outside, I mediated an agreement to solve the problem. Knowing that Julia is very active outside and quickly gets uncomfortably hot and sweaty, I told her that although she had to wear a jacket because of the cold weather, she could leave it unzipped. Julia readily agreed to this, her mood brightened instantly, and she was out the door in a flash.

Julia's behavior about wanting the "librarian" job was something new and more difficult to understand, so I responded to it with an educated guess. I said to her in a sympathetic voice, "Julia, I know that you really want to be the librarian. Let me try to help you" (**de-escalated** emotions and **validated** her feelings and needs). Then I said, "Please sit up and look at me. When you are able to use a calm voice (encouraged her to **de-escalate** further and to control her emotions), you may ask Max if he would be willing to trade jobs with you. He may not agree, however" (**educated** her and the other children about one way to **negotiate** to resolve a conflict). As it turned out, Max preferred the "waiter" job, so he was glad to trade. If he had not agreed, I had mentally prepared another possible solution (**anticipated**): Julia could ask Max if looking directly at the child, "I hear you, but I'm ignoring you. When you are calm and ready to let me help you, I'll pay attention to you, but now I'm ignoring you." Fortunately, few young children are able to catch the irony!

Investigate Causes

There is a cause, reason, and purpose for every problematic behavior. Although in many cases it can be difficult to determine the cause or reason, it is important to try. If the chosen solution strategy does not address the cause, fully or in part, the result will either be a superficial, short-term fix or no fix at all. Investigating the cause may entail talking with children, conducting a home visit, having discussions with parents, getting expert advice, reading books and articles, and/or conducting a focused and thorough observation of the child, among other strategies. Meeting with parents to support their efforts in dealing with their child's behaviors can open the door to discovering the cause(s). A great deal is often revealed during a home visit. A family's values, priorities, approach to discipline, parenting style, view of the child, and much more become readily apparent. Parents are more likely to open up when they feel comfortable on their own turf. The root causes of serious problematic behaviors, the vital needs that are not being met, and the reasons that they are not being met usually come down to complex problems in the family and/or poor parenting skills.

Physical or biological problems are other possible causes. Check the child's file for any medical information that might tell you something. Possible physical causes include certain kinds of allergies, mild types of autism, sensory integration problems, and more. Request a medical checkup, as it may reveal the possible causes of the behavior problems. This is often a good place to start the process of helping the child, because it takes the blame for the behaviors off the parents, the child, and the teacher.

Here's a case in point. A three-and-a-half-year-old child in my class had a problem of occasionally but regularly biting other children . . . hard. His parents were concerned, cooperative, and at a loss at what to do. We tried everything we could think of to eliminate the behavior. We blamed ourselves for not being consistent and vigilant enough. We were frustrated and felt like failures. Finally, after much prodding, his parents took him for a psychological evaluation. During the intake interview, his parents were asked if he was taking any daily medication. He was. I did not know about this, nor did I know what problem he had for which he needed daily medication. The medication was changed and the biting stopped.

Continue to investigate possible causes for problem behaviors while you work on changing the behaviors in the classroom. Although you will not always be able to fully or conclusively determine the cause of problematic behaviors, you will gain useful insights that will help you be more empathetic to the child's problems. And you can still do many things to help the child and to reduce or eliminate the behaviors.

Julia's Story (Part III)

I arranged for and made a home visit one evening. Among the most striking things I saw was that Julia's older sisters did just about everything for her—washed her face, put on and tied her shoes, and even fed her when they wanted her to finish so they could clear the table. While Julia was playing in another room, I sat in the kitchen, where Julia's sisters were doing homework, and described my concerns to Julia's mother, Cynthia. Before Cynthia finished her dinner and headed off to her second job, I asked if she had noticed any similar behaviors or other changes at home. "The only thing I noticed," she stated, "is that Julia started to complain that she doesn't like school." I suggested to Julia's sisters that it would be good for Julia if they involved her more in household chores and encouraged her to do more for herself. The sisters said that it was too much work for them: "Little kids just make more of a mess when they try to help. Plus she's so slow, we'd never get our homework done. And this year, we have even more homework and more tests."

Fortunately, I was given an opportunity to observe Julia closely over several days, when a student teacher took over the class. While taking on the role of an assistant to the student teacher, I carefully observed Julia, keeping in mind what I learned from the home visit and my previous interactions with her. Although Julia was just another happy child most of the time, by the second day, there had been enough incidents that I was able to see a pattern in Julia's behaviors. It appeared that Julia's mood and behaviors would change when she was faced with a challenging (for her) fine-motor task, such as cutting out a circle with scissors and pouring water from a pitcher into a cup. Most of the time she found inconspicuous ways to avoid these tasks, but when she could not, she created a minor distraction and occasionally a major distraction. Julia cleverly circumvented activities or tasks that made her feel and look incompetent. The connection between Julia's problematic behaviors and her fine-motor struggles was difficult to see because the behaviors happened *before* she engaged in those types of activities and she was usually successful at avoiding them.

Update Strategies

In response to what you've learned from investigating, make any and all changes necessary to address the problematic behaviors more effectively, to prevent the behavior from recurring, and to prevent similar behaviors from occurring with other children. The changes may involve rearranging the physical environment, responding to the behaviors in a different way, modifying the daily schedule, altering the curriculum, making activities less or more complex and more engaging, or accessing assistance from a health or social service professional. You will likely need to provide families with support and assistance. Have resources such as books, articles, and videos available for parents on positive guidance strategies. Make sure they know that they can ask you for advice any time about children's development and about guidance and discipline. Focus more on helping them anticipate and prevent problematic behaviors and less on how to respond to those behaviors. If necessary, refer them to community resources for family counseling and health and nutrition assistance. This is important because it will be much easier to help children in your classroom if their families are improving their child-rearing skills.

Julia's Story (Part IV)

Upon realizing that Julia used a variety of problematic behaviors to avoid fine-motor tasks, I shifted my focus from figuring out how best to respond to the behaviors to helping Julia with her fine-motor and self-image struggles. This was a major change in the way I viewed and therefore regulated the problem, and many positive developments resulted. I allowed Julia to opt out of such tasks and "save face" by offering several choices of activities to all the children. I was also careful not to put Julia in too many situations that required good fine-motor skills and found ways to assist her that were supportive and called little attention to her difficulties, usually by offering the same assistance to all the children. I talked with Julia's mother and sisters about once a month to get updates on Julia's progress, to answer questions, and to continue offering suggestions for helping Julia improve her skills and for allowing her to gradually do more for herself. While Julia's skills were improving, she and I found clever ways to compensate: she waited to pour the juice at snack until it was nearly empty and asked someone to hold the cup, I put grips on all the markers and pencils, we figured out how to take off and put on a jacket without unzipping it all the way, among other strategies. The problematic behaviors became less frequent and disappeared within a few months.

1. LITTLE VOLCANOES: CHILDREN WITH EXTREME OR DANGEROUS BEHAVIORS

These are the children who are most likely to be expelled from preschool programs. The behaviors are beyond problematic and most of the prevention and mediation strategies described above are not effective enough. These children almost always require assistance from a mental health specialist and in some cases a treatment program of some kind.

In my classes, I have had more than a few children with extreme behaviors. And I had more of them when I was teaching in wealthy communities than in low-income communities. In every case, the children were eventually placed in special therapeutic programs, but they had not yet been "identified" when they were enrolled in my class. This is one reason for the high rate of expulsions in preschools compared to primary schools. Often preschool is the first place that a child's extreme behaviors are recognized and addressed. By the time the child is age-eligible to attend kindergarten, she is likely to be receiving help and have better behavior or be in a treatment program and not actually attend kindergarten. The children in my class with extreme behaviors were not so much expelled as transferred to a more appropriate program, though it often took several months for the transfer to happen. However, in one case, the family would not accept the severity of their child's behavior until we informed them that the child could not stay in the program unless they agreed to seek help. But the question we asked ourselves was *not* "Should this child be expelled?" It was "What is the best way to help this child?" Expulsion should always be the very last resort and only after a suspension was offered or tried. Any suspension should involve assisting the family in finding help and giving them clear instructions about the length of the suspension and the conditions under which the child can return. If your state has rules and regulations regarding this issue, follow them carefully.

What are extreme or dangerous behaviors? Although many children will occasionally exhibit one or two of the behaviors listed below, if a child has several of these behaviors or if they occur regularly, often, and/or intensely, then the behaviors are extreme and possibly dangerous. The child needs intensive and immediate help. Extreme or dangerous behavior in a young child would include the following:

destroys property for no apparent reason

acts depressed and despondent, very withdrawn, and slow to respond

has extreme fears and phobias

has extreme and frequent mood swings and temper tantrums

obsesses about a particular detail or item

plays with feces

eats items that are clearly not food

displays unusual emotions such as laughing when hurt

has unusual and intense habits such as hair pulling, rocking, head banging, or excessive masturbation/self-stimulation

runs away

makes suicidal statements

places himself in physical danger

hurts himself

threatens to hurt or kill others

is intentional and deliberate about causing pain to others

takes pleasure in hurting or being cruel to others; likes to ruin other children's work

targets another child to bully and victimize

manipulates other children in sophisticated ways, sexually or otherwise

There may be a physical or biological reason for these behaviors, such as birth trauma or autism, or the child may have been traumatized by abuse, neglect, or violence. Some children who exhibit these extreme behaviors have access to special education services and can receive a diagnosis, such as behavior disordered, conduct disordered, oppositional defiant disordered, attention-deficit/hyperactivity disordered (ADHD), reactive attachment disordered, sensory-integration dysfunction, and obsessive-compulsive disorder (OCD), among others. However, there are many, many children with these extreme behaviors who are not getting the special services they need. The reasons are numerous, from the reluctance to put a stigmatizing label on a young child to the lack of money or availability of services. This is especially true in smaller, more rural communities. The major barrier to services, however, is that too often the health care system and some health care providers are not able to offer children with extreme or dangerous behaviors the same level of intensive intervention that is provided to children with serious cognitive disabilities (such as Down syndrome) and physical disabilities (such as spina bifida or cerebral palsy).

Anticipating and Preventing Extreme or Dangerous Behaviors

- When children enroll, ask parents how they discipline their child, how often, and for which behaviors. Ask if their child behaves in any way that is unusual or that concerns them. Ask about any birth trauma, traumatic events, and medication. And ask if the child or family is now or has been in counseling or treatment, or involved with social services. Parents will be reluctant to say anything negative about themselves and their child, particularly if they think she will not be accepted into the program or will be viewed as a "problem" from the start, so they may not answer these questions fully or honestly. Nonetheless, it is important to ask these questions. In some cases parents will decide not to enroll their child with extreme behaviors when they are asked these questions and when they have read your policies, procedures, and approach to behavior issues.

- Having a written policy about issues related to children with extreme or dangerous behaviors is not just a good idea; it's a necessity. If you work in a school or licensed child care facility, there are most likely state and local laws and rules that govern what can and cannot be included in the policy. It's a good idea to refer to behaviors more generally than specifically. It's better to say "an action that causes another child to bleed or to bruise" rather than "biting," "scratching," or "kicking." It's also a good idea to include information about resources and supports that are available to families, the program's referral process, parental consent requirements, and how extreme or dangerous behaviors are handled. Include the program's policy about restraining children. The document should clearly describe what parents would need to do to prevent their child from being expelled and what the teachers and administrators will do to ensure the safety of all children and to help their child.

Solving Problems Related to Extreme or Dangerous Behaviors

While you are working on getting help for a child with extreme or dangerous behaviors, there are a number of things you can do for the child and for the other children in the class.

- It is usually necessary to meet with or notify all other families about a child in the class with extreme behaviors. They need reassurance that their children will not be hurt and that the program or school is doing everything possible to address the issue quickly, thoroughly, and effectively.

- Children with extreme or dangerous behaviors come into the classroom in the morning depleted of positive feelings about themselves and in dire need of attention. Be proactive. As soon as such a child comes in the door (if not before), give her a great deal of attention and affection. Do not wait for her to express her needs, as they are likely to be expressed inappropriately. As previously stated, these children arrive with their emotional tanks empty of the fuel that sustains them: positive attention. So fill them up before the lack of fuel leads to a breakdown and maybe even a crash.

- While it is a good practice to give more attention, assistance, and support to a child who is very emotionally needy than to other children, you cannot neglect the needs of the other children. If this is the case, then you are not receiving enough support. You must request changes to the current arrangement, such as having the child spend fewer days or hours per day in your classroom, more classroom assistance by a trained aide, and/or more intensive in-class and at-home interventions for the child.

- Do everything you can to convince the parents that their child needs to be referred for evaluation and a more appropriate placement. Keep detailed and objective notes of the behaviors you observe in the classroom to help other professionals determine the best placement for the child. (See "Is the Child Just Immature or Is There Really Something Wrong?" on pp. 112–16 for information on identifying children with special needs.) Usually your local school district serves as the place to make a referral. For other sources of help, check with your state or local department of special education, health department or department of social services, and advocacy organizations for children's mental health.

- Keep written, dated records of your conversations with parents, especially if they refuse help or deny a problem exists. There have been cases where parents have successfully sued early childhood programs for failing to make them aware of their children's problems while they were attending. For the benefit of the child, you are obligated to tell parents what you have observed about the child and advise them to seek a referral.

- In her classic book *Teacher* (1963, 1986), New Zealander educator Sylvia Ashton Warner described her fearful, angry, and needy five-year-old Maori children as having minds like volcanoes with "... two vents: destructiveness and creativeness. And to the extent that we widen the creative channel, we atrophy the destructive one" (p. 134). Give children with extreme behaviors many creative outlets, particularly those that are also sensory activities such as working with clay. Observe the child carefully to determine what calms her down and which activities hold her interest for extended periods.

- Teach the other children how to interact with and assist the child with extreme behaviors. Assure them that you will keep them safe. If you can effectively support the child with extreme behaviors so that she can control herself and successfully participate in most activities, the other children will feel secure knowing that you are responsive and able to control the difficult situations and people.

- Protect any child who has been singled out to be bullied or victimized. Observe carefully so you can intervene and mediate the situation before or immediately after a child is victimized by another child. Teach the child who has been victimized the skills and words to use to stand up for himself.

Anger

Anger is what ignites the eruptions inside these little volcanoes. Very young children have the capacity to feel very strong emotions, and anger is the strongest of emotions. The ability to feel a wide range and depth of emotions is one of the few aspects of human development where there is very little difference between young children and adults. The angriest child I have ever seen was a tiny three-year-old with a cherubic face, bouncy red curls ... and tremendous lung capacity! Her wise Head Start teacher was empathetic, tolerant, and helpful. She knew that her classroom was the only place this child could safely express her justifiable anger, her rage. Extreme and dangerous behaviors are often the by-product of such rage, but for this child it was all vocal. Her teacher just carried her out of the room to a place where she could scream and sob without disturbing the class and stayed with her until she was drained, exhausted, and ready to be held and comforted.

Unless the child has a serious physical problem, the source of the rage almost always lies in the child's unfair and (likely) abusive life circumstances. When there's no clear or immediate remedy for a child's anger, as in the example above, then she needs to be able to express her anger in ways that work for her, but also work for the classroom. In most cases this involves a negotiation between the child and the teacher, although the Head Start teacher in my story was able to accommodate the child's behavior rather than change or redirect it. Of course, it's easier to accommodate a behavior that isn't violent or dangerous. Other ways to redirect anger that can't be remedied is to invite the child to pound and work with clay, hammer nails into a stump, throw beanbags into a bucket or at a target on a wall, or run around outside as fast and as long as she can. Once the child is a bit calmer, drawing can be a good outlet for feelings. The child usually then needs help to "regroup." This may involve holding the child close or reading a book to her while she sits on your lap, though she may prefer to look through a book on her own. Listening to music while lying on a mat is very comforting to some children, or the child might be able and willing to quietly join the class activities while staying close by your side, with or without a teddy bear to cling to.

A different approach is necessary to help a child when there *is* a remedy for his anger. This is the more common kind of anger that early childhood teachers deal with: children having a conflict over a toy, a child who feels he was treated unjustly, a child whose delicate spaceship construction was just knocked over, or a child who was not finished playing when it was time to come inside for lunch. The main strategies to use in all these situations is to help the children express their anger with words (they can learn to use an angry voice without shouting) and to teach them the skills they need to reach a positive resolution, whether the conflict is within themselves or with another person. Angry responses to injustices and unwanted challenges will start to disappear when a child has confidence in his ability to deal with them successfully.

Restraining a child

You may have to deal with children who have or are about to seriously hurt you, another child, or themselves. Often the child in this situation is having a tantrum and has lost all control over his actions. You are left with no choice but to restrain the child.

- Insist on receiving training from an expert on how to restrain a child without hurting him. The description that follows is for your information and does not eliminate the need to get direct training and to practice. The most common technique to restrain a child safely involves sitting on the floor behind the child and holding his wrists so that his arms are crossed firmly across his chest, using the least amount of force or pressure possible. If the child butts his head against your chest, then lean in to close the space. Keep talking with the child the whole time using a calm, steady voice about what you are doing, why you are doing it, and that you will release him when he is calm for one minute. When this happens, release the child slowly while still talking with him. Lead him to a place where he can choose between two quiet activities that will further calm him. Stay with him as long as is necessary.

- Unless you are teaching in a school or program that intentionally serves children with behavior disorders and/or you have the supports, resources, and training needed to effectively serve such children, the first time you restrain a child should be the last time you restrain that child. Your supervisor has to take charge of the situation. As the program's policies should state, the child's family needs to pick up their child as soon as possible and meet with a manager or principal to discuss the situation and to agree to terms and conditions for his return or placement in a program better suited to his needs.

- Nonetheless, a child with extreme or dangerous behaviors can be successfully integrated into your class if you or an assistant is trained to help such children, and if you and the family have support services from a mental health specialist. But even then, it might be better if the child attends on a part-time basis, at least until the behaviors improve significantly. A regular classroom is, after all, the best place for him to see and interact with children who model appropriate behavior and to learn to get along with peers.

- When a child who has had extreme behaviors, or only occasionally still has them, can be successfully included in a regular classroom, it is likely to be a positive experience for you, the child, and even for the other children in the class. They will learn to be accepting and tolerant of others with special needs.

2. "YOU CAN'T MAKE ME!": DEFIANT BEHAVIOR AND POWER STRUGGLES

Do certain behaviors really "push your buttons"? The child with defiant behaviors most likely knows the answer better than you do! For some teachers it is an in-your-face "NO." For others it is whining, cursing, shouting, or hitting. It's important to be aware of the behaviors that make you particularly upset so you can (try to) avoid responding impulsively or overreacting. Power struggles often happen at naptimes, meals, cleanup times, and transitions. These are the activities in which children are expected to do things that they may not want to do. Children who feel powerless figure out quickly that starting a power struggle with the teacher by refusing to lie down, eat, clean up, or come inside is a great way to feel more powerful and in control. They bait the teacher, who has limited options and may be unsure of how to respond. But there *are* effective ways to respond. You just have to reach into your toolbox for the right tools.

Anticipating and Preventing Defiant Behaviors

- Forewarn children of what will happen next and what they will need to do prior to the activities that children typically resist. Tell them what will happen after as well. "As soon as we clean up the room and put away all the toys, we will go outside. If everyone helps and works hard, we can get it done quickly."

- Give choices whenever possible so that children will feel more powerful and in control. For example, "Fernando, would you like to work with Kayla to put away the blocks or with Lena to put away the games?"

- Reduce or eliminate the common triggers that may cause children to act defiantly. For example, having children clean up after themselves before moving on to another activity and put away toys and materials as soon as they are done playing with them means there will be very little to do during cleanup time. If children know that after they rest for thirty minutes they can get up from their napping cots or mats and choose a quiet activity, then they are less likely to resist lying down to begin with. It also helps if they can see a clock or timer.

Solving Problems Related to Defiant Behaviors

- When confronted with defiance, first stay calm. Upsetting you and rattling your composure is often the goal of the behavior, as the child then is in control of you.

- Do not completely ignore the behavior, as that can send a message that the behavior is okay.

- Respond to defiant statements like "You can't make me" by saying calmly, "I know you don't want to do this and I see that you are upset. Yes, I can't make you clean up, but tell me how I can help you so it's not so hard." Avoid explaining why she should do this, as that is not the issue at this point. If the child still resists, ask her if she would like your help or if she would like to do it on her own. If this is not successful, try the strategies below.

- Disengage from the power struggle. Remove yourself from the interaction emotionally and, as much as possible, physically. This makes the power struggle ineffective. First, tell the child as calmly as you can, "I will talk with you later when you are calm and can use a respectful voice and words." Then walk away if the child's health and safety will not be compromised and if the behavior is not very disruptive. This will give you time to calm yourself and for the child to calm down. It should stop the power struggle before it gets fully in gear.

- If the child continues trying to engage you in a power struggle, tell her something like this: "I hear you, but I am ignoring you now. When you are calm and respectful, I will help you solve your problem."

- After she has calmed down, talk to her and tell her that if she is angry, unhappy, or needs something, you will be glad to help her if she uses a respectful voice, words, and actions. Help her learn some words and actions she can use, such as tapping your arm gently to get your attention (rather than yelling, hitting, or grabbing) and have her practice them. Then respond calmly to her needs or concerns as best you can.

- The next time she attempts to engage you in a power struggle, stop her quickly and say calmly, "Remember to talk to me calmly and respectfully if you need to tell me something or if you need my help."

- Have her practice better ways of expressing her needs during small-group or work-play times, not during an incident or when she is upset.

3. PERPETUAL(LY IN) MOTION: ACTIVE AND EASILY DISTRACTED/ATTRACTED

Almost every classroom has at least one child who has difficulty concentrating or sitting still even for a short time. These children have much shorter attention spans than other children of the same age. The causes for this are many and varied. Most children like this have little control over their problem, though they really do want to control it. At the extreme, such children may have attention-deficit/hyperactivity disorder (ADHD). The average age for when children with severe ADHD are diagnosed is five years old (Center for Disease Control and Prevention 2013). A combination of drug, individual, and family therapy can be very helpful. However, the use of medication with young children (stimulants like Ritalin are most common) is controversial because many health professionals, educators, and parents feel that it is being overprescribed and that, for some children, it is used more for the convenience of teachers and school systems than to benefit the child. Also, about three times as many preschool-age boys are diagnosed with ADHD than girls. As boys' development lags behind girls' development at this age, the diagnosis may have more to do with adults' unrealistic expectations than a disorder in the child. The medications for ADHD are very effective at reducing active behaviors, which may be why they have become overused. Even for a child who clearly has ADHD and really needs medication to function, the effects of the medication will be greater and longer lasting if there are also changes in the classroom and the home and the child is helped to manage his behavior. This chapter offers numerous ideas for helping active and easily distracted children feel successful and gain at least some self-control and self-respect.

Anticipating and Preventing Problems Related to Children Who Are Active and Easily Distracted/Attracted

- To avoid a classroom that is overstimulating, reduce the busyness in your room while keeping it aesthetically pleasing. Use warm, soft colors; cover or store teacher supplies and materials; and arrange things neatly. Have a small number of photos, posters, children's artwork, and signs on the walls. Choose posters that are soothing, such as nature photos and reproductions of artworks that are beautiful to you.

- Label all shelves and containers. See that everything has its proper place in the classroom. This will help the active or distracted child, as he often has trouble organizing himself and his surroundings.

- Inform all children of what to expect ahead of time. Tell them, "We will be going outside for thirty minutes. When the bell rings, we will come inside for snack. Now you may put your coat on and walk to the door." This is particularly helpful for the active child, but you may have to repeat it several times.

- Set up and follow daily routines and rituals. Make your schedule essentially the same every day, alternating active times and sedentary times. A "good morning" song to start each day is an example of a ritual. This provides a sense of security to a child whose world otherwise feels ungrounded.

- Add action and interaction to all your activities. Teach children some basic sign language and use it during discussions, songs, and stories. This will give them something to do with their hands while also teaching them a helpful skill. Help all children improve their self-regulation skills by embedding self-regulation practice into many activities and routines. For example, play a version of "Simon Says" in which the children must follow your actions, not your words. If you say, "Simon says touch your head" while touching your shoulders, then the children must touch their shoulders. When they are able to do this pretty well, switch to having them do what you say, not what you do. Alternate to keep them challenged. A third variation for even more challenge is to have the children touch any part of their body *other than* the ones that you say and do. (In all these versions, we eliminate the traditional aspect of the game in which the children have to stay still when the leader omits the "Simon says" command.)

Solving Problems Related to Children Who Are Active and Easily Distracted/Attracted

- Appreciate the positive aspects of having an active child in your class. Look at the child as being very attracted to the wonderful things you have provided. Use the active child as your barometer for determining if your activity has gone on too long or is not very interesting to the children. Having a high activity level can be a great asset for the child when she grows up. She will likely be productive and able to accomplish more in a shorter time than most people.

- Provide a curriculum and activities that do not require a great deal of sitting or passive tasks. Avoid too many activities that only involve fine-motor tasks. Have at least one hour of work-play and thirty minutes of outside or gym play for every four hours of class time.

- Keep group times short and meet in small groups. Many active children have a hard time concentrating in groups, especially large groups, but do much better when receiving individual instruction.

- Physical contact helps some active children feel more in control of themselves. To help a child focus better during group times, an adult can have him sit on her lap, touch or rub his back gently, or hold his hand. However, for some active children physical contact has the opposite effect.

- Give the child something to hold during group times, such as a doll or teddy bear, a soft (partially deflated) rubber ball or spiky ball, or something smooth to rub like an oiled piece of wood or a polished stone.

- Give the child things to do during group time. The child who can't sit still during a flannel board story can place the flannel figures on the board and move them around. She can turn the pages of the book being read.

- Give the child the option to use a small, freestanding cardboard divider to keep visual distractions from interfering with his attention while he works at a table activity. Use a large divider during naptimes.

- Give instructions clearly and specifically for any task you are requiring children to do. Do not give more than two or three directions at a time. Reinforce the directions visually by demonstrating them and by drawing a picture that the children can refer to while carrying out the activity.

- Some active children benefit from individualized, specific assistance. Tell the child specifically how to focus on a task. For example, "Look at the line on the paper. Hold your paper tight with one hand and open your scissors with the other hand. Put the top blade on top of the line, and then close the scissors while slowly moving it forward."

- Provide many outlets for the child's energy that will not cause problems. Give her beanbags to throw at a target or into a bucket. Provide a gym mat to jump on and roll around.

- Change your expectations. Allow the child to spend less time at activities and to move around during some activities. He can stand or play with a quiet activity at a table nearby during circle time rather than having to sit the whole time.

- Whenever possible, substitute items that are easier to use and that help the child focus. If she can't keep her chair still while seated at the table, provide her with a beanbag chair instead.

- As often as you can, catch the child when he is calm and let him know when his overactive behavior is improving: "You've been listening for a long time. You must feel very proud of yourself."

- Give more direction and more verbal and physical assistance during activities and routines to the active child than you do for other children.

- Although many in the medical community claim there is no proof of a link between food and behavior, many teachers and parents have seen clear evidence that certain foods, food additives, chemical substances, or even some synthetic fabrics affect behavior. Suggest to parents that an allergist or pediatrician test for these reactions. Working on changes in the diet often makes for a positive first step for teachers and parents to help a child. There is no blame on anyone, and positive, direct action is being taken. Some diets can be very challenging to maintain, however, and will require effort and vigilance. A dietary approach to dealing with active behavior should be used alongside the other approaches discussed. If a child is on a modified diet and her behavior does not change, help the parents seek family counseling and try some of the other solutions discussed above.

4. THIS PROBLEM REALLY BITES!

Children who bite usually do so because they are frustrated or angry. For example, they want a toy that another child has or want the toy back that another child has just taken. They bite less out of aggression toward the other child than to vent frustration and to get what they want. They often act quickly and impulsively, too young or immature to stop themselves or make another choice. There tends to be more biting in small, crowded classrooms. Teething can also contribute to biting. The age when biting is most frequent is between thirteen and twenty-four months. Some children bite because their language skills are not good enough to say what they want; their cognitive development is more advanced than their language development, which is very frustrating. When children older than three years bite, it is a much more serious issue. They are likely being more intentional than impulsive, they may bite very hard, and it can be more difficult to change the behaviors. For these children, follow the recommendations about children with extreme or dangerous behaviors in chapter 1 of this part on pp. 185–89.

Anticipating and Preventing Biting

- Have at least two of each toy, especially for toddlers. This prevents disputes over particular toys, which causes frustration. Make sure you have an ample supply of toys that are interesting to the children and that can engage them for extended periods. Rotate toys so they do not become boring for the children.

- Attend to the teething needs of toddlers through use of individual teething rings and other safe, soothing things to bite on.

- Create an environment with few frustrations or stresses. Give children easy access to many materials and opportunities to participate in many engaging activities. Be equally responsive to their need for clear limits and their need for control. Give ample time for work-play choices and for outdoor/gym play.

- Observe children carefully and be ready to intervene as soon as you see signs of frustration. Help them solve their problems or resolve their conflicts. Encourage them to express their feelings with words and with actions that are socially acceptable and not hurtful. Provide toys to pound, nails to hammer, clay or playdough to mold, sand and water play to experiment with, and beanbags to throw.

- Help children calm themselves down when they are upset. Suggest that they listen to music, look at a book, draw, or ask to be held.

- Help children express their feelings with words or with vocalizations for very young children or children with language disabilities. Interpret their words to other children, if necessary: "Rosa, Sara is saying 'Me. Me.' She is telling you she would like a turn."

- Provide a great deal of individual positive attention. Some children bite out of the frustration of feeling invisible.

Solving Problems Related to Biting

- Carefully watch the child who bites to determine what, if anything, causes this behavior. Check for times of day, certain types of interactions, interactions with particular children, or particular situations.

- In most cases, changing biting behavior requires stopping the child *before* she actually bites. This means you must be extremely vigilant and stay as close to the child as possible for as much time as possible. You must be able to step in as soon as you see any sign of frustration or other indication that biting might occur and prevent it. Say to the child in a sharp voice, "Stop! That will hurt." Physically come between the children if necessary. For most children, it doesn't take too many such interventions to stop the biting.

- Validate the child's feelings. Teach the child words she can use to express her anger and frustration, and have her practice them, if she is not too upset. If the biting was not provoked by a frustrating situation, give her a teething ring or something similar to bite on. Move her quickly away from other children and give her a toy or an activity to engage in.

- If you are unable to mediate before the biting happens, comfort the child who has been bitten and say in a sharp voice to the biter, "You hurt Zach." Use a stern face so she will know that you disapprove. Be brief so as not to give the biter too much attention and then involve her in comforting the bitten child. Have the biter help put a bandage on the wound.

- If the children are too young or are unable to negotiate a resolution, then help them by giving the child who grabbed the toy away another toy, setting a timer for turns, presenting a toy they can use together, or giving the two children two different toys.

- Even screaming when frustrated is far preferable to biting. Give specific feedback to the child whenever she uses words or vocalizes when upset and doesn't bite: "Using your words is the best way to get what you want." If necessary, assist so that using words does resolve the problem. Work on the screaming or vocalizations to gradually reduce the volume.

- If the child seems to bite only one particular child, keep them separated as much as possible and watch closely when they are together. (See the "No One Likes Me!" on pp. 155–56 for information about helping children who are victims.) Consider moving the child who bites to another class. The biting often stops when the child is with older children because now she is more stimulated or because the older children won't let her bite.

- Make changes in your routines or schedule, if necessary. If biting happens most often close to lunchtime, make sure the child has a midmorning snack to ward off hunger or arrange for lunch to be served a little earlier. It's not that the child bites because she is hungry, but rather that being hungry makes her irritable.

- In extreme cases, you may have to help the child's parents find another program, perhaps temporarily. Some children do not thrive in a large-group setting and may stop biting when attending a program with fewer children, such as family child care. (See the information about expulsions in "Little Volcanoes" on pp. 185–89.)

5. HE SAID A BAD WORD, TEACHER: CURSING, NAME-CALLING, AND FOUL LANGUAGE

This is a challenging problem because foul language usually can't be ignored even though it should be. Children use swear words for one of the following reasons:

- to get attention by causing adults to focus energy and time on correcting or admonishing them, or to get attention from other children by making them laugh, look at them, or talk to or about them

- to empower themselves by causing adults or other children to get upset, agitated, concerned, or excited

- to empower themselves by putting down others

- to act and sound like an adult

- unintentionally as an automatic response when they get angry or frustrated; they hear parents or siblings use these words at home, and they hear them on television, in movies, and in the neighborhood

You can usually determine why children curse by observing them carefully. Is the child looking for a response from you or other children? Does he increase the volume of his voice? Is it targeted directly at another child? Or does he just say the words in a matter-of-fact way? Base your approach to dealing with the problem on the purpose of the behavior. The key to eliminating the behavior is to take away the power of the words, to make children feel powerful in acceptable ways, and to teach them better responses to anger or frustration.

Anticipating and Preventing Foul Language

- Establish a classroom rule: "Use your hands and words to help, not hurt." Regularly remind children of this rule. Tell them that using "bad" words does not help and it does hurt.

- Let children know that negative feelings are okay and that everyone has them. Teach them that saying to another child, "It really makes me angry when you grab my toy. I want it back!" is more likely to get the toy back than yelling bad words. And remind them that if that does not work, they should ask a teacher for help.

- Help children learn appropriate words that describe negative feelings—such as frustrated, embarrassed, hurt, put down, angry, humiliated, and upset—to replace curse words. Encourage children to talk about what makes them feel this way. Use pictures or take photos to help children connect the feeling words to facial expressions. Give them opportunities to practice saying the words by doing simple role plays.

- When children express their feelings by using appropriate phrases rather than cursing, give them positive feedback: "It's great that you used words to let us know how you feel. Now I can help you solve the problem."

Solving Problems Related to Foul Language

- If the goal of cursing is to get attention, ignore it if possible. If other children respond by telling you about what was said, say to them calmly, "I heard the words. I am ignoring them, and you can ignore them too." Show no agitation or anger, as this is just what the child wants.

- If the child curses as a response to frustration or anger, talk to him about the "helpful words" rule. Tell him that no one knows what he is upset about if he uses bad words instead of saying what he needs. Help him find other words he can say instead. For example, "That hurt me!" "I don't like it when you do that!" or "Stop it!" Help children learn strategies to prevent frustration and anger from developing.

- If a child curses to get other children to laugh and get excited, invite him to instead make up silly rhymes or stories, tell simple jokes, or lead an active movement game.

- If saying these words involves hurting others through name-calling, help the child practice expressing his feelings and needs using different, acceptable words. Also teach him strategies for solving conflicts respectfully. Talk with the other child involved in the altercation about her options. She can say, "If you call me names, I won't play with you," and then walk away.

- If using these words is unintentional (an automatic response or an imitation of adults), intervene quickly but calmly. Tell the child to use different words because those words can hurt and upset others. Ask him, "What other words can you use?" Recommend some if he can't think of any. Have him practice saying the more appropriate words out loud. If the swearing has become a habit, you may need to intervene many times before he will use better language.

Complaints from parents about foul language

Some parents are concerned that their children will learn or have learned foul language at school. The reality is that the children in your class have heard these words long before they came to your class, but they are now at an age when they are interested in trying them out.

- Tell parents about your approach to dealing with these behaviors and reassure them that you are doing many things to prevent and eliminate foul language. Let parents know that you are being intentional when you respond minimally to cursing and, under certain circumstances, you may not respond at all.

- Involve parents in helping solve the problem. Don't contradict the parent or act defensively because, after all, the allegation may be true. Tell the parent that you are concerned about cursing in the classroom and explain your approach and strategies for dealing with the behavior. Ask the parent for suggestions and ask what you can do to help his child.

- Brainstorm with parents on ways that you can help each other and agree to consistently use similar methods for dealing with the problem at home and school. (See "Beyond Feedback" on pp. 228–31 for ideas on responding to parents who complain.)

6. THE ART OF NONVERBAL COMMUNICATION: EXCESSIVE CRYING OR WHINING

This behavior is more common in children who are new to the center. (See "Right from the Start" on pp. 14–18 and "New Kid on the Block" on pp. 158–59 for ideas on helping a new child.) Also, children who are temperamentally sensitive or fragile will cry and whine more than other children. Adjust your expectations for these children because a child's temperament rarely changes. However, you can help them (as well as all the children) by teaching them new coping behaviors. Try to determine the root cause of the behavior. Although it is often an attention-getting strategy, there may be a more serious reason, such as chronic pain or a recent stressful event. Whining is so common among children because it is very effective. Adults find it so annoying that they will give in to the child or at least pay attention to him.

There was a three-year-old in my class who cried often and regularly from her first day to long past the time most children feel safe and comfortable and stop crying. Our sympathy and support did not reduce the crying at all. Her mother told us the child talks happily at home about all the activities at the center and sings all the songs and fingerplays. We were in disbelief because the child almost never participated in these activities. This discussion gave us the information we needed to stop the child's crying. We realized we had been inadvertently reinforcing her crying behavior, so instead we said firmly, "You're okay. You don't need to cry" and then we guided her to an activity. The crying stopped quickly after that.

Anticipating and Preventing Excessive Crying and Whining

- If you have an engaging, active curriculum, and you are organized and manage your classroom and schedule smoothly, there should be very little crying and whining.

- Provide individual attention and a great deal of positive regard to all children.

- In all you do, strive for a healthy balance between support (making children feel cared for and safe) and challenge (activities that stretch children's thinking and muscles a bit).

- Give little attention to any negative or inappropriate behavior. Give a great deal of energy and attention to acceptable behaviors. Help children learn words and strategies that help them get their needs met in ways that are positive and productive.

- Help children learn to avoid situations or activities that will cause them to get frustrated, angry, or humiliated. They may need to choose to play with certain children rather than others, and choose certain toys or games rather than others.

- Use many cooperative games and activities. Reduce competition. Almost all young children have a very difficult time dealing with losing and the stress of competition. More fragile children fare even worse. Teaching the skills of cooperation and negotiation provides children alternatives to interacting with others competitively. (See "The need to belong" in "Accommodate Needs" on p. 177 for more ideas about cooperative games.)

- Deal directly and effectively with all acts of aggression and hurtful behaviors among children. Help children interact with each other positively.

Solving Problems Related to Excessive Crying and Whining

- Give minimal attention to the child who cries excessively to get attention. Tell the child kindly, "I'm sorry that you feel sad. I'll be glad to help you (or pay attention to you) when you talk to me without crying." Support the child's feelings while helping him change the behavior.

- Cut off a whiny voice as soon as it begins by saying, "Please use your regular voice so we can understand you better."

- Give positive attention to the child when he is not crying or whining. Say something like "Thank you for using a regular voice. I can understand you so much better."

- Tell the child who is crying excessively that he can cry as much as he needs to where his crying won't disturb everyone else. Help him move to an area that is safe, visible to adults, but away from the other children. Tell him, "When you are ready to talk about what is making you unhappy, I will listen because I really want to help you." This will let him know that crying and feelings are okay but that you won't let this behavior disrupt the classroom, worry other children, or be a successful attention-getter.

- Observe carefully to determine if the behavior happens mostly at particular times of the day, when the child plays with certain children, or when he is with specific staff members. For example, the child may cry more near lunchtime because of hunger or in the middle of the afternoon because of tiredness. Be flexible and, if possible, make any necessary changes to meet his needs.

- Validate the child's intense feelings while helping him find other ways to deal with them. For example, help him learn that he can ask for a snack when he is hungry or to rest when he is tired. Follow through consistently on these requests so he will know that they are more effective than whining or crying.

- Talk with parents to determine possible reasons for the behavior. Brainstorm possible solutions together. Suggest an examination from a pediatrician to rule out any physical problems.

- Ask your supervisor or a respected coworker to observe you with your children to make sure you are not inadvertently supporting and promoting the behavior. It can be difficult to ignore this behavior and any attention you are paying to it may be giving the child just what he wants. Ask your supervisor or coworker for suggestions for changing the behavior.

7. THE HITS JUST KEEP ON COMING: PHYSICAL AGGRESSION

Hitting, kicking, scratching, pinching, and other types of physical aggression are the greatest behavior concerns of teachers. It is important to realize that a certain amount of this behavior is normal and to be expected with young children. Many children are not fully able to stop themselves from acting impulsively on their strong feelings. They are also not able to fully understand the consequences of their actions. In some families and communities, children are actually encouraged to hit and act aggressively. They also see this behavior among adults, especially in the media. Nonetheless, young children can learn to act differently in different places. In fact, this is a very useful skill to help them develop. They can learn to accept that hitting may be allowed at home but words must be used at school. Physical aggression is seen more often in boys than girls. The reason for this is probably a combination of male hormones, societal expectations, child-rearing practices (from birth, boys are handled and talked to differently from girls), and all the male "role models" who are admired for their physical aggressiveness—from athletes to cartoon characters to movie superheroes. Aggressive girls tend to be socially and verbally aggressive rather than physically aggressive. (See the next chapter, "Mean Girls, the Prequel" on pp. 204–6 for more information about aggression among girls.) Observe behaviors carefully because they may not be truly aggressive but are meant to be playful or they are unintentionally aggressive. This often happens with rough-and-tumble play. (See "Puppies at Play" on pp. 209–11 for information about roughhousing.)

Physical aggression includes any behavior meant to deliberately hurt another person, including punching, pinching, kicking, biting, and pulling hair. The essential task is to teach children how they can get their needs met—get the toy they want, express their anger or frustration, respond to meanness or aggression from other children—through methods other than physical aggression. All children need to know that aggression toward others is not acceptable at school. Remind them often, "This is a safe classroom. We use our hands and words to help, not hurt."

A child who continues to be aggressive, endangering the safety of other children, even after you have tried the ideas in this chapter, needs more intensive help. (See "Little Volcanoes" on pp. 185–89 for more information on help for children with extreme or dangerous behaviors.)

Anticipating and Preventing Physical Aggression

- Read the first few chapters of this section carefully (starting on p. 173) for many ideas that will help you prevent aggressive behaviors from happening.

- Teach all children social skills for getting along with others. Do this on an ongoing basis. Do it both when there are conflicts and during small- or large-group times. There are numerous social skills and violence prevention curricula you may find helpful, such as *Second Step* (www.cfchildren.org/second-step) and *PATHS* (*Promoting Alternative THinking Strategies*) for preschool/kindergarten (www.channing-bete.com/prevention-programs/paths/paths.html).

- Read books, use role plays and puppets, or use a social skills curriculum to teach children negotiating strategies and how to resolve conflicts peacefully.

- Create a physical environment and emotional tone in your class that keeps frustrations to a minimum. Provide many different types of toys, games, activities, and projects and give children ample time to engage with them. As much as possible, eliminate situations in which children have to wait, be still, or be quiet. When such times are unavoidable, start a fingerplay, song, or thinking game.

- Separate children who tend to "set each other off" at large- or small-group times.

- Watch for conflicts between children, especially if either child has been physically aggressive before, and intervene quickly so you can teach them how to de-escalate their emotions and resolve the conflict before it gets to the point where there is hitting or other aggression.

- Give children plenty of time to play outside or in a gym where they can engage in big, loud, physical play. Children will be less likely to channel the need for such play in aggressive ways.

- Provide many opportunities for children to have power and control in acceptable, age-appropriate ways. Give them many choices throughout the day: which books to read, which songs to sing, how much snack to eat, whether to play indoors or out, and so forth. There is little, if any, aggression in classrooms where children have many opportunities to have power and control by making choices, having "jobs," taking responsibility, being treated with respect, and having their feelings supported and their frustrations attended to.

- Use or develop a variety of games and activities in which children interact with each other physically. Many young children have a strong need for physical contact with each other and, if not given opportunities to do so positively, they may do it aggressively. Often they don't intend to be aggressive (their intention might even be to show affection), but it feels like aggression to the child on the receiving end.

Solving Problems Related to Physical Aggression

- Teaching new behaviors to a child who acts aggressively requires vigilance and persistence. You can't let any act of aggression go unnoticed and unmediated. You will undoubtedly have to help a child who acts aggressively many times before the new behaviors stick.

- When you mediate an act of aggression, attend first to the child who has been hit and give him sympathy and support. Keep the child who did the hitting with you also, but give him minimal attention. If possible, involve the aggressor in comforting and taking care of the child who has been hurt. Then calmly help both children negotiate on a more equal basis: help the targeted child stand up for himself emotionally and verbally, and help the aggressive child express himself peacefully.

- If, after many attempts to teach negotiating and turn-taking strategies, a child continues to act aggressively, he most likely does not yet have the cognitive ability or emotional maturity to do anything else. If this child is older than three and has similar impulse control challenges and difficulties during other activities, then he needs further evaluation and help. (See "Is the Child Just Immature or Is There Really Something Wrong?" on pp. 112–16.) If the child has been identified with a behavior disorder and is receiving services, ask for additional support and advice from his therapist(s).

- If a particular child is targeted by an aggressive child, teach him to stand up for himself. (See "No One Likes Me!" on pp. 155–56 for ideas for helping children who are too easily victimized.)

Grabbing toys

- Use this situation as an opportunity to teach social skills. Help the child negotiate a turn-taking system, a trade, or some fair method of sharing the toy. Give as much help as necessary, but no more. Make sure all the children have easy access to a timer or a clock to help them negotiate a solution on their own.

- Help the child find a good strategy to deal with having to wait for a turn. Offer a choice, if necessary: "While you are waiting, you can watch Lynn play with the toy, draw a picture, or choose another activity."

- Often the children who grab toys repeatedly are less mature or younger than other children. These children will eventually develop better behavior with your kind guidance and patience.

Wrecking other children's projects

A typical aggressive act in an early childhood classroom is when a child intentionally knocks down the carefully constructed block structure other children have spent a great deal of time and effort creating. Whenever a child deliberately knocks down blocks, tears up a drawing, or scribbles on another child's painting, it is an act of aggression meant to hurt others, even if it is not directly physical aggression. Such behavior also informs you that this child needs your help. Some children do this in a clumsy attempt to interact with other children and be part of their play because they don't know a better way. Through this aggressive act, the child at least gains their attention, as well as yours. In some cases the purpose of the behavior is to get revenge on another child (jealousy of a popular child, perhaps), to test your ability to set limits, or to get your attention.

- Just as with all aggressive behaviors, give minimal attention to the behavior itself but help the child get what he wants, express his feelings, and, perhaps, join the play in a socially acceptable way. Give sympathy and support to children whose project was wrecked. Work along with the aggressive child and together fix the destroyed object: tape the picture, hang a fresh sheet of paper on the easel, or pick up the blocks.

8. TOO BOSSY: GETTING CONTROLLING UNDER CONTROL

This is the child who tries—and often succeeds—to control what other children do. He dominates situations and believes that he has the best ideas . . . and he may. Even if there is no conflict because the other children accept the behavior, and some even welcome it, it is important to intervene. The child who acts bossy needs help to interact more equitably and cooperatively with others, and the other children need help to assert themselves and have opportunities to be leaders, at least on occasion.

Some children who act bossy are among the oldest children in the group or among the oldest siblings in their family. Telling other children what to do comes easily and naturally.

Common bossy behaviors include taking all the roles in social imaginary play scenarios: director, script writer, and lead actor; speaking for other children; and dominating discussions and conversations. Many of these children are highly intelligent, creative, and caring. They can see possibilities and consequences that other children cannot and want to share their knowledge with their peers. They have a greater awareness of social protocols and rules and have a keen (but often inflexible) sense of right and wrong. It is important for ECED teachers to see the positive aspects of the behavior and to not overreact.

Anticipating and Preventing Problems Related to Children Who Act Bossy

- Create processes for leadership roles to rotate among the children. For example, rotate the job of "teacher" so that it is assigned to a different child each day and all children have many opportunities to have the job. More information about job charts can be found in "Right from the Start" on pp. 14–18.

- Teach children to use a variety of turn-taking strategies and support their use. Encourage the children to take turns for who has the lead role(s) in an imaginary play scenario and, if necessary, facilitate the process. Have pieces of paper posted or attached to clipboards on which children can add their names to have a turn and then cross them off after their turn. Children who cannot yet write their names can just write the first letter or make marks on the paper that to her represent her name. Have a timer available so each turn is equal and for a reasonable amount of time.

- Help children collaborate when developing and sustaining ideas for play scenarios, constructions, projects, etc. Encourage the use of phrases such as "I have another idea," "That's a good idea and we can also . . ." "Who has another idea?" "What should we do if . . ." "Maybe we can . . ."

- Teach all children strategies for helping others without doing the task for them. For example, when helping another child tie her shoelace, first see if she can do the initial step or if you can teach her the initial step. Then ask her to watch how you do the rest. Describe what you are doing while you do it. Or, when helping another child zip up a jacket, get it started in the bottom stop, but let him pull up the slider to close it. More ideas can be found in "Reversed Roles: Children Who Are Too Responsible" on pp. 151–52.

- Before the start of an activity or routine that tends to elicit the bossy behavior (i.e., imaginary play, games, constructive play, outside play) remind the child to allow other children to speak, contribute ideas, and be leaders.

Solving Problems Related to Children Who Act Bossy

- When a child attempts to control the actions of other children, help him soften his tone, restate his command as a suggestion, and ask questions. Rather than stating, "I'll be the pilot and you be the passengers," he can ask, "May I be the pilot first? We also need co-pilots, flight attendants, and passengers. Who else do we need?"

Rather than demanding, "Go get some pens," he can say, "Do you want to get some pens and I'll get the paper and glue?"

- Help the children who are being controlled to assert themselves. They can use strategies such as playing with other children or in a different area; asking to take turns; saying, "No, I don't want to" and, if so inclined, offering to do something else; giving their own ideas to replace or to add to the idea given by the child who is being bossy; and responding to a command rather than accepting it by asking, "What will you do?" or stating, "Let's do it together" or "I'll do it, if you. . . ."

- Assist the child who acts bossy to be a leader in appropriate ways: offering to help others, modeling good behavior, being kind and having positive interactions with others, engaging in problem-solving and compromise, and being flexible, fair, and accepting of differences.

9. MEAN GIRLS, THE PREQUEL: VERBAL AND SOCIAL AGGRESSION

Of course young boys can be verbally and socially mean and aggressive, just as girls can be physically aggressive. However, aggression among girls is much more likely to involve social exclusion to hurt another girl on the inside, while aggression among boys is much more likely to involve hurting another boy on the outside. All mean behaviors are disturbing to see. We worry about children who seem to have mastered the art of making another child cry and then have no remorse about doing it, or worse, actually enjoy doing it.

Why is verbal and social aggression more common among girls? There are many factors involved. Girls have (on average) more advanced language and social skills than boys. They are socialized early to be attuned to feelings, their own and others', and to value social cohesion. Even some girls as young as three know that the most hurtful thing they can do to another girl is make her feel bad by making her a social outcast. "You can't come to my birthday party" is much more impactful and painful to most girls than a punch. There are other effective ways as well to be verbally and socially aggressive: forming cliques; making certain children take subservient roles in play; making cruel comments "behind the backs" of other girls but just within hearing range; and making up "rules" that others have to follow, then breaking the rules and remaking them to suit the aggressive child.

Children who are intentionally and deliberately mean may be that way because they have not securely bonded with a loving adult or because they are being mistreated themselves, perhaps by an older sibling or another child in the neighborhood. For some, being mean to others is an inappropriate way that they channel their anger and pain. But for most children, it is a way to feel powerful and in control and to feel better about themselves by diminishing others. To a child, being mean may feel like a perfectly acceptable way to behave, because this behavior is all too common in our culture and because adults rarely intervene.

However, children have to learn that verbal aggression is *not* acceptable. This requires teachers to mediate whenever the behaviors happen just as they would for physical aggression and help children resolve conflicts or express their feelings respectfully and peacefully.

At the same time, children who are being mean need to feel secure and good about themselves so they don't have the need to make themselves feel better by devaluing others. It can be very difficult to feel positive toward a child who is so unlikeable, but it is a bit easier when you understand that the child hurts others because she is hurting inside. Children develop consciences—an internal moral compass—as a result of experiencing an adult's unconditional positive regard and care. You can provide this for children even if no other adult in their lives can. Give them a great deal of positive encouragement and attention when they are acting in acceptable ways or just acting neutral. As soon as you start having a positive impact on the child's self-worth, you will see the behaviors improve.

Anticipating and Preventing Verbal and Social Aggression

- Create a classroom environment where kindness and respect are actively promoted and expected. Establish classroom rules: "Use your hands and words to help, not hurt" and a no-exclusion rule such as "Everyone's included, everybody plays." Remind them of these rules often. Model kindness and respect in your interactions with coworkers and with children. Many of the chapters in "Daily Dilemmas" that starts on page 13 offer ideas for creating a sense of community.

- Teach children negotiation, conflict-resolution, and turn-taking skills on an ongoing basis. Keep promoting the importance of including everybody in all activities, and help make this happen as necessary.

- Provide many outlets for children to express their strong feelings safely. Be available to talk with them and write stories together. Give them plenty of time for large-motor play. Validate their feelings often and give them ample amounts of positive energy and attention *before* they need it.

- Give children ways to express positive feelings about other children. Have each child say something good about another child during a group time. This way all the children receive a turn to both express positive feelings about others and receive positive comments about themselves and what they do.

- Make books throughout the year about each child. Invite every child to draw a picture and write or dictate positive information about the child whose book is being composed. Then put all the papers together to form a book.

- When a child does something positive for another, such as helping zip up a coat, assist the child who received the help to express his appreciation.

Solving Problems Related to Verbal Aggression

- Don't allow verbal and social aggression to be an acceptable behavior in your classroom. Intervene and mediate every time this happens. If the mean behavior involves social exclusion, remind the aggressive child that "Everyone's included, everybody plays." For example, "Marina, when you said to Ana, 'We don't want to play with you; go away,' she felt very hurt inside. Look at her face and you can see how hurt she feels. Please speak only for yourself and use words that help, not hurt. Help Ana by giving her some ideas for how she can join your play and make it even more fun." Then give as much assistance as necessary to ensure that Ana joins the play. Withdraw from the area as soon as you are able.

- Help the verbally and socially aggressive child see the good in herself independent of comparisons to others: "Everyone is unique and important. You really enjoy art and are fun to play with." Use many other methods to instill a positive sense of self-regard. Be physically affectionate, if the child likes it and needs it, and tell her when you see her being kind: "You helped Jason tie his shoes. You are a good friend, and you help make this a happy classroom."

- Help the child who is the object of the cruel behavior stand up for herself by coaching her to say such phrases as "Yes, I *can* play here." Be sure that the child knows ways to successfully join in play. (For more information, see "No One Likes Me!: Children Who Are Social Outcasts or Easily Victimized" on page 155.)

- You cannot make children like each other, but you can teach children (and expect them) to respect each other and get along. In this way, you are helping children develop the very important skills and dispositions to appreciate and partner with a wide variety of people.

10. I DIDN'T DO IT, TEACHER!: THE TRUTH ABOUT LYING

All young children lie occasionally. All adults lie too and much more than we would like to admit. Children lie and stretch the truth to build themselves up in the eyes of others, as many adults do when describing their accomplishments. We may be trying to be kind in complimenting a friend's new haircut we don't like, but it's still a lie. We may think we're being clever and saving a lot of money in coming up with a good excuse to get out of paying a parking ticket, but it's still a lie. Just as adults do not see these lies as something wrong or immoral, children do not view the lies they tell as wrong or immoral. They believe it is acceptable to lie if the lie prevents them from being viewed as "bad" or from being punished. In fact, viewed this way, they believe that lying is the "moral" thing to do. Yet, too many teachers mistakenly resort to lectures and punishments in response to children's lies.

A better strategy is to avoid putting children in situations that require them to lie in order to save face. We should forgive the occasional lie as a typical behavior of young children, but a child who lies often or to cover up a serious issue needs our help.

Anticipating and Preventing Lying

- Help children see the difference between what is real and what is imagined (made up) whenever the opportunity arises: "It's fun to play Batman, but is he real?" If necessary, explain that he is a pretend character that a man named Bob Kane invented from his imagination. He drew pictures of the Batman character the way he imagined him and made up stories about him. Then other people made movies from these stories. However, it would be exciting if he were real.

- Do not put children in the position of having to lie to protect themselves from negative consequences or from being seen as "bad." Instead of asking, "Did you grab the toy?" say, "Tell me what happened in your argument over the toy." Children will not feel the need to protect themselves or save face by lying if you help children solve their differences fairly, take a teaching and problem-solving approach to problematic behaviors, and avoid punishments.

- Build self-esteem by making sure children are accepted and appreciated unconditionally for who they are and not only for what they can do or say. Do this by saying many positive things to all children: "Your sweet smile brightens my day" or "I really enjoy being with you every day" or "I like you, just because you are you." Be physically warm and affectionate. Give children many opportunities to be responsible and expect that they can handle their responsibilities, even if this means offering a little (or a lot of) assistance.

- As lying can often be an attention-getting behavior, give all children a great deal of individual attention. Know their strengths and weaknesses well and be responsive to their needs.

Solving Problems Related to Lying

Young children will often make up improbable stories and insist they are true. This is not so much lying as it is fantasizing. Support the child's ability to imagine and the fulfillment he gets through the story: "You tell wonderful stories that are fun to listen to. You have a great imagination." This sends the child a positive message and at the same time lets him know that you know the story is a fantasy. Avoid asking if the story is true, as that only puts the child in a position of having to lie.

- Compulsive lying, or lying that happens frequently and consistently, is usually a sign that the child feels a great deal of shame about himself. He has the need to build himself up and to be seen as always good and right in order to protect his weak sense of self from further damage. Help this child feel more confident and better about himself through a variety of strategies. Help him see all that is actually positive about him, without exaggerating. For example: "You really know how to be a good friend to Amanda," "You threw that ball so far!" or "You worked very hard and long on your picture. I really like the way you put all the colors together."

- Try to determine if there is a purpose for the lie, such as to get sympathy, get attention, or feel validated. Tell the child how he can achieve his purpose in a better way. Make yourself available to talk with the child whenever he seeks your attention, and increase the amount of unsolicited positive attention that you give him.

- When the child lies directly to you, do not confront him with the lie. If the lie has to do with telling about an untrue incident—claiming to be hit when you know he wasn't—respond by validating the feelings behind the lie: "You feel hurt and feel badly treated. I'm glad you came to tell me and that you didn't hit back." Then move on to helping solve the conflict (if there actually was one) or to help him engage in an activity.

- If a child denies wrongdoing that you suspect is a lie—"I didn't take Celia's crayons!"—say, "I know you are a good person. Everyone makes mistakes sometimes. Let's talk with Celia and figure out how to solve the problem." The statement that "Everyone makes mistakes" is purposely ambiguous. It could refer to Celia's claim that her crayons were taken or to the child's act of taking them. This avoids accusations, affirms the child's self-worth, and leaves the door open for a number of solutions.

- Work with parents to try to determine the root cause of the problem and to discuss ways to help the child. Encourage parents to be positive with the child and not punish her.

- If the lying persists or gets worse in spite of using the strategies in this chapter, recommend or refer the family for counseling. A young child who lies compulsively and insistently has serious emotional needs, and the child and the child's family would benefit from the help of a mental health professional.

11. IN THEIR COMFORT ZONE: MASTURBATION AND SELF-PLEASURING

It is not unusual to see this behavior with young children. They are not masturbating in a sexual sense but are comforting or stimulating themselves by rubbing their genitals. For most children, it means they are bored and/or anxious. In my many years observing in early childhood classrooms, I have seen this behavior during very boring story times and circle times, during naptimes, and when children were put in "time-out" for long periods.

If a child does this often and overtly, help arrange for an examination by a pediatrician, as the child may actually be trying to alleviate discomfort from an infection or other medical problem. Suggesting there may be a medical problem is a good place to start to avoid the perception someone is casting blame or being blamed. However, the results might reveal a condition that could be or is likely the result of sexual abuse. It is the doctor's obligation to report this. If there are no medical issues, then the child and family would benefit from the help of a mental health professional. The child may have an intense level of anxiety and the source of the anxiety needs to be addressed. And there is still a possibility that she is being abused. (See "Little Volcanoes" on pp. 185–89 about children with extreme or dangerous behaviors and "Save the Children" on pp. 237–39 about parents who may be abusive.)

It is difficult for young children to figure out complex social rules and follow them. It's even difficult for adults sometimes. This is why children pick their nose in public, sing loudly in a store, take their shoes off in a restaurant, and, yes, masturbate at school. Learning social protocols is a long, slow, gradual process so be patient, understanding, and a little persistent.

Anticipating and Preventing Self-Pleasuring

- Make sure your schedule is meeting your children's needs for action and that your curriculum activities are individualized, engaging, and a little challenging. Boredom is a very common reason for such behaviors.

- Do not use time-out or other behavior management strategies that require children to sit still and do nothing for long periods.

- Provide many opportunities for children to express and relieve their anxieties every day through drawing and many open-ended sensory activities such as sand and water play, clay, and playdough.

Solving Problems Related to Self-Pleasuring

- Use the behavior as a cue that the activity you are doing is not meeting children's needs. Stop and alter the activity, do something different, or move on to the next activity in your schedule.

- Give the child a stuffed toy animal to hold and stroke, a soft rubber ball or spiky ball, or other object that may satisfy her need for calming herself or for stimulation.

- At a later point, away from others, talk to the child about the behavior. For example, "I know it feels good to rub your vagina, but this is something you can do at home, not at school. It's just like how you have to wear shoes at school, but at home you can be barefoot. Let's think of something else that you can do instead to feel calm."

- If it is a habit, help her realize when she is masturbating by giving her a nonverbal cue. This will signal her to stop and do the more socially acceptable behavior instead, without embarrassing the child.

- Talk to the parents about the possible reasons for the behavior, their view of it, and suggestions for helping their child. Develop a plan together to change the behavior. Tell the parents not to punish their child for the behavior or to be overly concerned.

12. PUPPIES AT PLAY: ROUGHHOUSING

Rough-and-tumble play is part of childhood for many boys and some girls. It is a way of expressing affection for some children, again mostly among boys. In our macho culture, it is just about the only socially acceptable way for boys to have close physical contact with each other. For some boys, it's the primary way they interact with their friends. While roughhousing is quite functional for puppies and many other young animals, it is a problematic behavior for young human beings because it is a low-level form of play and interaction that too often ends with a child getting hurt. Young children do not always know when and where it is appropriate (or inappropriate) to engage in rough-and-tumble play, or how to keep it from getting out of hand.

If you have two or more children who really want to roughhouse, rather than spending a lot of effort stopping them, allow them to do it in a safe, limited, and reasonable way. At the same time, you will be helping them develop the skills to control and limit the behavior, to learn that there are particular times and places for such activities, and to know how to avoid injuries.

Anticipating and Preventing Roughhousing

- Provide many opportunities for children to have physical contact with each other in a safe way. For example, play movement games and teach simple dances, yoga, or exercises in which children interact physically with partners. Make the rules and directions very clear to avoid accidental injuries.

- Give children many outlets and plenty of time for loud, big, fast, physical play. This will of course need to happen outdoors or in a gym. Place the play within an imaginary scenario full of action, other than playing pirates or ninjas, such as fighting fires, making emergency rescues, saving elephants, and searching for (and escaping from) wild animals to photograph. This helps focus the active play and keep it from degrading into roughhousing.

- Before the start of any organized activity, physically separate children who often interact with each other by roughhousing.

- Teach children other ways of expressing physical affection for each other, such as hugging, holding hands, and putting arms around each other's shoulders. Suggest to children that they ask before they touch other children, particularly children who do not like to be touched, by saying, for example, "Kim, do you want to hold hands with me?" Follow this suggestion yourself. Children need to be sensitive to and respect the feelings and bodies of others. However, most children enjoy spontaneously receiving and giving physical affection, and it's important not to dampen that impulse.

Solving Problems Related to Roughhousing

- Teach children other ways to interact: "Use words. Say to your friend, 'Let's play with the blocks.'" Assist the children in this process until they are able to do it on their own and are no longer relying on roughhousing as their main form of interaction.

- Once or twice per week, offer a mediated version of roughhousing on a gym mat as a choice during work-play time. Children will need to follow certain rules and a teacher will need to monitor the activity carefully. Rules might include the following:
    - No more than two children on the mat at one time.
    - No punching or kicking.
    - When one child says stop, the other must stop.
    - Only stocking or bare feet on the mat.
    - No other objects can be on the mat.
    - The round will end after three minutes.
    - Two other children may then roughhouse on the mat for three minutes. However, no pair of children can start a second round until they have had a break for at least another three minutes.

- Provide intensive assistance at first until you are sure the children are able to follow the rules on their own. If they are not able to follow the rules after repeated assistance, eliminate the activity and help them engage in other forms of active play. The section above offers many ideas on anticipating and preventing problems.

- If children are roughhousing at an inappropriate time, such as during circle time, tell them, "Now is a time for listening (or singing, sharing, and so on). During work-play time, you may choose the gym mat." Separate the children who are roughhousing.

- Give children who roughhouse during sedentary times something active to do with their hands, such as holding a toy stuffed animal or rubber spiky ball, or have them sit on an adult lap or right next to a teacher.

13. THESE BOOTS WERE MADE FOR WALKING: RUNNING INSIDE

Young children need to be active, and running is a natural way for them to move. Changing this behavior to ensure their safety requires doing many things. You have to eliminate the temptation to run, establish clear expectations, give many reminders, and allow children plenty of time during the day to run outdoors or in a gym. It is often best to redirect children who are running inside into another, safer activity, rather than trying to get them to walk. For example, a chasing game requires running. It makes no sense to walk and chase someone. However, redirecting both children into a different game or activity will stop the running. Remind them that they can chase each other later outside or in the gym.

Anticipating and Preventing Running Inside

- Establish a class rule: "Only walk inside." Be very consistent about enforcing this rule. Explain that the reason for the rule is to make sure no one falls or runs into another person and gets hurt.

- Remind children before they enter the classroom from outside and before transitions to other activities that they need to walk in the room.

- Arrange your equipment and furnishings so there are no long, open corridors that invite running.

Solving Problems Related to Running Inside

- Recognize the positive aspects of the behavior: the child is excited and wants to get to an activity as soon as possible. Tell her: "It's great that you are excited to play, but walking will keep you from getting hurt." Start walking with her to get her going successfully. Show her how to walk quickly without running.

- Pair the child who tends to run with another child who is good about walking. Have them be partners when it's necessary to walk somewhere.

- Remind the child why walking is important. Through role play, demonstrate in slow motion how a person coming around a corner can have a serious accident with a child who is running because he cannot see the child in time to stop. Have children practice this.

- Remind children that when they are outside, they will get to run all they want.

- Let children who are walking know that you appreciate the appropriate behavior: "Thank you for walking in the room. You know how to be safe."

14. CHILDREN WHO ARE TOO SILLY: BETTER TO BE GOOFY THAN BE NOBODY

This is a common behavior in young children, especially four-year-olds. Making faces or noises, talking in an exaggerated voice, laughing way more than is warranted, pretending to cough, sneeze, or fart, and other such behaviors are problematic if they happen too often or at inappropriate times. The usual reason for the behavior is to get the attention and the admiration of other children. A child who feels invisible and in need of attention can successfully make herself feel better this way. This is also known as the "class clown syndrome." When the child can get many other children to join the silliness (which is not hard to do) and create a "mass hysterical" disruption, she feels even more powerful.

A child who is silly a great deal of the time may be using the behavior to cover up a painful issue in her life. When you try to have a serious discussion with the children, the pain she may have to face during that discussion is too great. Acting silly is her way of avoiding this pain. Another common reason for silliness is boredom. Children who feel unchallenged or not engaged by activities you have developed may act silly as a way to relieve the stress of boredom.

Anticipating and Preventing Silly Behavior

- Provide many opportunities for children to be silly and even encourage silliness at times that are appropriate, such as work-play and outside. When the children are silly, let them know that this is a good time to be silly because it doesn't disturb others or make it hard to talk about important things.

- Just before starting a serious discussion, such as about good and bad touches, let children know that during serious talks everyone listens and only one person talks at a time. If this is difficult for them, use a talking stick or other object so that only the person who has the stick can talk.

- Give children many opportunities to express their feelings, and when they do, show interest and be responsive. Take their feelings seriously and help them to understand what they are feeling and why. Help them to find outlets for their feelings and appropriate ways to express them.

- Make sure your curriculum and activities are engaging and challenging. Provide extra challenges to children who are advanced or gifted.

- Give lots of positive attention to children throughout the day. For most children, this eliminates any need to get attention by acting silly. Review the ideas for accommodating the needs of individual children, particularly related to the need to be valued and cared for and the need for positive regard, in the introduction to this section on pp. 173–84.

Solving Problems Related to Silly Behavior

- Stop the child as soon as he starts being silly by saying, "In ten minutes when we go outside, you can make any kind of noise you want. Thank you for listening to the story now and letting others hear it." If the behavior persists, offer the child to sit next to you and turn the pages of the book or give him some other task. Later, talk with him about better ways to get your attention. Assure him that if he says your name (or taps you gently on the arm, or does whatever works best for you) that you will respond. Help him to learn a variety of more acceptable ways to get the attention of other children. Have him practice these new behaviors with you in role plays.

- If the behavior appears to be an attempt to push your buttons, respond calmly and minimally. For example, "Would you like to tell me something in your regular voice so I can understand you?"

- For the child who is inappropriately silly very often, meet with her parents to determine possible causes of the problem—the pain that the child is avoiding. Do whatever is in your power and ability to help the child and his family. If necessary, make a referral to a social service agency or mental health specialist, or provide a list of community resources.

- Try to spend one-on-one time with the child away from other children. If he is not near his peers, he might be willing to talk seriously. Use books, dolls, role play, and stories to help bring out his feelings. Give him opportunities to draw pictures that do not have to be shown to anyone else.

- If several children start acting silly during a planned activity, it probably means the activity is boring. Change the activity to make it more engaging or stop the activity and do a movement game or song, or move on to your next planned activity.

15. SPIT HAPPENS!

Spitting is usually the result of anger and frustration. It is an aggressive act when done intentionally, directly at another child. (See "The Hits Just Keep on Coming!" on pp. 200–2 for more information on aggressive behavior.) Also, the child who spits may have learned that it will get adults very upset and therefore is a good attention-getter.

Anticipating and Preventing Spitting

- Let children know that it is okay to be angry. Help them express their anger appropriately, as described in "Little Volcanoes" on pp. 185–89.

- Tell stories and lead role plays in which children act to prevent themselves from getting in frustrating or infuriating situations. Examples include deciding not to play with an older child in the neighborhood who doesn't play fairly, changing the rules of a game to reduce or eliminate competition, and setting some basic ground rules before an activity to ensure fairness and flexibility.

- Tell stories and lead role plays in which children express their anger nonviolently and effectively.

- Do all you can to keep frustrations and stress to a minimum. Have a challenging curriculum and nurturing and supportive environment, keep sedentary activities short, and allow much time for active and interactive play and for safe risk taking.

Solving Problems Related to Spitting

- Don't overreact or get upset. Say calmly and firmly, "I know you are angry, but I can't let you spit. It is hurtful and can make people sick. Let me help you find words you can use to solve the problem."

- Soothe the child who has been spit at.

- Have the child who spit help to clean it up. Show her how to do it safely and avoid direct contact with it by using a tissue or paper towel.

- A bit later, when the child is calm, talk to her about spitting. For example, "Spitting is not safe. You cannot spit. Let's think together about what you can do instead the next time you are angry." Among the alternatives are using angry words and asking an adult for help.

- Determine what situations lead to spitting and help the child avoid getting into them. It may mean not playing with certain children or doing certain activities, and choosing activities that are comforting rather than complex.

- The child's frustration level should not rise to the point that she feels the need to spit if she has negotiating and turn-taking skills. Teach these skills when opportunities come up as well as during group times using stories and role plays.

16. STEALING: THE NEED IS TOO MUCH AND THE TEMPTATION TOO GREAT

Most children who intentionally and persistently steal do so because they feel deprived. Because they do not get enough or any affection and attention, they collect material objects for themselves to fill the emotional emptiness inside. As they cannot buy things themselves and have long exhausted their parents' patience asking for things, they feel compelled to steal. If they do not have good self-regulation, then the temptation is overwhelming. The act of stealing can also give a child, who otherwise feels incapable or invisible, a sense of agency. She feels a bit more powerful by taking action against her circumstances with an immediate and tangible result. She feels skillful and cunning in her deceits. This is one of the few problematic behaviors without an element of attention-getting. However, stealing is ultimately unsatisfying because it does not solve the real problem. So she does it again and again. Many adults do this too, by buying themselves presents (shopping therapy) or eating sweets when they feel unhappy or unloved.

Anticipating and Preventing Stealing

- Make the development of self-regulation and self-efficacy a primary goal for children and a central part of your curriculum. A child with self-efficacy knows himself, his needs, and his strengths and weaknesses. He feels he has agency in his world, appropriate for his age. He has confidence in his ability to access resources to get his needs met. He will ask adults for what he needs in a way that makes them want to give it and, if necessary, keeps asking until he gets it.

- Maintain good parent communication so you know what problems a child might be facing. You can then be helpful, empathetic, and supportive to the child.

- Create a strong sense of community. Let children know that the toys and materials belong to the school, but they are for everyone to use. Follow the ideas about building a classroom community in "Circle Time and Group Time" on pp. 18–22.

- Have a class lending library for children to borrow inexpensive books or toys. Create a checkout system to track who borrowed what. Set clear guidelines about how long something can be borrowed and make it clear that the item must return in good condition. A borrowed item must be returned before another item can be checked out.

Solving Problems Related to Stealing

- Have empathy for the child. He likely has very little in the way of emotional and/or material goods. A positive aspect of the behavior is that he really appreciates the many great toys and materials in the classroom.

- If you catch a child stealing, support his needs and feelings: "You really like that toy and want to keep it. I wish I could give it to you, but other children want to play with it too. It will be here for you to play with tomorrow. Let's make a list for using it tomorrow and put your name first." Then ask, "Would you like to put it back on the shelf or give it to me and I'll put it on the shelf?" Do not shame or humiliate the child.

- Give a child who is stealing positive verbal feedback at least daily (or more often, depending on how often he steals) when he does not steal. Tell him: "Thank you for leaving the toys here so that everyone can play with them." Give the child a hug or high five so he will know that acting appropriately will get him positive attention and affection.

- If you're not sure that a child actually took something, intentionally or otherwise, but suspect that he has, give him the benefit of the doubt. Here's one idea of what to say to an individual child: "If you borrowed a toy, please bring it back tomorrow. Maybe we can add it to the lending library." Or say to everyone, "We seem to be missing the little red car from the shelf near the block area. Can everybody please check your pockets in case you put it there by mistake?"

- Meet with the child's parents to coordinate strategies to deal with the problem. Make them aware of the importance of being empathetic and positive and not punishing the behavior. Ask them if they are aware of any possible causes for the behavior. Help them with ways that they can build their child's positive self-image.

- Give the child many opportunities to be a leader and helper in the classroom. This will help him to feel important.

- If the other children are aware of the stealing, talk to them about ways that they can be helpful. They can say directly to the child, "Please don't take the toy. It belongs to our class. It's for everyone to play with." If the child still takes the toy, then they can ask you to help.

- If the problem persists, team with the child's parents to get help from a mental health specialist.

17. DO TELL!: TATTLING

The child who tattles usually does this to make herself look good by making other children look bad. But a child who tattles may also be telling you something that you need to know about another child, which you are not aware of. So, it is important to listen carefully, as it may be necessary to help the child or mediate a conflict. Often, it is not the tattler's message that is problematic but the intent of the message and the way it is delivered.

Anticipating and Preventing Tattling

- During small-group time, talk with the children about tattling. Read or make up stories in which children choose alternatives to tattling. Have them practice the alternatives through role plays.

- Establish a classroom rule: "Talk *to* your classmate before you talk *about* your classmate." Help children understand the rule. If they are concerned about another child's behavior in the class, then they need to first talk to that child directly about their concern before telling the teacher what the child did or didn't do.

Solving Problems Related to Tattling

- Give minimal attention to the tattling, but do not stop it or cut it off. There is no way to know if the child might be giving you some important information about other children until you hear it.

- After listening, thank the child who tattles: "I'm glad you care and are concerned about your friends." Then talk with the child about alternatives to tattling, including the following:
  - "When you see another child breaking a rule or doing something you don't like, talk directly to him. Remind him of the rule. Tell him what you don't like and why. Suggest what he can do instead. If that doesn't work, or there is a serious problem, then you can ask a teacher for help."
  - "If you need to tell a teacher something about other children, do it in a helpful way. You can say, 'I think Jason and Elijah need your help to stop fighting' or 'I'm worried that Elijah is getting hurt.'"
  - "When you need to talk to a teacher, talk about yourself, not just about other children. Say what you want or need. You can say, 'My feelings were hurt when they wouldn't let me play. Can you help me to play with them?' or 'I don't like hearing bad words. Can you help me ask Carrie to stop?'"

- If the child doesn't say what she wants or needs when tattling, ask her, "What would you like me to do?" or "How can I help you?"

- Involve the child who tattles in addressing the behavior of concern. This may mean agreeing to ignore it. For example, you can tell her: "I usually ignore it when children use bad words. They stop it quickly that way. Would you like to try ignoring it too?" It can also mean helping the child to find the right words and actions to express her concerns directly to the other child: "I didn't like it when you wouldn't let me play. Our rule says, 'Everyone's included, everybody plays.'"

- Ask children who tattle to tell you about the positive behaviors of other children: "I'd love to hear about the good things Madison does."

- Encourage the child when she is talking to you without tattling: "I enjoy talking with you when it is not about other children."

18. TEMPER TANTRUMS: SAVE YOURS FOR AFTER CLASS!

Unlike most of the other behaviors discussed in this section of the book, temper tantrums are rarely attention-getting behaviors. Although they can bring a great deal of attention, their purpose for the child is to get something he wants or to vent anger and frustration, or both.

This behavior is fairly common in toddlers, but is a cause for concern if seen in children older than three and a half. Toddlers throw tantrums because they do not have the language to express strong needs or the emotional maturity to deal with them. All their frustrations in understanding and coping with the world of "giants" build up to the point where they explode. However, children older than three and a half are usually able to express their needs with words; they can think abstractly enough to get their needs met with other people; and they have more self-control and emotional maturity. The older child who does have temper tantrums and who is not developmentally or language delayed is probably under emotional duress or has a lot of anger. He and his family may need the help of a professional counselor or similar assistance, especially if the tantrums are extreme, occur often, and the child has other problematic behaviors. (See "Little Volcanoes" on pp. 185–89 for information about children with extreme or dangerous behaviors.)

In some cases, tantrums can be caused by medical problems, such as chronic pain or lack of sleep, or from an adverse reaction to medication. Tantrums may persist among children older than three and a half because they have been overly indulged and rewarded for such behaviors (usually unintentionally). The tantrums work and the child gets what he wants.

Having carefully observed parent and child interactions over many years, I have seen numerous examples of children having *justifiable* tantrums. That is, parents create the circumstances that make children feel so powerless, frustrated, and angry that having a temper tantrum is a reasonable response. In almost all cases, parents do this out of ignorance and sometime with good intentions. The problem is often made worse when the child gets blamed for his "awful" behavior. One of the more common ways that parents do this is by making promises, stringing their child along emotionally with more promises, and then breaking them. Another example is when a parent offers the child a choice but then makes a different choice for him in the end.

Anticipating and Preventing Tantrums

- Provide many outlets for children to express their emotions and strong feelings in safe, acceptable ways.

- Reduce frustrations by offering children many choices of a wide variety of hands-on, self-directed activities for most of their time at school. Make sure your activities are not too challenging or too easy for children. Have high but reasonable expectations of the abilities of your children. Do not make them sit and listen for more than a few minutes at a time if they do not yet have the capacity to focus for longer periods. (See "Daily Dilemmas" that starts on p. 13 for more information on the appropriate length of time for various activities.)

- Observe carefully. As soon as you see children get frustrated, step in to help them solve their problems, as needed. Teach them problem-solving skills rather than solving the problem for them. Help them to learn to control situations and make choices that prevent them from reaching the point where they are too frustrated.

- Provide parents with resources such as books and videos on positive guidance strategies for dealing with tantrums. Offer your help to answer their questions about these issues.

Solving Problems Related to Tantrums

- Observe when the tantrums tend to occur and what seems to set them off. Respond by making adjustments in your schedule or environment, if needed.

- If the tantrum is causing a disruption or the child is in an area where he may get hurt, move him quickly to a safe area away from other children, preferably onto a gym mat. Tell him calmly, "It's okay to be frustrated and angry, but it's not okay to disturb others, and I won't let you get hurt. When you're calmer, I will comfort you or help you solve your problem." Watch the child carefully and stay relatively close in case you have to intervene for safety reasons.

- If an interaction with one other particular child tends to trigger the tantrums, separate the children after a few minutes of play to ease the tension or stay next to them while they play. As soon as tensions start to build, help them to de-escalate. Offer them activities that are less likely to cause tensions between them.

- Help the child find ways to calm himself down. He can generate his own ideas and/or you can suggest that he listen to music, look at a book, sing, talk, draw, or play with sand, water, or clay.

- When the child is calm, help him to think of other ways he can deal with the issue that made him so angry. Help him practice the words and actions he can take to get his needs met. For example, he can tell the child who has just knocked over his block structure to help build it back up again or to put the blocks away. He can also ask an adult to assist him.

- Invite a respected peer or supervisor to observe in your classroom. She can help you see if anything may be inadvertently contributing to the behavior and give ideas for changing the behavior.

- Meet with the child's parents to discuss possible causes of the problem. Brainstorm possible solutions together. Recommend counseling or the help of a social service agency if the above strategies do not significantly decrease the tantrums.

19. THUMB SUCKING: COMFORT ALWAYS AT HAND

For children under four and a half years old, thumb sucking is not a problem and should be ignored. Some doctors and dentists consider it a concern for children who are four and a half and older because the risk of dental problems increases as permanent teeth begin to come in. If a child who sucks her thumb is insecure, socially isolated, depressed, or has similar issues, ignore the thumb sucking and concentrate on helping her emotionally. Thumb sucking may be an important comfort for the child.

Anticipating and Preventing Problems Related to Thumb Sucking

- You are very unlikely to see a child suck her thumb in child-centered classrooms with many engaging, hands-on activities where children feel secure and happy.

- At the time of enrollment, ask parents about their children's habits and how they comfort themselves. If they say that their child sucks her thumb, ask them how they feel about it and what they do in response, if anything. At this time, you can share information and hopefully make an agreement about a consistent approach to use at home and at school that respects the child and is responsive to her needs.

Solving Problems Related to Thumb Sucking

- If the thumb sucking is a new behavior or has recently returned, meet with the parents to determine if there are any changes at home that might be causing stress. If the stressful situation will be temporary, ignore the problem for now.

- If it is not a new behavior, it is likely a habit, making it an unconscious behavior and difficult to change. Often children will stop sucking their thumbs at around four years of age because other children will poke fun at the habit. While this can be an effective way of ending the habit, the child will need your emotional support and assistance to find alternative ways to comfort herself when she feels stressed.

- Take no action on thumb sucking without consulting the child's parents. They may want you to ignore the behavior, or they may have some good ideas about how to deal with it.

- As soon as a child starts sucking her thumb, suggest a comforting activity that requires using both hands, such as holding and stroking a stuffed animal or lying on a soft pillow and looking at a book.

- Even a child who is ready and wants to stop thumb sucking will most likely need some help. Because habits can be unconscious behaviors, the child will sometimes not realize that she is sucking her thumb. Use a prearranged visual or physical cue to remind the child that she is sucking her thumb. For example, giving two "thumbs-up" signs or three quick, gentle taps on her shoulder.

- Comforting habits are very hard to break. When she has not sucked her thumb for a time, tell her often but privately, "You are making a great effort to stop sucking your thumb. You must be really proud of yourself."

20. TOO LOUD: SILENCE ISN'T GOLDEN BUT NEITHER IS NOISE

A healthy, happy classroom full of active learning is one that has a fairly constant, medium noise level. Expect your class to sound that way. Don't be jealous of the ultraquiet class next door. Important development of social skills, language, creativity, and a variety of other skills cannot happen in silence Young children cannot get their learning needs met without actively talking and doing. In your classroom, focus on dealing with talking only when it is overly loud or strident. Be aware that a child who seems to always have a loud voice may have a hearing loss.

Anticipating and Preventing Problems Related to Children Who Are Too Loud

- Establish a classroom rule: "Use regular voices inside." Enforce it consistently. Explain the reason for the rule: "When our room is not too loud, we will be able to hear each other and no one will get a headache. When we use a regular voice, we won't hurt our throats."

- Remind the children of the rule before entering the classroom from outside or before work-play time begins.

- Use a calm, slighter quieter than "regular" voice yourself. Children will lower their voices to match your level. Give children plenty of opportunities to talk and to be loud when such behavior is appropriate—outside, in the gym, or when singing an energetic song.

Solving Problems Related to Children Who Are Too Loud

- Tell all the children to remind other children of the classroom rule about regular voices when they hear someone being too loud.

- Ask the child who is being too loud to tell you the rule about using regular voices inside. Remind him that he will get a chance to be as loud as he wants to be outside: "You have a big strong voice; use it when you get outside."

- Support the child when he uses his voice correctly: "Thank you for speaking in your regular voice. Now I can easily hear what other children are saying."

- The child who continues to be loud after many attempts to help him most likely has a physical or medical problem that is causing a hearing loss. This is not unusual among young children, as it is common for them to get ear infections or have serious seasonal allergies. Refer the child for an examination from a physician and a hearing test from an audiologist.

21. CAT HERDING 101: CHILDREN WHO DON'T LISTEN OR FOLLOW INSTRUCTIONS

These children are not defiant and the behavior is not intentional, but they act as if your words are meant for everyone else but them. They have no idea what to do next, even though you just told them. They embody the expression "In one ear and out the other." Sometimes they will try to figure out what to do by watching what the other children are doing and following them. But sometimes they just do whatever they feel like doing, even if it is completely counter to what you just asked them to do. What's going on? Some of these children are just highly active and distracted and have difficulty focusing on pretty much anything. (See "Perpetual(ly in) Motion" on pp. 191–94 for information on active children.) Some may have a hearing loss, poor vision, or other physical problem that makes it hard to focus. Many, however, are a bit immature and need extra support, guidance, and patience.

Anticipating and Preventing Problems Related to Children Who Won't Listen

- Most young children listen better when told something individually rather than as part of a group. Your undivided attention directed at a child tells her clearly that the information is meant for her; it makes the child feel important and helps her to attend. When individual attention is not possible, meet in small groups with some individual follow-up.

- When talking with children, remove distractions, such as extraneous noises and enticing toys.

- If possible, back up your verbal information with something visual and with physical action. Most people (especially children) are visual learners, but everybody learns best by actually doing or practicing the skill. For example, if you want your children to wash their hands properly, tell them how to do it while showing them. Then have them practice. As a reminder, post pictures above the sink showing the steps of proper hand washing.

- Ask each child to repeat back to you the information she received. Expressing it verbally helps to set it in children's minds.

- Use a great deal of variety in your voice. Change the pitch (high and low), speed, and volume often. When you need to make an important point, use a slightly lower and slower voice than you normally use.

Solving Problems Related to Children Who Won't Listen

- Determine if the child has a hearing loss or other physical issue. If natural opportunities arise at times when there is very little noise, stand behind the child and say her name in a soft, but clearly audible, voice. Do this several times, as a hearing loss can fluctuate. If she doesn't respond all or most of the time, she likely has a hearing loss and should be referred to an audiologist. If she does respond all or most of the time, she may still have a hearing loss, but it would be a mild one and you can rule this out as the cause for not listening.

- Some children can't listen because they are overwhelmed by their feelings and emotions. They have too much anxiety. Be patient, nurturing, and supportive. Provide many outlets for children to express their feelings safely, including through creative art. With your care and guidance, in time their anxiety will ease and they will be more able to pay attention.

- Ask the child to look at you just before you give verbal instructions or information.

- Give children a specific visual cue along with your words and voice tone. For example, if you want children to remember to walk from the circle area to the door, use a slow rhythmic voice and move your arms slowly to emulate walking while you say, "Please walk to the door." If needed, the children can repeat the actions and words while walking to the door.

- Because some children listen better when they are active and have something to do with their hands, teach your class some words in American Sign Language. Also, give the child a soft toy animal or similar item to hold to help her listen.

- Allow the child to change her position to be more comfortable. This can greatly improve listening skills for some children.

- Try using a slightly louder voice, a quieter voice, or a slower voice to get the child's attention.

- Make physical contact with the child (a hand lightly on the shoulder) when talking with her.

Partnering with Families to Raise Happy Children: It's a Team Effort

ALTHOUGH SOME PARENTS will present a variety of challenges, most parents are appreciative and look to you for support and advice. Parents are under great pressure. Most parents of young children are young themselves, early in their careers, and not earning as much as they need. This is a particularly difficult time, and the United States is a particularly difficult place to raise a family. Almost all other industrialized countries have child and family policies that are more supportive and generous—offering paid parental leave, more paid vacation time, and government-funded early childhood programs for all children. Like early childhood teachers, many young parents are underpaid, underappreciated, and overworked. While we work to change this situation, the best strategy for coping is to be mutually empathetic and to partner with parents for the benefit of the child.

A partnership is a very different relationship than a customer-client, amateur-professional, or needy person–helper relationship. It is an equal relationship where both parties have important contributions to make. You and parents both have expertise in particular, and usually different, areas. By working together, you are both better off and your jobs are easier; however, the child is the big winner!

You can do many things to establish and maintain a partnership with families. Don't leave it to chance or just let it happen; that will result in partnerships with only the few families with whom you have an affinity. You can establish partnerships with many more of your families by taking deliberate actions to reach out to every family.

WHAT TEACHERS BRING TO THE PARTNERSHIP

Among the abilities, skills, and knowledge that teachers uniquely have are the following:

- distance and perspective that comes from not having the intense emotional involvement with children that parents have

- an understanding of children and their development in relationship to other children; knowing what is typical and expected behavior for a child at any age

- experience working with many different children and families, and expertise in certain areas

- knowledge of good resources—people, agencies, and print and online materials

- ideas and a variety of strategies for helping solve problems

- an empathetic ear

WHAT PARENTS BRING TO THE PARTNERSHIP

Among the abilities, skills, and knowledge that parents uniquely have are the following:

- deep knowledge of their children and their history from pregnancy (or from the time of adoption) to the present in the context of the home, family, and neighborhood; many children act very differently at home than at school

- a strong emotional connection to their child and great concern

- advocacy for getting the best for their child

APPROACH ALL INTERACTIONS AS A PARTNERSHIP

Your attitude about families gets expressed in every interaction—often nonverbally and unintentionally. When you meet with families at the school or center, sitting next to each other or across a table sends a "partnership" message. When you sit behind a desk or on an adult chair and they sit on a small chair, it sends a very different message.

- Don't assume. Instead, ask for information or make tentative statements. For example, "What have you already tried to solve the problem?" or "Am I correct in thinking that your wife is Jason's stepmom?"

- Offer yourself as a resource and support, rather than an expert.

- Choose your words carefully. When a parent picks up a child who is being fussy at the end of the day and you say, "I didn't have any trouble with him today," the parent may interpret that as meaning "I can handle your child better than you." Instead, say, "Many children are fussy at the end of the day. What can I do to help?" (Galinsky 1988).

- If you have expertise, offer it only when asked for. If neither you nor the parents have the needed information, say, "Let's find some resources to get more information."

- Approach all issues from a "strengths-based" perspective. Find the strengths and positive aspects of your families, and assume they are doing the best they can.

- In disagreements with families, usually you both have the same goals for children but different ideas for how best to reach those goals. You and the parents both want their children to be successful in school; however, you believe that positive dispositions for learning—motivation, curiosity, initiative, and persistence—are necessary to be ready for school, while parents likely believe that children only need certain skills and knowledge to be ready for school. Focus on the common goal rather than the strategies to reach it. Make an agreement with families to help them with ideas that they can use at home to teach their child the skills and knowledge they believe are necessary, and that you will support and encourage their child to use and practice those skills in the classroom. At the same time you will continue to develop the child's positive dispositions for learning.

- Make sure all written materials reflect a partnership approach. The "voice" used in written materials, including policies and procedures, should be supportive and express concern for the well-being of the child and family. That is, after all, the reason to have policies and procedures.

- Start off right. Early in the year, arrange home visits with families if they feel comfortable with them or meet with them in neutral territory, such as a park. Use most of your time in those first interactions to establish a trusting relationship. If later there are conflicts or difficult issues to deal with, you are much more likely to get a positive response and willingness to work together to help the child.

- In your first meetings, keep the information on program requirements to a minimum. Ask such questions as these:
  - "What do I need to know about your child to be a good teacher for her?"
  - "What are her strengths and interests and favorite activities?"
  - "What three adjectives describe her best?"
  - "How does she deal with stress?"
  - "What are your goals for her this year?"
  - "What are your hopes and dreams for her in the future?"

- Clearly explain your approach and expectations early in the partnership, especially for potentially controversial issues like celebrating holidays, teaching academics, and addressing problematic behaviors.

NONTRADITIONAL FAMILIES: THEY'RE QUICKLY BECOMING TRADITIONAL

In the United States, nontraditional families include any family that is not headed by a heterosexual English-speaking couple who are the biological parents of their child. As of 2016, the "traditional" family represents less than half of all families in the country (Pew Research Center 2015). When policies and materials developed for parents (such as parent handbooks, newsletters, and announcements) assume that all families are like the traditional family, nontraditional families may feel invisible and discounted. In the classroom, all children need to see their own families reflected in books, pictures, and discussions.

Anticipating and Preventing Problems Related to Partnering with Nontraditional Families

In your communications with families and discussions with children, be sure to recognize the broad spectrum of family types: single parents, adoptive parents, foster parents, stepparents, gay and lesbian parents, parents who don't speak English, and others. In addition to validating nontraditional families, it is important to understand their issues so you can be responsive and sensitive in your interactions with them. This will go a long way toward developing positive relations, which are vital to sharing the task of raising happy children.

- Respond to the needs of children by using the ideas from "Modern Family" on pp. 136–39 about children from nontraditional families and "Going with the FLOE" on pp. 139–42 about children from families who do not speak English at home. It is important that the children see their unique families represented and that they are as valid as any other family. This helps counteract the many other instances when their particular family is invisible or diminished. It also provides tremendous support for parents.

Solving Problems Related to Partnering with Nontraditional Families

- Read reliable information from websites and blogs and, if possible, talk with someone who can give you insight into the issues, challenges, needs, and strengths of the particular types of nontraditional families in your classroom. Resources related to nontraditional families can be found under "Cultural Responsiveness and Diversity" on page 285. Share some of these resources with your families if you think they will be useful to them.

- At your initial meeting, ask, "What can I do to make sure your family and your child have a great experience in our school and in my classroom?"

- Ask families how they prefer to be described and the terms you should use. What do they call each other? Is a stepfather called "Dad" or called by his first name or a nickname? Are both lesbian parents called "Mom," or is one called Mom and the other by her first name, or are both called by something else? Does a foster parent call her foster child "my son," "my foster son," or something else? Does a biracial family want to be considered black, white, or biracial, or do they prefer not to have any particular racial identity? When you use the same terms that families use for themselves, it supports and validates the families and is comforting to the child.

- Talk about your approach to discussing and including all families throughout your curriculum and ask for suggestions to improve or expand your approach.

- Provide translations of materials in the families' languages and arrange for interpreters at meetings. If there are no funds for this, often a community agency can assist, or the family may have a relative or friend who is bilingual and willing to help.

2. A SPECIAL PARTNERSHIP: PARENTS WITH SPECIAL NEEDS

You will occasionally work with parents who may have a disability, such as an intellectual impairment, hearing or vision loss, physical disability, or mental health issues, including addiction. This can create challenges in communicating with the parents and including them in their child's education and in the school community. You will need to ensure that the child will get all he requires to be fully supported and successful. This is of particular concern with parents who have a cognitive disability or have mental health issues, as these tend to threaten children's healthy development more than other disabilities.

Anticipating and Preventing Problems Related to Partnering with Parents with Special Needs

- Compile a list of local resources that assist with several types of the special needs that you are most likely to encounter among families and that put their children most at risk, such as intellectual disabilities and mental health issues, including drug and alcohol abuse. The resources should include social services agencies, service organizations, treatment centers, nonprofits, and charitable organizations, among others.

- If possible, visit these organizations and meet with staff. Ask them how young children are impacted when their parents have a particular disability or special need. This will give you important information about the services they provide and a little about the quality of those services.

Solving Problems Related to Partnering with Parents with Special Needs

- In most cases, the parents will have a caseworker and other support people, such as relatives. Meet with them to get information about the family and to learn about the various ways that you can be helpful.

- Request permission to access all of the key health professionals involved with the family throughout the year so you can quickly get information as issues, concerns, and questions arise.

- Meet with the parents early, often, and regularly to stay on top of issues. Ask open-ended questions to determine how to best support them and their child. For example: "What can I do better?" "How can I be more helpful and supportive of your family and your child?" and "What does your child need to be happier at school?"

- Take any concern you have directly to the parents without delay. Use your knowledge of the family to approach the issue in a supportive way that the parents will understand. If the problem does not get resolved, then seek assistance from their support persons.

- Find out as much as you can about the particular disability and how it is manifested in adults and in the child's parents in particular. Get information about the typical needs of children whose parents have that particular disability. Health providers and organizations (charitable, professional, and parent-led) that focus on the disability are a good source for this information.

- Individualize your interactions with the child. Get to know the child well and do not make assumptions. Every child who has parents with disabilities will have unique needs. I once had a child in my class whose parents both had intellectual disabilities, but she did not. She needed help with hygiene skills and support to feel more confident. But she eagerly and quickly absorbed basic and essential information and knowledge that were second nature to all the other children in the class, and she enthusiastically rose to the cognitive challenges I gave her.

- After you have tried the strategies discussed here and in related chapters, if the child regresses or if you have serious concerns about the child's welfare, take your concerns to the family's support persons. Be sure to have clear and objective evidence of your concerns. If you suspect that the child is being abused or neglected, see the suggestions in "Save the Children" on pp. 237–39.

3. BEYOND FEEDBACK: PARENTS WHO COMPLAIN

Most parents are very reasonable and simply want the best for their children. Provide a variety of ways and many opportunities for them to give you feedback. Don't ignore complaints, as they are often helpful, even if they are not delivered in a helpful way. Take their input seriously and act on the requests that are reasonable. When parents see that you are responsive, you will win their favor and support. Some parents, however, make unreasonable requests or complain very often. These chronic complainers seek attention, try to exert power where they can, and unload their anger and unhappiness on whomever they see as an easy target. The suggestions in this chapter will help you minimize complaints from parents and give you constructive ways to deal with unreasonable, chronic complainers.

Anticipating and Preventing Complaints from Parents

- Meet with parents before or soon after the child enters your class. At this meeting, make your goals, philosophy, and expectations clear to avoid misunderstandings. Provide this information in writing as well and in the parents' native language.

- Let parents know that they are welcome in your classroom to observe and participate at any time.

- Give them a parent handbook about your center, school, and/or classroom. If your program does not have a handbook, volunteer to be on a committee to develop one. In any case, write one for your classroom because they are a must for good parent relations.

- Ask for input from parents about their expectations. What would they like their child to experience? What, if anything, do they worry about? What are some things you should know about their child to ensure that she will be happy?

- Offer parents opportunities to help in the classroom or in another way, such as participating in a field trip or making a pillow for the book area. Welcome parents to be involved with your class in any way or on any level that feels comfortable to them.

- Before presenting material to children that may cause some parents concern (information such as sex abuse prevention strategies or antiracism education), send written information home about what you will be doing and arrange a meeting that any and all parents are welcome to attend to discuss the issue.

- Tell parents often about the great things their children say and do. Record or write down these comments for them. Take photos and videos (with permission) to share with individual parents and post them to your website. Send notes home or e-mail often to let parents know about the wonderful things that are happening in your class.

- Schedule regular parent meetings (perhaps one every other month) to allow parents to speak their minds, express concerns, and ask questions. Whenever you meet with a group of parents, arrange the chairs in a circle.

- Communicate with parents and encourage them to communicate with you as much as possible. Use e-mail, phone calls, text messages, bulletin boards, letters home, forms for parents to return, a notebook that children can carry between school and home daily (this makes children feel grown up too), informal chats, meetings, conferences, and so on.

- Request to visit the families in their homes, and at least once during the year invite all the families to your home (perhaps for a backyard barbecue) or on a field trip. Or, if you prefer, host smaller gatherings of families at your home, inviting one or a few at a time.

Solving Problems Related to Parents Who Complain

The chronic complainer

- Act quickly, as unresolved concerns make matters worse and an unhappy parent may be talking with other parents.

- Assume that there is a misunderstanding or miscommunication. Take a positive, problem-solving approach. Stay calm, be empathetic, and express your concern and willingness to do whatever you can to remedy the situation. For the parent who wants a conflict and confrontation, this will have the effect of "taking the wind out of his sails." However, for some parents it will result in them feeling that they are "in the right" and will encourage them to complain even more. When these parents' complaints become unreasonable and/or happen too often, follow the suggestions under "A Last Resort" on page 231.

- Set up a meeting with the complaining parent, you, and your supervisor to get at the root cause of his unhappiness. It may have to do with the rates, a recent loss of income, marriage problems, guilt about not being home with his child, or some other reason over which you have little or no control. A sympathetic ear may be a big help. Ask for parents' advice about how you can assist them in solving the problem.

Behind your back

A parent, or a few parents, may be unhappy about the program, a policy, the food, a child with problematic behaviors, or another concern, but they will not talk about it directly with you or the director/principal. Instead, they will network with other parents to get support for their cause. In time everyone's ire builds, and suddenly, one day, you feel as if you are being confronted by an angry mob. Worst of all, you will not even have known there was a problem. Parents do this because they want their concerns validated and because there is safety and power in numbers.

- Don't try to deal with the problem without preparation and help from your supervisor, supportive parents, and other staff. If necessary, give yourself space by saying, "I'm not ready to respond to your concerns right now. I need to think about it and discuss it with my supervisor. I will get back to you tomorrow." Arrange for a meeting where all the people involved can get together. Invite a neutral third party to mediate at the meeting, such as a supportive parent, sympathetic board member, or respected member of the community.

The angry parent

- When confronted with an irate parent, regardless of the cause, just listen at first. Don't defend yourself, even if the parent is clearly misguided or misinformed. Remember that challenging the person only fuels the fire of her anger. If the parent is shouting, tell her that you will listen carefully to what she has to say if she says it without shouting. Listen intently and sympathetically and use active listening techniques. Try reflection: "What happened is really upsetting. That is a serious problem." And use clarification: "What I hear you saying is that . . ." or "Tell me more about exactly what happened when you . . ." This should defuse much of the anger.

- Apologize. Even if the problem was clearly not your fault, you can apologize for the anguish that the misunderstanding caused the parent. In many cases, this is all the parent is looking for.

- Tell the parent that you will do what you can to ease her concern. If you need more information or advice about the problem, tell her what you will do and when you will get back to her. Even if the parent feels that the end of the world has come, waiting a day or two to answer will often put the problem in its correct perspective. Some form of compensation can help a great deal: "I wish I could replace the lost jacket. I can't, but I can offer you one of the jackets from our extra clothes box. I'm sorry I can't do better."

- When the person's immediate anger has cooled, you may be able to offer an explanation or a rationale—your side of the story. Be aware, however, that some people are not interested in, or able to, reason. If this is the case, empathize with their concern and say what you have done to make sure the problem will not happen again. Leave the situation at that.

Complaints about your curriculum or style

This problem typically happens over clashes in values. You believe, for example, that children have the right to know the facts (appropriate to their age level) about sexual orientation, bodies, death, and other delicate subjects. However, some parents believe that young children should not hear this information or that it should come only from parents. These parents may get very emotional and clearly express their concerns.

- Meet with the parents to give them a forum for their concerns. Let them know that arguing with you in your classroom during class time is not acceptable. Invite all interested parents, but make sure that some who attend the meeting support your approach. Discuss your perspective calmly using documented principles of early childhood development or recommendations from experts. Be prepared to debunk myths with facts and data: "Sexual orientation is not about sex, but about who a person is attracted to." "There is no gay 'agenda' and it's no more a choice than being heterosexual is a choice." If possible, invite a local child development expert to the meeting.

- Acknowledge the validity of the parents' concerns and feelings. Agree to some reasonable compromises, but don't abandon your approach.

A last resort

If you are not able to end the complaining using the ideas in this chapter, give the parent a choice of two options. Tell him, "It is clear that you are still unhappy with our program and we have done all that we can do and will do to address your concerns. At this point, you can choose to accept the program as it is or I can help you find another school/center for your child. What would you like to do?" Remember that no program can meet the needs and desires of every family.

4. BEYOND BUSY: PARENTS WHO ARE ALMOST ALWAYS IN A HURRY

Parenting today is very hard. Many parents are single or are struggling financially. Even well-off two-parent families have difficulty trying to balance work and family obligations. Most parents feel they have put in forty-eight hours at the end of each day. Be understanding of their situation and why they are always in a hurry. Some parents hurry out the door for helpful reasons. They know that their child will continue to cry or act out until they leave. Because they do not want to prolong the problem, they leave quickly out of consideration for you and the class. At the end of the day, they may need to pick up another child from a different school or center before it closes, or they may have to get to a doctor's appointment. Many such tasks have to be done during a very small window of time, after work and after they pick up their child but before the clinic or business closes.

Anticipating and Preventing Problems Related to Parents Who Are in a Hurry

- Say a kind word to parents when they pick up their child at the end of a hard day. Avoid talking about their child's problematic behaviors or other concerns at this time.

- Set up an area where parents can sit for a few minutes, charge their phones, make calls, or just unwind. Provide coffee, tea, water, or juice. Offer comfortable seating and some magazines, helpful parenting books, short videos, and articles. By doing this, you send a clear message that parents are welcome and that it is important to be calm—or at least not frantic—when they pick up their children.

- Provide many convenient ways for parents to communicate with you.

- Include information in your parent handbook and talk with parents about how important it is for children to have nonstressful transitions from home to school and from school to home.

Solving Problems Related to Parents Who Are in a Hurry

- Ask parents who are always in a hurry to try to rearrange their work schedules and appointments and to adjust the time that they leave their homes and offices.

- Provide clear evidence that always rushing negatively impacts their child, and offer suggestions to help solve the problem. To the child, being rushed adds insult to injury. She not only feels powerless because her parents and other adults control her schedule, but she also has to act a certain way—hurry—to adhere to their schedule. Describe to parents how and why their child's behavior changes late in the day. Some rushed children run away and hide when their parents come to pick them up. Hiding is a very clever way for a child to start a power struggle with a parent who is in a hurry. It gives the parent three (bad) choices: physically pick up the child and leave, offer a bribe, or miss the appointment, meeting, or whatever the parent is in a hurry to get to. Let parents know that you will talk to their child about the behavior and try to prevent her from hiding, but it may not be possible. The only real solution is to find a way not to be in a hurry.

- Request that the parents text or call to let you know that they will be arriving shortly and need to pick up their child quickly. Then you can help their child be ready, alleviating a potentially stressful situation. However, reiterate that you can do this only occasionally when it is necessary, but not on a daily basis.

5. BEYOND HELPFUL AND FRIENDLY: PARENTS WHO LINGER

Another result of stress in the lives of parents may be their need for support wherever they can find it. Early childhood teachers are very empathetic and caring people, and some parents will take more than full advantage of this. You may have parents who demand your time and attention when you need to focus on the children or get home to your own family. The stress facing parents at work or at home may induce them not to leave promptly. They may also find the classroom to be a comfortable, enjoyable place—a pleasant break from work or home. Another reason parents may linger is that they have trouble separating from their children. They feel guilty or remorseful about leaving them.

Anticipating and Preventing Problems Related to Parents Who Linger

- Have a written statement in your parent handbook with guidelines for dropping off and picking up children. In the statement, recommend that parents stay in the classroom for no more than five minutes at the start and at the end of the day, unless they are actively participating in the morning's activities or helping to close up in the evening. If they need to talk to teachers longer or privately, request that they make an appointment.

- Post a message pad by the door. This will allow parents to leave you notes without disturbing your work with the children. Also post a sign-up sheet listing your available appointment times for those parents who need to talk with you longer or more formally.

Solving Problems Related to Parents Who Linger

- Involve the parent in an activity that helps you, such as preparing some art materials, cleaning, or giving one-on-one assistance to certain children. If he will continue to be involved in the classroom, request that he provide a regular schedule and formally sign up as a volunteer.

- Tell the parent: "I enjoy talking with you, but I can't give you my full attention when the children need me. Also, I'm concerned that mornings might be stressful for Anna. The longer you stay, the more she thinks that you won't be leaving and the greater her disappointment when you do. I have some ideas for helping and you probably have some too." Discuss possible solutions together. One possibility to consider is for the parent to establish a consistent routine: Read one book to Anna, give her one quick kiss, say one quick "good-bye," and then promptly leave. Remind Anna of the routine just before she enters the classroom. Tell the parent that consistent routines are vital for young children to feel secure.

- If the problem happens at the end of the day, try one or more of the following ideas:
  - Tell the parent you would love to chat longer but must attend to the children and be ready to leave by a specific time.
  - Set an appointment to meet with the parent when it would be more convenient for you.
  - Tell the parent you will call her later that evening.
  - Ask the parent to write you a note or send a text message or an e-mail.
  - Ask the parent to help you clean up, close up, and leave on time.

6. BEYOND LATE: PARENTS WHO ARRIVE AFTER THE CENTER CLOSES

This is a very common and persistent concern for many teachers working in child care programs. Waiting for a parent, not knowing when he might finally show up, is annoying to say the least. It can also cut into your personal time. The child almost always feels worried, hurt, and abandoned. This chapter includes ideas to greatly reduce, if not eliminate, the problem.

Anticipating and Preventing Parents from Arriving after the Center Closes

- State in your parent handbook your policy on this issue and why parents need to pick up their children on time. Discuss the impact it has on the child and the need for staff to have time with their own families. Explain the fees that parents will need to pay to cover the cost of staff overtime and extra resources (heating or air conditioning, electricity, materials). State the limit on the number of times that parents can arrive after closing before they're considered in violation of their contract: more than twice in any week, more than three times in any month, or more than four times in total. Offer assistance to help them find another program. Make an exception if the parent has never arrived later than five minutes after closing. The policy should also state that if one hour after closing a child has not been picked up, there have been no phone calls or texts, and the staff have not been able to reach any family members or emergency contacts, a staff member will call the local child welfare agency for assistance.

- Post a large sign in a conspicuous place stating the opening and closing hours and thanking parents for picking up their children on time. In smaller letters, remind them of the consequences of being late.

- Discuss with your supervisor the need to levy fees for late pickups if the center doesn't already have them or to raise existing fees. For some parents a few extra dollars for being late is a cost they're willing to pay. However, programs that charge four or more dollars for every minute a parent arrives after closing usually have fewer problems with lateness. Even free, government-funded programs can charge child care fees after their regular hours. As these are fees to cover the cost of extra care beyond working hours, they should go directly to the teacher who is staying late for he should be compensated at one and a half times his hourly salary.

- Thank parents who are always on time. Follow up your verbal thanks with a letter of appreciation midway through the school year and again at the end.

Solving Problems Related to Parents Who Arrive after the Center Closes

- Meet with parents who have arrived after closing when it happens the second time. Discuss ways to solve the problem. Let them know how much it impacts their child and the extent of the problem it causes you. They need to get the message that this is a serious problem. Often, this will turn things around.

- Meet with your supervisor and discuss your concerns. Make sure she clearly understands the depth of your unhappiness about staying late. Come prepared with several possible solutions in mind, including raising fees for being late.

- Request to have your shift changed, if possible, so that you are not on the final shift.

- Request that your supervisor or another person stay late with any children who have not been picked up before closing or that the task is rotated between different staff members. Because maintaining positive relations with parents is so important, you should not have to be the only one to confront late parents.

- End services to a family only as a very last resort, because this family may be among the most needy in your program for stable, quality education and care for their children.

- If the problem is that parents bring their children in late in the morning, meet with them to discuss the impact this has on their children. Tell them what the child misses, how the adjustment to the day is more difficult, and how it may impair their child's ability to form friendships. Offer your help in devising solutions to the problem.

7. HAVING "THE TALK": DISCUSSING CHILDREN'S PROBLEMATIC BEHAVIOR WITH THEIR PARENTS

Many teachers dread having to confront parents with information about their child's behavior. They worry that the parents may become upset, be defensive, blame the teacher, or perhaps be too punitive to their child. However, it is worse not to keep parents informed about their children. This chapter offers ideas for talking with parents that will minimize strong negative reactions. If you work in a full-day program, be sure to avoid the all-too-typical routine of informing parents at 5:45 p.m. how "awful" their child has been that day. At this time everyone is short-tempered, tired, hungry, and irrational. There is no time or space to deal with the concerns properly. Use the following suggestions as a guide to alternatives.

Anticipating and Preventing Problems Related to Discussing Children's Problematic Behavior

- Throughout the year, share a great deal of positive information about children with their parents. Do this as often as possible. Win the trust of parents through helpful, positive, and supportive communications. Show empathy and understanding, and be responsive to their children and to their concerns. When parents know that you have their child's best interests at heart, they will be open to and interested in hearing your concerns.

- On an ongoing basis, inform parents about how their children are doing. Meet with them when you first see signs of a problem. Don't spring any big, unpleasant surprises. Teachers often avoid doing this because it is difficult and stressful, and they hope that they can remedy the problem themselves or that the child will adjust or mature. However, you must inform parents early in case the problem does not improve or gets worse. They may also be able to give you vital insights into the concern or know of simple solutions. This can save you weeks of stress.

Solving Problems Related to Discussing Children's Problematic Behavior

- Don't talk to parents about problems when you are in a hurry or will have distractions. Set up a meeting when you will both have ample time to fully work through the concern. Meet in a place that is relaxing, as there will naturally be stress. Arrange the seating so that you are near each other or directly across from each other at the same table. This gives the message that you are working together on a problem. Set a specific starting and ending time.

- When you schedule a meeting, tell parents the concern specifically and briefly. For example, "I've noticed that Mark is hitting other children. Let's set up a time to talk about helping him." Avoid statements such as "We need to talk about Mark." This phrase gives parents great anxiety.

- Set an agenda with parents before you start, such as the following:

    You: Share objective observations

    Parents: Share their thoughts and concerns and possible reasons for the behavior

    You: Share any additional insight and your current strategies for dealing with the problem at school

    Together: Brainstorm possible solutions and strategies for school and home

    Together: Develop a plan of action for the best solution. Set a date to meet again to discuss the effectiveness of the plan and make any needed changes

- Start the discussion by talking about the child's strengths and good points. End the conference on a positive note by restating those strengths.

- When sharing your concern, present objective information. You might say: "Mark punched a child in the chest at 9:05 a.m. when he wanted the toy the child was playing with. After I talked with Mark about other ways to get a turn, he grabbed a toy away from the same child at 9:22. At 10:45, he pushed another child to the ground when the child accidentally bumped into him on the playground. The child hit his head on the ground but fortunately was not seriously hurt. At 12:30, during lunch, he shoved the child sitting next to him and the child fell off his chair; I did not see a reason for this. Although this child also did not appear to be seriously hurt, he acted very distressed, crying hard for about five minutes. Before I tell you more and talk about what I did at that point, I would like to hear your reactions and thoughts."

- Consider parents to be the experts on their children. Take their suggestions seriously and listen to their ideas.

- Follow your agenda and end the meeting on time. If it lasts too long, parents will be reluctant to meet again. Keep written notes of what was discussed and the strategies you have agreed on.

- If parents refuse to meet with you, write to them about your concerns and keep a copy of your letter. Some people take written remarks more seriously. This also ensures that you have a record that you made the parents aware of your concerns.

8. SAVE THE CHILDREN: PARENTS WHO MAY BE ABUSIVE OR NEGLECTFUL

Each state has laws on reporting child abuse. Know the laws in your state. The information should be on the websites of your state agency that deals with child abuse (usually called Child Protective Services, Children's Services Division, Bureau of Family Services, Child Welfare Division, or a similar name). You can also access the information through the federal Child Welfare Information Gateway (www.childwelfare.gov). E-mail or call any of these agencies if you have specific questions. In all states, Washington, DC, and U.S. territories, you, as a teacher and caregiver, are required to report suspected child abuse. Not doing so is illegal. In turn, you are protected from wrongdoing if you are mistaken, as long as the report was made in "good faith."

Be as vigilant and concerned about neglect, sexual abuse, and emotional abuse as you are about physical abuse. Of course these are harder to detect, but they are as damaging to children as physical abuse. Emotional abuse can result in negative and antisocial behaviors that last a lifetime. An emotionally abused child is one who is often and consistently picked on, punished arbitrarily, humiliated, punished cruelly (such as being locked in a closet), and/or psychologically tortured. Some states are able to handle reports of emotional abuse and have procedures and trained staff to investigate. Other states focus more on abuse where there is physical evidence, particularly if protective service funds are in short supply.

Anticipating and Preventing Problems Related to Parents Who May Be Abusive or Neglectful

- Attend training sessions, usually sponsored by the state agency responsible for investigating child abuse, so you will know signs of abuse and neglect and exactly what to do if you suspect abuse. You will also learn the process that the state follows when they receive a report.

- Teach children personal safety as described in "Too Much Too Soon" on pp. 145–48.

- Ensure that parents know your program's policies and procedures about reporting abuse and about the state reporting requirement.

- Become familiar with resources for parents, programs that are effective at preventing abuse, and the causes and impacts of abuse and neglect. Prevent Child Abuse America (www.preventchildabuse.org) and Parents Anonymous (http://parentsanonymous.org) offer good information on these issues.

Solving Problems Related to Parents Who May Be Abusive or Neglectful

Children get many cuts and bruises, so determining whether the child is being physically abused can be difficult. However, making a mistake and overreporting abuse is better than taking a chance on missing abuse. At the very least, keep a written record with detailed descriptions of the child's cuts and bruises, including the date that you first see them. If possible take photos. Many small cuts, bruises, or burns over a period of time or wounds that do not seem to be healing are likely a result of abuse or neglect.

Reporting abuse can be very positive and something to feel good about, as you may be the person who starts the process that will help a family change for the better, and you may even save a child's life.

Signs or indicators of abuse and neglect

The following lists give you a quick guide to the most common signs or indicators of neglect and physical, emotional, and sexual abuse. Except where noted, one indicator or occasional indicators are likely not the result of abuse. In most cases, you should suspect and report abuse if there are two or more indicators and they are consistent or regular over time. However, any single indicator, if severe, such as extreme hunger or a serious burn, should be reported. A report should also be made if the parent or child gives explanations for bruises that are highly unlikely to have caused those injuries; if the child freely tells you that her injury was the result of being hurt by a parent, another adult, or an older child; or if the child tells you she injured herself when she was left unattended.

Indicators of Neglect

- always hungry
- chronically tired and listless
- dressed inappropriately for the weather
- smelling bad
- wearing very dirty clothes
- needing medical attention that does not get taken care of
- failing to grow and gain weight
- tells you she was left alone at home or in the care of a sibling who is younger than eleven or who is not mature enough for the responsibility

Indicators of Physical Abuse

- visible bruises or injuries in places unlikely to be hurt from a fall or a bump, such as around the eye or on the buttocks, genitals, neck, torso, thigh, and backs of legs
- bruises in a pattern, such as belt marks or handprints
- frequent burns or burns in unusual places or shapes, such as from a cigarette or clothes iron
- large bite marks that appear to be from an animal, adult, or older child
- numerous bruises in various stages of healing

Indicators of Emotional Abuse

- displays extremes of emotions (overly happy, depressed, withdrawn), which are often expressed at inappropriate times or in odd ways, such as laughing when hurt
- physically hurts herself
- isolates herself from others
- displays strange or intense habits, such as hair pulling, rocking, or head banging
- destroys property or sets fires
- has extreme fears, many fears, or unusual fears
- is cruel to other children or animals
- is obsessed with minute details
- steals compulsively
- lies compulsively
- bites (if three and a half or older)

Indicators of Sexual Abuse

- experiences difficulty sitting or walking due to soreness in the genital and/or anal area
- has stained or bloody underwear
- experiences itchiness in the genital and/or anal area
- displays sexually provocative behavior and adultlike knowledge of sexuality
- has an extreme fear of men or behaves seductively toward men
- draws pictures that depict adults with erect penises or other sexual scenes

What to do (and not to do) when you suspect abuse or neglect

- Keep a written record of any bruises. Record where it is on the body and the time and date you noticed it. Include any comments made by the child and/or parent. If you suspect neglect, sexual abuse, or emotional abuse, write down the signs, symptoms, and comments the child made. Be specific and objective. Then call your local child protective services or abuse hotline to make a report.

- Keep your report in a safe place. This is important because several days may pass before a caseworker investigates. Also, one incident may not be considered a cause for concern by the caseworker, but a number of incidents over time will be. In many states, a written report of abuse is required.

- Let your supervisor know that you have filed a report and request that she take over from this point so you can focus on your work with the children.

- Never discuss your suspicions with parents. Because you care about your families, you may want to let the child's parents know about the bruises you saw or even inform them that you will have to report the possible abuse. This is not a good idea. Abusive parents may take their child and leave. You will probably not be able to find them, nor will the caseworker. The parents also may be able to talk you out of reporting, which you may later regret. Your first responsibility is to protect the child. Abusive parents often do not begin to get help until they are involved in the legal system.

If a parent asks for your help

Parents Anonymous is a great resource for a parent who asks for help because he is worried he will abuse his child. As an alternative to Parents Anonymous, you can suggest a counseling agency, social service agency, or the state child abuse agency. Keep the telephone numbers of Parents Anonymous and the other agencies handy in case a parent requests help. To be supportive, you may want to offer to be present when the parent makes the call. Admitting publicly to a weakness and being willing to do something about it is a very difficult, life-changing step for anyone. A parent who does this needs and deserves support.

If a parent asks for help because he is already abusing his child, the abuse must be reported. Do not tell this to the parent, however, as she may try to talk out of it or flee. Instead, be supportive of the parent's willingness get help. Refer the parent to the local Parents Anonymous organization, if there is one. The national number is 855.4AParent or 855-427-2736. Their website is www.parentsanonymous.org. Then report the abuse immediately after the parent has left.

Problematic Behaviors Take 2: This Time It's the Adults!

WE'VE DISCUSSED A NUMBER OF children's behaviors that are problematic because they are too adultlike: caretaking of other children, being too responsible, acting sexually precocious, and being manipulative, for example. Here we discuss a number of adult behaviors that are problematic because they are too childish. Joking aside, problems with coworkers and supervisors are very stressful and will take the pleasure out of what would otherwise be enjoyable work. These problems make the hard job of being an early childhood teacher that much harder, so it is important to solve them. Working with supportive and positive people in an emotionally healthy environment makes your work so much easier and more enjoyable.

1. BULLIES, BUMBLERS, AND OTHER BAD BOSSES

Fortunately, there are many more supportive and reasonable bosses in the early childhood field than there are difficult bosses, probably because most people drawn to the field are nurturing, caring people. However, like any profession, there are a great number of supervisors who do not manage their employees well and who have trouble running a complex organization. Many supervisors in our field have proven their worth as teachers and have moved up into supervisory positions with little knowledge or training in management and supervision. And, like the staff they supervise, they are typically overworked, underpaid, and stretched to capacity. They may really desire to be more flexible or responsive with their staff, but the leaky roof just has to take priority over a teacher's concern about a child. This does not mean you should just accept a poor relationship between you and your boss or accept difficult working conditions. There are many things you can do to improve the situation.

Anticipating and Preventing Problems Related to Difficult Bosses

- Know the management style you work under best. You may prefer to be basically left alone and given a great deal of autonomy, or you may prefer to get more direction, feedback, and support from a supervisor. Your preference may be based on whether you are an experienced or a new teacher, but it may also just be the way you work best.

- During your initial interview when applying for a new position, ask your potential supervisor questions that will reveal her style of managing. If her style is very different from what you prefer, determine if you can accept the discrepancy before taking the position.

- In the interview, ask the supervisor about her short-term and long-term goals for the organization. This will help you determine how well your goals fit with hers. Make sure your teaching style, curriculum approach, and values will be accepted and supported by the supervisor before accepting the position.

- During your first weeks on the job, discreetly ask your new coworkers about your boss's strengths, weaknesses, and idiosyncrasies. Use that information to establish positive relations with your boss.

- Make your supervisor aware of the wonderful things you are doing in your classroom. Give her samples of your children's artwork for her office. Offer her some of the good food your children make in cooking projects. If you do special projects for holidays, ask one of the children to volunteer to make something for your supervisor. Most children enjoy this and especially enjoy presenting it to her.

- Bosses need praise and support as much as anyone. When your boss does something you appreciate, let her know. Praise her good qualities to others.

- Request regular individual meetings with your boss to discuss concerns and problems before they become crises. If there are no problems to discuss, use the time to offer and receive positive feedback or to get to know each other better.

Solving Problems Related to Difficult Bosses

- Talk to your coworkers who seem to get along well with your boss to determine how they do this. You are sure to get some good ideas. Whenever you have a complaint or concern, request to meet with your supervisor at a time that will be good for both of you. Ask for her undivided attention and request that phone calls be held. Come into the meeting with at least two reasonable ideas for solving the concern.

- Do not circumvent your boss and go to her supervisor or to the board of directors unless this is absolutely necessary. An example would be if she violates personnel policies or does something illegal. In all other cases, take your concern directly to your boss first. If the issue does not get resolved, then you may talk with her supervisor. But discuss the concern with your boss first or you will not likely get a sympathetic response from her supervisor, and it may make matters worse for you. If you must talk to her supervisor, be absolutely certain that any allegations you make are correct and that you can provide proof.

- Accept that you probably will not change your boss, so work on ways you can change your own behavior, thinking, and reactions. For example, if your boss demands more paperwork than you think is necessary and discussions with your boss have not resolved the problem, find ways to do the work quickly and efficiently. Don't continue to waste time and energy complaining or being angry about the foibles of your boss.

When you have a new boss

- If there is a change in supervisors, ask to meet individually with the new supervisor to discuss how you can best work together. Clarify your approach to teaching young children and determine his expectations and goals. Offer to help in any way to make his transition into the position easier and smoother.

- Invite your new boss to spend time in your classroom—before he has a chance to request it. Ask for his input and feedback about a specific concern you have. Have your children make a gift and provide a welcoming party (perhaps during a snack-time). Have the children give him a tour of the room and talk about their favorite activities. Sing a favorite song or two for him.

The authoritarian boss

- A boss who is overly controlling, demanding, demeaning, unapproachable, and intimidating is probably insecure about the organization and her ability to manage it. She may also (incorrectly) believe that this management style will get the best performance out of people. Get to know her on a personal level and offer empathy, understanding, and help. If you do this, she will likely feel more positive toward you and treat you with more respect.

- Keep a complete and detailed written record of examples of your boss's actions and statements that cross the line from directive to dictatorial or that are unreasonable or punitive. Write down direct quotes accurately.

- Know your legal rights as an employee and the personnel policies of the school or organization you work for. However, even if your legal rights are not being violated, you have a moral right to be treated respectfully and professionally. Speak up for yourself without being angry or defensive. An authoritarian boss expects compliant and weak behavior and almost always gets it. When you change your behavior patterns and take more control of the interactions between you and your boss, she will likely change her behaviors as well.

- Seek support and assistance from coworkers and friends, and stop expecting it from your supervisor.

The incompetent boss

- Your boss may seem incompetent because he has more to do than he can possibly handle. Offer to take responsibility for a task that you would like to do, that will give you some additional job experience, and that will look good on a résumé. For example, volunteer to organize "Week of the Young Child" events, find a trainer for a music workshop, or take responsibility for keeping up the parent bulletin board.

- Your boss may be incompetent because he is not capable of handling the job responsibilities or because he is preoccupied with personal problems, or both. Offer your support and assistance, but take on no more than you can handle. Remember that you may help just by being a good listener. If your boss is smart but new, he will become competent with experience. If he seems to be steadily improving, give him time and be helpful and supportive.

- Decide if you can still do your job well and your school or center can provide quality services to children and families under an incompetent boss. If not, consider finding another position or, if many things about your program are good, try the ideas below.

- Discreetly keep a written, dated log of specific, observable behaviors that show your supervisor's inability to do his job as it affects you. For example, you might note the following: "6/24—Did not show up for staff meeting. Later, at 2:00 p.m., he said that he forgot." Enlist other concerned coworkers to also keep a log. Write at home and keep your log there. Your log may be an important document to support, if not directly lead to, his supervisor or the board asking for his resignation. You can choose to take your log directly to them, but be prepared that you will not be appreciated and may even be fired for doing so. If other staff members (preferably all of them) join you in the process, your concerns will undoubtedly be taken more seriously.

If all else fails

- If you have given a great deal of time and effort to getting along with your boss but still find the situation difficult, make a decision to stay or leave. If you choose to stay, accept your boss's limitations and find a way to be at peace with your life at work. If your choice is to leave, determine what other employment options you have and begin to discreetly seek those out before resigning. You have a right to work in an environment that helps you be effective in your job. You and the children you care for and teach deserve the best.

2. BEING A BOSS WITHOUT BULLYING OR BUMBLING: MANAGING ASSISTANTS, VOLUNTEERS, AND OTHERS

While you may not have an official management position, if you are a lead teacher, you do have to manage other people, such as assistants and volunteers. To be a good manager, you must understand and appreciate the skill and knowledge level of each person you manage and to know their strengths and challenges. Then you can help them improve from wherever they are. It is also important to know what motivates them, how to most effectively communicate with them, how they learn best, and what they believe and value in regard to supporting families and nurturing children's development. Managing people well is a difficult task requiring effort, time, and skills in a variety of areas: counseling, organizing, communicating, and more. However, it is worth the time and effort, as having positive working relationships with capable assistants and volunteers will help create a successful and happy classroom and make your job easier and more enjoyable. The suggestions in this chapter will assist you in giving the people you manage the knowledge, tools, and support to perform well.

Anticipating and Preventing Problems Related to Managing Others

- Give a thorough orientation to any new people who will be working with you. The time this takes will be worthwhile because ultimately you will have to deal with fewer problems, misunderstandings, or conflicts.

- During the orientation, review your approaches to and reasons for the way you teach, guide children's behavior, set your daily schedule, use and store materials and supplies, work with parents, handle transitions, and deal with crises. Clarify roles and tasks by specifying who will do what and when. Make your expectations and personal priorities known. For example, "Coming on time or a few minutes early is very important to me. Mornings are hectic and there is so much to be done."

- Have some written information for your orientation. In addition to a staff handbook that outlines your program's general policies and procedures and the job description for the new employee or volunteer, provide written information specific to your class and your procedures.

- If you will be giving or participating in your assistant's job evaluation, give him a copy of the form that will be used. Make sure the form is specific and detailed and that it includes such items as talking positively with children, smiling at children, doing assigned tasks willingly, staying focused (not talking or texting while with children), coming to work on time, maintaining confidentiality, being friendly to parents, showing initiative, and learning more about child development.

- Request to be involved in hiring and placing new staff or volunteers. You should be the manager of any person who works under your supervision. This means doing their performance evaluations, recommending (or not recommending) an end to probation, proposing disciplinary measures, and, if necessary, requesting termination for just cause—with the final approval of your supervisor. If you have the responsibility of making sure your assistant does a good job but are not given the authority of a manager, you are in an untenable situation. If you have neither the responsibility nor the authority, then you are only in a difficult situation. If there are problems with your assistant's work, you will have to continually go to his actual supervisor with your concerns and wait for that person to take some action. Some programs have been able to make this work by developing a detailed process for sharing the authority and responsibility between a manager and the teacher. However, this requires excellent and frequent communication between them and compatible beliefs and management styles, which is difficult to achieve and maintain. Consider talking to your supervisor about restructuring lines of supervision so you can have both the rights and the responsibility. Help her see how this chain of command will benefit her by reducing her workload and stress.

- Avoid establishing close personal friendships with any person you supervise. Also avoid having a friend hired as your assistant. If there is a work-related problem, the friendship makes dealing effectively with the situation difficult. It's rare that friends stay friends for very long if one supervisors the other.

- Meet regularly and individually with the people you directly work with. Use the time to discuss problems, successes, and new activities to try. Read books and articles, attend workshops, and talk to experienced people about being a good boss. Most teachers have no training in this area, yet being an effective supervisor can be a big factor in your job satisfaction.

- Be positive with the people who work with you. Thank them often for what they do. Keep a stack of attractive thank-you cards to use. A written appreciation, which can be kept and looked at over and over again, has a more lasting impact than a verbal thank-you, though that's important too. Ask your staff what you can do differently to make their jobs easier or more pleasant.

Solving Problems Related to Managing Others

Whether the problem you have with your assistant or volunteer is that she is inefficient and lazy, interferes with what you do, acts inappropriately with the children, doesn't do the tasks assigned to her, or anything else, the best approach to dealing with the problem is basically the same. Write down your concerns and be very specific and clear. In collaboration with your supervisor or human resource specialist, carefully follow the school's policies regarding disciplinary action. Most personnel policies require immediate termination for serious violations that endanger the safety or well-being of the children or other staff. However, addressing less serious problems usually involves developing an assistance plan outlining the specific, measurable behaviors required to improve job performance to an acceptable level and a time frame in which to do it. If your school's process is inadequate or unfair—or if there is no specific process in place—consider using the one below.

- Keep a detailed, objective written record or journal of exactly what your assistant does or does not do and the way it impacts you, the children, and/or families. Include dates and times.

- Set up a meeting with your assistant at a time when you both can be relaxed, have no interruptions, and are not rushed for time. Say, for example, "I'm frustrated about not getting the help I need in the morning. Let's set up a time to discuss ways to address my concerns." This keeps the focus on how the behavior affects you rather than on what is wrong with her. Because she will not feel threatened or accused, it should promote dialogue and better communication.

- Start and end the meeting with positive statements about what the assistant or volunteer does well.

- Brainstorm possible solutions to the problem together. Be creative and don't lock yourself into a solution. Trying to change the behavior directly rarely works. The best ideas usually involve a structural change or the addition of resources: training, adjustments in the environment, changes in assigned tasks or schedules, clarification of roles, or helpful reminders. Choose one or two of the best potential solutions and make a plan of action. Write down who will do what and when. Set another time to meet to evaluate how the plan is working.

- Give her a great deal of feedback while executing the plan. Tell her specifically what she is doing well and what she is not doing well. Enlist help from someone who does not supervise her, such as a highly skilled teacher, consultant, or board member, to coach her in the classroom on the specific skills or behaviors that she needs to improve. An hour or two of coaching, two to three days per week, should be sufficient, in most cases. Continue to keep a detailed journal.

- If the problem is not fixed after two meetings over two weeks, meet with your supervisor to create an assistance plan and place her on probation for two weeks, if she is not already on probation. Tell her that she will be dismissed if she does not meet the improvement targets on the plan. Ask her what supports she needs to improve. Follow through on the consequences, if necessary, and don't accept a small, partial improvement. You and the children need and deserve to be with people who are competent, committed, and caring.

3. COPING WITH CONFOUNDING COWORKERS

You may have coworkers who make your job difficult or who lower the quality of your school or program because of their poor teaching skills. This puts you in a tough spot because they are your peers and you don't supervise them. But you have a right and the moral duty to express your concerns, as long as you do so tactfully. Antagonizing your coworkers will only be counterproductive. Most people do the best they can with what they know, so correcting problems often means getting more information and support to your coworkers. This chapter will offer you ways to do this without making your coworkers feel defensive.

Anticipating and Preventing Problems with Coworkers

- Establish positive relations with your coworkers. Treat them with respect. Be helpful to them by sharing your materials and ideas without acting superior. Ask for their assistance and ideas when you have a problem. Set up a system where each person on staff does a training session for other staff in an area in which he feels particularly strong.

- After attending a conference, share what you have learned with other staff members and ask them to share what they have learned.

- Actively work toward improving communications and relations between you and your coworkers. Help organize and participate in staff meetings, training sessions, and social events with other staff members.

- Suggest holding a staff retreat where there is a relaxing atmosphere and ample time to get to know each other better, solve problems, learn new skills, clarify and agree on a philosophy and program objectives, set exciting goals, eat good food, and have fun.

- Start a study group to read and discuss new ideas and potential solutions to shared problems.

- Suggest that the program invite consultants to do team-building workshops with staff.

- Think of new and better ways to communicate—e-mail, in-school mailboxes, a memo system, a phone/texting tree, a sharing time before each staff meeting, and so on.

- Work with your supervisor on developing personnel policies and staff evaluations that include such personal capacities as being friendly with other staff, supporting the growth of other staff, working as a team, and sharing resources. This makes it clear that getting along with coworkers is a vital part of the job.

Solving Problems Related to Confounding Coworkers

Among the most common concerns that teachers have about their coworkers are that they are lazy, incompetent, and untrained; too strict or too lax with children; divisive, arrogant, or uncooperative. These concerns fall into two categories: behaviors that affect you directly and behaviors that affect children, families, and the program or school.

Problems with coworkers that affect you directly

- Coworkers who hoard supplies or take your supplies, lie to you, or belittle you in front of others create problems that directly affect you, your ability to do your job, and your happiness with your work. This is particularly true when a coworker does this to you often over an extended period of time. If this happens, confront the person directly. Although this is difficult, avoiding this step may create more problems in the end. Say, for example, "I would like to talk with you. I feel hurt by your comments, which you probably didn't intend. Can we meet at five o'clock for about fifteen minutes?" When you state it this way, you will hopefully avoid a defensive response from your coworker.

- Meet at a time and place conducive to relaxation, privacy, and no interruptions. Explain how her actions made you feel and ask what her intention was. Be very objective: "I felt put down when you said, 'That's a ridiculous idea.' Did I hear you wrong? Did I misunderstand you?" After her response, specifically ask for what you want and state the consequences: "I would like an apology and a promise that if you disagree with me, you will do it respectfully and professionally. If you put me down again that way, I will make a formal complaint to our supervisor."

- If you get a denial or no cooperation, and the behaviors continue, follow through on your stated consequence. Keep written records documenting objectively what the person did and said, when it happened, and the contexts or circumstances. Talk with other staff members to determine if they have similar concerns. If so, ask them to keep written records too. Complaints from several people to a supervisor carry much more weight than from one.

- Use all legal and appropriate channels to stop the problem. Keep written documentation of all your meetings and the responses you received. If your supervisor clearly intends to do nothing about the concern, go to his superiors (board of directors, for example) and/or a lawyer, if appropriate. A lawyer can help you determine if your rights are being violated because of sexual harassment, racial or other biases, or other reasons. But a hostile work environment itself is a violation of the law in most states. Being regularly harassed or bullied by a coworker would be considered a hostile work environment, especially if you have made every attempt to stop it and a supervisor is unable or unwilling to deal with it. Be prepared for almost certain negative responses from your supervisor and others if you do this.

- If all else fails, decide whether or not you can live with this troublesome coworker. Either find ways to be happy in your job or start looking for a better situation.

Problems with coworkers that affect children, families, and the program or school

Certain concerns you have about others may involve how they interact with other staff, children, or parents. These concerns do not affect you directly; however, you still feel compelled to do something because you care about all the children and families and the quality and reputation of the program or school.

You may have a very different approach toward teaching young children than other staff in your program. Perhaps other teachers use direct teaching methods, worksheets, few choices, and little time for children to play, reward systems, time-outs and other punishments, or teaching to the whole group for long periods. Suggest to your supervisor that the program develop and adopt a unified philosophy on teaching young children and some guidelines for carrying out that philosophy. Alternatively, a new curriculum could be adopted. Recommend that a group of teachers work together with your supervisor to develop the philosophy and guidelines or to select a new curriculum, either of which will be later approved by the whole staff. Volunteer to be a part of the group.

- Offer your assistance to other teachers in a supportive way: "I noticed you had some difficulty with the children in the gym. I used to have the same problem. Would you like some ideas that might help?"

- If the concerns continue, meet with your supervisor and ask her to observe. Make no accusations and try not to indict your coworker. State objective facts about what you saw and why you are concerned: "Two children in Helen's class were sword fighting outside this morning with pointy sticks. She told them to stop, but when they continued, she took no further action. I was concerned for their safety, so I gave them some foam swords to use instead. I think it might be helpful to Helen if you gave her some pointers."

- If your supervisor does not act to improve the situation, take detailed, objective notes of your coworker's behavior and bring them to *her* supervisor or a board member. Get additional written evidence of problems from other concerned staff members, if possible. If your coworker's behavior endangers the health, safety, or well-being of children, and you get no action from a supervisor, take your concerns to the appropriate authorities, such as the child care licensing department, advisory council, or board of directors.

- If other concerns you have do not threaten the health, safety, or well-being of the children, then you may have to either accept your coworkers or find work in a program that shares your approach and philosophy.

- Disparities among teachers in their ability to teach and their commitment to the work exist in almost every program. You can reduce these disparities by being helpful and supportive to others and by creating excitement and enthusiasm through sharing ideas, organizing a staff retreat to a beautiful place, or using other suggestions listed earlier in the chapter.

Take Care of the Caretaker: Attending to Your Own Needs

YOU CAN'T REALLY TAKE GOOD CARE of others if you are not taking good care of yourself. I have heard it said that to stay mentally healthy, a person needs at least one hour a day of uninterrupted "me" time. That is, time for yourself and by yourself to do whatever "feeds your soul" at that moment. If you are a teacher and a parent of young children, you are probably thinking "In my dreams!" However, if you don't try, if you don't plan for it, arrange for it, ask for it, and (gasp!) even expect it, then it *definitely* will not happen. Even if you are able to get this time only once or twice per week, it will make a difference in how you feel. Other important ways to take care of yourself are to eat healthy, nutritious food, to take control of your time and work, and to have a good balance of activity and rest, and work and leisure.

1. NEVER ENOUGH TIME: WHEN LIFE FEELS LIKE A GAME OF BEAT THE CLOCK

Although this is a particularly difficult problem for people who work in full-day programs, almost everyone working in early childhood programs feels short of time. This is largely because there are not enough funds to pay people for the planning time they need. In spite of this, there are undoubtedly some things you can do to organize your time better.

Anticipating and Preventing Problems Related to Never Having Enough Time

- Take the time to make time. Here are a few tried-and-true tips:
  - Keep yourself well organized. One of the biggest time wasters is the time you spend looking for things. Get the tools you need to keep organized: file cabinets, folders, labels, shelf space, clear plastic boxes of various sizes, and so on. If you are computer savvy, get a fast scanner and a well-organized electronic file system.
  - Use a calendar planner, actual or virtual, to keep track of appointments and tasks. Don't rely on your memory.
  - Make a list of tasks you need to get done each day. Do this the night before. Prioritize the tasks to ensure you get the important ones done. If possible, tackle the biggest and/or most unpleasant task first.
  - Use your phone's voice recorder function to immediately record important thoughts or ideas and anything that you need to remember. Technology has made it unnecessary to waste your time and brainpower memorizing phone numbers, shopping lists, and other trivia. As soon as you are able, transfer the information from the voice recorder to your calendar, address book, task list, or wherever it needs to go.
  - Eliminate distractions and don't try to multitask. Put your phone on "airplane mode" when you are with children, working on lesson plans, in meetings, or taking time for yourself to relax. This will eliminate the temptation to answer the phone or respond to text messages but will still allow you to use it as a voice recorder and for most other functions that do not require Wi-Fi.
  - Don't be a perfectionist, at least not all the time. As the saying goes, "Perfect is the enemy of good." "Good enough" is usually doable in a reasonable amount of time, but there is never enough time for perfection. Save your perfectionism for the few tasks that are really important to you and that you have ample time to accomplish.
  - Delegate tasks as much as possible. Your assistant or volunteers may be able to do a few more things than they currently do. Give them opportunities to develop new skills and practice them. This will also help their career development. For example, if you take the time to help your assistant become good at reading stories to children, you will save a great deal more time by having him lead "read-alouds" often. Also, the children in your class, as well as your own children at home, can likely do more for themselves than they

do now. And they will actually enjoy some of these tasks, such as setting the table, vacuuming and sweeping, and making their own sandwiches.

- ▸ If you are interested and ready to make a significant change in your life to be better organized, check out David Allen's book and training program *Getting Things Done*, which is very popular in the business world (http://gettingthingsdone.com). Rather than a series of tips, it is a comprehensive approach to time management, so it requires a significant commitment of time and effort initially to learn the system and get it set up.
- ▸ Think "long term" and "big picture." Decide on one or two personal and professional goals that you can achieve in a year, and one or two that are five to ten years down the road. Break these long-term goals into smaller steps to help you get there and so they don't feel overwhelming. It is too easy to let daily, mundane tasks and crises eat up all your time. Make sure you allow time to work regularly on your longer-term goals.

Solving Problems Related to Never Having Enough Time

Short on planning time

- If you never have enough time, you may not be asking for the time you need to plan and get organized. To improve your situation, assert your needs to your family, coworkers, or supervisor. Planning and organizing are essential to doing your job well and staying in control. And these steps will ultimately save time.

- Collaborate with other teachers so you can cover for each other and use the time to plan.

- Keep a file for each theme that you implement. These can be electronic or actual paper files. Make or scan copies of the lesson plans you created for that theme to put in the file, along with notes, photos, and so on. In subsequent years, draw from these files when planning, and modify and update them to improve them and to match the needs and interests of each new group of children.

- Plan classroom activities at least two weeks in advance to allow time to gather supplies, arrange field trips, and so on.

- Use an effective planning tool to reduce the time and effort needed for planning. Trying to work with a generic form may result in inadequate planning. Find or develop a lesson plan form that works for your specific needs. The form should reflect your classroom schedule, priorities, and goals. Use a one- or two-page monthly planning form to plan themes, projects, field trips, and other broad and more general activities. Then use a weekly or daily planning form (or both) to plan more specifically and in more detail.

Time seems to slip away

- To manage your time well, set personal goals for yourself and for your teaching. If you set a personal goal of earning a college or more advanced degree, the time you spend working toward that goal will be fulfilling. Goals for your teaching might include encouraging the children to be more independent, involving them more actively in science activities, or adding more variety to the outside play area in terms of equipment and activities. Not having goals will make you feel frustrated—as if time is slipping away from you. Accomplishing goals will make you feel that your time has been well spent.

- Start by choosing one realistic shorter-term goal to work toward. Make sure you can achieve it. Doing so will help you feel successful, in control, and motivated to work on more challenging and longer-term goals.

- Track children's progress toward the goals you and their families have set for them. Use a systematic format for recording their progress. Performing ongoing informal, observational assessments of children will allow you to regularly see the positive impact you are making on their development.

- Mark and celebrate successes and milestones—the end of a complex project or unit, the anniversary of your start in teaching, the completion of a restructured playground, and so on.

Too many committees and meetings

- Early childhood teachers too often try to be all things to all people. For your own mental health, limit your activities and commitments to what you can realistically handle and to only those that are very important to you. Learn to say, "No, but thank you for asking!"

- Set a time limit for how long you will stay at a meeting, particularly for meetings that tend to run over their allotted time. At the start of the meeting, say, "I apologize in advance, but I will have to leave right at 5:00."

Rushed and hassled

- If possible, go to work about an hour early to organize yourself and the day's activities and to do some planning. Most people work better and are more efficient in the morning. Feeling ready and prepared when children start arriving can make the whole day go well. Plus, once you are involved with the children, getting any time for yourself will be difficult.

Procrastinating

- We tend to procrastinate when faced with a particularly large, difficult, and/or unpleasant task. We fool ourselves into believing that we will feel more inclined to do the task sometime later. But, of course, we won't. So the key to stop procrastinating (or at least to procrastinate less) is to do such tasks early in the day so that the rest of the day can be enjoyed. Create a plan to manage a large task incrementally over time.

- Break down large tasks into small steps and accomplish them one day at a time. For example, making more handmade games for your classroom can be a big, time-consuming job. But if you plan to make one game a week, the task will be manageable. Design the game one day, make the game board the next day, make the pieces/cards and directions the following day, and make the spinner or dice and laminate the game on the final day. In a month, you will have four new games.

2. JUST NOT FEELIN' IT: BURNED OUT AND FED UP

Feeling burned out is unfortunately an occupational hazard in our field. There are two main factors that contribute to burnout. One is internal—the job itself and the working conditions. The other is external—job status, wages, and demands and expectations. Research conducted by Hossain, Noll, and Barboza (2012) revealed that early childhood teachers like their jobs; they love working with children. They tend to accept the long hours and the physical exhaustion that comes with the job. They have more autonomy and control in their own classrooms than most other teachers, except professors. Unless there are tense relationships with coworkers, parents, or bosses, they are satisfied with their working conditions. What they don't like is everything else. The aspects of the job that cause burnout and lead nearly one-third of early childhood educators to quit each year are the meager wages and benefits and the lack of respect.

Burnout is the by-product of the disconnect between the low status of the job and the actual job, which requires special expertise, entails a high level of risk and responsibility (the health, safety, well-being, and development of young children), and is subject to the unreasonable expectations and demands of supervisors, parents, primary school staff, funders, and state regulators.

Anticipating and Preventing Burnout

- Get involved politically to advocate for more funding, children's rights, quality enhancements, or other issues in support of the field and of children and families. You will be actively doing something about the problem and feel less helpless. This is also a good way to meet people with whom you will have much in common. Political work can be stressful too, however, so don't take on more than you have time for and don't expect immediate results.

- Join or get more involved in your local chapter of the National Association for the Education of Young Children (NAEYC). You can find contact information for your local chapter through the NAEYC website (www.naeyc.org).

- Find a like-minded colleague in a program that serves children who are different from the children you serve, such as ethnically different or in a rural area if you are in an urban area. Partner up by having the children visit each other's classrooms and sharing play and project ideas.

- Be nurtured by your environment. Take the time to set up and maintain a classroom that reflects your taste and aesthetic values—one that is beautiful, comfortable, and bright but peaceful. This will be a classroom you will want to return to every day. Keep one comfortable adult-size chair in the room. Constant sitting on small, hard children's chairs is stressful on your body. Although being on the same level with the children is important, an occasional stint on your chair—during naptime or to read to a child—will be good for everyone.

- Provide yourself with a space that you can call your own, even if it is just a few shelves. This is your private area. You can set it up as you like and it can contain your important materials and books. (One teacher I know keeps a jar of hot peppers in her area as a daily pick-me-up in the afternoons, though I would keep chocolate.) A small file cabinet just for your own use, containing activity ideas, notes, and articles from magazines, will make your job easier. It can also hold children's files and personal information if it can be locked.

- Take a break. Get out of the classroom and take small breaks and a full lunch break every day. Take a brisk walk, jog, exercise, go window shopping, or read a good novel. Give yourself a mental vacation and get a change of scenery in the middle of every day.

- Take care of your health. Start an exercise group with your coworkers. Eat healthy foods and sleep as much as you need. Stay home when you are sick. If your energy level is good, you will be better able to meet the challenges of the day. A hurt or aching back is a common health problem for teachers of young children. Working with a bad back will increase your stress tremendously. Avoid back problems by doing the following:

  - When standing for long periods, bend your knees slightly, keep your legs apart (directly under the shoulders), have one foot slightly in front of the other, and distribute your weight evenly over both legs.

  - Avoid sitting for long periods, but when you do sit, put your feet on a cushion or a low box so that your knees are slightly higher than your hips.

  - When you need to reach up to get something from a high place, stand on a stepladder or stool designed for that purpose. Don't stand on your toes. Keep your knees bent slightly to avoid losing your balance.

  - When standing at a sink to wash your hands, bend your knees and rest them against the cabinet below the sink. If the space below the sink is open, put a low box there and put one foot up while washing.

  - Push, rather than pull, heavy items.

  - When lifting a child, get down in a squat position with one knee on the floor. Put your other leg forward, bent at the knee with your foot flat on the floor. Keeping the child close to your body, lift with your legs. Or, you can bend your knees slightly so you are steady, hold out your arms, and, on the count of three, have the child jump up into them from a *standing position*.

- If at all possible, don't work alone. Do you have an assistant? In programs for young children, it is best practice that there are at least two capable adults in every classroom at all times. Guiding children, maintaining order, and individualizing are almost impossible with only one adult, but of most importance are safety concerns. If there is an emergency, someone needs to be with the hurt child while another person is in charge of the rest of the children. Tracking down a supervisor or another adult at this time may leave children unsupervised. Working with other adults also helps keep you from burning out. You will have someone with whom to discuss ideas, problem solve, and share funny things that children do and say. If at all possible, avoid working in programs where there is only one person in a classroom for children under six years of age.

- Don't overinvolve yourself in the lives of your families and children. It may not ultimately be helpful to them, because they can develop a dependency on you and never learn to solve problems for themselves. Be a resource and support for solutions, not the solution itself.

- Set goals. Everyone needs to feel like she is going somewhere, heading in a direction. Set goals as a way to achieve that feeling. You will be much less likely to burn out. You may want to be a head teacher, education coordinator, director or principal, business owner, teacher of older children, consultant, the president of the United States, or just a better teacher. Whatever the goal, have one. Then write down in detail the steps needed to achieve it and target completion dates for each step. Begin working toward it immediately. Every day do something that brings you closer to your goal, even if you only have time to read one page of a book.

Solving Problems Related to Feeling Burned Out

- Find a support group. Being involved in associations with networking meetings can help by giving you support for your feelings and frustrations. Be assured that many teachers have common concerns and have similar problems. Much can be gained by sharing them and discussing solutions that have worked for others.

- Learn something new. Attend workshops and classes to give you fresh new ideas, as well as to validate your current abilities. Visit teachers in other programs to learn new ideas and to connect with peers. Request time to do this from your supervisor as part of your professional development. The expense to your program of paying a substitute for the day is well worth the return of increased quality.

- Teach something. Offer to give a class or workshop to your program colleagues, at a conference, or through a local college. You probably have a particular area of expertise or a special skill that others would love to learn about. If not, cultivate an area of expertise that is particularly interesting to you. For example, study and practice to become the local expert on emergency preparedness or the use of computers with young children.

- Take control. The lack of control over numerous aspects of your job can be a huge source of stress. All adults need to feel that they can try out their ideas, take chances, learn from mistakes, and make changes. Schools that use programmed curricula with daily activities spelled out take that sense of control away from the teacher. This is also true for teachers who have to accept whatever materials and equipment are supplied to them. If you are in a situation where either of these is true, work cooperatively with the powers that be to make some changes. Start with a modest request such as a small monthly budget with which you can purchase supplies. This is a reasonable request and might be a place to start to gain more control. This is important because a flexible, responsive curriculum that has relevance to your particular group of children is a vital part of a quality ECED program. For example, if two children in your class have mothers who are about to give birth, you need to be able to do a unit on babies. Your supervisor should be able to see this as an issue of improving the quality of the program. If she cannot or if she does not have control over the decision, consider implementing your ideas anyway. Many teachers work through the required curriculum quickly and minimally and then use the extra time to implement their own activities. If you cannot impact this issue, consider taking your skills and talents to a program that gives more control to teachers.

- If you teach by yourself, work on ways of getting an assistant. Consider the following ideas: parent volunteers, college or high school students (through service learning programs or student teachers), community volunteers, chapters of service clubs and charitable organizations. Or assist the program director to restructure the budget to include another position.

- Know your limitations. Early childhood teachers are generally very giving, caring, generous people, but sometimes they have trouble saying no. Taking on the role of therapist for a troubled family or spending your hours after work helping a family in need find resources are noble things to do, but not required. You can easily burn out by taking on more than you can cope with or have the skills for. This will impact your ability to be a good teacher, and being a good teacher is the first obligation you have to your children, their families, and yourself.

- Experiment. View yourself as a "researcher." Take some risks by trying out new and different ideas with your class. Evaluate the results and discuss them with coworkers to determine what worked, what can be improved, or what needs to be scrapped completely. For example, try a completely new curriculum approach (with permission), change the class schedule, create an automobile service station imaginary play area, or create a theme around television—visit a TV studio, teach critical viewing skills (media literacy), create and record a TV show in the classroom.

- Have fun. Making your job more fun may be the single most important thing you can do to prevent burnout. Some of the many ways you can do this include the following:
  - Have regular parties with other staff members.
  - Use humor (not sarcasm) with your children.
  - Share the funny things your children say and do with parents and other staff.
  - Sing silly songs.
  - Get a little outrageous. Paint your face and the kids' (use a cold cream base and add coloring). Plan and create a carnival and invite other classes, staff, and parents to "test their luck" at the games. Make footprint pictures, fingerpaint a huge mural, have a fancy dress-up day and set up an expensive restaurant imaginary play setting, or have a backward day when you reverse your schedule and routines.

There isn't a better job in the world for having a fabulously fun time than teaching young children. Just think, you could be working in an office all day!

3. WAGE OUTRAGE: UNDERPAID IS AN UNDERSTATEMENT

The entire field of education is underfunded, but in early childhood education, the problem is severe. Ironically, programs for young children need the most funding because class sizes are smaller and there are more teachers per child, but they receive the least. Early childhood teachers, especially in child care programs, are one of the lowest paid of all classes of workers. You will likely have to accept that wages are low, have been low for many years, and will most likely continue to be low for quite a while. This does not mean you should be apathetic. Without many people becoming actively involved in fighting for better wages, conditions will never improve. This does mean coming to terms with living on less, for now, and finding satisfaction from the work you do. This is important for your own mental health. (For more information about getting involved in improving salaries, see "'A' Is for Advocacy" on pp. 266–67.)

Anticipating and Preventing Problems Related to Being Underpaid

- Know what you are worth in the early childhood job market based on your years of experience, expertise, education, and so on.

- Before you take any job, find out as much as you can about the organization. Know what the salary range is and how it is determined, so you can know if you are getting a reasonable offer. Also find out about wages in similar programs in the same community.

- Do not accept the position unless you are sure you can live with the salary. Do not necessarily believe promises of future increases, or at least do not count on them.

- Continue to work toward a more advanced degree or to gain new skills that will lead to more lucrative work with young children.

- Be creative and entrepreneurial. Carve out a unique service, product, or program that is marketable, is helpful to families or teachers, and promotes the healthy growth and development of young children.

Solving Problems Related to Being Underpaid

- Make a list of the positive aspects of your job. Include the things that satisfy you most. The list might include the following:
  - I learn a lot about myself from the children.
  - I get joy from seeing happy children.
  - I know the children love, trust, and respect me.
  - I get positive feedback from satisfied parents.
  - I am doing a great service to society by keeping children safe and happy and by helping them learn and grow.
  - I am helping secure a bright future for society by helping bring up well-adjusted children.
  - I am making an important contribution to society and to families by allowing them to work without worrying about their children.

- ▸ I am good at what I do.
- ▸ I have fun at my job.
- ▸ I have the respect of my boss, coworkers, and parents.

- Keep the list where you can read it every morning or when you are feeling depressed about your low wages.

- Many early childhood educators cut their personal expenses by sharing housing, joining co-ops, clipping coupons, using public transportation, carpooling, shopping for sales, and frequenting discount stores, flea markets, and garage sales.

- Perhaps there are other sources of income you can find to supplement your current income without burning yourself out. Write books or a blog; offer workshops or consulting services in your particular areas of strength and expertise. Start a small business out of your home or obtain a low-stress part-time job.

Finding the better paying jobs in early childhood education

- If staying in the field and earning more money are both important to you (and I hope they are), set some career goals for yourself. Here are some suggestions:
  - ▸ Open your own program. The experience and expertise you gain as a teacher will be a great asset as an owner. Although few people make a great deal of money as child care/preschool owners, the potential is there. You often need to own several sites (expanding after you have been successful) before you can earn substantially more than working for someone else. However, running your own business based on your own ideas, values, and methods can be tremendously rewarding.
  - ▸ There are some well-paying jobs in the field, but they often require a master's degree or doctorate, specialized training, and/or years of experience. These include college or university instructor, trainer, consultant, writer of adult or children's books, editor, publisher, center director, education coordinator, program administrator, researcher, state certifier of child care centers, and manufacturer and seller of toys, playground equipment, or classroom supplies and furnishings. There may be a job here that you can aspire to, but be prepared that even these jobs may not pay as well as similar jobs in other professions.
  - ▸ Early childhood teaching can also lead you into higher paying jobs in closely related fields, though specialized training and advanced degrees will most likely be necessary. Teaching in early childhood education requires a wide variety of skills, and these provide good training for related careers. The careers include social worker, business owner, school principal, human resource specialist, family life educator (in hospitals), parenting instructor, recreation director, extension agent, journalist, politician, therapist (also psychologist and counselor), community education director, child development specialist, health educator, public relations director, pediatric nurse, and pediatrician.

Grants

You may want to get involved in helping your program write grant proposals. Many programs have been able to increase salaries and expand job opportunities by obtaining grants for setting up new programs or services, expanding existing services to serve younger or older children, instituting a new program for families, participating in research projects, and forming partnerships with other programs. Grants are offered from the federal, state, and local governments, school districts, foundations, advocacy organizations, charitable organizations, service organizations, and more.

- Start with an idea or project that you have passion for and that meets an important need, as it will require a great deal of work and time to refine your idea, to find and apply for funding, and to get the new project or service going if you are funded.

- Develop projects with other organizations in your community, such as mental health programs, parent education agencies, child nutrition programs, or programs for children with disabilities. Agencies that give grants usually prefer projects in which two or more agencies collaborate to help children and families. When you collaborate, more expertise is available, services are consolidated, and dollars can be stretched.

4. IN OVER YOUR HEAD AND OVERWHELMED: HOW TO TREAD WATER UNTIL YOU LEARN TO SWIM

If you work with young children and have less experience or training than you need to do the job well, you are not alone. Many people start out that way and learn on the job. Experienced teachers often look back on their first year or two on the job and wonder how they and the children ever survived. Many teachers have found the same problem happening when they switch positions to work with a different group of families or in a different setting, even if they have many years of experience. An example would be moving from teaching a half-day toddler program for children of middle-class families to a full-day program for four-year-olds from low-income families.

Anticipating and Preventing Problems Related to Being Overwhelmed

- Do not let a fear of being "in over your head" stop you from taking a job or working with a different group of children in a different setting. New challenges can be very rewarding and rejuvenating.

- Before you start the new position, learn as much as you can about the job and the program. Ask to observe there and also try to observe a similar classroom in a different program. If there is a current teacher who is leaving, request time to meet with her. Get as much information as you can from trusted websites, books, and articles.

- Be honest and open about your strengths and weaknesses with yourself and with others.

Solving Problems Related to Feeling Overwhelmed

Don't muddle through by pretending that you know what you are doing. Accept that you will make mistakes. People who know their weaknesses and actively work on overcoming them get far more respect and are "cut more slack" than people who make similar mistakes but pretend to be skilled.

- Ask for help from coworkers who are competent. They will most likely be flattered by your request and be glad to offer suggestions and assistance. Other teachers in your own program are apt to know practical ways of dealing with problems specific to your situation.

- Ask for more training from your supervisor. He will probably be very willing to help you. Supervisors sometimes put training needs on the bottom of their priority list (coping with numerous crises comes first) but are responsive when asked directly.

- Read books and magazine/journal articles. Specialty publishers, libraries, and bookstores are carrying more and better books about early childhood education. More full-text articles are available online than ever before.

- Delegate some of your work to other coworkers or supervisors. Ask others to take on some tasks that are particularly difficult for you while you learn ways to do them better. (This will free up some time and energy to train yourself on other aspects of your job.)

- Develop a network of support people who can help you solve problems and who can answer questions. Include local health professionals, early childhood education instructors, trainers, consultants, and experienced teachers. Although most of these people charge for their services, they often are willing to help occasionally for a short time at no charge or for a small favor in return.

- Have confidence in your ability to learn and to improve. Take the pressure off yourself by giving yourself two years to gain the skills and knowledge you need to be really good at your job through experience and by attending classes, workshops, reading, asking people with expertise, and so on.

Being a Professional in a Semi-Professional Profession: The A, B, C, D, and E of Working in the Field of Early Childhood

OUR FIELD IS "SEMI-PROFESSIONAL" because it has some of the elements of a true profession but is lacking in other significant ways. Some early childhood teachers have at least a bachelor's degree and a license or certification but many do not. Some programs require this but many do not. In addition, some of those degrees and licenses are not specifically focused on working with children three to five years old, and even fewer on working with children birth to three. In fact, some degrees and licenses involve only a minimum amount of coursework in early childhood. Are there many great teachers who do not have a bachelor's degree or a license? Yes. Are there many incompetent teachers who have a master's degree and multiple licenses? Of course. But within all true professions, there is a large ongoing effort to try to ensure a high-quality workforce. And they all do it essentially the same way: by requiring evidence of having in-depth and comprehensive knowledge (a college degree or more) and good skills (gained through a license, internship, student teaching experience, apprenticeship, and so on) *specific* to the work of the profession.

There is much more to any profession than knowledge and skill requirements, however. Again, we have some of these elements but not others. We *do* have professional organizations and conferences, scholarly and practical journals and magazines, a code of ethics, principles of best practices, and evidence of effectiveness from research. But we have only a voluntary national accreditation system for programs. We do not have cohesion, consistency, or collaboration among the many different types of programs that fall under the early childhood umbrella; nor do we have the wages, clout, recognition, and respect that is associated with most other professionals and their professions. Why is it important for our field to be a true profession and for early childhood teachers to be professionals? Because the work we do is so important, complex, and impactful.

Therefore, continue your own education by working toward a higher degree and/or credential, taking classes, attending conferences, watching videos, and reading. Subscribe to or use library or online copies of magazines and journals in the field to keep current. The Internet is your best tool for keeping current. All professionals make extensive use of computers for communicating, getting information, storing and sharing photos and documents, and staying organized. But early childhood teachers use technology infrequently, particularly compared to people in other professions (Blackwell, Lauricella, and Wortella 2014). Although computers and the Internet can be maddening to use at times, knowing a few key "tricks" will minimize frustrations and save you time.

- If you have trouble finding an article, try entering the entire name of the article within quotation marks in the search box on Google, Safari, Bing, or another search engine.

- Once you have your search results, you can narrow down your search and get the most current information. For example, when using Google, click on "search tools" then on "any time." Choose an option from the drop-down list, such as "past year," to get just the results that have been posted within the past twelve months, or set a specific date range by clicking on "custom range." Other search engines have a similar tool to narrow your search.

- If you enter a website address in the address bar and you get an error message, try using the root address (this is the part that begins with "http://" and usually ends with ".com" or ".org" or ".net"). You can also start over and just search for the name of the organization, if you know it, such as "NAEYC." This will bring you to the main page of the website. If there is a search box on this main page, enter in the name of the article or resource you are looking for there. If there is no search box, try to find it by clicking on logical headings, such as "publications" or "for teachers."

- When looking for information on a topic from multiple websites, use the tab function of your web browser. Open up a new tab to search on another website and keep the current tab open. Use your right mouse button. This will bring up a menu where you can choose to open the link in a new tab. Using tabs will allow you to easily go back and find all the web pages that you opened on the topic.

- Learn how to take a screen shot (also called "print screen" or "PrtSc"). This will allow you to save an electronic copy of exactly what you see on your computer screen, which will eliminate the need to spend time writing down long web addresses or taking notes on the content.

Conducting and promoting yourself as a professional will benefit not only the families and children you serve, but ultimately yourself. Unless the general public perceives early childhood teachers as professionals, better salaries and benefits, more respect, better working conditions, and more public funding may never happen. Professionalism is largely based on public perception, and public perception can be swayed. You, as an individual, can have a great impact on helping families and promoting the cause of quality care and education for young children, even if the only thing you do is have a great classroom.

1. "A" IS FOR ADVOCACY

The authority that comes with being a professional also comes with responsibility. One such responsibility is to be an advocate. Advocacy for early childhood teachers happens on two levels: (1.) *Social advocacy* for more and better quality early childhood services, programs, and schools, and for more family-friendly policies; and (2.) *Child advocacy* for ensuring that children are nurtured, safe, happy, healthy, and secure. Often these mesh. Better quality child care services certainly directly benefit children and families.

Social Advocacy

- Educate yourself about current political issues related to the field. Get involved in helping pass beneficial state and federal legislation and elect candidates who support working families and who care about young children. Do not feel that you have to be an expert or a great public speaker or that you have to invest a huge amount of time. There is a great deal of work to do and any help, from stuffing envelopes to gathering signatures on a petition, would be an important contribution.

- Know what the opposition is and why it is there. Many people would like to keep early childhood teachers from becoming more professional because they do not want the cost of care to increase. Others believe that it threatens the "sanctity" of motherhood and family. Work together with parents to fight for more state and federal funds and business contributions to help them pay for the high-quality care their children deserve and the better salary you deserve.

- Know about key research studies that support your work and be able to describe them simply and clearly. Stay informed so you can update these as new research brings new knowledge. It is particularly important to know about early brain development and its implications for supporting children's optimal development. (See the resources under "Brain Development" on p. 284, and under "Advocacy, Public Policy, and Research" on p. 282.)

Child Advocacy

As adults who care for children, we need to understand that growing up today involves complex challenges that are equal to but different from the challenges that children faced in previous generations. Our main tasks, however, are the same: protecting children from harm and helping them thrive. Yesterday's challenges for children centered primarily on their basic *physical* health and safety, while today's challenges center primarily on their *psychological* health and safety. Surviving childhood was the main concern for thousands of years. Injury and death from fires, accidents, poisoning, infectious diseases, and so on were commonplace. Much of our earliest children's literature focused on physical and personal safety, such as "Little Red Riding Hood" and the "The Wolf and the Seven Little Kids." While these stories have engaging plots and interesting, sympathetic characters who survive their traumatic experiences, many other stories were moralistic lessons designed to terrify children into avoiding dangers, such as Hans Christian Andersen's "Little Match Girl."

Today nearly all children survive childhood and, in spite of too much gun violence and too many acts of terrorism, very few children will be victims themselves or suffer serious injury—though even one child is too many. Because of safety devices such as car seats, airbags, smoke alarms, and sprinkler systems and the actions of the Environmental Protection Agency, the Food and Drug Administration, the Centers for Disease Control and Prevention, and the Consumer Product Safety Commission, among others, children living in the United States have never been physically safer. Today, however, we must protect our young children from dangers to their psychological well-being and their emotional and nutritional health. Disturbing images—from porn to explosions to beheadings to natural disasters—on ever larger, increasingly ubiquitous electronic devices with screens have made it almost impossible to protect young children from seeing inappropriate, frightening images meant for adults. Even adults have difficulty coming to grips with these images. And fast-food businesses, junk food manufacturers, and toy and video game makers, along with their partners in the advertising industry, use sophisticated strategies and spend billions of dollars to make children desire things that they don't need, shouldn't have, and, in many cases, are bad for them. Younger and younger children are feeling increasingly stressed as a result of pressures to do everything sooner, better, and quicker—from speaking to potty training to reading. Children in the United States are given more tests and at earlier ages than ever before. Being a child advocate means protecting children from all these threats, directly as their teacher and indirectly as a professional and activist.

- Be serious about your role as a protector of children and childhoods. Get involved in fighting policies that hurt children and in supporting policies that help them. Do what you can, even if it is very little. Be knowledgeable about these issues, take a stand, and discuss them with family members, friends, and neighbors. You won't bore or annoy them if you talk about the issues using stories of how they impact your work and the children and families you serve. (See the resources under "Advocacy, Public Policy, and Research" on p. 282 to keep up to date on issues affecting young children and to learn ways to get involved.)

- Teach media literacy. Provide specific activities that teach children how to watch television critically and not be fooled by advertisers. Help children understand that advertisers try to get them to want things, many of which are bad for them, so that they will beg their parents to buy them. Show examples of how advertisers make their products look better than they actually are. (See the resources for media literacy under "Technology and Media Literacy" on pp. 296–97.)

2. "B" IS FOR BRAVE: MALE TEACHERS OF YOUNG CHILDREN

As a male early childhood teacher for many years, I would love to see the day when there are about equal numbers of men and women teaching in early childhood programs. All children need many nurturing men in their lives, and they need a teacher who can make Papa Bear's voice really sound like a PAPA BEAR! But this is not likely to happen any time soon.

In 2014, only about 4.5 percent of child care teachers were men, and the rate was even lower among preschool/kindergarten teachers at just under 3 percent. Surprisingly, however, nearly 10 percent of assistant teachers were male. But the really disappointing data is that the percentage of male teachers has not changed much over the twelve-year period between 2002 and 2014. While the percentage of men has fluctuated year to year, ranging from 1 to 3 percent for preschool/kindergarten teachers and from 4.4 to 5.9 percent among child care teachers, the most recent figure of 4.5 percent is almost as low as it has ever been (U.S. Census Bureau data as reported by Men Teach at www.menteach.org).

Low salaries are clearly *not* one of the main reasons that there are so few male early childhood teachers. There is a much higher percentage of male assistant teachers than male teachers, and their salaries are even lower. Also, the percentage of male teachers in primary schools increases with each grade level, though the salaries are the same. So the barriers to increasing the number of men working with young children are nearly all social and psychological.

In addition to everything else that is challenging about working in an early childhood program, male teachers have to deal with widespread negative perceptions of men who choose to do low-status "women's work" and who are in close relationships with young children who are not their own. Being considered "suspicious" is a serious burden and risk that female teachers do not have to deal with.

When I was a program director, a young man I hired to run an after-school program was accused by a parent of sexually abusing her daughter. The girl complained of pain in and around her vagina, and the family doctor confirmed that there was serious bruising. The accusation was ridiculous for many reasons, including the fact that there was no time or place where this could have happened. It turned out that the girl had fallen, crotch first, onto a lower bar from a higher bar on a piece of climbing equipment. Older children on the playground had seen this happen. But, while the incident was being investigated, I had to suspend his employment for about a month. Although cleared of wrongdoing, he felt he could not return. He had been too humiliated and his reputation was damaged. This would not have happened to a female teacher. Fortunately, he found another job running an after-school program, which coincidently was at the school my own child attended, and ran a very successful, highly regarded program for many years.

Men also have to accept being in a very small minority, if not the only male in the building. Many men who would be great teachers and who would love the work avoid it for this reason. In addition, many program managers are reluctant to hire male teachers because they are worried about parents' (biased) perceptions and, perhaps, because of their own deep-seated biases that they may not readily admit to. It's a self-reinforcing cycle that is hard to interrupt. Having so few men in early childhood reinforces the notion that it is "women's work," which keeps men from entering the field (particularly when it involves so much risk), and so the percentage of men stays low.

But men and women want to become early childhood teachers for mostly the same reasons: the work is enjoyable and important, children's development is fascinating, children need caring and capable teachers, helping families means making a positive contribution to society, it's more creative and satisfying work than teaching older children, and they have some talent or proclivity for the work.

Female Teachers with Male Coworkers or Assistants

Female teachers are critically important allies for male teachers. They can contribute to increasing the number of men in the profession by being helpful and supportive of the male teachers they work with. That said, men should expect help and support from their male colleague(s) in equal measure. Male and female teachers usually have some complementary abilities. He may be able to get more fathers involved and she may be able to reassure parents on his behalf.

- Appreciate that breaking down gender barriers involves men working in traditionally female occupations, not just women working in traditionally male occupations.

- Avoid constantly relying on your male coworker to lift heavy things for you, assist with an out-of-control child, or take on similar tasks. Use him, but don't abuse him.

- Women should not hold their male colleagues to a higher or lower standard than their female colleagues. They should keep their criticisms or concerns about a male coworker separate from the issue of his gender.

- Female teachers with male assistants should help them become teachers, if they have the interest and capability. They need opportunities to develop and practice teaching skills such as story reading, leading a circle time, developing a theme, and introducing a new song. Female teachers can help male teachers with assignments for the classes they take toward becoming full-fledged teachers.

Male Teachers

Thank you for breaking barriers! Being a male early childhood teacher involves a good deal of risk and a strong commitment.

- As happens to women in traditionally male occupations, you will probably be held to a higher standard than your female colleagues. Live up to the challenge. Use this as a spark to inspire you to be a great teacher. Work continually to improve your skills by taking classes, attending conferences, reading relevant materials, observing good teachers, and responding to feedback from parents, colleagues, and supervisors. Carefully review the ideas in the next chapter about professionalism.

- Be prepared for the possibility that you will be misunderstood and subjected to bias. Some of your colleagues may view you as a threat or with suspicion, particularly at first. Making a suggestion to a female coworker may be seen as being domineering. It's better to be available and wait to be asked, or to offer general assistance—"Let me know if I can be helpful in any way"—than to give unsolicited, specific advice or assistance.

- Make it clear to parents, coworkers, supervisors, and others that you will be physically affectionate with children, but appropriately so, and that children will occasionally sit on your lap. It's not possible to be a good early childhood teacher and do otherwise.

- Avoid being the only adult in the room with children, as much as possible.

- Connect with other male early childhood teachers and join Men Teach (www.menteach.org). Feel supported and inspired by other male teachers. Check out Teacher Tom's blog (teachertomsblog.blogspot.com).

- If you feel unfulfilled, find additional, complementary ways to expand your horizons. For example, Tom Hobson started his blog, "Teacher Tom." Get involved with national and international efforts to recruit more men to jobs in early childhood. Offer to speak about being a male teacher to groups of students taking early childhood classes at high schools and colleges. Develop some training sessions that you can offer at conferences or as a consultant. Write articles or a book.

3. "C" IS FOR COMPORTMENT: PROMOTING A PROFESSIONAL IMAGE AND REPUTATION

We can all contribute to the effort to become a true profession by acting and dressing professionally.

- Treat parents and coworkers with respect. Talk with them attentively, use professional language, and speak clearly. Avoid slang, cursing, gossip, and talking behind anyone's back.

- Maintain confidentiality. It's not only an important way to show respect, but it's probably a legal requirement in your state.

- Be involved, alert, and focused when with children.

- Dress appropriately but nicely and neatly. Wear clean, fashionably conservative, and comfortable clothes. Keep a change of clothes at work, just in case the entire jar of orange paint lands in your lap, and, for lesser catastrophes, don't get too far away from a stain-remover stick or spray. Wear sturdy shoes or sneakers with rubber soles for comfort and for running with children, but do not wear torn, dirty sneakers. Keep a good pair of shoes on hand for meetings or for parent conferences.

- Join professional groups, clubs, political groups, and civic organizations. These should not only include those within the profession but groups such as Kiwanis, Lions, Rotary, Knights of Columbus, American Association of University Women, Junior League, political clubs, city clubs, League of Women Voters, National Organization for Women, and so on. Many of these groups consider issues related to educating and caring for young children an important part of their work. They will benefit from your expertise, and you will benefit by being recognized as a valuable community member.

- Inform parents about your professional background, including work history and education. Request that your supervisor inform parents that criminal background checks and references are thoroughly checked on all staff members before they are hired.

- Learn the jargon used in the field. For good or bad, all professional groups have their own jargon. Help parents and new colleagues understand the jargon. (See the "Glossary of Common Terms and Jargon" on pp. 299–308.)

- Be helpful to others in the field. If you are an experienced teacher, be a mentor to a new teacher, offer to help a coworker solve a problem, share your children's favorite songs and activities.

- Build bridges between yourself and colleagues who work in other types of programs (Montessori, public school, private child care, Head Start, and so on). Focus on all the things you have in common, including challenges and problems, rather than on the few differences between your programs.

- Let parents know they are welcome to visit or participate in your classroom at any time. Explain that calling ahead is appreciated but not necessary. Consider setting up a webcam in the classroom that parents can access via the Internet at any time. Every parent will need to give their written consent for a webcam, and parents will be required to use a password so that the website is not public.

- Protect yourself from the possibility of false accusations of wrongdoing or abuse by taking the following precautions:
  - Make an official accident report for all injuries to children. The report should include a detailed description of the injury, how it happened, where it happened and when, and any first aid or treatment that was given.
  - If it all possible, have another person working with you at all times. Your assistant teacher should also not work alone. Join with another teacher if you find yourself alone with only a few children (typically at the beginning or end of the day), as long as you can still adhere to staff-child ratio requirements.
  - Have an "open-door policy" as described above.

4. "D" IS FOR DILEMMAS: EVERYDAY ETHICAL ISSUES

A major hallmark of a professional is the ability to confront an ethical dilemma and make a good decision about what to do based on a sound set of ethical principles. The National Association for the Education of Young Children developed such a code of ethics in 1989 and revised it in 2005 (NAEYC 2005). It is important to be familiar with this code; however, it should be viewed as a starting point for ethical conduct rather than a "how-to" manual. Early childhood teachers face tough ethical decisions almost daily. For example, should you force a child to stay on her cot during naptime even though she is clearly not tired? If so, for how long? Should you physically restrain a child who is hurting another child, and if so, with how much force? Do you follow a father's wish that his child not take a nap because he doesn't fall asleep at home until 11:00 p.m., even though he is very tired at naptime? Do you follow a mother's request that the child's father not be allowed to pick up the child, because he has been abusive, until she can get a restraining order? Should you follow a father's request that his child not be seen by his estranged wife because she has threatened to kidnap the child? Should you allow a child to use a bathroom inside the building alone or should you accompany her, leaving the other children to play outside by themselves? Do you report your own program to state authorities if your supervisor tells you to do something that violates licensing laws?

A Third Way: Resolving Ethical Dilemmas

The following recommendations are for your consideration when dealing with ethical dilemmas. They are meant as helpful guidelines. Ultimately, you have to do what you believe is right after you have carefully thought through the issues and the potential consequences, good and bad.

- Remember that your children's health, safety, and well-being are your main priorities. Choose a child's well-being over the wishes of a parent or a supervisor or the smooth running of your classroom. Above all, do no harm and allow no harm to any child.

- Carefully determine the best way to put children first without hurting yourself or your program. Licensing standards are established to protect the health and well-being of children, and therefore any major violation has to be reported. You can do this, however, without giving your name, so your supervisor or anyone else cannot retaliate. Your own health, well-being, and job security are important considerations in making this type of ethical decision. Anything that jeopardizes these is not a good choice. Not only will you be hurt by it, but your children will be harmed if you lose your job.

- Nearly all ethical dilemmas can be resolved with a creative "third-way" solution. For example, if a parent asks you to keep her child awake during naptime, but the child is very tired and cannot stay awake, it might work to have the child sleep for half of the naptime. Then help the parent with strategies to establish a consistent bedtime routine at home at 8:30.

- Obey all laws and rules related to your work, but if following a rule may harm a child, then a third-way solution must be found. For example, if a parent cannot legally stop her child's father from picking him up, then you cannot keep him from the child. However, if you believe that the child may be harmed if his father picks him up, then you have an ethical responsibility to protect the child. A third-way solution is to have the parent keep the child home or with a relative until she obtains a restraining order. It is important that you, or anyone else in the program, does *not* know the location of the child so that you can honestly say the child's whereabouts are unknown to you. You can also agree to call her if the father shows up looking for the child.

- One solution to the dilemma of the child who has to use the bathroom when the class is outside is to gather all the children together and go inside with all of them for a few minutes. Several children probably need to use the bathroom anyway. Although this is harmful to the children who are outside because it shortens their gross-motor time and disrupts their play, it is less harmful than the potential dangers that come with leaving any young child unsupervised. An ethical rule of thumb is to choose the course that will cause the least harm and negatively impact the fewest children.

- Continue to monitor the results of your decision. Often situations change or new information is obtained. Few decisions are irreversible.

- Work on developing policies and procedures that will help eliminate, or at least minimize, ethical dilemmas. Being alone with a group of children will put you in dilemmas over and over again. Work with your supervisor on solving the problem. Perhaps an intercom system, security camera, and/or two-way radio can be purchased while you both work toward minimizing or eliminating the amount of time that you spend alone with children.

- Every decision has repercussions. What seems like a good choice now may not ultimately be good for a family. For example, you may decide to help a family out of an immediate crisis, but the long-term result is that they become dependent on you to bail them out of subsequent crises. Assist families to help themselves.

- During a staff meeting, or as an exercise with your coworkers, describe a variety of ethical dilemmas and discuss strategies for resolving them. Thinking through dilemmas and possible solutions will help you tremendously when you inevitably have to face one.

5. "E" IS FOR EGREGIOUS: HOW CAN WE SOLVE OUR PROFESSION'S MOST PRESSING, LONG-STANDING PROBLEMS?

Here it is, thirteen years after the second edition of this book, twenty-five years after the first edition, and forty years since I entered the field as a teaching assistant, and many of the major problems I faced and wrote about over those decades are still with us. There has been little or no progress toward their solution, and some problems, like low salaries and "pushed-down curriculum," are even worse. We also have some new problems to deal with. The job of the early childhood teacher is more challenging than ever.

In spite of decades of advocacy, early childhood teachers, especially those working in child care centers, are still among the lowest-status and lowest-paid workers in the workforce, particularly when considering their level of education and the demands of the job (Bornfruend 2015; PayScale.com 2015; Whitebook, Phillips, and Howes 2014). Nor does it appear that working conditions have improved during this time, as turnover remains high; about 30 percent of early childhood staff leave their jobs each year. (Porter 2012; Whitebook, Phillips, and Howes 2014). And certainly, children's behaviors, families' needs, and parent-teacher-school relations have not become any easier to manage.

Adding to the challenges is the pressure to teach content and use methods that are contrary to how young children learn and develop best. Today we know so much more about children's development and have so many more effective tools to optimize their development than we did twenty-five years ago; however, the gap between what we know is right and what we are pressured to practice is wider than ever (Gramling 2015). As mentioned in the introduction, all over the United States, kindergarten is not what it used to be or should be. Its original purpose was to boost children's social skills and offer them a positive introduction to school as a way to ease the transition to first grade. Now it is first grade! Unfortunately, this means that it falls on early childhood programs to ease the transition to kindergarten. And not, we are told, by boosting social skills and offering engaging learning experiences, but by teaching children simpler versions of the academics they will learn in kindergarten (which they actually should be learning in first grade), using the same tedious and ineffective methods. Something is terribly wrong when children require a preparatory program to be successful in kindergarten.

Although the pushed-down curriculum problem has been with us for a very long time, it has become a much bigger problem in the last ten years. The path and timing of children's development has not changed in the last one hundred years (Gesell Institute of Child Development 2012), so today's unrealistic expectations inevitably lead to developmentally and educationally inappropriate practices, which cause stress, or worse, for children, teachers, and parents. Stress impedes young children's learning and healthy development, and it leads teachers to burn out or to leave the profession before they have a chance to burn out. To accept this situation would change the very concept of who we are as a field and what we do: from facilitators of happy, healthy, and stimulating childhoods—which is actually the ideal preparation for success in school and life—to "child trainers" focused on a narrow set of superficial skills. It would be a shift from serving the needs of children and families to serving the needs of school systems.

So how can these problems be solved or, at the very least, stopped from getting worse? As with all problems, especially large, intractable problems, it is important to try to fully understand the problem and to look for the root causes. Albert Einstein said, "If I had an hour to solve a problem, I'd spend fifty-five minutes thinking about the problem and five minutes thinking about solutions."

So, after thinking and investigating long and hard (for much more than fifty-five minutes), I believe that the root causes of the low status and low pay of our profession are (1) The prevailing view that what we do is not much more than babysitting, (2) The fact that we work with the youngest children, and (3) Sexism. Early childhood workers are viewed as nonprofessionals doing low-skilled labor who don't really know how to teach. They "let them just play all day" instead of preparing them adequately for school. The low salaries then reinforce this image and the image keeps the salaries low. Also, pay and status are directly connected to the age of students. On average, early childhood teachers earn less than elementary school teachers, who earn less than secondary school teachers, who earn less than college teachers. However, the biggest pay gap by far is between early childhood teachers and elementary school teachers (Payscale 2015). In addition, women still earn less than men in every profession, and women-dominated fields, like ours, tend to be among the lowest paid professions. These three causes have deep and wide roots in our society's value system and economic structure, making it very hard to change.

The main causes for the pushed-down curriculum problem is the anxiety produced by the overemphasis and misuse of test scores and the general lack of knowledge about child development. Student test scores have become the primary way of measuring the quality of teachers, schools, districts, states, and even countries. This means that funding levels and educators' reputations and job security can be impacted by students' test scores. Poorly developed and implemented Early Learning Standards at the state level and the misguided (and misnamed) Common Core State Standards for K–12 at the national level, add fuel to the fire. The more pressure and anxiety K–12 leaders and educators feel, the more narrow the curriculum and the more pedantic teaching practices become. Often this anxiety infects parents. Because all parents want their children to be successful, they want their preschoolers to be taught lots of "academics" to meet the rigors of kindergarten and first grade and to do well on all the tests they will have to take. Child development is complex, and our knowledge of it is changing rapidly as advances in technology and science lead to new understandings. Most educators in the K–12 system have not taken a child development course that focuses on the early years. Many of them, and the general public, do not know about young children's need for imaginary play and how it benefits their development. They do not know the many ways that young children learn differently from older children and that it is not effective to offer lessons separated into distinct subject areas.

Is There Any Good News for Our Field from the Last Twenty-Five Years?

Very little, unfortunately. But there is one very significant positive development. Within about a ten-year period starting in 1989, the Department of Defense (DOD) transformed its very large, international child care program from a low-quality, chaotic, costly system into what experts widely agree is a model system of high-quality care and education. And it keeps on improving. Let's explore the DOD program by using a problem-solving strategy called "benchmarking." Benchmarking entails finding an example of a successful and excellent program (or teacher, school, school system, and so on) and examining it in detail to learn what makes it so good and how it got there. The DOD program is an example from the United States of a large-scale system that successfully improved wages, working conditions, and the quality of classrooms according to principles of developmentally appropriate practice. This is just what we are looking for to help us better understand our major problems of pushed-down curriculum, low status, and low wages.

The improvements at DOD were spurred by the increasing numbers of active-duty women and couples with children and the realization that child care issues were negatively impacting the work of many of its soldiers and other employees. With open-ended funding from Congress, the DOD ended its practice of subcontracting with many different companies and organizations for child care services and started to run the program themselves. Then they changed . . . just about everything! But they did it with clear goals and high standards to work toward and the funds to make it happen. One such goal was that all centers would be accredited by an outside, nationally recognized organization.

The result is that now teachers earn about 60 percent more than the national average salary of early childhood teachers and they have excellent benefits. Military families pay for care on a sliding scale based on family income amounting to, on average, about 8 percent of their income, as compared to about 25 percent for the typical civilian family. Parent fees cover about one-third of the operating costs; the other two-thirds is federally funded. It is a complex, responsive, well-organized, and well-regulated system that includes networks of family child care homes and support for some families to use community-based child care programs. Classrooms are well equipped and teachers receive ongoing training. Nearly all centers are NAEYC accredited, attesting to their quality and use of child-centered, active, play-based practices (Floyd and Phillips 2013). There is no pressure to change those practices pushing down from the DOD-operated K–12 school system. Their 80,000-plus students outperform civilian students at every grade level in spite of a 30 percent annual student turnover rate (the military is a mobile workforce). In a 2014 report on early childhood salaries, the authors describe the changes the DOD made this way: "The Department of Defense re-invented its early care and education system as a compact with service members that their children would be well cared for by competent, adequately compensated teachers while they were at work" (Whitebook, Phillips, and Howes 2014, 85). So, they reinvented the system from a service that they offered to an obligation, from a burden on their workers to a workplace quality enhancement, and from the responsibility of individual families to the responsibility of the employer: the federal government and the DOD.

What Are Some Lessons Learned?

Here are just three of the many helpful lessons that I see in the DOD example:

1. The positive changes are the logical result of acting on the beliefs and values embedded in their new, revised vision of what they do and who they are. Their commitment was not to specific outcomes, such as better salaries or classroom quality; it was to their employees' families. Issues like improving the status of the early childhood workforce were not directly addressed but were a result of all the other positive changes, particularly of hiring teachers and other staff as federal employees with salaries and benefits commensurate with similar jobs outside of the child care program.

2. Politicians are fond of saying that throwing money at a problem won't fix it. But if Congress did not "throw" substantial amounts of money at this problem, it would not have been fixed, even with all the thoughtful planning, the competent and strong leadership, and the capable and committed staff.

3. Many people think that large federal government–run programs are always inefficient, wasteful, bureaucratic, and of poor quality. They are told that the private sector can always do it better and cheaper than the government. But the opposite is true in this case. To reach the level of quality they were aiming for and to make the program efficient required the DOD to operate it directly and remove the private-sector providers.

So, What Are Some Practical Solutions?

Well, for problems on this grand scale outside of the military, no solution will be very practical. But it will certainly be more practical to pursue solutions that might actually work than to continue to do what has not worked for decades. The problems can't be solved by tackling each of them individually and directly if the root cause of all these problems is how the early childhood system was conceptualized, or invented. The solution, then, requires reconceptualizing or reinventing the system. The field needs to be reconceptualized from its current status as a marketplace of nonprofessional services staffed by low-skilled workers to that of an occupation vital to both the economy and society as a whole. As such, it should be funded through businesses, much like Social Security and workers' compensation, and through taxes, as are public schools and intervention programs. The primary responsibility would then be spread among employers and federal, state, and local governments, rather than entirely on families. When this occurs, it is almost certain that status, wages, working conditions, and curriculum practices will all improve, as they did at the DOD. Actually, this is exactly how it is done in most other countries in the world, particularly in Western Europe.

Another potential model program is in Seattle, Washington. The city government developed a program that provides full-day child care and integrates classrooms by family income.

While free for low-income families, higher-income families pay fees on a sliding scale basis, although no family pays the full cost. In addition to these subsidies for families, the Seattle program recruits existing providers, including family child care providers, and heavily invests in them to increase salaries, train teachers, fund operations, improve facilities, and more. The funds come from a voter-approved property tax levy earmarked for this purpose. At the time I am writing this (winter of 2015–2016), the Seattle program is just starting its first year of operation. Hopefully, it will be successful and can provide another example of a model system in the United States and one that is locally funded.

What Will It Take to Reinvent Our Profession?

My best thinking on this is to hold up the example of the DOD program, not just as a model and as proof that it can be done, but as a necessary and reasonable benefit that should be available to all government employees who need it. Of course I think it should be for *all* employees, not only government employees, but I think it is a good strategy to first expand the model to other federal branches. After all, it seems hard to justify giving federal employees in one branch a needed, high-quality service but not giving it to employees in the other branches who have the same need. Currently, many parents who use DOD child care centers, or who get subsidies, are not enlisted (civilian employees) and work in a range of jobs typically found in all the other non-military branches of the federal government: office workers, engineers, programmers, health professionals, and so on. Once it is established in other federal agencies, I believe that the program will inevitably spread to state government employees and then to everyone else.

The unfortunate reality is that most child care programs in the United States are of fair or poor quality and few are excellent (Vandell and Wolfe 2015, 4). It is important that the general public knows that the only children in the country who are *assured* of being in an excellent child care program are those whose parents are in the U.S. military or are very rich. I think that young couples, parents, and grandparents—the future, current, and former users of early childhood services—should carry the banner in this effort, and that we professionals should support them or join the effort as parents ourselves.

Could This Ever Really Happen?

There are three reasons to be hopeful. One is that in nearly all of the other higher-income countries in the world (and many lower-income countries), the national government views child care the same way as the DOD views it and with the same positive results. The second reason is that something similar has happened with health care insurance in the United States. It took a very long time, but a national system to cover (nearly) everyone was finally established in 2010. The primary responsibility to obtain affordable health insurance shifted from individuals to state government agencies, though the service is still provided by an array of mostly for-profit private companies. And the third reason is that the DOD *is* a federal government agency and they are subsidizing increasing numbers of community (non-military) child care centers for their civilian employees.

· · · · ·

I hope that the next update of this book will have much better news to report. I want to believe that things will have changed so much that this chapter will make no sense and its replacement, " 'E' is for Excellent," will be about the problems of how to spend all the money flooding into our programs, how to deal with the leadership responsibilities that go along with being a child development and education expert, and how to cope with all the requests from primary school teachers, principals, and superintendents to help them create child-centered, active, and joyful classrooms.

Until we get there, do the best you can, enjoy your work and your children, and remember that you are appreciated more than you will ever be told or could ever know. Please keep in touch at http://practical-solutions.net and please keep creating happy, healthy, and stimulating childhoods.

Resources

THE FOLLOWING IS A LIST of key print materials, websites, and videos. Many of the websites have full-text articles on a variety of subjects and links to videos and to other websites and resources. I have only included sites that provide direct access to free resources for teachers and families. Some websites are targeted to parents but have helpful information for teachers and give teachers ideas for helping parents; Parenting Science is one such website. The first main group of resources are comprehensive or general in nature, providing information on a wide array of topics or of broad issues. The websites in this comprehensive group are categorized by the type of organization that hosts the website in the following order: professional associations and nonprofit organizations; government agencies; research institutes and universities; individuals and blogs; public awareness campaigns; and social media. The other main group of resources is categorized by topic in alphabetic order, from "Advocacy" to "Testing."

The videos that are listed in both groups have been selected for their quality and relevance and can be seen for free on YouTube. If a link does not work, then enter the title of the video into the search box on the YouTube main page.

COMPREHENSIVE RESOURCES

Print Materials

Allen, David. (2015). *Getting Things Done*. (http://gettingthingsdone.com).

Bruno, H. E., D. R. Sullivan, J. Gonzalez-Mena, and L. A. Hernandez. (2013). *Learning From the Bumps in the Road: Insights From Early Childhood Leaders*. St. Paul: Redleaf Press.

Elkind, D. (2015). Giants in the Nursery: A Biographical History of Developmentally Appropriate Practice. St. Paul: Redleaf Press.

Falk, B. (Ed.). (2012). *Defending Childhood: Keeping the Promise of Early Education*. New York, NY: Teachers College Press.

Gramling, M. (2015). *The Great Disconnect in Early Childhood Education: What We Know vs. What We Do*. St. Paul, MN: Redleaf Press.

Hyson, M., & Tomlinson, H. B. (2014). *The Early Years Matter: Education, Care, and the Well-Being of Children, Birth to 8*. New York, NY: Teachers College Press.

Mooney, C. G. (2013). *Theories of Childhood: An Introduction to Dewey, Montessori, Erikson, Piaget & Vygotsky*. Second Ed. St. Paul: Redleaf Press.

Pianta, R. C. (Ed.) (2012). *Handbook of Early Childhood Education*. New York: Guilford Press.

Websites—categorized by the type of host organization

Professional associations and nonprofit organizations

National Association for the Education of Young Children (NAEYC) (www.naeyc.org). This site has access to many full-text articles from past issues of Young Children, Teaching Young Children, and Voices of Practitioners: Teacher Research in Early Childhood Education. Also, there is access to position statements on a wide variety of issues. Links to many other useful websites and resources are throughout, including archived audio interviews with experts on important topics.

Zero to Three: National Center for Infants, Toddlers, and Families (www.zerotothree.org) is a national nonprofit organization that provides parents, professionals, and policymakers the knowledge and the know-how to nurture early development. Its mission is to ensure that all babies and toddlers have a strong start in life. The website is rich with many excellent free resources (not only about babies), including podcasts, videos, and print materials on topics such as preventing preschool and child care expulsions, brain development, abuse and neglect issues, problematic behaviors, and a separate portal with resources for parents.

Also see *Division for Early Childhood* under "Disabilities, inclusion, children with special needs."

Government agencies

Resources for Early Childhood (REC) (http://rec.ohiorc.org/). REC is a collaboration between the Ohio Resource Center for Mathematics, Science, and Reading and the Ohio Department of Education's Office of Early Learning and School Readiness. It has content specific to Ohio's Early Learning Standards and Kindergarten Readiness initiative, but also has a vast amount of information helpful to early childhood teachers everywhere. Main topic tabs include: Learning Experiences, Inclusive Classrooms, Inquiry Projects, Bookshelf, Research/References, and Assessment. The Bookshelf includes suggestions for high-quality books to read to children in sets of about ten organized by themes, as well as related activity ideas. Each theme is sub-categorized by age group: Infants/Toddlers, Preschool, and Transition to K. Themes include: It's Fall! It's Back to School!; Numbers and Counting, Helping Children Understand Disabilities, Fun on the Farm, Polar Animals, Picture Books that Support Early Investigations, and many more.

Illinois Early Learning Project (http://illinoisearlylearning.org) is funded by the Illinois State Board of Education. It has three main sections: Resources for Teachers and Caregivers, Resources for Families, and The Project Approach. While organized around and in relation to the Illinois' Early Learning Standards, the website has many useful resources, including a very large and excellent collection of videos (typically two to three minutes in length) illustrating ways that teachers and caregivers use child-centered, play-based strategies to promote children's development in all areas. Each video has a transcript and a guide to the content in English and in Spanish.

Research institutes and universities

The Encyclopedia on Early Childhood Development is produced by the Centre of Excellence for Early Childhood Development (CEECD) (http://www.excellence-earlychildhood.ca) at Université de Montréal and the Strategic Knowledge Cluster on Early Child Development (SKC-ECD) (http://www.skc-ecd.ca) at Université Laval (Quebec, Canada). Most topics are explored from three perspectives: development, services, and policy. The papers gathered under each topic are written by internationally renowned experts. Syntheses and information sheets (called "Eyes on...") provide summaries of the most essential knowledge in simple, jargon-free language. The site includes many short but well-produced and informative videos. Information is categorized by behavior; education and learning; health and nutrition; pregnancy; family; and services and policy, and are available in five languages.

MOOCs and other free online classes and courses

MOOCs are Massive Open Online Courses. Enter the terms you are interested in—such as early childhood, child development, inclusion—into the search boxes.

Academic Earth (http://academicearth.org)

EDX (www.edx.org)

MOOC List (www.mooc-list.com)

Open 2 Study (www.open2study.com)

Udemy Free Courses (www.udemy.com)

Individuals and blogs

Not Just Cute | Intentional Whole Child Development (http://notjustcute.com). Amanda Morgan's blog has stories, articles, and activities that include developmental objectives to help teachers and parents foster children's full potential in all areas, particularly creative expression, social skills, physical control, language skills, and critical thinking. The blog also has a four-session course on Positive Guidance. Preschool activities can be cute as long as they are "not just cute" but also intentionally promote children's development.

Parenting Science (www.parentingscience.com). This site has many objective, in-depth articles written at a high level by Gwen Dewar who has a PhD in Anthropology. Dewar began the site when, after becoming a mother, she was unsatisfied with the literature she found targeted to parents. However, her articles are not just for parents and are based on current best evidence from research. She clearly states what we know about a topic and what we don't know because there is no research or because the findings are contradictory or inconclusive. Articles are categorized by these topics: Babies, Preschoolers, Big Kids, Parenting, Behavior, Learning, Play, Sleep, Well-Being.

The Spoke: Early Childhood Australia's Blog (http://thespoke.earlychildhoodaustralia.org.au) is hosted by Australia's main professional organization, Early Childhood Australia (ECA). The site is a treasure trove of information on a wide range of topics, all with very direct implications for teachers. Topics include recent research findings on many aspects of children's development; the importance of teaching thinking skills; language development in bilingual children; issues related to sharing; dealing with stress; and more. There is very little in this blog that is not applicable to early childhood programs in the United States.

Teacher Tom: Teaching and Learning from Preschoolers (http://teachertomsblog.blogspot.com). Tom Hobson is a preschool teacher, a writer, a speaker, an artist, and the author of *A Parent's Guide to Seattle*. For over 14 years he has been the sole teacher at a parent co-op preschool in Seattle and posts thoughtful, well-written blogs almost daily about issues that arise in the course of his work and with his own family. His opinions are clearly explained and supported with insight and logic. The hundreds of blog posts can be accessed by topic (from about 50 topics): Art, Community, Fairness, Education Reform, Outdoor Play, Love, Media, Parenting, Teaching, Science, Dramatic Play, Emotions, Kindergarten.

Videos and Video Collections

Dr. Lilian Katz: "Professional Emergencies" (www.youtube.com/watch?v=XXel4dZV7D0). Keynote Address at the World Forum on Early Care and Education, Honolulu, Hawaii. 2011. Containing important insights, wisdom, and advice from our "Sage," this is one of Dr. Katz's best speeches. If you only watch one video from this list, watch this one!

California Early Childhood Educator Competencies (www.cde.ca.gov/sp/cd/re/ececomps.asp) has twelve videos, one for each competency, as well as a seven-minute introductory video. The titles of the videos, which are the same as the titles of the competencies, are: (1) Child Development and Learning; (2) Culture, Diversity, and Equity; (3) Relationships, Interactions, and Guidance; (4) Family and Community Engagement; (5) Dual-Language Development; (6) Observation, Screening, Assessment, and Documentation; (7) Special Needs and Inclusion; (8) Learning Environments and Curriculum; (9) Health, Safety, and Nutrition; (10) Leadership in Early Childhood Education; (11) Professionalism; and (12) Administration and Supervision. The videos range from 12.5 minutes to 22 minutes and all are very high quality in terms of production and content. Every concept is illustrated with a video clip from an early childhood classroom.

Early Childhood Australia Learning Hub (www.youtube.com/user/EYLFPLP). Among the many high-quality videos on this site are a set of four videos on intentional teaching (intentionality), a set of three videos on adventurous play outdoors, and a set of five videos on the physical environment. A number of these videos align with the National Quality Standard (NQS), which has seven areas: 1. Educational program and practice, 2. Children's health and safety, 3. Physical environment, 4. Staffing arrangement, 5. Relationships with children, 6. Collaborative partnerships with families and communities, and 7. Leadership and service management.

Early Childhood Videos (www.youtube.com/channel/UCmPfoBQuoI_sPfOpr0WzH9Q). This excellent set of videos is provided by the Center for Early Childhood Education, which is a multidisciplinary research and training institute at Eastern Connecticut State University. The videos average about seven minutes in length, although the series of videos on investigations are longer. Investigations are something between theme-based and project-based learning. They are highly focused topics—rocks, trees, pathways, containers, balls, nature, "going green" (taking care of the earth)—that are explored in depth and from different angles through a variety of planned activities. Unlike with most projects, teachers carefully plan the activities in advance, which are often discrete rather than connected or sequential, and which do not necessarily emanate from or respond to children's interests.

Top Ten Signs You're an Early Childhood Educator (www.youtube.com/watch?v=QNdeX_5XPlM). This is a very funny presentation from Richard Cohen. Spoiler alert: Number 10 is "You find yourself humming 'Wheels on the Bus' in the shower." Enjoy!

Also see the **Illinois Early Learning Project** under "Websites" above as they have links to many videos.

RESOURCES BY TOPIC
Advocacy, Public Policy, and Research
Print Materials

Ochshorn, S. (2015). *Squandering America's Future: Why ECE Policy Matters for Equality, Our Economy, and Our Children*. New York, NY: Teachers College Press.

Pica, R. (2015). *What If Everybody Understood Child Development?: Straight Talk About Bettering Education and Children's Lives*. Thousand Oaks, CA: Corwin.

Sykes, M. (2014). *Doing the Right Thing for Children: Eight Qualities of Leadership*. St. Paul: Redleaf Press.

Wright, A. C., & Jaffe, K. J. (2013). *Six Steps to Successful Child Advocacy: Changing the World for Children*. Los Angeles: Sage Press.

Websites

The Alliance for Childhood (www.allianceforchildhood .org) promotes policies and practices that support children's healthy development, love of learning, and joy in living. They conduct effective public education campaigns as a voice for children to protect their vulnerability and to promote their promise for creating a more just, democratic, and ecologically responsible future. They conduct research in support of their advocacy for children and have produced many widely read publications on topics such as the use of computers with young children, inappropriate expectations and practices in kindergartens, and the importance of play for children's development.

Center for the Study of Child Care Employment (www.irle.berkeley.edu/cscce) conducts research and proposes policy solutions aimed at improving how the United States prepares, supports, and rewards the early care and education workforce. In 2014 they produced the report "Worthy Work, STILL Unlivable Wages: The Early Childhood Workforce 25 Years after the National Child Care Staffing Study," which is available to download from the website.

Defending the Early Years (http://deyproject.org) works to support and nurture the rights and needs of young children. Their advocacy focuses on teaching practices that are responsive to children's developmental needs and abilities and on protecting children from the harm caused by inappropriate expectations, tests, and teaching methods.

National Institute for Early Education Research (NIEER) (www.nieer.org). NIEER conducts and communicates policy-related research to support high-quality, effective early childhood education for all young children and offers advice and technical assistance to policymakers, journalists, researchers, and educators. Since 2002, they've produced an annual report, the "State Preschool Yearbook," that tracks funding, access, and policies of state preschool programs.

Research Connections (www.researchconnections .org) promotes high-quality research in child care and early education and the use of that research in policy making. The website provides access to thousands of research articles and data resources. Research Connections is a federally funded partnership between Columbia University and the University of Michigan.

Videos

What Is Advocacy and Why It's Important (www .youtube.com/watch?v=K75jEgzBIfc). This six-minute video was filmed in 2010 at a workshop sponsored by the Chicago Metro chapter of NAEYC. The presentation is from Kathy Ryk, a former state legislator and, at the time, an advocate with Illinois Voices for Children.

Art and Aesthetics
Print Materials

Fox, J. E., and R. Schirrmacher. (2014). *Art and Creative Development for Young Children*. Stanford: Wadsworth Publishing.

Moomaw, S., and B. Hieronymus. (2002). *More Than Painting: Exploring the Wonders of Art in Preschool and Kindergarten*. St. Paul: Redleaf Press.

Pelo, A. (2007). *The Language of Art: Inquiry-Based Studio Practice in Early Childhood Settings*. St. Paul: Redleaf Press.

Websites

Art in Early Childhood (http://artinearlychildhood .org) is an international professional association. Their website is, of course, lovely, but it also has two types of excellent resources: full-text academic articles from all issues of their journal, and presentations of art-based projects. The project presentations, primarily connected to nature, need to be downloaded (pdf files), and most are in the format of PowerPoint slides. All have many photos and thorough, engaging descriptions.

Videos

Reggio Emilia Philosophy: Aesthetics (www .slideshare.net/oscarcompass/reggio-presentation). While not technically a video, this slide show with over 200 slides shows the "art of esthetics" taken to a very high level in the preschools of Reggio Emilia, Italy. Although American teachers are awestruck by the beauty and sophistication of the children's artwork, art is just the medium that is used to deliver the "curriculum." The curriculum is about fostering community and promoting all areas of children's development through sustained inquiry and exploration. The choice of art as the primary medium aligns with the cultural values, history, and practices in Italy and the high aesthetic sense of the teachers and parents, as seen in the way they create beautiful classroom and school environments.

Behavior Issues, Positive Guidance, Classroom Management, and Social/ Emotional Development

Print Materials

Appelbaum, M. (2013). *How to Handle Hard-to-Handle Preschoolers: A Guide for Early Childhood Educators.* New York: Skyhorse Publishing.

Bilmes, J. (2012). *Beyond Behavior Management: The Six Life Skills Children Need.* 2nd Ed. St. Paul: Redleaf Press.

Cross, A. (2009). *Ants in Their Pants: Teaching Children Who Must Move to Learn.* St. Paul: Redleaf Press.

Heidemann, S. and D. Hewitt. (2014). *When Play Isn't Fun: Helping Children Resolve Play Conflicts.* St. Paul: Redleaf Press.

Hirschland, D. (2015). *When Young Children Need Help: Understanding and Addressing Emotional, Behavioral, and Developmental Challenges.* St. Paul: Redleaf Press.

Jacobson, T. (2008). *"Don't Get So Upset!": Help Young Children Manage Their Feelings by Understanding Your Own.* St. Paul: Redleaf Press.

Janko Summers, S. and R. Chazan-Cohen. (2011). *Understanding Early Childhood Mental Health: A Practical Guide for Professionals.* Baltimore, MD: Brookes Publishing.

Kaiser, B. and J. S. Rasminksy. (2011). *Challenging Behavior in Young Children: Understanding, Preventing, and Responding Effectively.* Third Ed. Upper Saddle River, NJ: Pearson.

Kinnell, G. (2008). *No Biting: Policy and Practice for Toddler Programs.* 2nd Ed. St. Paul: Redleaf Press.

Langworth, S. E. (2015). *Bridging the Relationship Gap: Connecting with Children Facing Adversity.* St. Paul: Redleaf Press.

Lewis, K. R. (2015. July/August). "What If Everything You Knew About Disciplining Kids Was Wrong?" *Mother Jones.*

Oehlberg, B. (2014.) *Making It Better: Activities for Children Living in a Stressful World.* 2nd Ed. St Paul: Redleaf Press.

Rice, J. A. (2013.) *The Kindness Curriculum: Stop Bullying Before It Starts.* 2nd Ed. St. Paul: Redleaf Press.

Riley, D., R. San Juan, J. Klinker, and A. Ramminger. (2007.) *Social & Emotional Development: Connecting Science and Practice in Early Childhood Settings.* St. Paul: Redleaf Press.

Schweikert, G. and J. Romanoff. (2016.) *Winning Ways for Early Childcare Professionals: Supporting Positive Behavior.* St. Paul: Redleaf Press.

Schweikert, G., J. Romanoff, and J. Decker. (2016.) *Winning Ways for Early Childcare Professionals: Guiding Challenging Behavior.* St. Paul: Redleaf Press.

Schweikert, G., J. Romanoff, and J. Decker. (2016.) *Winning Ways for Early Childcare Professionals: Responding to Behavior.* St. Paul: Redleaf Press.

Websites

Preventing Expulsion from Preschool and Child Care (http://zerotothree.org/policy/preschool-expulsion) is a set of resources from Zero to Three, including research reports, videos, and print materials for teachers and parents on coping with problematic behaviors and supporting positive social and emotional development.

The Center on the Emotional and Social Foundations for Early Learning (CSEFEL) (http://csefel .vanderbilt.edu) is funded by the Office of Head Start and the Child Care Bureau to disseminate research and evidence-based practices to early childhood programs across the country. The website includes links to many helpful resources, including a five-module training course on responding to problematic behaviors and creating environments that nurture positive behaviors, with accompanying videos; and dozens of training kits on topics ranging from behavior issues for multiple-language learners to transitions to deciphering the meaning and function of children's behaviors.

Also see *Healthy Sexual Behavior in Children and Young People* under "Sexual development, sex roles, and gender identity."

Videos

Discipline and Conflict (www.youtube.com/watch?v=gr8zqwRxd2g). This is a brief, under two-minute video in which Tom Hobson (better known as Teacher Tom) explains how we help children resolve conflicts. Good advice from an experienced, working preschool teacher.

Relationships, Interactions, and Guidance (https://www.youtube.com/watch?v=avWLBUMo_5Q). This 20-minute video was developed by the California Department of Education and First 5 California as part of their Early Childhood Educator Competencies program. Topics include "Supporting Children's Emotional Development," "Social-Emotional Climate," and "Socialization and Guidance."

Understanding Challenging Behavior in Young Children (www.youtube.com/watch?v=acAJsiEKxzg). In this video provided by Eastern Connecticut State University, early childhood teachers and experts discuss some of the possible influences and causes of children's behavior and how to respond objectively.

Children's Books

Death

Everett Anderson's Goodbye by Lucille Clifton. Austin, TX: Holt, Rhinehart and Winston, 1983.
Lifetimes: The Beautiful Way to Explain Death to Children by Bryan Mellonie. New York: Bantam, 1983.

Divorce

Two Homes by Claire Masurel. Cambridge, MA: Candlewick Press, 2001.

Fears, worries, feelings

Lots of Feelings by Shelley Rotner. Minneapolis, MN: Millbrook Press, 2003.
Scaredy Squirrel by Melanie Watt. Toronto, ON, CAN: Kids Can Press, 2010.

Hospitalization

Franklin Goes to the Hospital by Paulette Bourgeois. Toronto, ON, CAN: Kids Can Press, 2011.

Moving

I Know Here by Laurel Croza. Groundwood Books/House of Anansi Press, 2010.

New baby in the family

Pecan Pie Baby by Jacqueline Woodson. East Rutherford, NJ: Putnam Press, 2010.

Separations

My Day, Your Day by Robin Ballard. New York: Greenwillow Books/HarperCollins, 2001.

Trauma

A Terrible Thing Happened by Margaret M. Holmes. Washington, D.C.: Magination Press, 2000.
Brave Bart. A Story for Traumatized and Grieving Children by Carolyn H. Shepard. Grosse Pointe Woods, MI: The Institute for Trauma and Loss in Children, 1998.

Brain Development
Print Materials

Darling-Kuria, N. (2010). *Brain-Based Early Learning Activities: Connecting Theory and Practice.* St. Paul: Redleaf Press.
Galinsky, E. (2010). *Mind in the Making: The Seven Essential Life Skills Every Child Needs.* New York: William Morrow.
Gellens, S. ((2012). *Building Brains: 600 Activity Ideas for Young Children.* St. Paul: Redleaf Press.
Sprenger, M.B. (2008). *The Developing Brain: Birth to Age Eight.* Thousand Oaks, CA: Corwin Press.

Websites

Brain Development from **Zero to Three** (www.zerotothree.org/child-development/brain-development) has an interactive "Baby Brain Map" and "Tips and Tools for Brain Development," a podcast featuring Dr. Alison Gopnick, an interactive quiz, and more.

Videos

PBS *The Secret Life of the Brain: "The Baby's Brain"* (www.youtube.com/watch?v=MS5HUDVNbGs). This short video contains segments from the first two parts of a five-part PBS series on the developing brain across the life span: Part one is "The Baby's Brain—Wider than the Sky" and part two is "The Child's Brain—Syllable from Sound."

Child Development
Print Materials

Galinsky, E. (2010). *Mind in the Making: The Seven Essential Life Skills Every Child Needs.* New York: William Morrow.
Merryman, A., & Bronson, P. (2011). *Nurtureshock: Why Everything We Thought About Children Is Wrong.* London: Ebury.

Mooney, C. G. (2013). *Theories of Childhood: An Introduction to Dewey, Montessori, Erikson, Piaget & Vygotsky. Second Ed.* St. Paul: Redleaf Press.

National Research Council (2000). *Neurons to Neighborhoods: The Science of Early Childhood Development.* Washington, D.C.: National Academy Press.

Redleaf Press. (2015). *Redleaf Quick Guide Developmental Milestones of Young Children. Revised Ed.* St. Paul: Redleaf Press.

Schweikert, G. (2012). *Winning Ways for Early Childhood Professionals: Understanding Preschoolers.* St. Paul: Redleaf Press.

Websites

Gesell Institute (gesellinstitute.org) has promoted the importance of understanding children's development for educators, parents, administrators, and policy makers since 1950 through their highly respected research, assessment tools, training workshops and materials, public education campaigns, and more. A 2012 research report, the Gesell Developmental Observation—Revised Technical Report (www.gesellinstitute.org/technical-reports) found that children's developmental milestones have not changed for 100 years. They also produce a lively and informative blog (www.gesellinstitute.org/blog).

Videos

The Science of Early Childhood Development (www.youtube.com/watch?v=tLiP4b-TPCA). This four-minute video gives an excellent overview of brain development and its implications for child rearing and education. It's presented by Jack Shonkoff, Harvard professor and lead author of *Neurons to Neighborhoods.*

Child Development and Learning (www.youtube.com/watch?v=TLi0mvqIWik). This 16.5-minute video was developed by the California Department of Education and First 5 California as part of their Early Childhood Educator Competencies program. It includes up-to-date information, engagingly presented and well-illustrated with video clips from a variety of diverse classrooms.

Cultural Responsiveness and Diversity

Print Materials

Ramsey, P. G. (2015). *Teaching and Learning in a Diverse World: Multicultural Education for Young Children.* 4th Ed. New York: Teachers College Press.

Sullivan, D. R. (2016). *Cultivating the Genius of Black Children: Strategies to Close the Achievement Gap in the Early Years.* St. Paul: Redleaf Press.

Wolpert, E. (2005). *Start Seeing Diversity: The Basic Guide to an Anti-Bias Classroom.* St. Paul: Redleaf Press.

Websites

The **National Black Child Development Institute** (www.nbcdi.org) has two excellent publications available as free downloads: "Being Black Is Not a Risk Factor" and "A Framework That Works: How PreK-3rd Can Be a Smart Strategy for Black Kids, Families, and Communities."

The **National Resource Center on Hispanic Children and Families** (http://www.childtrends.org/nrc) was established in 2013 with funding from a federal grant to improve the lives of low-income Hispanic families in three areas: early care and education, marriage and fatherhood, and economic sufficiency.

Videos

Culture, Diversity and Equity (www.youtube.com/watch?v=3a7QRDZC_2M). This 17-minute video was developed by the California Department of Education and First 5 California as part of their Early Childhood Educator Competencies program. It covers the topics: respect for all differences and similarities, culturally responsive approaches, culture and language development and learning, and culturally inclusive learning environments.

Embracing Diversity with Children's Literature (www.youtube.com/watch?v=XATm0nXvunk). In this seven-minute video, Dr. Helene Harte reviews several different types of children's books that promote diversity in various ways. She also recommends a book for teachers.

Children's Books

All the Colors We Are / Todos los colores de nuestra piel: The Story of How We Get Our Skin Color / La historia de por qué tenemos diferentes colores de piel by Katie Kissinger. Redleaf Press, 2014.

We're Different, We're the Same (Sesame Street) by Bobbi Kates. New York: Random House Books for Young Readers. 1992.

The Family Book by Todd Parr. New York: Little Brown Books for Young Readers. 2010.

Rosie's Family: An Adoption Story by Lori Rosove. Asia Press. 2001.

Black, White, Just Right! by Marguerite W. Davol. Morton Grove, IL: Albert Whitman & Co. 1993.

Curriculum and Project-Based Learning

Print Materials

Curtis, D. & M. Carter. (2007). *Learning Together with Young Children: A Curriculum Framework for Reflective Teachers*. St. Paul: Redleaf Press.

Gronlund, G. (2016). *Individualized Child-Focused Curriculum: A Differentiated Approach*. St. Paul: Redleaf Press.

Helm, J.H. (2014). *Becoming Young Thinkers: Deep Project Work in the Classroom*. New York, NY: Teachers College Press.

Stacey, S. (2011). *The Unscripted Classroom: Emergent Curriculum in Action*. St. Paul: Redleaf Press.

Stacey, S. (2008). *Emergent Curriculum in Early Childhood Settings: From Theory to Practice*. St. Paul: Redleaf Press.

Wien, C.A. (2014). *The Power of Emergent Curriculum: Stories from Early Childhood Settings*. Washington, D.C.: NAEYC.

Wurm, J. P. (2005). *Working in the Reggio Way: A Beginner's Guide for American Teachers*. St. Paul: Redleaf Press.

Websites

Project Approach. Illinois Projects in Practice (http://illinoisearlylearning.org/illinoispip) and Early Childhood and Parenting (ECAP) Collabortive (http://ecap.crc.illinois.edu/poptopics/project.html) websites have information about how to develop and implement projects and examples of projects, each with very detailed information and many photos, including teachers' reflections. There are also links to article, resources, blogs, and more.

The following websites are sources of information about specific curricula. They are categorized by four descriptors or quadrants as explained and illustrated in the chapter "Curriculum Conundrums" on pp. 59–68.

Quadrant A curricula: Relatively more responsive to children's needs and interests and children have relatively more agency

Reggio Emilia approach. The Illinois ECAP also has website dedicated to the Reggio Emilia approach (http://ecap.crc.illinois.edu/poptopics/reggio.html) with links to further information and a wide variety of resources. The North American Reggio Emilia Alliance (http://reggioalliance.org) is a membership organization of and for schools that use the Reggio Emilia approach with a focus on advocating for its wider use. Many of the resources are available only to members or for purchase, but there are numerous links to articles and books (click on Free Resources under the Resources

tab), international associations, job postings, and events such as conferences, exhibits, and study trips to Italy. Also see the video, "Reggio Emilia Philosophy: Aesthetics," under "Art and aesthetics."

Step by Step (www.issa.nl) is an international curriculum used in about 30 countries, mostly in Central and Eastern Europe and Central Asia, but not in the United States. It focuses on developing the skills and dispositions to engage in a democratic and civil society. It focuses on child-centered teaching methods and the content and cultural elements of the curriculum vary by country.

Emergent Curriculum (http://elc.utoronto.ca/about/pedagogy). The University of Toronto's Child Development Center website provides a clear and detailed description of this approach. It is also closely linked to the Reggio Emilia Approach, the Project Approach, and many of the curricula listed here, as they all use children's interests and needs as the basis for developing the curriculum.

Australia's Belonging, Being, Becoming (www.dss.gov.au type "belonging" into the search box). This culturally responsive, anti-bias curriculum framework was developed as part of a comprehensive nationwide effort involving all sectors of the government to address the wrongs committed against its Aboriginal people. National "Sorry Day" is held annually on May 26.

New Zealand's Te Whāriki (www.education.govt.nz type "Te Whariki" in the search box). This framework is a model for weaving family and community culture throughout the early childhood curriculum.

Finland's Core Curriculum for Pre-School Education (www.oph.fi/english type "pre-primary" in the search box). Each education provider is obliged to develop a local curriculum based on this national core curriculum. The general principles emphasize developing children's individuality, active learning, and the importance of being a group member. Its focus is on instilling a positive outlook on life and developing initiative through a play-based curriculum.

Quadrant B curricula: Relatively less responsive to children's needs but children have relatively more agency

Creative Curriculum (www.teachingstrategies.com). This is the most widely used curriculum in the United States. It has a linked computer-based child assessment system and numerous materials: a set of booklets on the theory and research foundation of the curriculum, six teaching guides that span a school year to "guide teachers moment-by-moment through the day," "intentional teaching cards," and "mighty minutes," which are ideas for transitions.

High/Scope Curriculum (www.highscope.org) is another widely used curriculum. The developers describe the approach as "active participatory learning." It focuses on 58 key developmental indicators, which are early childhood milestones that guide planning of activities, interactions with children to support learning, and assessment. There is an aligned assessment tool, COR (Child Observation Record) Advantage. The indicators are embedded in activities categorized by approaches to learning, social and emotional development, physical development and health, mathematics, creative arts, science and technology, social studies, and language, literacy, and communication.

Montessori Curriculum (www.montessori-namta.org) was originally developed around 1900 by the Italian physician Maria Montessori for children with developmental delays. It has a strong emphasis on developing independent and focused learners. Children choose activities from within a prescribed range of options, work in uninterrupted blocks of work time (ideally three hours), and learn concepts from working with Montessori-specific self-correcting materials, rather than by direct instruction. Activities are categorized by practical life, language arts, mathematics, cultural activities, and sensorial activities. Teachers must receive training and certification from a MACTE (Montessori Accreditation Council for Teacher Education) accredited training program.

Tools of the Mind (www.toolsofthemind.org) was developed by Dr. Deborah Leong and Dr. Elena Bodrova based on the developmental theories of Lev Vygotsky. The developers describe the goal of the curriculum as giving "teachers the tools to ensure every child becomes a successful learner, developing the underlying cognitive, social and emotional skills needed to reach his or her highest potential." It has a strong focus on the development of self-regulation through social imaginary play and curriculum-specific activities. It also has an innovative and effective approach to literacy development through "scaffolded writing."

Quadrant C curricula: Relatively more responsive to children's needs and interests but children have relatively less agency.

An **IEP (Individual Educational Plan)** contains curriculum activities developed specifically for a child with special needs. The activities are designed to meet short- and long-term goals for the child and tend to be detailed and prescriptive as they need to be understood and agreed upon by a multi-disciplinary team that includes parents. Also, the IEP specifies the criteria for measuring the success of the activities in meeting the child's goals on a continuous basis. Especially if they are well developed, IEPs are highly responsive to the needs of a child, and are, therefore, a good example of this type of

curriculum. Excellent information about IEPs along with samples can be found on the **Early Childhood Technical Assistance Center**'s website (www.ectacenter.org) and from the **Kansas In-service Training System (KITS)** housed at the University of Kansas. (http://kskits.org). Their packet of resources on the role of curriculum in Early Childhood Special Education is particularly relevant and useful (http://kskits.org/ta/Packets/RoleOfCurriculum.shtml).

Curriculum developed for **Tutoring** is another form of this type of curriculum. The Bank Street College of Education provides a template and samples of tutoring curricula on their website (www.bankstreet.edu/literacy-guide/sample-tutoring-lessons).

Quadrant D curricula: Relatively less responsive to children's needs and interests and children have relatively less agency

Waldorf early education curriculum (www.waldorfearlychildhood.org) focuses on routines and repetition, imitation (teachers model behaviors and skills for children to copy), seasons, Christian holidays, crafts, baking, natural materials, and appreciation of nature. The approach was developed by Rudolf Steiner in the early 20th century based on the spiritual philosophy he developed, anthroposophy, which attempts to synthesize spirituality and science.

Everyday Math (http://everydaymath.uchicago.edu/teachers/pre-k) is an early childhood math curriculum that aligns with the Common Core State Standards, with activities in the areas of number and numeration, operations and computation, data and chance, measurement, geometry, patterns, functions, and algebra.

Waterford Early Learning (www.waterfordearlylearning.org) is a completely computer-based, self-paced program. It has three curricula: literacy, mathematics, and science.

Frog Street Pre-K (www.frogstreet.com) is a bilingual, bicultural complete curriculum that includes ten teacher guides covering nine themes. There is a supplemental social skills curriculum and a computer program with literacy and math lessons, as well as a child assessment tool. The curriculum includes children's books, music CDs, math manipulatives, wall charts, pocket charts, and other classroom materials.

Scholastic's Big Day for PreK (www.scholastic.com enter "big day prek" in the search box) is a complete curriculum developed to "ensure kindergarten readiness." It includes eight themes, each with a "road map" for daily lessons and activities in Circle Time, Story Time, Small Groups, and Learning Centers. The curriculum materials include children's books, wall charts, formal and informal assessment tools, a music and finger-play

CD, manipulatives, magnetic letters (including Spanish letters), number cards, letter cards, etc.

Videos

Learning Environments and Curriculum (www .youtube.com/watch?v=PWxTA9IjakI&feature= youtu.be). This 21.5-minute video was developed by the California Department of Education and First 5 California as part of their Early Childhood Educator Competencies program. It addresses the following topics: "Curriculum and Curriculum Planning," "Environments, Schedules, and Routines," and "Strategies to Support Learning and Development."

Reggio Emilia (www.youtube.com/watch?v= m0mvbWEd61M) is a six-minute video that provides a good introduction to the program. The photos are not very clear, but it is still one of the better videos on the approach.

Thinking Big. Extending Emergent Curriculum Projects (www.youtube.com/watch?v=G-y4gUEbuW8) is a superb example of developing curriculum in response to children's needs and interests; creating a "Reggio Emilia inspired project" with great depth and breadth; teaching and learning that is inquiry-based, hands-on, engaging, creative, and intellectually challenging. Hosted by Margie Carter of Harvest Resources, every minute of this 25-minute video is inspiring.

Disabilities, Inclusion, and Children with Special Needs

Print Materials

Cross, A. (2010). *Come and Play: Sensory-Integration Strategies for Children with Play Challenges.* St. Paul: Redleaf Press.

Dimitriadi, S. (2015). *Diversity, Special Needs and Inclusion in Early Years Education.* Thousand Oaks, CA: SAGE Publications.

Gadzikowski, A. (2013). *Challenging Exceptionally Bright Children in Early Childhood Classrooms.* St. Paul: Redleaf Press.

Hewitt, D. (2011). *So This Is Normal Too?* 2nd Ed. St. Paul: Redleaf Press.

Hirschland, D. (2015). *When Young Children Need Help: Understanding and Addressing Emotional, Behavioral, and Developmental Challenges.* St. Paul: Redleaf Press.

Langworthy, S. E. (2015). *Bridging the Relationship Gap: Connecting with Children Facing Adversity.* St. Paul: Redleaf Press.

Roffman, L. & Wanerman, T. A. (2010). *Including One, Including All: A Guide to Relationship-Based Early Childhood Inclusion.* St. Paul: Redleaf Press.

Websites

Division for Early Childhood (DEC) (www.dec-sped .org) is a branch of the professional association, the Council for Exceptional Children (CEC). They publish a very helpful and practical guide called Recommended Practices, which can be downloaded for free from the website by clicking on the "Recommended Practices" tab.

Learn the Signs. Act Early (www.cdc.gov/ncbddd/ actearly) is hosted by the Centers for Disease Control and Prevention (CDC) and has an array of great resources related to early identification and referral for young children. It focuses on observing and screening and includes developmental milestones lists for children two months through five years and a free, high-quality four-module course specifically for early childhood teachers, called Watch Me! Celebrating Milestones and Sharing Concerns. It also has links to early intervention contacts in every state and territory.

National Center for Family/Professional Partnerships (NCFPP) (www.fv-ncfpp.org) is a project of Family Voices (www.familyvoices.org), a national, nonprofit organization dedicated to promoting family-centered health care, particularly for families with children with disabilities. NCFPP, funded by the U.S. Maternal and Child Health Bureau, provides training, technical assistance and resources to build the capacity of families and professionals for mutual understanding, linguistic and cultural competence, and joint decision-making. They also work to increase access to family-centered services.

Videos

Special Needs and Inclusion (https://www.youtube .com/watch?v=3Lc9zJcfsnE). This 28-minute video was developed by the California Department of Education and First 5 California as part of their Early Childhood Educator Competencies program. The video addresses "Philosophy, Policies, and Practices," "Developmentally and Individually Appropriate Practice," "Collaboration with Families and Service Providers," and "Environmental Access and Adaptive Equipment."

Preschool Inclusion: Drew (www.youtube.com/ watch?v=GR6Tl1EhQ8c). This six-minute video is one of seven excellent videos on inclusion from the SpecialQuest Group of the Napa County Office of Education (www.specialquest.org). It focuses on the successful transition of a little boy with developmental delays from a home-based intervention program to an inclusive Head Start classroom. The video presents the perspectives of Drew's family, his teacher, and all of the key members of the multi-agency team that facilitated the transition and supported his full inclusion.

Children's Books

Dan and Diesel by Charlotte Hudson. Dugort, Ireland: Red Fox Press. 2006.

The Invisible Boy by Trudy Ludwig. New York: Knopf Books for Young Readers. 2013.

Just Because by Rebecca Elliot. Oxford, UK: Lion Children's Books. 2011.

Leah's Voice by Lori DeMonia. Halo Publishing Intl. 2012 .

Looking After Louis by Lesley Ely. Morton Grove, IL: Albert Whitman & Co. 2004.

Susan Laughs by Jeanne Willis. New York: Henry Holt & Co. 2000.

Environments: Indoor and Outside
Print Materials

Cross, A. (2011). *Nature Sparks: Connecting Children's Learning to the Natural World.* St. Paul: Redleaf Press.

Curtis, D. & Carter, M. (2014). *Designs for Living and Learning: Transforming Early Childhood Environments.* St. Paul: Redleaf Press.

Daly, L. & Beloglovsky, M. (2014). *Loose Parts: Inspiring Play in Young Children.* St. Paul: Redleaf Press.

Harms, T., Clifford, R.M. & Cryer, D. (2014). *Early Childhood Environment Rating Scale. Third Ed.* New York: Teacher's College Press.

Nelson, E. (2012). *Cultivating Outdoor Classrooms: Designing and Implementing Child-Centered Learning Environments.* St. Paul: Redleaf Press.

Olsen, H. M., Hudson, S. D. & Thompson, D. (2015). *Safe and Fun Playgrounds: A Handbook.* St. Paul: Redleaf Press.

Sobel, D. (2015). *Nature Preschools and Forest Kindergartens: The Handbook for Outdoor Learning.* St. Paul: Redleaf Press.

Zane, L. (2015). *Pedagogy and Space: Design Inspirations for Early Childhood Classrooms.* St. Paul: Redleaf Press.

Websites

Let the Children Play (www.letthechildrenplay.net) is a website hosted by Jenny, an Australian early childhood specialist. The website "celebrates the importance of play in the lives and education of our children by . . . providing inspiration, tips and information to help parents and teachers alike put the play back into childhood." Her focus, however, is on creating playful environments indoors and outside. This website is fabulously rich with information and beautiful photos. Here are links to three inspiring postings:

Beautiful Learning Spaces in Reggio Emelia Inspired Preschools (www.letthechildrenplay .net/2010/05/beautiful-learning-spaces-in-reggio .html). This is a post from 2010 with dozens of photos of creative, aesthetic spaces for children.

How to Create a Natural Outdoor Play Space (www .letthechildrenplay.net/2010/04/8-tips-for-creating-inspiring-outdoor.html) consists of 10 separate posts on this topic that follow the design and development of a play space that every child deserves.

Twenty Playful Ideas for Using Pallets at Preschool (www.letthechildrenplay.net/2013/10/20-playful-ideas-for-using-pallets-at.html). Before this post, I had never seen anything that I liked made with pallets. But I was completely converted by these incredibly creative and beautiful ideas. It's hard to pick a favorite, but the outdoor kitchen and the shoe rack are near the top of my list.

Videos

Bambini Creativi, a Reggio Inspired Preschool in Kansas City (www.youtube.com/watch?v=kQdAU7Dm9A0). This five-minute wordless slide show presents this program's inspiringly beautiful physical environments. Even the bathrooms are lovely.

Preschool Head Start Early Childhood Classroom Decorating (www.youtube.com/watch?v=l6p4MlZgX0o). This short slide show presents some wonderfully simple but very aesthetically pleasing environments and materials. It was posted by a person who goes by the name "Go Tell a Teacher," and the slides apparently depict her early childhood special education classroom.

Family Language Is Other Than English
Print Materials

Espinosa, L.M. (2014). *Getting It Right for Young Children from Diverse Backgrounds: Applying Research to Improve Practice with a Focus on Dual Language Learners.* Upper Saddle River, NJ: Pearson.

Nemeth, K.N. (2009). *Many Languages, One Classroom: Teaching Dual and English Language Learners.* Beltsville, MD: Gryphon House.

Sancho Passe, A. (2012). *Dual-Language Learners: Strategies for Teaching English.* St. Paul: Redleaf Press.

Websites

Language Castle (www.languagecastle.com) is a website hosted by Karen N. Nemeth, a presenter, a consultant, and an author of numerous books on the subject of teaching and including young children whose family language is other than English. The site includes Ms. Nemeth's blog posts and links to resources and information.

Planned Language Approach (http://eclkc.ohs .acf.hhs.gov/hslc/tta-system/cultural-linguistic/ planned-language-approach). This is a website of the federal Head Start office that provides resources to support a systematic and multi-faceted approach to promoting children's language development. It has a strong focus on dual-language learners. Its components include a **research base** in children's language development in one or more languages; **home language support** as the foundation for developing English language skills; **strategies to support dual-language learners** to thrive in their home language(s) and English; **policies, practices, and systems** that sustain language and literacy development; and the **five key elements of early language and literacy development** needed for school readiness and success: background knowledge, oral language, and vocabulary; book knowledge and print concepts; alphabet knowledge and early writing; and phonological awareness.

Videos

Dual-Language Development (www.youtube.com/ watch?v=AMA528GGL8A). This 21-minute video was developed by the California Department of Education and First 5 California as part of their Early Childhood Educator Competencies program. It covers these topics: dual-language program models and strategies; development of the home language and of English; observation and assessment of young dual-language learners; and relationships with families of dual-language learners.

Supporting English Language Learners in the Preschool Classroom (www.youtube.com/ watch?v=09PrmLppQ1A). Dr. Ann Anderberg stresses the importance of continuing to support first language development in children and gives suggestions for assisting these young learners in their acquisition of English. This video was developed by the Center for Early Childhood Education at Eastern Connecticut State University.

The Benefits of a Bilingual Brain (www.youtube .com/watch?v=MMmOLN5zBLY). Mia Nacamulli details the three types of bilingual brains and shows how knowing more than one language keeps the brain healthy. This is an engaging animated lesson from TED-Ed.

Family Partnerships
Print Materials

Gonzalez-Mena, J. (2013). *50 Strategies for Communicating and Working with Diverse Families.* 3rd Ed. Pearson.

Keyser, J. (2006). *From Parents to Partners: Building a Family-Centered Early Childhood Program.* St. Paul, MN: Redleaf Press.

Websites

Building Partnerships: Guide to Developing Relationships with Families (http://eclkc.ohs.acf.hhs .gov/pgor/). This is a resource from Head Start's Early Childhood Learning and Knowledge Center. Topics include Getting Started: Family Engagement and Positive Goal-Oriented Relationships; Tools: Strengths-Based Attitudes and Relationship-Based Practices; Reflective Strategies: Sustaining Effective Practice; and Additional Resources

Videos

Involving Families (www.youtube.com/watch?v= RTVLtIn29I0). This 5.5-minute video from Eastern Connecticut State University covers the importance of building strong, trusting relationships with families and providing a variety of opportunities for families to become involved in classrooms and in programs, which will have a positive impact on their child's learning and development.

Best Practices in Family Engagement (www.youtube .com/watch?v=RgdUvQ6sRSI). Filmed at Sheltering Arms School, Educare of Atlanta, this eight-minute video is very inspirational. It clearly shows how a strong and honest effort, using multiple approaches and strategies, creates true partnerships with families, and has positive impacts for everyone.

Health, Safety, and Nutrition
Print Materials

DK. (2012). *First Aid for Babies and Children Fast: Emergency Procedures for All Parents and Carers.* London: Dorling Kindersley.

Marotz, L.R. (2014). *Health, Safety, and Nutrition for the Young Child.* 9th Ed. Australia: Wadsworth Publishing.

Sorte, J. & Daeschel, I. (2013) *Nutrition, Health and Safety for Young Children: Promoting Wellness.* Boston: Pearson.

Websites

Let's Move! Child Care (https://healthykidshealthy future.org/) is a campaign to counteract obesity in young children led by First Lady Michelle Obama. However, the sensible approach and strategies offer a way to promote good health in general. The five areas of focus are good nutrition, healthy beverages, physical activity, limits on screen time, and promoting breast-feeding. The site, which has a Spanish language version, has links to additional information, activity ideas and games, resources (including some for parents), online courses, and more, for each focus area.

Center on Media and Child Health (http://cmch.tv). Located at Boston Children's Hospital, the center is led by pediatrician, father, and former movie producer Michael Rich (the Mediatrician). They conduct research on the benefits and ill effects of media use on children's health. Their goal is to foster the use of media to promote children's health and development.

Videos

Health, Safety, Nutrition (https://www.youtube.com/watch?v=CHLxyS6mCSs). This 17.5-minute video was developed by the California Department of Education and First 5 California as part of their Early Childhood Educator Competencies program. This video addresses these topics: Environmental Health and Safety, Emergency Preparedness, Nutrition, Response to Health Requirements, Child and Family Health, and Physical Activity.

Literacy and Language

Print Materials

Bettelheim, B. (2010). *The Uses of Enchantment: The Meaning and Importance of Fairy Tales.* Vintage Book Edition. (1975 original copyright). Vintage.

Curenton, S. M. (2015). *Conversation Compass: A Teacher's Guide to High-Quality Language Learning in Young Children.* St. Paul: Redleaf Press.

Grimm, J., & Grimm, W. (2014). *The Original Folk and Fairy Tales of the Brothers Grimm: The Complete First Edition.* (J. Zipes, Editor & Translator). Princeton, NJ: Princeton University Press. Note: This edition is the first English translation of the first edition of the fairy tales. These versions of the stories make more sense logically and psychologically, have more sexuality, and have less gratuitous violence than the versions commonly heard today. The female characters have much more agency. Cinderella puts her own slipper on and her sisters are beautiful; it's their vain and mean personalities that are ugly. Rapunzel gets pregnant as a result of the prince's visits. The stories were later sanitized of their sexuality, bad children were more harshly punished, if not killed, and all of the evil mothers became evil step-mothers in subsequent editions (there were six over a 40-year period) in order to make the books more marketable to mothers. Over the years, the stories were altered again and again by various interpreters, especially the folks at Disney studios. They removed even more of the stories' sexuality and gutted their psychological meaning and function.

Hansen, H. S. & Hansen, R. M. (2009). *Lessons for Literacy: Promoting Preschool Success.* St. Paul: Redleaf Press.

Jalongo, M. R. (2015). *Literacy for All Young Learners.* Boston: Gryphon House.

National Association for the Education of Young Children and Editors of Teaching Young Children. (2015). *Learning about Language and Literacy in Preschool.* Washington, D.C.: NAEYC.

Weitzman, E. & Greenberg, J. (2010). *ABC and Beyond: Building Emergent Literacy in Early Childhood Settings.* Toronto: Hanen Centre.

Websites

Early Language and Literacy Series (https://pdg.grads360.org/#program/early-learning-language-and-literacy-series). This is a free comprehensive 14-module training program supported by video webinars, which was developed with federal funds from the Preschool Development Grants program. It includes access to a facilitators guide and all materials. This is a fabulous resource.

Language and Literacy in Child Care (http://articles.extension.org/pages/25721/language-and-literacy-in-child-care). There is access to articles (many include links to videos) on topics such as emergent literacy, story-stretching ideas, read-alouds, promoting understanding, writing, learning new words, choosing books, and many more.

Videos

Five Predictors of Early Literacy (www.youtube.com/watch?v=HqImgAd3vyg). This 6.5-minute video from the Center for Early Childhood Education at Eastern Connecticut State University covers oral language development, phonemic awareness, alphabet awareness, concepts about print, and early writing with inventive spelling. There are video clips showing how these concepts are promoted by teachers in their classrooms.

Reading with Your Children (www.youtube.com/watch?v=6QVfbYvPaAM). This three-minute video from the British Council of Singapore nicely covers the key strategies for making stories come to life and promote literacy skills.

Math

Print Materials

Erikson Institute Early Math Collaborative. (2014). *Big Ideas of Early Mathematics: What Teachers of Young Children Need to Know.* Boston: Pearson.

Moomaw, S. (2013). *Teaching STEM in the Early Years: Activities for Integrating Science, Technology, Engineering, and Mathematics.* St. Paul: Redleaf Press.

Moomaw, S. and B. Hieronymus. (2011). *More Than Counting: Math Activities for Preschool and Kindergarten.* Standards Ed. St. Paul: Redleaf Press.

Omohundro Wedekind, K. (2011). *Math Exchanges: Guiding Young Mathematicians in Small-Group Meetings.* Portland, ME: Stenhouse Publishers.

Rosales, A. (2015). *Mathematizing: An Emergent Math Curriculum Approach for Young Children.* St. Paul: Redleaf Press.

Shumway, J. F. (2011). *Number Sense Routines: Building Numerical Literacy Every Day in Grades K–3.* Portland, ME: Stenhouse Publishers.

Websites

Center for Early Education in STEM (www.uni.edu/ceestem). The center, housed at the University of Northern Iowa, provides a large number of recipes and games categorized by age/grade. Click on links under "Resources for Educators."

Erikson Institute Early Math Collaborative (http://earlymath.erikson.edu). The goal of the collaborative is to improve early math instruction through research, professional development, and the dissemination of materials and information. This website is their main strategy for dissemination, and it provides access to a huge number of resources, particularly in the "Idea Library." Their video collection is listed below.

Videos

Erikson Institute Early Math Collaborative Video Collection (www.youtube.com/channel/UC9Mf7 YgfhmoZNwMxeQ1YOJQ). There are dozens of videos posted to this YouTube channel by the Erikson Institute Early Math Collaborative. I'm particularly fond of the third and fourth videos in the four-video set of the "Shoe-Graph" Lesson.

Using Math Talk to Support Learning (www.youtube .com/watch?v=TLmm3U0eYX4). This five-minute video from the Center for Early Childhood Education at Eastern Connecticut State University covers ways to promote mathematical thinking within all activities and throughout the day.

Observation, Assessment, Reflection, and Documentation

Print Materials

Curtis, D. and M. Carter. (2013). *Reflecting Children's Lives: A Handbook for Planning Child-Centered Curriculum.* 2nd Ed. St. Paul: Redleaf Press.

Curtis, D. and M. Carter. (2012). *The Art of Awareness: How Observation Can Transform Your Teaching.* 2nd Ed. St. Paul: Redleaf Press.

Gronlund, G. and B. Engel. (2002). *Focused Portfolios: A Complete Assessment for the Young Child.* St. Paul: Redleaf Press.

Gronlund, G. and M. James. (2013). *Focused Observations: How to Observe Young Children for Assessment and Curriculum Planning.* St. Paul: Redleaf Press.

Losardo, A. & Syverson, A. (2011). *Alternative Approaches to Assessing Young Children, Second Edition.* Baltimore, MD: Brookes Publishing.

Stacey, S. 2015. *Pedagogical Documentation in Early Childhood: Sharing Children's Learning and Teachers' Thinking.* St. Paul: Redleaf Press.

Websites

Monitoring, Documenting and Assessing. (www .qcaa.qld.edu.au/kindergarten/professional-topics/monitoring-documenting-assessing). This website from the Queensland, Australia, Curriculum and Assessment Authority includes links to several videos and observation samples.

Framework for Effective Practice: Ongoing Child Assessment (http://eclkc.ohs.acf.hhs.gov/hslc/tta-system/teaching/practice/assessment). The Early Childhood Learning and Knowledge Center is a project of Head Start and offers helpful resources on a wide array of topics. Assessment topics include preparing for assessment, collecting and using information, interpreting information, and strengthening your program. Among the documents for which there are links is *Understanding and Choosing Assessments and Developmental Screeners for Young Children Ages 3–5: Profiles of Selected Measures.* Many of the assessments reviewed are observational.

Videos

Observing Young Children (www.youtube.com/watch?v=t1Xtr3RKjGc). This seven-minute video from the Center for Early Childhood Education at Eastern Connecticut State University covers various types of observations and how to plan observations to get the most useful results. Four early childhood teachers also describe their use of formal and informal observation strategies to identify the individual strengths and needs of children and to plan instruction.

Planning for and Documenting Children's Learning (https://www.youtube.com/watch?v=9Io85mky6D0). This six-minute video from the Queensland, Australia, Curriculum and Assessment Authority describes the connection between intentional teaching and planning and documentation, and ways to involve children in documentation.

Focused Observation Video Clips (www.youtube .com/playlist?list=PLknl7Z_QI4MzaXeOe3CjFqL _CLQa44yWO). This collection of 25 video clips accompanies the book listed above by Gronlund and James (2013), published by Redleaf Press. The first video in the series is an introduction by the authors.

Play

Print Materials

Daly, L. & Beloglovsky, M. (2014). *Loose Parts: Inspiring Play in Young Children*. St. Paul: Redleaf Press.

Gadzikowski, A. (2015). *Creating a Beautiful Mess: Ten Essential Play Experiences for a Joyous Childhood*. St. Paul: Redleaf Press.

Gronlund, A. (2010). *Developmentally Appropriate Play: Guiding Young Children to a Higher Level*. St. Paul: Redleaf Press.

Heidemann, S. and D. Hewitt. (2009). *Play: The Pathway from Theory to Practice. Revised Ed.* St. Paul: Redleaf Press.

Johnson, J.A. & Dinger. D. (2014). *Let's Play: (Un)Curriculum Early Learning Adventures*. St. Paul: Redleaf Press.

Johnson, J. A. & Dinger, D. (2015). *Let's All Play: A Group-Learning (Un)Curriculum*. St. Paul: Redleaf Press.

MacDonald, S. (2001). *Block Play: The Complete Guide to Learning and Playing with Blocks*. Lewisville: Gryphon House.

Murphy, L. (2016). *Lisa Murphy on Play: The Foundation of Children's Learning. 2nd Ed.* St. Paul: Redleaf Press.

American Journal of Play (www.journalofplay.org) is a scholarly journal published three times per year since 2008. The full text of all articles in all issues are available free online. The site has a search box that will find results for search terms from all issues.

Websites

Strong National Museum of Play (www.museumofplay.org/education) is located in Rochester, New York. They are a national leader in promoting the understanding and value of play. The website has many resources for teachers.

KaBOOM! (http://kaboom.org) is a national nonprofit dedicated to ensuring that all kids get a childhood filled with the balanced and active play needed to thrive. In addition to providing thoughtful information and resources, this organization takes a unique and innovative approach to the play deficit program. They promote the concept of "playability" and seek to integrate it into the fabric of everyday life.

Videos

Kathy Hirsh-Pasek on the Importance of Play (www.youtube.com/watch?v=_jZbL8669uk). This is an inspiring talk by Dr. Hirsh-Pasek, author and professor of psychology at Temple University. It's 28 minutes long and was recorded live in Chicago in 2012 by Chicago Access Network Television.

The Decline of Play—Dr. Peter Gray (www.youtube.com/watch?v=Bg-GEzM7iTk). In this TEDx Talk recorded in 2014, Dr. Peter Gray compellingly argues that over the past 60 years there has been a gradual but overall dramatic decline in children's freedom to play with other children. Over this same period, there has been a gradual but overall dramatic increase in anxiety, depression, feelings of helplessness, suicide, and narcissism in children and adolescents. Dr. Gray cites research showing that free play is essential for children's healthy social and emotional development and suggests ways to bring free play back to children's lives.

Also see the websites Parenting Science under "Comprehensive Resources," and Alliance for Childhood under "Advocacy, Public Policy, and Research."

Professionalism: Professional Development and Quality Programs, Classrooms, and Teaching

Print Materials

California Department of Education and First 5 California (2011). *California Early Childhood Educator Competencies*. Sacramento, CA: California Department of Education. This is available to download free from www.cde.ca.gov/sp/cd/re/documents/ececompetencies2011.pdf.

Feeney, S. (2012). *Professionalism in Early Childhood Education: Doing Our Best for Young Children*. Boston: Pearson.

Feeney, S., Freeman, N. K., & Pizzolongo, P. (2012). *Ethics and the Early Childhood Educator: Using the NAEYC Code. Second Edition*. Washington, D.C.: NAEYC.

Goffin, S. (2015). *Professionalizing Early Childhood Education as a Field of Practice: A Guide to the Next Era*. St. Paul: Redleaf Press.

Heidemann, S., B. Menninga, and C. Chang. (2016). *The Thinking Teacher: A Framework for Intentional Teaching in the Early Childhood Classroom*. Minneapolis: Free Spirit Publishing.

Lewin-Benham, A. (2015). *Eight Essential Techniques for Teaching with Intention: What Makes Reggio and Other Inspired Approaches Effective*. St. Paul: Redleaf Press.

Mooney, C. G. (2014). *Theories of Practice: Raising the Standards of Early Childhood Education*. St. Paul: Redleaf Press.

Robertson, R. & Dressler, M. (2009). *Prove It!: Achieving Quality Recognition in Your Early Childhood Program*. St. Paul: Redleaf Press.

Sancho Passe, A. (2015). *Evaluating and Supporting Early Childhood Teachers*. St. Paul: Redleaf Press.

Websites

Accreditation of Programs for Young Children (NAEYC) (www.naeyc.org/academy) is a national, voluntary accreditation system to set professional standards for early childhood education programs, and to help families identify high-quality programs. Established in 1985, it is also known as the NAEYC Academy for Early Childhood Program Accreditation.

Competent Educators of the 21st Century: Principles of Quality Pedagogy (http://www.issa .nl/content/issa-quality-principles) is a document that defines quality teaching practices in working with children from 3 to 10 years old and their families to optimally support children's development and well-being. Developed by an international network of leaders of Step by Step programs, it is available as a free download in English, French, Spanish, and Russian.

Quality Teacher/Child Interactions: Resources from Teachstone (http://teachstone.com). Teachstone provides training on the Classroom Assessment Scoring System (CLASS), which focuses on measuring teacher/child interactions as the key indicator of quality of early childhood classrooms. Click on the "Resources" tab, as well as the "Blog" tab to access an array of helpful resources available to everyone at no cost.

Position Statement on the Code of Ethical Conduct and Statement of Commitment: NAEYC (www .naeyc.org) was updated 2011 with supplements for administrators and for adult educators. It has three primary purposes: to help educators of young children understand the meaning and importance of having a code of ethics, to recognize ethical dilemmas that occur in our work, and to make sound ethical decisions. To access the document, enter "position statement ethical conduct" in the search box and click on the link.

Professional Development (http://eclkc.ohs.acf.hhs .gov/hslc/tta-system/pd). Provided by Head Start's Early Childhood Learning and Knowledge Center, this site has a huge number of resources organized into four categories: Professional Development Systems, Foundation for Staff Development, Individual Career Development, and Professional-Development-to-Go (access to dozens of complete training workshops for facilitators/trainers with videos). Although the focus is on Professional Development in Head Start, there is very little that does not apply to any early childhood program.

Videos

A Few Good Men (www.youtube.com/watch?v= KHWrCfAIVlE). This 11-minute video from New Zealand features the research and views of Dr. Sarah Farquhar and portraits of several male teachers. It delves deeply into the role that gender bias and stereotyping play in keeping men out of ECE in spite of clear research evidence of the benefits of men working with young children. Apparently, this video helped double the percentage of men in ECE in New Zealand from 1% to 2%!

Professionalism (www.youtube.com/watch?v= nU-KPaw3wc4). This 20-minute video was developed by the California Department of Education and First Five California as part of their Early Childhood Educator Competencies program. The video addresses Professional Development, Professional Conduct and Behaviors, Competence in a Specialized Body of Knowledge, and Pedagogy.

School Readiness
Print Materials

Child Trends. (2015). *Child Trends Data Bank: Early School Readiness*. Child Trends. Retrieved 1/3/2016 from (http://www.childtrends.org/wp-content/ uploads/2012/10/07_School_Readiness.pdf).

Pianta, R., Cox, M. & Snow, K. (2007). *School Readiness and the Transition to Kindergarten in the Era of Accountability*. Baltimore, MD: Brookes Publishing.

Whitebread, D. & Bingham, S. (2011). *School Readiness: A Critical Review of Perspectives and Evidence*. TACTYC Association for the Professional Development of Early Years. Retrieved 1/3/2016 from http://tactyc.org.uk/ occasional-paper/occasional-paper2.pdf.

Websites

Maryland Model for School Readiness (MMSR) (http://marylandpublicschools.org) is an exemplary system for improving the chances of all children to be successful in school. Like most school readiness programs, it includes an assessment of children's readiness and progress. However, this program uses a portfolio-based assessment. All parts of the system align with each other. The items and expectations of the assessment match the developmentally appropriate content and methodology of the curriculum, which align with the professional development teachers receive. To access the site, enter "MMSR" in the search box and then click on the link.

Science
Print Materials

Chalufour, I. & Worth, K. (2003). *Discovering Nature with Young Children: Part of the Young Scientist Series*. St. Paul: Redleaf Press.

Chalufour, I. & Worth, K. (2004). *Building Structures with Young Children: Part of the Young Scientist Series*. St. Paul: Redleaf Press.

Chalufour, I. & Worth, K. (2005). *Exploring Water with Young Children: Part of the Young Scientist Series*. St. Paul: Redleaf Press.

Moomaw, S.(2013). *Teaching STEM in the Early Years: Activities for Integrating Science, Technology, Engineering, and Mathematics*. St. Paul: Redleaf Press.

Moomaw, S. & Hieronymus, B. (1997). *More than Magnets: Exploring the Wonders of Science in Preschool and Kindergarten*. St. Paul: Redleaf Press.

Neumann-Hinds, C. (2007). *Picture Science: Using Digital Photography to Teach Young Children*. St. Paul: Redleaf Press.

Plaster, L. & Krustchinksy, R. (2010). *Incredible Edible Science: Recipes for Developing Science and Literacy Skills*. St. Paul: Redleaf Press.

Websites

Collected Papers from the SEED (STEM in Early Childhood Education and Development) Conference, May 2010 (http://ecrp.illinois.edu/beyond/seed/index.html). This site from the online journal *Early Childhood Research and Practice* has links to eight papers, most of which have information that is more practical than academic.

Quality Teaching and Learning: Science (http://eclkc.ohs.acf.hhs.gov/hslc/tta-system/teaching/eecd/Domains%20of%20Child%20Development/Science). This resource, provided by Head Start's Early Childhood Learning and Knowledge Center, has links to webinars, materials, and all nine science themes, each with multiple topics and activities, from the publication *Marvelous Explorations through Science and Stories (MESS)*.

Videos

Science and Math Integrating Literacy in Early Childhood (www.youtube.com/watch?v=lNG6dTW9X70). This is a 21-minute video from University of California Television explores how early childhood educators and parents can encourage science and math literacy through real-world and classroom activities. Experts utilize research to show how math and science learning can be integrated into early reading activities.

Sexual Development, Sex Roles, and Gender Identity

Print Materials

Chrisman, K. & Couchenour, D. (2002). *Healthy Sexuality Development: A Guide for Early Childhood Educators and Families*. Washington D.C.: NAEYC.

Jacobson, T. (Ed.). (2010). *Perspectives on Gender in Early Childhood*. St. Paul: Redleaf Press.

National Child Traumatic Stress Network. (2009). *Sexual Development and Behavior in Children*. NCTSN. Retrieved 1/3/2016 from www.nctsn.org/sites/default/files/assets/pdfs/sexualdevelopmentand behavior.pdf.

Rutgers. (No Date). *Spring Fever: Relationships and Sexual Health Education*. Retrieved 12/10/2015 from www.rutgers.international/what-we-do/comprehensive-sexuality-education/spring-fever and www.springfever.org.uk.

Websites

The Case for Starting Sex Education in Kindergarten (www.pbs.org/newshour/updates/spring-fever). This is the transcript (with additional information and links to resources) from a PBS *NewsHour* program about the Dutch approach to comprehensive relationship and sex education called Spring Fever.

Healthy Sexual Behavior in Children and Young People (www.nspcc.org.uk), from the UK-based National Society for the Prevention of Cruelty to Children, can be found by clicking on the Preventing Abuse tab, then on Advice to Keep Children Safe, then on Healthy Sexual Behavior.

Videos

Dutch Kindergarteners Get Their First Lesson in Sexuality and Relationships (https://www.youtube.com/watch?v=il8HIi7wqQE). This is a 28-second video clip from PBS *NewsHour* (May 2015) that accompanies the program referenced above about starting relationship and sex education in kindergarten.

Five-Year-Old Boy Chooses to Live Life as a Girl (www.youtube.com/watch?v=_A6rd-QFWIg). This six-minute segment from an Australian news broadcast (November 2013) features a family's journey to accept and support their son's need to be a girl.

Life as a Five-Year-Old Transgender Child (www.youtube.com/watch?v=kVmau1cM5TU). This is a six-minute segment from NBC *Nightly News* (April 2015) about a family supporting their young daughter's need to be a boy.

Children's Books

Books about bodies

The Bare Naked Book (20th Anniversary Edition) by Kathy Stinson. Toronto: Annick Press. 2006.

Who Has What?: All About Girls' Bodies and Boys' Bodies (Let's Talk about You and Me) by Robie H. Harris. Cambridge, MA: Candlewick Press. 2011.

Books about sex and reproduction

What Makes a Baby? by Cory Silverberg. Triangle Square. 2013.

It's Not the Stork! A Book about Girls, Boys, Babies, Bodies, Families and Friends (The Family Library) by Robie H. Harris. Cambridge, MA: Candlewick Press. 2008.

Books about gender identity and sex roles

Not Every Princess by Jeffery Bone and Lisa Bone. Washington, D.C.: Magination Press. 2014.

I Am Jazz by Jessica Herthel and Jazz Jennings. New York: Dial Books. 2014.

Jacob's New Dress by Sarah Hoffman and Ian Hoffman. Morton Grove, IL: Albert Whitman and Company. 2014.

And Tango Makes Three by Justin Richardson and Peter Parnell. New York: Simon & Schuster Books for Young Readers. 2015.

Standards
Print Materials

Jacobs, G. & Crowley, K. (2006). *Play, Projects, and Preschool Standards: Nurturing Children's Sense of Wonder and Joy in Learning.* Thousand Oaks, CA: Corwin Press.

Jacobs, G. & Crowley, K. (2009). *Reaching Standards and Beyond in Kindergarten: Nurturing Children's Sense of Wonder and Joy in Learning.* Thousand Oaks, CA: Corwin Press.

Gronlund, G. (2014). *Make Early Learning Standards Come Alive: Connecting Your Practice and Curriculum to State Guidelines.* 2nd ed. St. Paul, MN: Redleaf Press.

Gronlund, G. & James, M. (2007). *Early Learning Standards and Staff Development: Best Practices in the Face of Change.* St. Paul: Redleaf Press.

National Association for the Education of Young Children. (2015.) *Developmentally Appropriate Practice and the Common Core State Standards: Framing the Issues. Research brief.* Washington, D.C.: NAEYC. http://www.naeyc.org/topics/common-core.

National Association for the Education of Young Children (NAEYC). (2009). *Where We Stand on Early Learning Standards.* Washington, D.C.: NAEYC. http://www.naeyc.org/files/naeyc/file/positions/earlyLearningStandards.pdf.

Strauss, V. (2013). "A Tough Critique of Common Core on Early Childhood Education." *Washington Post.* Retrieved 1/3/2016 from: www.washingtonpost.com/news/answer-sheet/wp/2013/01/29/a-tough-critique-of-common-core-on-early-childhood-education.

Websites

Kindergarten Math Standards from the Common Core State Standards (www.corestandards.org/Math/Content/K/introduction).

Kindergarten English Language Arts and Literacy Standards from the Common Core State Standards (www.corestandards.org/ELA-Literacy). The kindergarten standards are not grouped together. It is necessary to click on each area (reading, writing, speaking and listening, etc.) to find the standards for kindergarten. A critique of these standards can be found at **Defending the Early Years** (http://deyproject.org).

Also see the website Competent Educators of the 21st Century under "Professionalism."

Videos

Reading Instruction in Kindergarten: Little to Gain, Much to Lose (https://www.youtube.com/watch?v=DVVln1WMz0g). This four-minute video from Defending the Early Years is a sharp critique of the Common Core State Standard that kindergartners should be reading by the end of the year.

Technology and Media Literacy
Print Materials

Donohue, C. (Ed.). (2014). *Technology and Digital Media in the Early Years: Tools for Teaching and Learning.* New York: Routledge.

Guernsey, L. (2007). *Into the Minds of Babes: How Screen Time Affects Children from Birth to Age Five.* New York: Basic Books.

National Association for the Education of Young Children (NAEYC). (2012). "Technology and Interactive Media as Tools in Early Childhood Programs Serving Children from Birth through Age 8." A Joint Position Statement issued by the National Association for the Education of Young Children and the Fred Rogers Center for Early Learning and Children's Media at Saint Vincent College. Washington, D.C.: NAEYC. Retrieved 1/2/2016 from www.naeyc.org/content/technology-and-young-children.

Rogow, F. (2014). "Media Literacy in Early Childhood Education: Inquiry-based Technology Integration." *Technology and Digital Media in the Early Years: Tools for Teaching and Learning.* New York: Routledge.

Simon, F. (2012). *Digital Decisions: Choosing the Right Technology Tools for Early Childhood Education.* Lewisville, NC: Gryphon House.

Websites

Center for Media Literacy (www.medialit.org). The Center for Media Literacy (CML) promotes the ability to communicate competently in all media forms and to access, understand, analyze, evaluate, and interact with all technology and mass media. From this website you can access an article by Faith Rogow, *ABCs of Media Literacy. What Can Pre-schoolers Learn?* by clicking on "Reading Room" at the bottom of the home page, then typing "media literacy" in the search box.

Erikson TEC (Technology in Early Childhood) Center (http://teccenter.erikson.edu). The TEC Center at Erikson Institute gives early childhood educators the skills and knowledge to make informed decisions about the appropriate selection, use, integration, and evaluation of technology.

Fred Rogers Center for Early Learning and Children's Media (www.fredrogerscenter.org/initiatives/digital-media-learning). The Center helps children and adults thrive in the digital age and promotes the use of technology to complement children's social interactions, play, and other activities with caring friends and family.

Videos

Erikson TEC Center "Show Me Videos" (http://teccenter.erikson.edu/category/show-me-videos). The videos in this collection include topics such as: finding the balance between tech and no tech, technology and social-emotional development, apps that promote children's literacy, and introducing STEM into early childhood, among others.

Introducing Technology to Young Children (https://www.youtube.com/watch?v=29ylsrxof48). This 5-minute video from Eastern Connecticut State University features Dr. Douglas Clements who explains that when teachers carefully select and introduce children to appropriate software, computers can help young children not only learn new skills, but also make the connection between concrete concepts and more abstract ideas. Also Dr. Sudha Swaminathan stresses the important role of the teacher in supporting learning how to use technology, and provides tips for teachers for the successful integration of computers in the classroom curriculum.

Testing

Print Materials

Krasnoff, B. (2015). *Overview of Approaches to Kindergarten Entry/Readiness Assessments.* Portland, OR: Comprehensive Center, Education Northwest. Retrieved 1/2/2016 from: http://nwcc.educationnorthwest.org/webfm_send/433.

Snow, K. (2011). "Developing kindergarten readiness and other large-scale assessment systems: Necessary considerations in the assessment of young children." Washington, D.C.: NAEYC. Retrieved 1/3/2016 from http://www.naeyc.org/resources/research/kreadinessassessment.

Snow, C. E., & Van Hemel, S. B. (Eds.). (2008). *Early Childhood Assessment: Why, What, and How.* Washington, DC: National Academies Press.

Websites

FairTest: The National Center for Fair and Open Testing (http://fairtest.org/) works to end the misuses and flaws of standardized testing and to ensure that evaluation of students, teachers, and schools is fair, open, valid, and educationally beneficial. Enter "early childhood" into the search box to access numerous articles, stories, and documents.

Change the Stakes (https://changethestakes.wordpress.com) is a group of New York City parents and educators who are concerned about the harm high-stakes testing is causing our children and schools. They believe high-stakes testing must be replaced with valid forms of student, teacher, and school assessment.

Videos

Defending the Early Years Director Nancy Carlsson-Paige Acceptance Speech for Hero in Education Award (http://deyproject.org/2015/11/11/deys-nancy-carlsson-paige-receives-hero-in-education-award-from-fairtest/). Dr. Carlsson-Paige received this award from FairTest in November 2015. The audio is clear but the video quality is terrible (shaky cell phone). Minimize the video and listen.

Refuse the Tests (https://www.youtube.com/watch?v=2ayYajsQjg8). New York City parents explain why they refuse to have their children take the tests associated with the Common Core State Standards.

Glossary of Common Terms and Jargon

Accommodation: Term used by Jean Piaget to describe how children learn by altering old concepts to include new information. For example, a child alters his idea of "dog" to include small, short-haired creatures after seeing a Chihuahua for the first time. This is the second part of the adaptation process. Assimilation is the first part.

Accreditation: Certification by a legitimate organization (NAEYC, state Departments of Education, and so on) of having met a set of standards. It can be for a program or an individual and can range from meeting minimal to very high standards.

Action Research: Research that is done by teachers in classrooms. The teacher identifies a question he wants to know the answer to or problem to solve and carries out activities in the classroom to find the answer. For example, the teacher may try several different schedules over a period of time to determine which seems to best meet the needs of the children and make the class run smoothest.

Active Listening: A variety of techniques to be able to listen well, elicit information from others, and communicate effectively. Includes using "I-messages," restating what the person says, making eye contact, and asking clarifying questions.

ADA: See Americans with Disabilities Act.

Adaptation: Term used by Jean Piaget to describe how children learn by assimilating new information and accommodating their previous knowledge to incorporate this new information.

ADHD: See Attention Deficit Hyperactivity Disorder.

Affect: The emotional part of a person, including values, feelings, interests, and motivations.

Affective Development: See Affect.

Agency: The extent to which children are allowed to make their own decisions, direct their own learning, and contribute to the environment and activities. Prescribed curricula allow children very little agency, while emergent curricula allow them much more.

Americans with Disabilities Act (ADA): Federal legislation passed in 1990 that gives civil rights protections to individuals with disabilities similar to those provided to individuals on the basis of race, color, sex, national origin, age, and religion. It guarantees equal opportunity for individuals with disabilities in public accommodations, employment, transportation, state and local government services, and telecommunications.

Areas of Development: Typically includes social, emotional, cognitive, self-help, language, and small-motor and large-motor skills. Can also include dispositions, creativity, motivation, behaviors, play abilities, and more.

Assessment: A tool or system for determining a child's skills, abilities, or knowledge. Assessments can range from very formal (psychometric, standardized tests like the Wechsler Intelligence Scale for Children) to very informal (checklists of children's development). Screening tests, developmental assessments, readiness tests, and diagnostic tests are all types of assessment used for different purposes.

Assimilation: Term used by Jean Piaget to describe how children learn by taking in new information and sensations. For example, a child sees a Chihuahua and hears an adult say "doggie." This is the first part of the adaptation process. Accommodation is the second part.

Associative Play: Children playing together but in an unorganized way, without a central purpose.

At-Risk: A term used to describe a child with a number of risk factors for whom there is concern that he might not develop well or do well in school.

Attention Deficit Hyperactivity Disorder (ADHD): The inability of a child to concentrate or pay attention to something so that the child's behavior causes problems in learning or getting along with others. This behavior must happen consistently and in nearly all situations for a child to be diagnosed as having ADHD.

Authoring Software (or Tools): Computer software that enables one to develop a website or a complex document that can include text, photos, video, animation, and sound. It allows teachers to develop electronic spaces for children or to document class events or student work electronically.

Behavior Modification: Changing a person's behavior through rewards, punishment, or some system of reinforcement.

Behaviorism: Branch of psychology that ascribes the cause of all human behavior to how other people and the environment reinforce it or do not reinforce it.

Benchmarks: Expectations of what children should be able to do or know at a given age or grade level. It is usually used in relation to standards and testing. A benchmark is set for a particular standard and then the child is tested on his ability to meet that benchmark. For example, a benchmark in the area of literacy might be that a child can recognize his name when written in large block letters by four years old.

CDA: See Child Development Associate.

CDF: See Children's Defense Fund.

Child Development Associate: A national certificate certifying basic competence in working with young children. Administered by the Council for Early Childhood Professional Recognition.

Children's Defense Fund: Organization that educates and lobbies for better lives for children and families.

Classification: Grouping items by like characteristics. For example, sorting all red objects into a box.

Cognition: The process of thinking or coming to an understanding of something.

Cognitive Development: See Cognition.

Communicative Competence: The ability to make one's message clearly known to others by any means (words, sign language, writing, and so on).

Compensatory Preschool Programs: Programs such as Head Start and Title I that are designed to help children from low-income families compensate for some experiences and skills they may have missed due to lack of resources.

Computer Literacy: The ability to use computers and a variety of common software with a good degree of skill and accuracy for one's developmental level.

Conflict Resolution: A set of skills for solving a conflict peacefully. It usually involves brainstorming solutions, discussing possible consequences of the solutions, negotiating a compromise, and deciding on and taking a course of action.

Conservation: The principle that amounts of things stay the same even when they are moved or reshaped. For example, pouring a liquid from a short, wide glass into a tall, thin glass (conservation of volume), and flattening a ball of clay into the shape of a pancake (conservation of mass). Piaget stated that children younger than seven cannot conserve and cannot be taught to conserve. Subsequent research to verify this has found mixed results, but it is generally agreed that some children younger than seven can conserve and more can be taught to conserve.

Constructive Play: Play in which the child builds or creates something.

Constructivism: Term used by Jean Piaget to describe the process by which children learn. They construct their own knowledge of the world and how it works by interacting with real things and people. For example, a child invents or constructs for himself the idea of "half" by dividing up his playdough in equal amounts to give some to his friend.

Content: What is taught. Content typically refers to subject matter content (or content areas) such as math, science, and literacy. The concern for early childhood programs is that the content is developmentally appropriate, is individualized, and has a balance of breadth and depth. Another concern is that some content—math and science in particular—will not be adequately covered, accurately taught, or even covered at all.

Cooperative Play: Children playing together with a common purpose.

Criterion-Referenced Assessments: Tests whose scores are based on comparing a child's performance to certain, explicit criteria. These are typically observational assessments and use a rating system such as "No, Somewhat, Yes." These assessments are in contrast to norm-referenced assessments, where the score is based on a comparison to other children.

Cultural Competence: The ability to understand, work effectively, and be responsive to a variety of cultures. It involves a set of skills that includes sensitivity, respect, empathy, flexibility, careful listening, reading body language, the ability to get information about a culture from a variety of sources, and more.

DAP: See Developmentally Appropriate Practice.

Developmental Delay: A child's physical and/or cognitive abilities mature significantly more slowly than expected for her age, based on developmental norms.

Developmental Milestones: Major points in a child's life at which time growth and ability are measured and compared to norms. Examples include sitting up, height and weight, walking, first word, first primary tooth, hopping on one foot, counting to ten, and so on.

Developmental Psychology or Developmental Education: The branch of psychology or education that ascribes human behavior to the interaction between the growth/maturing process and the environment.

Developmentally Appropriate Practice: Guidelines by which teachers do activities, interact, and create environments that meet the needs of young children according to their age level and their individual strengths, weaknesses, and interests. These guidelines are described in *Developmentally Appropriate Practice in Early Childhood Programs Serving Children from Birth through Age Eight, Revised Edition*, edited by S. Bredekamp and C. Copple. Washington, D.C.: NAEYC, 1997.

Differentiated Instruction: Individualizing responses to children's learning needs and strengths. Teachers offer various ways for children to understand information within the same lesson.

DLL: See Dual-Language Learners.

Dramatic Play: Situations in which children interact while taking on roles. Some examples are children playing a family on a camping trip and firefighters putting a house fire out. Also called socio-dramatic play, make-believe play, pretend play, imaginary play, and social imaginary play.

Dual-Language Learners: This term is more accurate and descriptive of young children whose families speak a language other than English at home than the term English language learners, because all young children in the U.S. are learning to speak English.

However, some children are learning more than two languages and a dual-language learner could be a child whose primary home language is English.

Early Childhood Education: Abbreviated as ECE, this is the most common acronym for our field. Outside of the United States, however, it is more common to hear ECD for Early Childhood Development or ECDE for Early Childhood Development and Education,

ECE: See Early Childhood Education.

Egocentricism: Term used by Jean Piaget to describe the inability of young children to see the world through another's eyes, and the belief that events and actions are caused by or directed at them.

ELL: English language learners. See Family Language Other than English.

Emergent Skills: Abilities that are in the process of developing in children. For example, emergent literacy refers to a child's early attempts to write and read.

Empathy: The ability to understand and relate to how another person feels or thinks.

Empowerment: To give someone the ability to have control over a situation, themselves, or their lives. Children are empowered when they are given choices and encouraged to make meaningful decisions.

ESL: English as a second language. See Family Language Other than English.

Evaluation: Usually refers to a process for determining the effectiveness of a program. Sometimes called "Program Evaluation."

Expressive Language: The ability to use words or sounds to communicate.

Eye-Hand Coordination: The ability to use the hand and the eye together to complete a task, such as putting a peg in a hole or hammering a nail.

Family-Centered Practices: Ways of working with families that respect them as individuals and consider their needs, unique qualities, and strengths. Any assistance or intervention provided is based on that knowledge of families.

Family Language Other than English (FLOE): Children whose primary language and the dominant language spoken at home is not English. Also called DLL (Dual-Language Learners), ELL (English Language Learners), and ESL (English as a Second Language) among others.

Fine Motor: See Small Motor.

FLOE: See Family Language Other than English.

Forest Kindergartens: See Outdoor Preschools.

Functional Play: Repetitive, practice play in which the child performs the same action over and over.

Goals: Statements of what adults hope to help children gain, accomplish, or achieve. For a very shy, withdrawn child, an example of a long-term goal (one year or more) might be the following: "The child will play cooperatively with other children." An example of a short-term goal (a few months or less) would be: "The child will engage in associative play with one other child." The length of a goal depends on a child's ability level. Goal statements are typically followed by objectives.

Gross Motor: See Large Motor.

Guidance: Helping children develop self-control and self-efficacy.

High Stakes Tests: Tests whose results are used to evaluate the performance of a child, teacher, school, district, entire state, etc. Typically the evaluation is then used to make decisions about funding, placements, and the imposition of sanctions and rewards.

Hot-Housing: Pushing children to grow and learn faster than is appropriate for their age or ability.

Hyperactive: Behavior characterized by a very high activity level and the inability to remain still for even a short period of time. This behavior occurs consistently over time and in all situations.

IEP: See Individualized Educational Plan.

IFSP: See Individualized Family Services Plan.

Imaginary Play or Imaginary Social Play: Play in which children take on roles within a particular imagined scenario or setting. They improvise the dialogue and plot line using props and sometimes costumes. This is also called dramatic play, socio-dramatic play, make-believe play, pretend play, etc.

Inclusion: Fully involving all children in the activities and social fabric of a typical classroom. Also see Universal Design.

Individualized Educational Plan (IEP): Required by law for all children receiving special services, this plan details the child's current abilities, sets educational goals and objectives, lists the services the child will receive, and tells where the child will spend his time. A team of people including the teacher, specialists, and the parents develop the plan. Parents must approve and sign the plan before it can be implemented. It must be reviewed and updated periodically.

Individualized Family Services Plan (IFSP): Required for children from birth to age three with special needs, this plan is similar to an individualized educational plan, but it also includes supporting the needs of the family to aid the child.

Individualizing: Meeting the needs of each child by altering activities, interactions, the schedule, and the environment to optimize each child's learning and well-being.

Inquiry-Based Learning: This is also known as exploratory or investigative learning. Teachers guide children's acquisition of knowledge and understanding through an open-ended process in which children follow their interests and curiosity. There are no specific learning objectives or set timeframes. Subject matter content is integrated within the activities teachers develop in response to children's inquiries. This can be done with the whole classroom, a sub-group, or individually.

Instrumental Aggression: An aggressive act done in order to get something that the child wants. It is the most common type of aggression.

Integration: Serving typically developing children and children with disabilities in the same classroom. Integration differs from inclusion in that inclusion ensures the full participation of children with disabilities in all activities.

Intentionality or Intentional Teaching: All aspects of an early childhood program, from teacher-child interactions to the physical environment, are planned and implemented from a coherent and consistent pedagogical, philosophical, and psychological perspective to achieve particular goals for children and families.

Interactionalism: Vygotsky's theory that development happens, and is only understood, within interactions between people. Intelligence, in this theory, is not a fixed concept but will vary based on the people involved. The same person can be very intelligent in his community but not in a school setting, for example.

Intersubjectivity: Vygotsky's concept of mutual understanding between people. The implication for teachers is that too often teachers assume that a child understands what she means when that is not the case. Intersubjectivity must be achieved for true teaching and learning to take place.

Kinesthetic: Sensation or learning achieved through touching, feeling, or moving any part of the body. Petting real animals, feeling three-dimensional figures of animals, or moving the way various animals move are kinesthetic ways to become familiar with animals.

Lanham Act: Federal funding of child care during World War II that produced widespread, quality, affordable, or free child care, but ended when the war ended in 1945.

Large Motor: Skills related to using the head, arms, legs, and feet. Running and climbing are large-motor skills. Also called Gross Motor.

Literacy: The ability to read and write text or interact with books with a good degree of facility and accuracy for one's developmental level. It is emergent in young children but must be taught explicitly to be developed. Also see Numeracy, Computer Literacy, and Media Literacy.

Logical Consequences: This is essentially using a "punishment that fits the crime." The logical consequence of misusing a toy is lose access to that toy for a period of time. Its use has fallen out of favor as it is not an effective deterrent to problematic behaviors and does not teach the appropriate behavior.

Looping: The teacher stays with the same group of children for multiple years.

Loose Parts: Sets of objects that can be used in many different ways. Objects from nature such as stones, shells, and acorns are often used because they vary from each other in unique ways and are pleasing to look at and touch. The items can also be scrap materials such as wooden thread spools, wires of various colors and sizes, and bottle caps, as well as repurposed materials such as glass beads, buttons, shells, and clothespins. There are typically many objects in a set—50 stones, 100 buttons or beads—and the objects vary in size, color, and other attributes, in order to promote complex play and learning.

Mainstreaming: Process of integrating children with disabilities into classrooms that mostly contain typically developing children, either part or full time.

Manipulatives: Toys or activities consisting of small parts requiring the use of eye-hand coordination and spatial relations. They include construction toys, puzzles, and marble runs. They are also called table toys. Also see Loose Parts.

Media Literacy: The ability to critically view TV, film, video games, advertisements, and other media in order to understand its intents, purposes, strengths, and weakness, attempts at manipulation, and to discern fact from fiction. It is emergent in young children, but needs to be taught explicitly to be developed.

Meta-Cognition: The ability to think about how one is thinking. Even young children can begin to develop this type of self-awareness.

Modalities: Various senses by which children learn. These include visual, auditory, tactile, olfactory (smell), and taste. Most children learn better when several modalities are engaged.

Modeling: Demonstrating a behavior or action by showing how it is done. Adults who use polite words model good manners for children.

Multiple Intelligences: A theory developed by Howard Gardner that describes different people as having different types of intelligences, many of which are not valued in schools. This can put some children at a disadvantage in school even though they may have great strengths and abilities. A child with great interpersonal intelligence may get in trouble for talking too much if there are not enough opportunities to interact.

Natural Consequences: This is a disciplinary strategy in which an adult allows the child to experience the result of his problematic behavior rather than intervene. The natural consequences of hitting another child is getting hit back. However, this approach assumes that the child can connect the effect with the cause, can reflect on his behavior, and can stop himself from repeating the behavior at a future time by remembering what previously happened, reflect again on the behavior, and think of an alternative behavior. Without assistance, very few young children can be expected to do this.

Norm-Referenced Assessments: Tests whose scores are based on a comparison to a representative group. For example, a child who scores low on a screening test for language does not have as large a vocabulary as most other children his age.

Numeracy: The ability to use numbers and math to solve daily problems with a good degree of facility and accuracy for one's developmental level. It is akin to literacy, but relates to numbers rather than text. It is emergent in young children but needs to be taught explicitly to be developed.

Object Constancy: The principle that objects stay the same even when they are moved, turned, or felt rather than seen.

Object Permanence: The principle that objects still exist even when hidden from view.

Objectives: Statements of what children will do to meet a goal. Usually they are specific, measurable, observable, and follow a sequence. Objectives for the goal "The child will engage in associative play with another child" may be the following: (1) the child will play near another child for ten minutes each day; (2) the child will play with the same materials and near another child for ten minutes each day; and (3) the child will play with the same materials and with another child for five minutes each day. Objectives are typically followed by teaching strategies for implementing the objectives.

Onsets and Rimes: Onsets are the initial sounds in words and rimes are the ending sounds. Teaching about "word families" employs onsets and rimes. In the word *hat*, "h" is the onset and "at" is the rime. The word bat has a different onset but the same rime.

Outcomes: Expected results from an action, activity, or program. Outcomes for children from attending preschool might include the ability to get along with a wide variety of people, a love of books and learning, curiosity, the ability to negotiate and solve conflicts peacefully, and the ability to get his needs met appropriately.

Outdoor Preschools: These are programs in which children spend a great deal of time outdoors. Many common preschool activities such as circle time, art projects, and story time are done outdoors. The trend started in Nordic Countries to instill in children environmental awareness and appreciation and the habits of an active lifestyle.

Parallel Play: Children playing alongside each other, usually with the same materials, but playing independently.

Phonemes (Phonemic Awareness): The sounds of a language. Phonemic awareness refers to the ability to hear and say the separate sounds in words. It is considered by many to be an important precursor skill to reading.

Piaget, Jean: Swiss developmental psychologist who developed the constructivist theory of how intelligence develops in children. Most of his research was done by observing his own children.

Portfolio Assessment: The use of a set of tangible examples of a child's work or behavior to evaluate his skills, knowledge, and abilities. For example, a collection of a child's self-portraits done over the course of the school year to show growth and progress in motor and eye-hand coordination, sophistication of observation and detail, and self-concept.

Preoperational: Term used by Jean Piaget to describe the ages from about two and a half to eight. Children in this stage think concretely, are egocentric, and learn by actively interacting with real things.

Pro-Social Behavior or Skills: The ability to interact with others in positive, pleasing ways; the ability to make and maintain friendships.

Projects (Project Approach): Long-term, large-scale efforts through which a wide variety of subject matter and teaching and learning are integrated. Projects usually involve children working together cooperatively and results in a finished product such as a report, display, collection, book, video, and so forth.

Provocations: Questions or problems posed by teachers that provoke children to think at a high level.

Punishment: A negative consequence for a negative behavior, such as sitting in a time-out chair for hitting another child.

Receptive Language: The ability to understand what is said by another person.

Red-Shirting: Starting a child in school at an older age than he is eligible to start at so that he will experience academic success.

Redirection: Helping a child engage in a more acceptable activity than one that is causing a problem, but that will meet the same need.

Reggio Emilia: A town in north-central Italy known for its uniquely high-quality early childhood programs. Part of the approach of these programs involves helping children express themselves using a wide variety of art materials at a very high level of skill and creativity.

Reinforcement: Providing verbal or tangible rewards or punishment to increase a behavior.

Representational Art: Art that attempts to represent actual objects. Children's drawings of themselves, families, and houses are representational art, as opposed to drawings of shapes, squiggles, or designs.

Representational Play: See Symbolic Play.

Resiliency: A term used to describe certain children who have the ability to do well and have a healthy sense of self in spite of great obstacles and risk factors such as poverty, violence in their community, and so on. Factors that increase and support resiliency include a supportive relative or teacher, a safe place to go in the community, and access to resources such as books.

Risk Factors: A (problematic) term for challenging events or circumstances that put children "at risk" for not doing well in school or being successful in life and for becoming a dependent of the State or worse. Risk factors typically include low birth weight, developmental delays or other disabilities, living in a single-parent family, poverty, violence in the home or community, substance abuse among family members, homelessness, etc. The term is problematic because of its negative connotations and attribution. The term sends the message that these particular challenges will very likely lead to bad outcomes. The term "challenges" is more accurate and neutral.

Scaffolding: Based on Vygotsky's theories, it is a process of helping a child move up to his next level of development or learning by providing materials and assistance. Then when the child is fully capable on his own, helping move him to the next level, and so on.

Schema: A set of pieces of knowledge or skills that becomes automatic. People have schemas for everything from how to tie their shoes to how other people should behave. Set schemas help keep the world clear and organized; however, schemas for the same activities can vary greatly among people. Children are in the process of developing new schemas rapidly.

Screening: Determining (usually with a test) a child's general areas of strength and weakness. Typically a child who is weak in one or more areas of development is referred for further testing.

Self-Concept: The sense of who one is and how a person sees himself. This includes a person's view of his own roles (sibling, son, friend), abilities, interests, values, beliefs, and more. Children with good self-concepts have a realistic sense of their own strengths and weaknesses. They feel comfortable with who they are and with what they like and dislike.

Self-Efficacy: The ability to be resourceful and to have enough influence in one's environment to get needs met positively and intentionally. It also entails knowing oneself and having a realistic and accurate sense of one's own strengths, weaknesses, and unique qualities.

Self-Esteem: The feelings of one's worthiness. It is one part of self-concept. Children with good self-esteem generally feel competent, worthwhile, able, confident, and positive about themselves. However, building children's self-esteem in the abstract can result in a child having a false sense of ability and confidence because she actually does not have skills or ability she believes she has. Self-esteem should be tied to specific accomplishments, knowledge acquisition, and effort.

Self-Help Skills: The ability to take care of one's own basic needs such as toileting, dressing, washing, and eating.

Sensorimotor Stage: Term used by Jean Piaget to describe the first stage of life. It is characterized by learning through all the senses without language. For example, infants typically put things in their mouths to learn through taste what the object is.

Sensory Integration: The ability to fully integrate a number of related bodily feelings and skills such as balancing, knowing where you are in space, feeling one's weight in specific places, and so on. Most people have these abilities naturally, but a few do not to varying degrees.

Sensory Integration Dysfunction: The lack of ability to fully integrate a number of related bodily feelings and skills such as balancing, knowing where you are in space, feeling one's weight in specific places, and so on. Children with this disability have a hard time focusing, behaving appropriately, and performing simple motor tasks. There are specific strategies that physical and occupational therapists use to help children overcome the problems or compensate for them.

Seriation: Ordering items based on their size, weight, thickness, quantity, or similar quality.

Small Motor: The ability to use the hands and fingers, and to manipulate objects. Stringing beads is a small-motor task.

Social-Cultural Development: Vygotsky's theory that all development can only be viewed and understood within particular social and cultural contexts. Knowledge and intelligence is always culturally based. The long history associated with any society or culture has a great bearing on individual development.

Social Skills: The ability or lack of ability to interact, form, and maintain relationships with others.

Spatial Relations: The sense of how things relate to each other in terms of their position in space. For example, on, below, above, behind, to the left, and so on.

Standards: Agreed-upon expectations for what constitutes high-level, challenging teaching and learning in the content areas (reading, writing, math, and so on). A math standard for a young child might be the ability to use numbers to solve simple everyday problems, such as determining how many cups are needed so that everyone at the table has one.

STEM: Science, Technology, Engineering, and Math.

Strengths-Based: An approach to working with children and families that builds on what they can do well to help them do better.

Symbolic Play: Play in which the child substitutes pretend items for the real thing, such as using a block to represent a glass of milk.

Tactile: The sense of touch.

Temporal Relations: The sense of how things relate in time, such as knowing that a past event happened yesterday, last week, last month, or last year.

Transitional Objects: Items such as blankets and stuffed animals that help children make the transition from the security of home to another place.

Transitioning: Helping a child make a positive move from preschool to kindergarten or from any grade to the next.

Transitions: This term has two common meanings. One meaning refers to the change from one activity to another in the classroom. The second meaning refers to the change from one school or grade to another.

Trilemma of Child Care: Refers to the three issues of quality, affordability, and accessibility and how they interact with each other. Increasing or improving one often decreases the others.

Universal Design: Physical environments and teaching practices that benefit and are responsive to all children. This is in contrast to "accommodating" a child with special needs by altering the environment and practices specifically for that child. For example, reading a large picture book clearly, loudly, and not too fast helps every child engage with the story and understand it. If a child with low vision and hearing enters the class, the teacher would not need to do anything differently.

Verbal Skills: The ability to speak and to be understood.

Vygotsky, Lev S.: Russian developmental psychologist who espoused a social-cultural theory of human development. He believed that the development of all higher mental functioning starts in interactions between a child (interpersonal) and an adult—or more capable child—and then becomes internalized (intrapersonal).

Work: There are multiple meanings of this word, but in regard to young children, work either means "effort" or doing chores or tasks such as cleaning up or setting the table.

Work-Play: An invented term for the way young children spend much of their time: in effortful engagement in play and, less often, in playful engagement in tasks. It attempts to communicate the idea that for young children, work and play are often inseparable or can change quickly from one to the other.

Work-Play Time: The part of the program day when the children choose from a wide variety of activities and materials and make decisions about how to participate and for how long.

Zone of Proximal Development: Vygotsky's idea of the area between what a child can do on his own and what he can do with assistance from someone more capable. The implication is that teachers should target their assistance within that zone.

References

Barnes, S. (2012). *Making Sense of "Intentional Teaching."* New South Wales, Australia: Children's Services Central. Retrieved from www.cscentral.org.au/Resources/intentional-teaching-web.pdf

Blackwell, C.K., Lauricella, A. R., & Wortella, E. (2014). "Factors Influencing Digital Technology Use in Early Childhood Education." *Computers & Education 77*, 82–90. Retrieved from http://web5.soc.northwestern.edu/cmhd/wp-content/uploads/2011/06/Blackwell.Lauricella.Wartella.2014.Factors-influencing-digital-tech-use-in-early-education.pdf

Bloom, P. (2010). "The Moral Life of Babies." *New York Times Magazine*, 44–47. Retrieved from www.nytimes.com/2010/05/09/magazine/09babies-t.html?_r=0

Bloom, P. (2013). *Just Babies.* New York: Crown.

Bodrova, E., & Leong, D. J. (1998). "Scaffolding Emergent Writing in the Zone of Proximal Development." *Literacy Teaching and Learning, 3*(2), 1–18. Retrieved from www.earlyliteracyinfo.org/documents/pdf/doc_122.pdf

Bodrova, E., Germeroth, C., & Leong, D. J. (2013, Fall). "Play and Self-regulation: Lessons from Vygotsky." *American Journal of Play, 6*(1), 111–122. Retrieved from www.researchgate.net/publication/274898497_Play_and_self-regulation_Lessons_from_Vygotsky

Center for Disease Control and Prevention. (2013). *Summary Health Statistics for U.S. Children: National Health Interview Survey, 2012.* CDC. Retrieved from www.cdc.gov/nchs/data/series/sr_10/sr10_258.pdf

Chenfeld, M. B. (2006). "Wanna Play?" *Young Children. 61*(6), pp. 34-35.

Chicago Teachers Union (2014). *Arguments against the Common Core.* Retrieved from www.ctunet.com/quest-center/research/text/CTU-Common-Core-Position-Paper.pdf

Dweck, C. S. (2015). "The Secret to Raising Smart Kids." *Scientific American, Mind and Brain Special Editions, 23*(5). http://doi.org/10.1038scientificamericangenius0115-76

Epstein, A. (2007). *The Intentional Teacher: Choosing the Best Strategies for Young Children's Learning.* Washington, D.C.: NAEYC.

Finkelhor, D., Turner, H. A., Shattuck, A., & Hamby, S. L. (2015). "Prevalence of Childhood Exposure to Violence, Crime, and Abuse: Results from the National Survey of Children's Exposure to Violence." *Journal of American Medical Association Pediatrics, 169*(8), 746–754.

Finkelhor, D., Shattuck, A., Turner, H. A., & Hamby, S. L. (2014). "Trends in Children's Exposure to Violence, 2003 to 2011." *Journal of American Medical Association Pediatrics, 168*(6), 540–546. Retrieved from http://www.unh.edu/ccrc/pdf/poi130100.pdf

Galinsky, E. (1988). "Parents and Teacher-Caregivers: Sources of Tension, Sources of Support." *Young Children, 43*(3), 4–12.

Galinsky, E. (2010). *Mind in the Making: The Seven Essential Life Skills Every Child Needs.* New York: William Morrow.

Gardner, H. (2006). *Multiple Intelligences: New Horizons in Theory and Practice.* New York: Basic Books.

Gesell Institute of Child Development. (2012). *Gesell Developmental Observation—Revised and Gesell Early Screener Ages 3–6 Technical Report.* New Haven, CT. Retrieved from www.gesellinstitute.org/technical-reports

Gilliam, W. S. (2005). "Prekindergarteners Left Behind: Expulsion Rates in State Prekindergarten Programs." *Foundation for Child Development.* Retrieved from http://challengingbehavior.fmhi.usf.edu/explore/policy_docs/prek_expulsion.pdf

Greene, P. (2015, Summer). "Can we rescue the common core from the testing machine?" *Rethinking Schools, 29*(4). Retrieved from www.rethinkingschools.org/archive/29_04/29-4_greene.shtml

Hamlin, J., Newman, G., & Wynn, K. (2009). "Eight-month-old infants infer unfulfilled goals, despite contrary physical evidence." *Infancy, 14*(5), 579–590.

Hamlin, J., Wynn, K., & Bloom, P. (2007). "Social evaluation by preverbal infants." *Nature, (450),* 557–559.

Hart, B., & Risley, T. R. (2003, Spring). "The Early Catastrophe: The 30 Million Word Gap by Age 3." *American Educator (American Federation of Teachers),* 4–9. Retrieved from www.aft.org//sites/default/files/periodicals/TheEarlyCatastrophe.pdf

Honig, A. S. (2008). "Supporting Men as Fathers, Caregivers, and Educators." *Early Child Development and Care, 178*(7&8), 665–687. Retrieved from www.researchgate.net/publication/247499918_Supporting_men_as_fathers_caregivers_and_educators

Hossain, Z., Noll, E., & Barboza, M. (2012). "Caregiving Involvement, Job Condition, and Job Satisfaction of Infant-Toddler Child-Care Teachers in the United States." *Education Research International, 2012,* 1–9.

Howes, C.; Burchinal, M.; Pianta, R.; Bryant, D.; Early, D.; Clifford, R.; Barbarin, O. (2008). "Ready to Learn? Children's Pre-Academic Achievement in Pre-Kindergarten Programs." *Early Childhood Research Quarterly, (23)*1, 27–50.

Knapton, S. (2015, September 17). "Obese three-year-old becomes youngest child diagnosed with Type 2 diabetes." *The Telegraph*. Retrieved from www.telegraph.co.uk/news/health/news/11869249/Obese-three-year-old-becomes-youngest-child-diagnosed-with-Type-2-diabetes.html

Lewis, K. R. (2015, May). "What If Everything You Knew About Disciplining Kids Was Wrong?" *Mother Jones*. Retrieved from www.motherjones.com/politics/2015/05/schools-behavior-discipline-collaborative-proactive-solutions-ross-greene

Mayo Clinic. (2015, November). "Childhood obesity complications." Retrieved from www.mayoclinic.org/diseases-conditions/childhood-obesity/basics/complications/con-20027428

Melker, S. De. (2015, May 27). "The case for starting sex education in kindergarten." *PBS News Hour*. Retrieved from www.pbs.org/newshour/updates/spring-fever

NAEYC (2005). *Code of ethical conduct and statement of commitment. Position statement.* Washington, D.C.: NAEYC. Retrieved from www.naeyc.org/files/naeyc/file/positions/PSETH05.pdf

New Zealand Ministry of Education (1996). "Te Whāriki: Early Childhood Curriculum." Retrieved from www.education.govt.nz/assets/Documents/Early-Childhood/te-whariki.pdf

Nichols, H. (2016, February 23). "Head lice: Causes, symptoms and treatments." *Medical News Today*. Retrieved from www.medicalnewstoday.com/articles/164492.php

Parker, G. (2015). "Teachers' Autonomy." *Research in Education,* 93(1), 19–33. Retrieved from http://doi.org/10.7227/RIE.0008

Patterson, C. J. (2009). "Children of Lesbian and Gay Parents: Psychology, Law, and Policy." *American Psychologist*, 68(8), 727–736. Retrieved from www.the7eye.org.il/wp-content/uploads/2015/07/lgbt-parents3.pdf

Robert Wood Johnson Foundation. (2016). "Declining Childhood Obesity Rates." Retrieved from www.rwjf.org/en/library/research/2016/02/declining-childhood-obesity-rates.html

Rutgers. (No Date). "Spring Fever: Relationships and Sexual Health Education." Retrieved from www.rutgers.international/what-we-do/comprehensive-sexuality-education/spring-fever and www.springfever.org.uk

Saifer, S. (2016). "Higher order thinking (HOT) skills for young learners: Pre-K through 2nd grade." Unpublished manuscript.

Saqlain, N. (2015). "A Comprehensive Look at Multi-Age Education." *Journal of Educational and Social Research*, 5(2).

Smarter Balanced Assessment Consortium (No Date). *About the assessments.* Retrieved from http://www.smarterbalanced.org/assessments

Torbert, M., and L. Schneider. (1993). *Follow me too: A handbook of movement activities for three- to five-year-olds.* New York: Addison-Wesley.

Townsend, C., & Rheingold, A. A. (2013). "Estimating a child sexual abuse prevalence rate for practitioners: A review of child sexual abuse studies." *Darkness to Light*. Retrieved from www.D2L.org

University of Toronto Childcare Resource and Research Unit. (2014). "What does the research say about multi-age grouping for infants, toddlers and preschoolers?" Retrieved from http://childcarecanada.org/sites/default/files/Multi-age_BN_Feb_12_14_0.pdf

U.S. Department of Education Office for Civil Rights (2014). "Civil rights data collection: Data snapshot (early childhood)." Retrieved from www2.ed.gov/about/offices/list/ocr/docs/crdc-early-learning-snapshot.pdf